Z O L A R ' S

Compendium
of
Occult
Theories &
Practices

Other books by Zolar

Zolar's Encyclopedia of Ancient and Forbidden Knowledge
Zolar's Encyclopedia and Dictionary of Dreams
Zolar's Book of Dreams, Numbers, and Lucky Days

ZOLAR'S

Compendium of OCCULT Theories & Practices

PRENTICE HALL PRESS
NEW YORK

Published by Prentice Hall Press
A Division of Simon & Schuster, Inc.
Gulf + Western Building
One Gulf + Western Plaza
New York, NY 10023

PRENTICE HALL PRESS is a trademark of Simon & Schuster, Inc.

Library of Congress Cataloging-in-Publication Data

Zolar.
Zolar's compendium of occult theories and practices.

1. Occult sciences. 2. Fortune-telling. I. Title.
II. Title: Compendium of occult theories and practices.
BF1411.Z635 1987   133   86-12396
ISBN 0-13-983990-9

Manufactured in the United States of America

10 9 8 7 6 5 4 3 2 1

First Edition

CONTENTS

PREFACE:
A CHAT
WITH
ZOLAR

People often ask, "How is it that an author decides to write a book? Why at a particular time? Where do the ideas come from?"

Out of fairness to my fans all over the world, I have to point out that Zolar doesn't *write* books! Books are written through Zolar—and as children are born: when they are supposed to be.

The work you are about to read is really a compilation of a number of books and lessons that belong together. The section of numerology provides you with a unique method for charting your day's activities, the Solar and Lunar guides will chart the course of your personality, and as cards and card reading have always been with us, it is only fitting that they, too, be included. And, in addition, I have given you, for the first time in book form, a series of lessons in psychic disciplines that were given for many years by the Academy of Mystic Arts. These contain a series of unique exercises, derived from the ancient mystery schools, that will increase and enhance your natural psychic ability!

I believe that everyone is psychic. One simply has to know how to develop these abilities. And so the publication of this work.

I must thank my stouthearted typists, Maria Binski and Mary Rodriguez, who introduced me to the wonder of word processing.

Enough said. Turn the page and begin a journey into your Self. It's sometimes lonely, but it's very exciting.

—Zolar
New York City

1.
Numerological
Secrets

---- ★ ----

Daily Numbers

Numerology, or the sacred use of numbers for divination, has existed throughout recorded time. I am not going to deal with the history of numerology nor make predictions for individuals but rather provide a means whereby anyone following these instructions can determine for himself the major events of each day as it passes. I am not writing this to convince the general public that some general planetary forces are at work in the life of every person on a particular day but rather to enable each individual reading these words to prove for himself the value of this very simple method.

I have ruled out and fixed three primary and three secondary planetary influences for each day. The primary planets play an important central role in determining events, while the secondary planets merely cast their shadows on human life.

It would be presumptuous of me to say that every incident mentioned in the following pages will occur on any given day. I have simply attempted to distill the qualities of six major planets to arrive at a fair assessment of the happenings of a particular moment in time. I have tested these methods for a great many years and now offer this information to the public for the first time. Four tables allow you to find your daily number, and succeeding sections identify the primary and secondary planets affecting that number and how they will influence the course of events. In addition, each section notes the lucky numbers for that day. These may be useful for playing the lottery, gambling, or any other numerical speculations.

Daily Number Tables

Following there are four tables. The horizontal column at the top of each table represents minutes, while the left-hand vertical column represents a particular day of the week.

To find your lucky daily number, note the exact time you awake. Take into consideration only the minutes. For instance, if you awaken at 7:31 A.M., only 31 counts, and you should locate this number in the minutes column of the table. Once you have done this, look at the corresponding day of the week. At the junction of these two intersections you will find your lucky number for the day. For instance, suppose that it is Thursday and you looked at the clock at 7:30 A.M. You will find the number 30 on Table 2 in the very last column. If you now move down in that column opposite the heading Thursday, you will find the number 91. This is your lucky number for the day.

Now turn to the section for 91. You will find that the primary planets for the day are the Moon, Mercury, and Saturn, while the secondary influences are Venus, Mars, and Jupiter. At the very bottom of this description you will find lucky numbers for the day—1, 3, and 6—which may be used for local lotto or lottery speculation.

TABLE 1

Minutes	1	2	3	4	5	6	7	8	9	10	11	12	13	14	15
Monday	27	94	72	10	25	98	11	41	88	76	7	85	57	84	8
Tuesday	93	99	37	95	59	60	4	87	22	86	31	58	3	45	21
Wednesday	51	18	96	26	17	97	49	74	9	36	56	77	35	107	40
Thursday	91	50	71	6	67	34	42	1	75	30	92	20	44	83	66
Friday	100	19	78	61	33	102	12	48	55	90	5	82	23	105	39
Saturday	101	70	63	16	69	2	54	89	24	47	81	32	65	46	13
Sunday	79	62	28	108	52	29	43	15	80	38	64	103	106	14	104

TABLE 2

Minutes	16	17	18	19	20	21	22	23	24	25	26	27	28	29	30
Monday	10	25	98	11	41	88	76	7	85	57	84	8	72	94	27
Tuesday	95	59	60	4	87	22	86	31	58	3	45	21	37	99	93
Wednesday	26	17	97	49	74	9	36	56	77	68	107	40	96	18	51
Thursday	6	67	34	73	1	75	30	92	20	44	83	66	71	50	91
Friday	61	33	102	12	48	55	90	5	82	23	105	39	78	19	100
Saturday	16	69	2	54	89	24	47	81	32	65	46	13	63	70	101
Sunday	108	52	53	43	15	80	38	64	103	106	14	104	28	62	79

TABLE 3

Minutes	31	32	33	34	35	36	37	38	39	40	41	42	43	44	45
Monday	11	41	88	76	7	85	57	35	8	72	94	27	98	25	10
Tuesday	4	87	22	86	31	58	3	45	21	37	99	93	60	59	95
Wednesday	49	74	9	36	56	77	68	107	40	96	18	51	97	17	26
Thursday	73	1	75	30	42	20	44	83	66	71	50	91	34	67	6
Friday	12	48	55	90	5	82	23	105	39	78	29	100	102	33	61
Saturday	54	89	24	47	81	32	65	46	13	63	70	101	2	69	16
Sunday	43	15	80	38	64	103	106	14	104	28	62	79	53	52	108

TABLE 4

Minutes	46	47	48	49	50	51	52	53	54	55	56	57	58	59	60
Monday	76	7	85	57	38	8	72	94	27	98	25	10	88	41	11
Tuesday	86	31	58	3	45	21	84	99	93	60	59	95	22	87	4
Wednesday	36	56	77	68	107	40	96	18	51	97	17	26	9	74	49
Thursday	30	42	20	44	83	66	71	50	91	34	67	6	75	1	73
Friday	90	5	82	23	105	39	78	29	100	102	33	19	55	48	12
Saturday	47	81	32	65	46	13	63	70	101	2	69	16	24	89	54
Sunday	38	64	103	106	14	104	28	62	79	53	52	108	92	15	43

Daily Number Analysis

1

Primary Planetary Influence: Mars, Neptune, Mars

Secondary Planetary Influence: Jupiter, Moon, Saturn

This morning you woke up in a cheerful frame of mind and with a sense of physical well-being. Your mood is a joyous one and especially humorous. You may very well tease your wife or partner by cracking jokes. A planned business trip may be canceled, to your great satisfaction. You may also hear something pleasant regarding your children's progress in school.

You will receive some letters giving you good news about the recovery of an ailing relative. You will make some very lucrative business deals. If you are involved in any speculation, it will profit you to be somewhat bullish. If you are employed in either the military or civil service, you may receive news in regard to a promotion of increase in rank.

From 6 P.M.on your mind will assume a somewhat romantic attitude, and you may find yourself in the company of a partner or loved one. You should also set aside some time to meditate and picture in your mind's eye the coming of great prosperity. This moment out will have a very tonic effect on your mind.

This is also a good day for purchasing luxury items. Be very cautious, though, not to ride a bicycle or scooter during the evening hours, as such an activity may likely result in an accident. End the evening by contemplating the God of your heart and giving thanks for your well-being. And be sure to consider those less well off than yourself.

Your lucky numbers for the day are 3, 5, and 9. The lucky hours of the day are 8 A.M., 4 P.M., and 7 to 9 P.M. These are especially good times for gambling of any kind.

2

Primary Planetary Influence: Mars, Neptune, Venus

Secondary Planetary Influence: Mars, Venus, Mercury

This is an especially lucky day for you. In the morning you will find yourself being extremely optimistic about finances and may decide to try your luck in some form of gambling. Family life is very happy and cheerful, and you may be in a very light mood with your partner. You may have a desire to clean and rearrange your room or office. A friend to whom you have lent money is likely to repay the loan before 10 A.M. You may be disappointed, however, when the mailman fails to deliver a letter that you have been expecting anxiously for some time. This is an especially good day to wear new clothes or to change your style of dress. Any meals you partake of will be extremely tasty, which means you must be very cautious not to overeat.

This day is also particularly lucky for doing business on a very large scale. If you occupy a bullish position in shares of gold or cotton, unload half of your holdings and cover this sale three days afterward, when prices of these commodities go down. Trade in shipping or rayon around 12 P.M.

★

If you're in the military service, you'll find that the day goes by without too much to do, and you will especially enjoy the hours after work. After 6 P.M. there is a great possibility of your meeting a very important person. As this period is ruled by the Sun, evening hours will be particularly pleasant. Spend some time reading an instructive book. Listen to the radio, as it will also bring you some very important news that you must hear. Expect to have a good night's sleep.

Your lucky numbers for the day are 2, 4, and 7. Especially lucky periods are from 6 to 10 A.M. and 12 P.M. to 3 P.M. Do not undertake any new work or perform any stock trading between 10 A.M. and 12 P.M.

3

Primary Planetary Influence: Mars, Neptune, Mercury

Secondary Planetary Influence: Jupiter, Venus, Moon

This day begins with your waking from an unusually funny and very symbolic dream. Unfortunately, this is not a day that brings a great many good things to you. Most likely you will postpone or cancel engagements scheduled for the rest of the morning. You are likely to feel somewhat saddened during the major part of the day.

Do not, under any circumstances, lend money to anyone, as repayment will be delayed. You will prefer to be left alone but will find this impossible as unwelcome calls from friends will continually disturb you. You will also find that you have less than your normal appetite and will not enjoy any of your meals.

During business or office hours, expect a great many problems that will disturb you greatly. It is definitely to your advantage to postpone any new business deals.

If you are in the government service, you will find this day a tough one as the pressure of work will be difficult for you to bear.

From 2 P.M. onward, you will find some relief from the worries of the morning and will begin to feel much more positive and optimistic. You are likely to enjoy your evening with family members at home. There is also a possibility of an old friend visiting you. You may also spend some of your time in searching for some misplaced papers or other articles. Expect to feel very sentimental about your children. Unlike the earlier part of the day, in the evening hours your household assumes a gay and festive mood. The possibility of some financial good luck or the receipt of a gift from a friend now comes to the fore.

If you are religious, meditation will bring some new spiritual under-standings, and you will have a peaceful and undisturbed sleep.

Your lucky numbers for the day are 1, 6, and 8. Lucky hours of the day are 10 A.M., 3 P.M., and 5 P.M. Any proposals, contracts, or speculations made around these times should prove successful.

4

Primary Planetary Influence: Mars, Neptune, Moon

Secondary Planetary Influence: Sun, Mercury, Venus

Today an event will occur that will make you feel unusually impor-tant. If you are a writer, expect to produce some inspired text; you are also likely to receive a long overdue check from an editor or acquaint-ance. This is a fairly good day, with the exception of health. You may feel a bit run-down and even suffer from a bad headache. Other matters remain normal, though. If you are a speculator, this is a good day to go for long-term investments and to purchase options. Much to your surprise, these will appreciate in value. If you deal in com-modities, it might be a good day to take a holiday from trading. If you are involved in retailing, do not expect many customers with large orders; in fact, do not use this day to replenish your inventory.

If you are in the military service, most likely you will be required to work long hours. You will return home exhausted. You may even feel blue and somewhat out of sorts. Take control of your mind, and don't let yourself get excited. Go out for a walk in the evening and gaze at the moon. Don't let imaginary worries come to mind. This is a transitory period you're passing through, and you need not worry about it. Do not expect to sleep too soundly this evening.

Your lucky numbers for the day are 5, 8, and 9. Of these 5 and 9 will be uppermost. Your auspicious periods are from 6 to 10 A.M. and from 6 to 7 P.M. Something good is going to happen to you during these hours.

5

Primary Planetary Influence: Mars, Venus, Sun

Secondary Planetary Influence: Mercury, Venus, Mars

This morning you spend a great deal of time pondering over unfor-tunate incidents from the previous day, seeking a means to straighten out what went wrong. In other ways, too, this is not a good morning for you. You find that you do not have sufficient funds to pay bills that are coming due, and even your body seems somewhat listless. You suffer from continual constipation and flatulence.

This is a good time to practice yoga by lying down, closing your eyes, and feeling the movement of incoming and outgoing breath. Such practices will make your mind tranquil and truly give you peace.

Don't be surprised if you miss your bus or train while going to work. If you are engaged in retailing, sales will be unusually good, and you can expect to spend a great deal of time with customers. Also, some of your long-standing credit sales will be paid up by the end of the day. If you are involved with the stock market, be somewhat bearish today. Be extremely cautious in contracting for future goods. This is an especially good day to trade in agricultural machinery and farm supplies. If you speculate in cotton, this day could set new records for the year.

Your evening hours at home will be much more successful than those of the morning. First, you feel better physically. Second, listening to good music on the radio will put your mind at peace so that you have a good night's sleep.

Your lucky numbers for the day are 3, 4, and 7. Of these, 3 is the most important. The luckiest periods of the day are from 1 P.M. to 2 P.M., around 4 P.M., and from 9 to 10 P.M.

6

Primary Planetary Influence: Mars, Venus, Mercury

Secondary Planetary Influence: Venus, Mars, Jupiter

Today you find yourself unusually romantic and happy, desiring a long overdue holiday. Your partner will be unusually loving and caring as he or she confesses to having had a frightening dream about you. To see you hale and hearty might even bring tears. There's a great deal of sunshine in the house. You feel yourself in a religious and pensive state of mind. Take some time to read some inspirational material, and realize that while you may enter the light, you will never touch the flame. Your luck is at an unusually high level, due to the influence of Venus, Mercury, and Jupiter.

In the office, expect much happiness, as your work will be appreciated by your employer. If you're in business for yourself, your position is comfortable. If you are in retailing, expect to sell an item that has been on your shelves for some time. In speculation, try to make the best of the day. Trading in cement and steel is very good. This is also a good day for those involved with agriculture, but speculation in ground nuts, cottonseed, and oils should be avoided.

The evening hours will bring a sense of comfort and well-being, but there is nothing special to record. You may feel an urge to read some unusually intellectual material that will put you to sleep very quickly.

Your lucky numbers for today are 1, 4, and 6. The luckiest periods are 3 P.M. to 7 P.M. and 9 to 10 P.M. This is an extremely lucky day.

7

Primary Planetary Influence: Mars, Venus, Venus

Secondary Planetary Influence: Mars. Jupiter, Saturn

Today begins with you worrying about the health of some member of your family. The morning hours do not appear very promising. You're likely to feel exhausted both mentally and physically. Immediately try some breathing exercises. They will provide the vigor that was missing when you first arose. If you are married or living with a partner, there's a great possibility of some misunderstanding. There may also be difficulties with household objects. Be careful that a fan or radio does not malfunction. Also, be especially careful of dropping or breaking dishes.

You will go to your office or place of business as usual. If you are involved in retailing, expect more female customers than usual. Also expect a particularly affluent woman to make a rather large purchase.

This is not a good day for speculation. Especially to be avoided is any trading in the bullion markets. If you are not cautious, you could lose a large sum of money.

On the other hand, this is a good day for those who like to go to the track. The best time to place your bets is 12 P.M. to 2 P.M.

If you are employed in the government service, the day is normal, the evening is particularly pleasant for you, and you feel unusually cheerful and happy. This day is very suitable for the purchase of fine and costly articles.

You may receive an unexpected visit from a couple with children and have a good time in their company. As Venus is active, you will feel more romantic than usual. Today is a good day for balancing your personal accounts. You will probably be pleasantly surprised to find that you are in sound shape. Expect to stay up into the wee hours and have a good night's sleep.

Your lucky numbers for the day are 1, 5, and 7. Of these, 1 and 7 will play important roles. Lucky hours are from 4 to 9 P.M. Anything undertaken during these auspicious times will be successful.

8

Primary Planetary Influence: Mars. Venus, Mars

Secondary Planetary Influence: Jupiter, Saturn, Saturn

This is a day on which you will very likely demonstrate some of your more martial qualities. You may receive letters that you will find disturbing. Don't answer them impulsively—set them aside for a few days. Don't be surprised if you become angry with your employees or just about anyone with whom you come into contact. There is a great possibility of hearing some unpleasant gossip about yourself from a fellow employee or neighbor. When this happens it will be best to simply observe silence.

Your appetite will not be exceptionally good because the events of the morning will somewhat discolor your day. After 12 P.M., all the negativity of the morning will be gone and you will be in a much more cheerful mood. If you are employed by another, expect your boss to make personal inquiries about you and your work.

If you are trading in the stock market, expect prices of gold and silver to remain more or less steady. This is also a good day to trade edible oil and various nuts grown on the ground. You might wish to enter into some option or purchase of stock, which will realize profits within a very short period of time.

The evening will be spent in material enjoyment. You may wish to go shopping and spend money on unnecessary luxury items. If you are interested in sports, you may have an opportunity to see an unusually good contest in baseball, tennis, or football. Expect to feel more optimistic in the evening and to have a relatively good sleep.

Your lucky numbers for the day are 4, 5, and 8. Number 8 has the most significance. Your lucky periods are from 10 A.M. to 12 P.M. and the rest of the afternoon and evening.

9

Primary Planetary Influence: Sun, Mars, Jupiter

Secondary Planetary Influence: Saturn, Saturn, Jupiter

Congratulations! Today the Sun is your ruling planet, which promises a very auspicious day. The morning hours will be filled with sunshine and happiness for you and members of your family. This is a good day to set aside some time for meditation. Books that you have lent to friends and forgotten about will very likely be returned to you unexpectedly.

If you are a government employee, this day will be particularly lucky for you. You might receive news of a promotion, a transfer, or an increase in salary.

For those who speculate in the market, this is also a lucky day. Look to acquire shares of chemical companies, as they will give you handsome profits in the long run. If you deal in oil, seed oils, caster-oil seeds, or any nuts grown on the ground and hold a bullish position, unload some of your stock and you will make a good profit.

Retailers who sell fabric, diamonds, stereos, and other such luxury items are likely to find that sales are high indeed. This is also a good day for renewing your inventory.

If you are interested in the racetrack, a last-minute change in the selection of your horse will reward you handsomely.

At the end of the day, stop at a florist and buy some flowers to brighten your environment. When you get home, light candles and spend time in meditation. New ideas will come to you, which, translated into positive action, will give you a financial life in the near future. Your lucky numbers for today are 0, 1, and 4. Number 4 has the greatest significance. The entire day may be considered unusually lucky.

10

Primary Planetary Influence: Venus, Sun, Saturn

Secondary Planetary Influence: Saturn, Jupiter, Mars

If you are recently married or living with someone, you and your partner will have a quarrel. Do not be exceptionally disturbed, as this is only a passing rain cloud; the influence of the Sun makes this a

---

★

---

bright day. However, this is a good day for financial improvement. If you are a writer, try to finish your work and mail it to your editor as soon as possible. What you have produced is your best effort. You may find yourself whistling with joy and enthusiasm. This day is especially favorable for those who sell books, for writers, and for persons doing any kind of intellectual work. If you have some photography to take care of, why not do it today, when the influence of the Sun will help it?

During your hours at the office, don't be surprised if you find yourself especially favored. Expect to be very liberal with expenses as you entertain your friends later on in the day.

If you speculate in the market, look for a blue-chip stock that has not been in the limelight until now. Make an investment, and wait for the harvest in the future.

If you trade in commodities, the trend will inspire confidence in you and your broker. Do not sell or buy, however.

While the day so far has been an exciting one, expect the evening hours to be extremely dull and uninteresting. It may be that you will have to stay home by yourself, listening to music and relaxing. If you practice meditation, memories of past lives may come to the fore, making you somewhat depressed and uneasy. When you retire, the activities of the day will be bathed in a peaceful sleep. Before going to bed, however, read some inspirational material in order to set your mind in the proper mode. Use the evening hours for relaxation and not for work.

Your lucky numbers for the day are 1, 3, and 4. Number 3 has the greatest influence. The lucky period is from 8 A.M. to 2 P.M.

11

Primary Planetary Influence: Venus, Sun, Saturn

Secondary Planetary Influence: Jupiter, Mars, Venus

Of your three primary planets, Saturn is in the most positive aspect. The daytime hours are active ones. Expect to experience disturbed conditions in your routines. If you have children, there is a possibility that one of them will suddenly become ill. You will be in great haste during the morning hours and may hear about an accident in the neighborhood. When you arrive at your office, you do so with a certain degree of depression and a lack of joy. Don't be surprised if you find some serious mistakes in your previous day's work. Correct these and attempt to be more positive.

For those in the market, this day is auspicious from 12 P.M. to 1 P.M. Market trends at first appear to oscillate, but afterward will be fairly steady. Traders in cotton will find this day very uneventful. Very likely they will find stock quotations holding steady and not indicating any particular trend. If you hold a bullish position in silver, now is a good time to think about unloading your holdings and getting out of this market. The silver market is very likely to decline within the next few days.

Those who favor the racetrack should pick chestnut horses and use to full advantage the lucky numbers given below. This is an especially lucky day for you at the races, in playing cards, or in other related forms of gambling. In the evening hours, look for some entertainment, but don't be surprised if your sleep is somewhat disturbed.

Your lucky numbers for the day are 4, 5, and 9. Number 9 will have the greatest influence on your general good luck. Lucky hours of the day are from 12 P.M. to 1 P.M. and during the evening.

12

Primary Planetary Influence: Venus, Sun, Jupiter

Secondary Planetary Influence: Mars, Venus, Mercury

You're indeed a lucky person if this is your daily number. The entire day is ruled by the very auspicious planets of Venus, Jupiter, and Mercury. You will find that the morning hours are particularly pleasant, and you will feel that all is well with the world. You will be pleasantly surprised to read newspaper announcements that are important to you personally, and your partner will be in an unusually good mood. Expect to find tasty food placed on your plate throughout the day. This sense of well-being will carry over into the office, and you may find yourself cracking jokes with your associates.

If you speculate in the market, for unexpected gains look to those companies that produce synthetic fibers. If you already occupy a bullish position in such stocks, do not sell; hold on, as prices are likely to soar higher within the next few days.

Retail dealers in luxury items will also have a good day: perfumes, cutlery, and cosmetics will enjoy good sales. Those who make their living with trucking or taxis will also find that today is a good one. Those in other businesses will find sales steady.

If going to the racetrack is your cup of tea, try your luck in the third race. It is not likely that you will be disappointed.

Spend the evening hours in some form of entertainment or by taking a casual walk. Be prepared to encounter strong sexual aspects coming to the fore in the later hours of the day.

Your lucky numbers for the day are 2, 3, and 6. Of these, 3 dominates. The entire day must be regarded as a very auspicious one.

13

Primary Planetary Influence: Venus, Moon, Mars

Secondary Planetary Influence: Venus, Mercury, Moon

Today is a fine day, with sunshine all around and nothing much to do. One of your neighbors is likely to call you for a chat. In your home life, you will feel unusually happy and comfortable. Most likely you'll spend some time reading old correspondence and sorting it out. If at all possible, wear clothing that is predominantly white. If you have a diamond ring, make sure you wear it for its Venusian planetary influence could bring you exceptional good luck. This is also a day for cleaning and organizing your work space. A member of your family who has been ailing may show distinct improvements in health from this day on.

This is a very lucky day for speculators in the stock exchange as well. Look to chemical companies and those that manufacture synthetic fibers. Buy these shares and hold them until you see a decent profit.

Those who deal with insurance or who work as commission agents will also do very well. Those who work in banks or other commercial lending institutions are likely to hear good news. This is also a favorable day for persons who speculate in silver, cotton, and copper.

Those who favor the racetrack should do well and should bet on white colts as often as possible.

During the evening hours from 6 P.M. on, however, do not expect to have a particularly happy time. Those who suffer from blood-pressure problems or asthma will have an especially bad evening. Have a glass of hot milk and retire early. Avoid any arguments during the evening hours.

Your lucky numbers for the day are 2, 3, and 8. The number 8 will have more influence over your activities than any other. Lucky hours are 8 A.M. to 6 P.M.

14

Primary Planetary Influence: Venus, Moon, Venus

Secondary Planetary Influence: Mercury, Moon, Mercury

Just as whatever King Midas touched became gold, everything you do today will be blessed by luck. This is a day full of romance, outings, picnics, and meetings with beautiful people. The morning is exceptionally fine, and you feel bright and cheerful. If you live with someone, you find yourself unusually sweet-tempered toward your partner. If you are engaged to be married, this is a good day to set a definite marriage date. If you are in love but living apart from a prospective partner, you may receive a very exciting letter from him or her. If you have an unmarried daughter, she may receive a marriage proposal. If you have misplaced stock certificates or currency, you may find them.

For those who speculate, today is a day for big business. Expect large increases in the general market trend. Shares of stock dealing with shipping motor vehicles will especially be in the limelight. This is a time during which you can turn existing shares into great profits. If you are involved in retailing medical supplies, such as a pharmacy or vitamin shop, business will be greatly favored. Those who sell textiles will also find this a very positive time. Today is also favorable for merchants who deal in ready-to-wear clothing, toilet accessories, and toys.

If you favor the racetrack, today is a particularly lucky day. Make sure you bet in the first race, though, and when you have won, take your profits and go home. Select a horse whose name begins with F or G.

During the evening hours, set aside some time for romantic endeavors. You might go to a movie with your partner. Be aware that you may find yourself looking at other men or women with thoughts that are sure to cause a certain amount of guilt.

Expect to have a disturbed sleep tonight.

Your lucky numbers for the day are 1, 5, and 9. Of these, 1 is of the greatest importance. Your luckiest period is the entire morning.

15

Primary Planetary Influence: Venus, Moon, Mercury

Secondary Planetary Influence: Moon, Moon, Sun

It is not likely that you will find a more favorable day than this during the whole year. You are indeed very lucky if you have chosen this number. The morning hours should prove particularly fortunate. A few moments glancing at the Sun when you begin your day will help you feel invigorated. Expect members of the family to be hale and hearty. You may spend a pleasant time in the morning hours in the company of a dear and close friend, who may offer to do you a great favor. You may receive pleasant correspondence from your friends or relatives. If you're thinking of traveling to a foreign country, this is the day to confirm your travel plans. If you are taking any examinations, your success is assured.

For those who engage in the stock market, the best profits can be yielded by selling short. This is a fairly normal day for other businessmen and traders, though it is a very auspicious one for placing new orders for medicines and imported articles. Those who speculate in cotton and oilseeds will have to mark time awaiting new price movements. Do not enter into any new contracts.

For those who are attracted to the ponies, plan to go to the track during the evening hours. Do not follow the advice of friends as to betting but use your own intuition. Bet on a horse with a white crescent moon on his forehead.

Evening hours are likely to be merry and pleasant, and you might wish to stop in at a fine hotel for a snack and a cup of coffee or tea. The early part of the night may be spent in romantic adventures, and you will pass the night in a deep, restful sleep.

Your lucky numbers for the day are 0, 1, and 3. The number 1 is the most significant. Your lucky periods are the entire morning and from 2 to 8 P.M.

16

Primary Planetary Influence: Venus, Moon, Moon

Secondary Planetary Influence: Moon, Sun, Mercury

Today is the day for misadventures. You must be extremely careful as to what you do, write, or speak. You may awaken with a bad cold or sore throat. Your eyes could also cause you some trouble. Some great hope that you have held for a long time will be smashed, and you may feel totally disillusioned. You may be required to visit a friend who has taken very ill. In an official capacity, you will find little interest in your work, and you may find yourself committing a great many mistakes. Be prepared to accept criticism from your boss. In other respects, however, the day is a fairly good one, especially in terms of home life.

For those who speculate in the stock exchange, this is a good day. Quotations may be seen to move very briskly during the last hour of trading. Buy blue-chip stock. Do whatever you can with a good margin of profit, and go home knowing you have made money. Gold and silver markets are likely to remain firm but with a great many price changes. Prices of oil and cotton are likely to show downward trends. This is not a day for selling short.

Those who prefer speculation at the racetrack or other forms of gambling should refrain from changing their selections at the last moment. Since this is a day of great mental confusion, such a change could cause a substantial loss.

Evening hours are very pleasant, and you may find yourself catching up on some new ideas. If you are unusually restless, have a cup of warm milk before going to bed.

Your lucky numbers for the day are 1, 3, and 4. Of these, 4 predominates. Your lucky hours are from 12 P.M. to 5 P.M.

17

Primary Planetary Influence: Venus, Mars, Sun

Secondary Planetary Influence: Sun, Mercury, Venus

You wake up with a great sense of fatigue and physical illness, possibly brought about by indigestion or a low-grade fever. It might be best to observe a complete fast or perhaps to drink only fruit or vegetable juices. The harmony that you usually enjoy at home is likely to be broken today. Expect to have some regrettable words with your partner or children. A radio, stereo, fan, or air conditioner is likely to go on the blink today. You may have a disagreement with a grocer or other shopkeeper who supplies you with goods at a very high price. Try to keep your temper, at least in the morning hours. Be careful that you do not get carried away and write offensive letters to those who really don't deserve them.

In the office, work is likely to be unusually heavy. You may find yourself doing the work of another employee who is absent. This is a

★

very unfortunate day for speculation on the stock market, where there may be a slight panic; those who indulge may suffer great losses. Those who deal in commodities can also be caught up in the net; the only exceptions are dealings in linseed oil.

If you prefer the racetrack, don't expect any killings today. It would be better to enjoy a pleasant evening at home, avoiding even such events as the friendly neighborhood poker game.

Your lucky numbers for the day are 3, 5, and 7. The evening is your only lucky period.

18

Primary Planetary Influence: Venus, Mars, Mercury

Secondary Planetary Influence: Venus, Mars, Mercury

The morning is extremely favorable for family life. You find yourself waking up unusually cheerful and totally oblivious to events going on around you. You may wish to take a stroll or visit an old, dear friend. This is a good day to purchase something new and exciting for your children. Meals served today will be unusually enjoyable, and you will especially enjoy your breakfast before going to work.

From 12 P.M. on, you fall under the pressure of a great many things that have to be completed and feel somewhat tired and exhausted.

For those involved in the stock market, expect a great many swings in prices. You may find yourself caught in the uncomfortable position of not knowing whether to buy or sell. When this happens, it is best to do neither. Those who deal in agricultural projects, however, will have a fine day.

For those who go to the racetrack, this is a day of mixed luck. Early stakes are very likely to fail, but by the end of the day things may prove much more advantageous. A horse whose name begins with or contains the letter D is a good horse to bet on. You may also wish to bet on a horse that has a prominent scar on his body.

The evening hours are quite normal and peaceful, and you will probably do nothing special. However, you may receive an important telephone call. Expect a peaceful night's sleep.

The lucky numbers for the day are 1, 2, and 6. The number 6 is more meaningful than the others. Lucky hours of the day are in the morning from 6 to 8 A.M. and in the evening from 8 to 9 P.M.

19

Primary Planetary Influence: Mercury, Mars, Venus

Secondary Planetary Influence: Venus, Mars, Jupiter

The atmosphere around you is unusually peaceful and comfortable. You may find yourself involved in a great deal of intellectual work. Expect some letters giving you good news about money or investments, You feel unusually optimistic about financial gains and easily imagine a more comfortable home life in the very near future. As the day advances, however, the morning glory begins to wilt, and you feel yourself encountering trouble ahead.

If you are in the civil service, this day is unusually difficult. You have a great deal of work to do and may be required to rummage through old correspondence. Expect some words with subordinates.

For those who speculate in the market, this day is not a favorable one. The strong influence of Mars will land all who speculate in trouble. It is better to simply stand by and not make any rash decisions. However, those who trade in firearms, machinery, or agricultural products will be much more fortunate. These persons will find themselves doing a very good business. The price of silver, however, is likely to fall.

For those who prefer the track, the day is one of mixed luck. Do not place bets on white horses. Do not play the ninth horse or the ninth race. If you play cards in the evening, however, especially if you are a woman playing with other women, you may find yourself earning a tidy sum. Evening hours generally make you feel homesick; you may wish you were visiting family members this evening. Expect a peaceful and sound sleep.

Your lucky numbers for the day are 4, 6, and 8. The number 8 is of greatest influence. Especially lucky periods are the morning hours and from 6 P.M. onward.

20

Primary Planetary Influence: Mercury, Mars, Mars

Secondary Planetary Influence: Mars, Jupiter, Saturn

With the exception of the morning hours, this will be a day of great troubles, anxieties, and physical illness. You may be called upon to contribute, unwillingly, to some charitable cause. In the family scene,

★

there are likely to be petty quarrels with a partner, and you will find yourself unusually harsh in dealing with offspring. Try to keep your temper, and avoid friends as much as possible. Very likely you will suffer from blood-pressure problems and stomach troubles. Take some light food, and attend to your office duties as best you can.

The office atmosphere is also likely to be unusually uncomfortable, and you will find that your heart is not in your work. A change of work requirements or a transfer to another department are not ruled out.

For those in the stock market, this day is very unlucky. It is advisable to abstain from seeking any new business. Anything you do today is likely to turn against you. Do not follow your intuition or seek the advice of astrologers, for the stars are especially unfavorable now.

Those who deal in articles that are colored red, on the other hand, are likely to benefit, because of the strong influence of the planet Mars. Other traders, however will find this day most unlucky. Prices of agricultural produce are likely to go down, causing a great deal of anxiety.

For those who favor the racetrack, this day is most unlucky. This holds true for cards and other types of gambling as well.

During the evening hours, guard against some kind of accident. If at all possible, spend the evening at home, reading. If you are a professional writer, you may find yourself worrying over the success of your current project, and thus you will have an unusually disturbed sleep.

Your lucky numbers for the day are 1, 7, and 9. The number 7 is more significant than the others. Your lucky period is only between 12 P.M. and 2 P.M.

21

Primary Planetary Influence: Mercury, Uranus, Jupiter

Secondary Planetary Influence: Jupiter, Saturn, Saturn

You are especially lucky if you have picked this number. The morning hours are particularly suitable for financial pursuits and gains. If you have been contemplating a particular financial idea for a long time, go ahead with it. This is an especially good day to recover debts. Family life will be very happy and comfortable. It is also a good day to meet individuals of wealth and property in a quite casual manner and an especially good day for purchasing valuable articles. If you have the good fortune to wear an astrological talisman ring under the influence of Mercury or Jupiter, expose it to the bright sunlight for some time before returning it to your finger. Don't be surprised if you have an unusual breakfast; when you reach your place of business you will be in an unusually cheerful frame of mind.

For the stock exchange fraternity, this day could be one of great, sweet surprises. Doing business contrary to your hunches will succeed. Today is a good day for bulling ahead. Iron, steel, machinery, and automotive shares are worth dealing in. This is a good day for trading in silver and other valuable metals. Dealers in very expensive dresses, toys, and jewelry will find this day especially lucky. This is also a good day for opening a new retail business or for signing contracts or other legal papers.

Those who prefer the racetrack will find their horses bringing them unusually good dividends. This is a day in which to earn more money than expected.

The evening hours are especially suited for some form of spiritual or uplifting activity. Your sleep will be unusually peaceful this evening.

Your lucky numbers for the day are 4, 5, and 9. Lucky hours are from 6 to 12 P.M. and from 3 to 8 P.M.

22

Primary Planetary Influence: Mercury, Uranus, Saturn

Secondary Planetary Influence: Saturn, Saturn, Jupiter

This is a strange day for you, since the planet Uranus is in close proximity to Saturn, a conjunction that usually indicates unusual happenings. In the morning hours you are likely to experience some unexpected good luck in regard to money matters. You may find yourself in the company of witty and bright friends. If you are in need of a typewriter or sewing maching for the home, today is a good day to purchase that item. Friends will appear, wasting a good deal of your time, and you may find yourself reaching your office late. Once there, you may be required to attend to some unusual and unique duties. The office hours will not be comfortable.

Those who speculate in the stock market must be extremely cautious. Market trends may be somewhat deceptive. This is not a good day to transact new business; instead, sit tight on previous holdings. This is, however, a good day for traders in machinery and luxury articles.

For those who prefer the racetrack, this is a good day indeed. Select horses whose numbers are 3, 5, and 6. Black horses are especially likely to win. You may meet someone at the track who has an eye on your earnings, so be forewarned.

During the evening hours, don't be surprised if you find some problems with teeth or with the ears. Sleep will be disturbed and unsound this evening.

Your lucky numbers for the day are 3, 5, and 6. The number 6 is more significant than the rest. Your lucky period is during the morning and at midday.

23

Primary Planetary Influence: Mercury, Uranus, Saturn

Secondary Planetary Influence: Saturn, Jupiter, Saturn

Today you experience the great influence of the planet Saturn in all your activities. Since Saturn is a materialistic planet, its conjunction with Uranus brings a number of unexpected enjoyments. Since you may be tempted to purchase articles that you don't really need, use your credit card rather than cash to ease any returns you may wish to make tomorrow.

The morning is especially pleasing, and your energy level runs very high. Expect the unexpected today. Your home is filled with sunshine. You find yourself arriving at the office before you really need to be there. In the office you are likely to encounter strange persons who wish to sell you things or to promote a new love interest.

If you are engaged in the stock market, expect very irrational sales. Try to make any purchases or sales before 1 P.M. This is not a good day for those who trade in valuable metals.

This is a good day for gambling. You can succeed with cards or any other form. For those who prefer racing, this day can prove very lucky indeed. You should choose the seventh race for a horse whose number is 7. As far as possible, limit your speculation to black horses. With the onset of the evening hours, you will feel somewhat depressed. Perhaps one of your children will be taken ill. Your sleep will be somewhat disturbed, and your partner may awaken with a nightmare.

Your lucky numbers for the day are 1, 5, and 7. The number 7 is the most significant of all. Lucky periods are in the morning and from 12 P.M. to 2 P.M.

24

Primary Planetary Influence: Mercury, Uranus, Jupiter

Secondary Planetary Influence: Jupiter, Saturn, Saturn

This is indeed an excellent day for family life and business. You arise with an idea that you have a distinct connection with the Cosmic. Strange things are likely to happen during the course of this day. You can add to the sense of oneness with all that is by devoting some time to meditation or by reading an inspirational book. You may receive long-expected letters. Because you are looking inward, it is possible that you will arrive at your place of business late.

The atmosphere at the office is much better than it was yesterday, and you may find yourself with far less anxiety about getting things done.

For those who speculate in the market, this is only a so-so day. Blue-chip stocks will drop, and you may find yourself able to make some very advantageous purchases. The catch of the day will be those companies dealing with iron, steel, machinery, and construction. High-priced electronic stocks are also favorable.

At the racecourse, flaunted favorites fail completely. You must use your own discretion and not rely on those who pretend to know of such things. Brown, white, or black horses are most likely to win. Speculation in the fourth race will bring you good luck. Do not stake too much money on the horses.

Evening hours can be spent in serious contemplation. Your sleep will be peaceful and restful.

Your lucky numbers for the day are 0, 2, and 5. The luckiest periods are from 8 to 10 A.M. and during the evening hours.

25

Primary Planetary Influence: Mercury, Jupiter, Mars

Secondary Planetary Influence: Saturn, Saturn, Jupiter

Today is a day for many difficulties, but they may be warded off by your innate wisdom. During the morning hours you find yourself in a very unhappy frame of mind. Perhaps you are dwelling too much on the past. If at all possible, to cheer yourself up, why not do some shopping? You may receive letters that bring disappointment and worry. You will not feel like doing anything and would much prefer a vacation to your work. The digestive system seems unusually toxic, and it is highly unlikely you will enjoy any of your meals.

At the office, a great deal of unforeseen work is placed before you.

For those who speculate in the stock market, this day is not favorable. Those who deal in oil and seeds, however, can make advantageous gains. Make the best of the day, and try to conclude your business before 3 P.M. so that you can go home early.

For those who go to the racetrack, today is an absolute loss. You would be better advised to stay home and save your money. Any judgments you make appear to go wrong. It would be far better to go to a good hotel for an enjoyable lunch or early dinner than to go to the track.

As the evening hours are controlled by the planet Mars, be especially careful while traveling. Also be very careful to watch your step. You might turn an ankle while stepping up or down from a train or bus. Evening hours are particularly troublesome, and you will not sleep very well.

Your lucky numbers for the day are 1, 3, and 7. The number 3 is most significant of all. Lucky periods are from 12 P.M. to 2 P.M.

26

Primary Planetary Influence: Mercury, Jupiter, Venus

Secondary Planetary Influence: Saturn, Jupiter, Mars

This is an exceptionally good day for you. You can expect great monetary gains. The morning is exceptionally bright, and you find yourself in a cheerful and happy frame of mind. This is a day for putting money into the bank rather than drawing it out. You are likely to meet individuals who will encourage you to enter into some sort of partnership, which might have something to do with a joint purchase of a book or some aspect of publishing. Breakfast seems exceptionally tasty, and you go to your office in high spirits.

The position of Jupiter, which rules expansion, during the period of 12 P.M. to 6 P.M. is especially favorable for you.

For those involved in the stock exchange, this day is a lucky one. The market shows a bullish nature, resulting in a good margin of profit. Those who deal in silver and cotton will find the day exceptionally lucky. The price of cotton should begin to advance.

For those who favor the track, consider betting on white horses.

Simply close your eyes and intently think of a horse; the horse that first comes to mind is your winner. Do not continue to play after the midday race.

During the evening hours, you may have to devote much of your time to family needs. Take some time to sit down and talk with your partner. Your sleep will be sound and refreshing.

Your lucky numbers for the day are 0, 1, and 2. The number 2 is especially significant. Most of this day is a lucky one for you, but the period from 12 P.M. to 6 P.M. is especially favorable.

27

Primary Planetary Influence: Mercury, Jupiter, Mercury

Secondary Planetary Influence: Jupiter, Mars. Venus

This is a day during which the goddess of wealth will visit you with a smiling face. Do something big. The morning hours are exceptionally favorable and lucky. You can make a partner happy by buying a much-needed article of clothing. Some older person from your partner's family may pay you an unexpected visit. This is a time during which you find yourself turning inward and your thoughts becoming more serious. If you feel so inclined, you may wish to spend part of the day in meditation.

Your work at the office will be normal.

For those who favor the stock exchange, this could be a lucky day. Textile shares are especially hot right now. If you have a bullish position, unloading some of your holdings will result in a good profit. Those who deal in silver will find themselves unusually successful today.

This is also a good day for those who lend money, such as bankers and pawnbrokers. Overdue loans advanced by them are likely to be repaid in full, with interest.

When it comes to the racetrack, however, look for the den of forty thieves. No matter how much money you take with you, you will not have enough. White or brown horses are likely to win. Horse number 3 in the fifth race can bring you a good dividend.

The evening hours are somewhat low-key, and sleep will be unusually refreshing.

Your lucky numbers for the day are 3, 5, and 7. The number 7 is most significant. Your lucky period is the morning.

28

Primary Planetary Influence: Moon, Jupiter, Moon

Secondary Planetary Influence: Mars, Venus, Mercury

Today you do things you would never have done yesterday, and the whole day's aspect is slightly topsy-turvy. The mischievous, fast-moving Moon is certainly at play. In the morning you receive some disappointing news. It may simply be that some important appointment has been postponed. If you have a dog or a cat, take special care of this important pet, for he may be involved in some kind of accident. You may have awakened with a cold or a sore throat. Fasting could be useful.

Once you get to the office, however, things can be happy and cheerful. You may be required to do some work that is apparently difficult and beyond your capacity, but if you persist all will be well.

As for those who are involved in the stock market, trading can be deceptive. Do not get caught up in short-term movements. If you feel you must invest, look toward those companies involved in shipping. It might be best to refrain from doing any business, however.

Persons engaged in other commercial activities will find the day to be a day of deception and great frustration.

For those who favor the racetrack, this is a most unlucky day; any selections made are most likely to result in failure. Remember that money not gambled is money gained. Make this your motto for today.

The evening hours are spent on a more positive note. If you have time, take a long walk, preferably in a country garden or along the seashore with members of your family. Your sleep will be sound and refreshing.

Your lucky numbers for the day are 1, 3, and 7. Number 1 is the most significant of all. This is not generally a very lucky day.

29

Primary Planetary Influence: Moon, Saturn, Sun

Secondary Planetary Influence: Venus, Mercury, Sun

Today is good day to enjoy material pleasures, such as good food, amusements, and sports. You awaken cheerfully from a sound night's sleep. As you gaze at yourself in the mirror, you look quite young, energetic, and very fit. This is an especially good day for those of the older generation, who will feel unusually healthy. This is a good day for senior citizens to associate with young boys and girls and perhaps to please them by buying sweets or a small toy. Some of your morning hours will likely be spent in office work that was not finished yesterday but brought home.

Writers and poets will find this day unusually inspiring and will produce a good many pages before the day ends. Musicians likewise will find this a very fulfilling day.

When you reach your office, you will find routines running normally. Your boss will not leave you alone, however, so expect to be on constant call.

For those who are involved in the stock market, this day should prove to be generally auspicious—a day for bears. If you are holding stocks bought under a bear market, you may wish to unload them and will feel unusually elated at your good fortune. This day is also most favorable for those who trade in oilseeds. They should buy at every rise, at least in lots of three.

Those who prefer the racetrack will also be lucky. Black horses are most likely to be winners.

Toward evening, you find yourself safe and financially sound. You will have a good night's sleep.

Your lucky numbers for the day are 1, 3, and 5. The number 5 is especially significant. The luckiest times are during the morning from 10 to 11 A.M. and during the evening from 9 to 11 P.M.

30

Primary Planetary Influence: Moon, Saturn, Mercury

Secondary Planetary Influence: Mercury, Sun, Moon

This day is generally a good day for you. The morning hours are unusually lucky, and you should use them to plan the balance of your day, especially in regard to any financial pursuits. You may wish to start the day with an invigorating cool shower. It is a day during which you will meet a number of friends whose company you will enjoy greatly. The morning hours are suitable for purchasing articles of luxury. You may also receive some very positive letters from unexpected quarters. If you have a relative living in a foreign country, you may receive some good news from him by mail or by telephone, and when you reach your office, you will find the same good luck following you. Work at the office, though, may be a bit heavy and taxing.

Those who are engaged in the stock exchange will find this to be a very lucky day. This is a good day for big business. Investment company, insurance, and bank shares are likely to show a great deal of activity. Those who trade in oil or oil-related products will find this day an extremely lucky one. If you are holding bullish contracts at this time, it is a good day to unload them.

For those who favor the racetrack, this is also a good day. Place your bets on black horses and on horses who carry the number 6. The sixth race of the day can also prove luckier than the others.

The evening hours are spent in a cheerful mood. You may visit a museum exhibit you have thought about for some time. You may wish to read an amusing book before falling into a peaceful sleep.

Lucky numbers for the day are 1, 2, and 6. The number 6 is most significant of all. The lucky times of day are 11 A.M. to 12 P.M. and 7 to 8 P.M.

31

Primary Planetary Influence: Moon, Saturn, Venus

Secondary Planetary Influence: Sun, Moon, Sun

This is an especially auspicious day from the point of view of family matters. The finalization of marriage plans for a son or daughter is possible. You will find yourself extremely happy in the morning. Those around you will be cheerful, too. A female relative is likely to pay you an unexpected visit. This is a good day to take out an insurance policy or to buy a lottery ticket. Meals are especially to your liking, and you go off to your place of business in an optimistic frame of mind.

Once in the office, however, work is likely to be a bit taxing and demanding. Give full attention to whatever you do.

For those you play the stock market, this day will hold good and bad luck in equal lots. While previous bullish holdings will appreciate in value, you may enter into some bearish transactions that will take you into deep water. For those who trade in oilseeds, this day may represent the top prices of current rises. Sell and reap whatever profit you may. For those who deal in silver, the day is a normal one without any unusual increase in price. Those who retail luxury items will find themselves busy throughout the day.

Racetrack lovers have great surprises in store for them. If you play your hunch, you will succeed. Especially lucky are horses with a mixed black and white coat. Avoid the third and sixth races.

The evening hours find you unusually romantic. You will have a good night's sleep.

Lucky numbers for the day are 0, 1, and 5. Number 1 is especially significant. The luckiest periods of the day are from 8 to 9 A.M. and 6 to 8 P.M.

32

Primary Planetary Influence: Moon, Saturn, Mars

Secondary Planetary Influence: Moon, Sun, Mercury

Today is likely to prove troublesome for you in many different ways. You wake up with a bad headache and upset stomach. Suddenly the world around you has assumed a somewhat sober aspect, and you feel somewhat saddened and downhearted. It's likely your temper will be bad, and you may find yourself having an argument with a partner. The best thing to do is to get out of the house and away from others. This is a day in which you must surrender yourself to the will of the Cosmic. Since your stomach will be upset for most of the day, you will not eat particularly well.

When you get to the office, you find a great deal of work mounted up, which may require you to work late into the evening hours.

For those involved in the stock market, today could be an unfortunate one. Prices will decline to an alarming extent, making those in bullish positions nervous. This could be a day of great loss for you. Those dealing in oil and cotton should be extremely cautious, as their ideas as to the trend of the market will be completely out of keeping with reality. Today is not the day to do any new business.

The racetrack is most unlucky. A horse you might select may stumble, and so will your finances. You may win a few races, however, if you approach your betting somewhat cautiously.

The evening is not particularly auspicious; you find yourself getting involved in some kind of accident or quarrel. As a result of your unpleasant day, your sleep will be disturbed and uncomfortable.

Your lucky numbers for the day are 2, 6, and 9. Number 6 is most significant. Your auspicious hours are those between 1 and 3 P.M.

★

33

Primary Planetary Influence: Moon, Mercury, Jupiter
Secondary Planetary Influence: Sun, Mercury, Venus

This should prove to be an unusually lucky day for you, as three strong planets are controlling your life's activities equally. You will wake up positive and cheerful and with an abundance of new ideas, which you should translate into positive action. This is an especially lucky day for poets and writers. Whatever they write will be well received by the public. Because of the strong influence of Venus, romantic literature will do especially well. The day is particularly lucky from the standpoint of monetary gains from unexpected sources. You may pass a pleasurable time in the company of members of the opposite sex. You will have a hearty breakfast and go off to the office with optimism and in a most positive frame of mind.

In the office, work will proceed normally, much to your liking.

If you favor the stock exchange, actions taken should be bullish. Shares purchased will shoot up within a short period of time. Especially active are shares in shipping, synthetic fibers, and other blue chips. You may also find some unusual activity in the silver market.

For those who favor the racetrack, white horses will do especially well. In fact, you may win on two consecutive races.

When you return home, you will find sleep unusually refreshing.

Your lucky numbers for the day are 1, 5, and 9. The entire day, but especially the evening hours, will prove extremely lucky.

34

Primary Planetary Influence: Moon, Mercury, Saturn
Secondary Planetary Influence: Mercury, Jupiter, Mars

This is generally a good day for you. The morning hours may be spent at home, possibly reading or arranging your personal effects. In fact, you may find some misplaced article that has been missing for some time. Relations with your partner will be more than cordial, and the two of you may discuss family problems that have come to the fore recently.

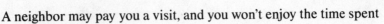

A neighbor may pay you a visit, and you won't enjoy the time spent in his company.

When you go to your office, you will find on your desk some long-pending work that needs clearing up. This may be an exhausting task, but you must put your attention to it once and for all.

For those who speculate in the stock exchange, the day is quite normal. The market appears to be somewhat bearish today. If you must invest, bank, insurance, and investment company shares are the catches of the day. This is also an excellent day for an investment in oil shares. Silver prices are likely to remain steady, with no real gains.

For those who favor the racetrack, this is a day of mixed fortunes. Be extremely cautious in the selection of horses. Brown horses are most likely to win.

During the evening hours, you find yourself plagued by some unnecessary worry, and as a result, your sleep is somewhat disturbed.

Your lucky numbers today are 0, 4, and 7. The number 4 is particularly significant. The lucky period is from 10 A.M. to 6 P.M.

35

Primary Planetary Influence: Moon, Saturn, Mercury

Secondary Planetary Influence: Venus, Mars, Jupiter

This should prove a very lucky day for you in terms of material gains. You wake up feeling romantic toward your partner and affectionate about any offspring you might have. The morning news-paper carries some astounding news. This is a particularly auspicious day for musicians, painters, and writers. Whatever is produced today will be highly appreciated and valued by the public.

Be especially cautious around water—either swimming or traveling by water.

As for the office, those who work in highly technical areas will find the day a good one. Work will be more or less normal and tedious. For those who play the stock market, this is a day with good profits in the offing. Shipping and synthetic fibers appear to be somewhat bullish. Enter the market as soon as it opens, because you may wish to sell out at the end of the day. For those who trade in oil or oilseeds, this is an especially lucky day. Profits can be beyond your expectation.

Racing fans will find this day unusually lucky. Both black and white horses are very likely to win. However, do not gamble on the last races. You're most likely to win in the first, fourth, and fifth races.

Expect to have a disturbed sleep, due to a barrage of minor physical ailments.

Your lucky numbers for the day are 1, 4, and 5. The luckiest period of the day is the morning.

36

Primary Planetary Influence: Moon, Mercury, Jupiter

Secondary Planetary Influence: Mars, Jupiter, Saturn

This is a good day for doing charitable work or undertaking some new literary assignment. The entire morning can be spent in writing. You may receive news about a birth in the family. The morning is unusually auspicious. You may find yourself doing the daily crossword puzzle or looking over the selection of the horses for the evening races. Expect to be visited by unusually happy friends and to enjoy time in their company. Nothing exceptional will happen at the office.

For speculators, the stock exchange is extremely lucky. Under the influence of the benevolent planet Jupiter, the market is likely to rise. Buy only blue-chip stocks and avoid trading in oilseeds.

Those engaged in the retail business, selling luxury items, ladies' dresses, toys, or cosmetics, will find this day especially favorable.

For those who favor the racetrack, today is also a good one. Be sure to play your hunch. Those horses that have been neglected are most likely to win. The third and fourth races are especially favorable. Select those horses on whose forehead there is a white mark resembling a crescent moon.

When the evening comes, you find yourself meditative. Your lucky numbers are 3, 4, and 7. The entire day will prove to be a lucky one, with the evening hours especially so.

37

Primary Planetary Influence: Sun, Neptune, Mars

Secondary Planetary Influence: Jupiter, Saturn, Saturn

This is a day during which you are likely to feel lonely and pessimistic. You will soon realize that your activities will never come to fruition unless it is the will of the Cosmic. You should devote a good deal of time to religious practices: meditation and prayer. Even though all is well with the world as far as you are concerned, there is a certain underlying gloom during the morning hours. Perhaps there will be a misunderstanding between yourself and your partner. You may find a missing document or article. As a result, you reach your office late. Long-pending and tedious work will have to be dealt with today. It is possible that you will exchange some hot words with your boss or a subordinate.

This is a black day for those who speculate in stocks. Do not enter into any new contracts or buy anything. You may feel like unloading shares, as prices seem to have remained stagnant for some time now, but do not be quick to throw the baby out with the bathwater. The market may receive some disturbing news that results in a minor panic. Traders in grain, however, may find this day a lucky one.

For those who favor the track, the day is not favorable. All judgments are likely to be bad ones, and if you bet, you will lose heavily. It would be better to stay away from the racecourse.

You find yourself unusually uneasy and restless during the evening hours, and your sleep will be somewhat disturbed.

Lucky numbers for the day are 0, 4, and 7. The number 7 is especially important. Lucky hours of the day are from 6 to 9 A.M. only.

38

Primary Planetary Influence: Sun, Neptune, Venus

Secondary Planetary Influence: Saturn, Saturn, Jupiter

This is a most auspicious day for older members of the family. They can expect to feel a great improvement in their health if they have been ill for some time. You may also receive a visit during the morning hours from older persons. This is a good day to take out an insurance policy or to make long-term investments. The morning hours are especially sunny and cheerful. If you are a writer, don't be surprised if you receive letters of appreciation from fans of your literary work. Breakfast seems especially good, and you go off to your office in an optimistic frame of mind.

At the office, work seems to be somewhat lighter than usual and much to your liking.

Those who trade in the stock exchange find the day a fairly good one. Synthetics seem to be in the limelight, and the market in general is somewhat bullish. You might wish to sell off some holdings with good profit. Do not do anything on hunch alone, though; rely on the

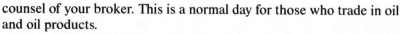

counsel of your broker. This is a normal day for those who trade in oil and oil products.

Those who deal in luxury and other valuable articles, however, will find this day a very lucky one, with record sales. Pawnbrokers and money lenders of other kinds will also have a good day. Some overdue loans will be recovered.

For those who prefer the racetrack, this is a lucky day. Chances are that fortune will smile on them for two or three races. Bet on older horses.

The evening hours are spent in a romantic way, and you will have a peaceful sleep.

Auspicious numbers for the day are 1, 3, and 9. The number 9 is especially significant. Lucky hours for the day are from 8 to 10 A.M. and from 4 to 7 P.M.

39

Primary Planetary Influence: Sun, Neptune, Mercury

Secondary Planetary Influence: Saturn, Jupiter, Mars

In general, this is a lucky day for you. You find yourself financially stronger and will spend the morning hours in some serious work. Those who are engaged in literary pursuits should write as much as possible, for the muses are especially inspirational. This is also a good day for those who are religious. It is a good time to enter into deeper levels of meditation and to forget the mundane plane of life. The morning is generally fine and cheerful. You are likely to receive some long-expected letters. Finding yourself in the company of older persons makes you unusually happy. A member of your family is likely to receive good news regarding an increase in salary or a promotion.

At the office, you find yourself being unusually responsible.

For those who are involved in the stock exchange, the day appears to be favorable for selling off long-standing shares. It is advisable to get out of the market for a few days. Any new business you engage in will result in your having to hold acquisitions for a much longer time than you would like. In other words, this is a time for long-term investments rather than short-term trading.

Today is especially favorable for those dealing in oil or oilseeds. Sell short in the cotton market, and wait for prices to continue to decline. Traders in metals will have an exceptionally busy time.

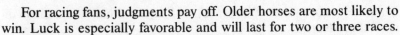

For racing fans, judgments pay off. Older horses are most likely to win. Luck is especially favorable and will last for two or three races.

In the evening hours, you may find yourself going out to stores and purchasing household items that have been needed for some time. You will find yourself somewhat happy and will have a sound, restful sleep.

Lucky numbers for the day are 1, 4, and 7. The number 7 is especially significant. Practically the whole day is lucky.

40

Primary Planetary Influence: Sun, Neptune, Moon

Secondary Planetary Influence: Jupiter, Mars, Venus

A day as bright as this is very rare. This is an excellent day for traveling or for planning a long future trip. You may find yourself the recipient of a financial windfall that will bring a great deal of happiness and enable you to do things you have put off doing for some time. Whatever is undertaken today will prove to be successful. The morning hours are particularly happy and cheerful. Throw away any imaginary worries regarding the past, and you will feel generally optimistic. You may receive good news in regard to a promotion or transfer. In fact, the transfer may even require relocation to a distant city or state. If such as offer comes, look at it very carefully, and don't be too quick to refuse it.

In the office, you will find yourself dealing with old correspondence and pending work. Your boss will be appreciative and will be cordial with you all day.

As to the stock exchange, this is a very lucky day for those who hold bullish positions. Shares of synthetics or steamship companies move up swiftly, and you should enter the market as soon as it opens. Dealers in very fine cloth, silk, and other luxuries will also have a busy day. This is an especially good day for receiving new orders, no matter what business you are engaged in.

For those who favor the racetrack, the day is lucky, and you are advised to play hunches. White horses and horses on whose forehead there is a crescent moon are likely to win.

During the evening hours, reading light books will bring a great deal of comfort. You may find yourself somewhat romantic toward a partner and will sleep well.

Lucky numbers for the day are 4, 7, and 8. The number 4 is especially significant. The lucky period for the day is from 2 to 7 P.M.

41

Primary Planetary Influence: Sun, Venus, Sun

Secondary Planetary Influence: Mars, Venus, Mercury

This is generally a very good day for you and your family. You wake up with a great deal of cheer, full of ideas for the future. You may receive good news from a relative announcing the birth of a son, a betrothal, or a long-expected promotion. Today is a good day to catch up on long-pending correspondence. You may find yourself visited by older persons and will spend a good time with them. Breakfast is unusually pleasant, as is the morning mail.

Once you get to the office, you will find youself receiving some very important work that will have to be done quickly but will be highly appreciated by your employer.

For those involved in the stock exchange, this is a generally good day, although prices will fluctuate greatly. Synthetics, oil, and sugar shares are likely to go up and with them, possibly, your assets. If you already hold shares in these areas, do not sell them now, but wait for further increases. Those who deal in luxury items, very fine cloth, and ready-to-wear garments will have a busy day.

For racing fans, this is an especially sunny day. Horses with black or white coats are most likely to win. Bet on races number two, four, and six. You can expect to score at least one good race.

During the evening hours, why not relax with a serious book?

Lucky numbers for the day are 1, 2, and 6. The number 6 is most significant. Lucky periods are during the morning hours and from 2 to 6 P.M.

42

Primary Planetary Influence: Sun, Venus, Mercury

Secondary Planetary Influence: Venus, Mercury, Sun

This is one of the luckiest days for you of the entire year. Good luck abounds in your work, family, and finance. The morning hours are extremely bright and cheerful. Why not spend some of these early hours with your partner and children? An eldest son or daughter will have some exceptional luck today. You may be invited by a neighbor for a cup of tea or breakfast meeting. If any business proposals are presented at this time, give serious thought to them. This is generally a good day for purchases.

You may find yourself getting to the office earlier than usual. Work will not be exceptionally heavy, and you will idle away much of the time. This could be because your boss is away on vacation. You feel unusually important in the office.

For those who favor the stock exchange, this is a good day for making money. As prices are likely to go down, you may find yourself selling short. Yoy may also find that there are some exceptional buys among blue-chip stocks. Moneylenders, pawnbrokers, and those who trade in luxury articles will have good luck.

At the racecourse, you will have a wonderful time. You should pay special attention to colts and white horses. Play your hunches, but avoid the sixth race.

The evening hours are pleasant, and your pockets will be full. You feel exhausted and weak at night, and your sleep is somewhat disturbed.

Lucky numbers for the day are 4, 5, and 8. The number 8 is especially significant. Lucky hours are from 4 to 7 P.M.

43

Primary Planetary Influence: Sun, Venus, Venus

Secondary Planetary Influence: Mercury, Moon, Moon

This is an especially good day from the family point of view. The day starts well both at home and in business. You may feel sorry for having had unpleasant words with a partner on the previous day; strained relationships can now be patched up. You may find yourself unusually romantic from the moment you awaken. If you find yourself in love, this is a very good day for confessions or proposals. If you have an unmarried son or daughter, today's news may bring some excitement in regard to a partnership.

At the office you will find yourself approaching a number of employees of the opposite sex. Work seems exceptionally light, so you can easily get into trouble if you allow yourself the freedom to do so. You may have to draft a report, though, or handle some correspondence, but this goes very quickly.

For those involved in the stock market, the day moves slowly. Prices move upward and downward within a very small range. This would seem to be a day to avoid making new commitments or selling shares already owned.

Those involved in printing, photography, cosmetics, and ladies' garments will find this day a busy one. New orders for such articles should seem unusually good.

For those who favor the racetrack, fate is unpredictable. If you must bet, bet on colts, and try your luck in the sixth race.

The evening hours are romantic and you will have a good, restful sleep.

Lucky numbers for the day are 2, 6, and 9. The number 6 is important. Lucky periods are from 8 to 10 A.M. and from 4 to 8 P.M.

44

Primary Planetary Influence: Sun, Venus, Mars

Secondary Planetary Influence: Moon, Moon, Sun

During the early morning hours you feel sickly and somewhat ill at ease. You may find yourself suffering from a headache or unusual stomach problems. You will probably feel anxious about a child's progress in school because of a report received the previus day. The fact that he or she is not achieving adds to your despondency. One way to handle this morning is to pay a visit to a close friend or relative and get away from your own problems.

An angry neighbor may approach you, or you may receive some letters requesting donations. Your appetite will be unusually poor, and you will find yourself reaching the office in a state of great depression. Once there, you get caught up in your work, which helps to relieve the discomfort of the early morning hours. Be sure that you keep your temper and observe silence as much as possible. Those around you will attempt to get you involved in their problems.

For those who speculate in the market, today is not a lucky one at all; you are likely to misjudge general trends. News from outside sources seems to shatter the general market morale and prices may plummet. Do not follow the crowd, however, but simply hold on and have patience. Do not enter into any new purchases. Generally speaking, those who deal in agricultural products will find the day better suited to financial gains.

For those who favor the track, winning and losing seem equally likely. Suggested are the first four races only. Brown horses are most likely to win. Small bets are most desirable; don't be surprised should you find yourself with some losses.

During the evening hours, the physical problems you began the day with seem to return, and your sleep is somewhat restless.

Lucky numbers for the day are 2, 4, and 5. The number 4 is especially significant. No particularly lucky periods can be predicted.

45

Primary Planetary Influence: Sun, Sun, Jupiter

Secondary Planetary Influence: Moon, Sun, Mercury

This day is an exceptionally lucky one. The morning hours may be spent in the company of political authorities. For those who are engaged in writing, this is a most auspicious day; work completed will have great philosophical merit. If you engage in public speaking, you may find yourself with an invitation to deliver a last-minute lecture in the evening or to preside over some unexpected meeting. This is an especially good day to enhance your fame in any endeavor, and you find yourself feeling rather important. The morning hours and noontime are unusually bright. If you felt somewhat ill yesterday, today you feel a great deal better.

At the office, you find yourself concluding some very important and confidential work. You may hear some good news regarding a promotion or advancement.

For the stock exchange, this is a good day. Blue chips are likely to rise, and the market is generally bullish. Don't trade your hunch today, but listen to your analyst. Those who are engaged in selling retail books or stationery, education, social work, or politics find this a good day.

The racetrack proves to be a lucky bet. White horses come to the fore. Why not bet on horse number 7 in the seventh race? During the evening hours you find yourself feeling religious and reach for books of an inspirational nature.

Lucky numbers for the day are 1, 5, and 7. The number 7 is significant. The entire day will be extremely lucky.

46

Primary Planetary Influence: Mercury, Sun, Saturn

Secondary Planetary Influence: Sun, Mercury, Sun

Financially this day is very lucky. You may recover some long-standing debts. You are likely to feel very comfortable during the entire morning. There will be a great deal of energy and exhilaration. This day is especially good for shopping for household articles, which you find available at bargain prices. You may begin the day thinking about one of your hobbies and will eventually arrive at your office in a cheerful and optimistic frame of mind.

Once there, you will find important work to be done and will solve a number of difficult problems. Your employer is going to be well pleased with you, and you feel very important.

For those who favor the stock exchange, this is not a particularly good day. Price trends are somewhat deceptive, and it is better to hold on to previous purchases than to expand your ownership. If you wish to purchase some new stocks, however, you might look at sugar. Those who trade in oil may find this a good day. Prices seem to rise without any apparent cause.

Those who favor the racetrack find this a difficult period. The only chance for them to reap any kind of benefit is by betting on the numbers 3, 6, and 7.

During the evening hours you feel worried, and your sleep will be restless.

Lucky numbers for the day are 3, 6, and 7. The number 7 is especially significant. All time periods are fairly good, with the exception of the nighttime.

47

Primary Planetary Influence: Mercury, Sun, Saturn

Secondary Planetary Influence: Mercury, Sun, Moon

This is generally a good day for you in terms of financial and family affairs. The morning hours are bright, and you find yourself cheerful and optimistic. You come into contact with a number of intelligent, people. You also feel quite proud of your offspring. This is a good day for purchasing costly items. If you own a vehicle of some type, however, it may not function well.

As the day advances, you come further under the influence of the Sun. You reach your office in a cheerful frame of mind. Work is to your liking, and everyone seems pleased with you. You handle important work easily and successfully.

For those who favor the stock exchange, the day is one of mixed fortunes. The general sentiment is bright and optimistic, and you will be tempted to enter into some bullish contracts. But the gains for the day may actually be rather meager. In fact, it is perhaps best not to do too much business at all. Shares of companies engaged in oil and soap may be in the limelight. This is an extremely good day for oil and oil-related businesses. Any new dealings will return handsome rewards. The day is also auspicious for those dealing in stationery or book sales.

As for the racetrack, this is a day of mixed fortune. Do not follow hunches. If you must bet at all, bet on black horses. Horse number 7 in the seventh race is particularly favorable.

The evening hours are not particularly cheerful, and your sleep may be somewhat disturbed.

Lucky numbers for the day are 0, 4, and 7. The number 7 is significant. Lucky hours of the day are from 2 to 6 P.M.

48

Primary Planetary Influence: Mercury, Sun, Jupiter

Secondary Planetary Influence: Sun, Moon, Sun

This is a very good day for you, as all three controlling planets are most fortuitous. The morning time is suitable for doing things for your fellowmen and for serious writing. You will find youself filled with many noble and inspiring ideas. Morning hours will prove very lucky from a financial point of view. This is an especially good day for taking out an insurance policy or investing in long-term securities. You may visit a close friend, whose advice regarding financial investments may prove extremely valuable.

Once you reach your office, you find yourself in an optimistic frame of mind. Work is quite normal, and you have a relatively easy time of it.

For those who favor the stock exchange, the day is extremely favorable and business should proceed at a good pace. Since you may find that end-of-the-day trading is particularly optimistic, buy as early in the morning as you can. Shipping companies and those engaged in

★

synthetics are the catch of the day. This is also a good day for those who engage in expensive luxury items. Those who deal in oilseeds, cotton, and silver will find no great movement in prices. It may, however, be wise to unload half of your cotton holdings at this time.

For those who favor the racetrack, white and older horses are likely to be in the limelight. Horse number 3 in the third race should prove lucky. The night is unusually pleasant, and you get a good sleep.

Lucky numbers for the day are 1, 3, and 4. The number 3 is significant. The entire day is quite lucky.

49

Primary Planetary Influence: Mercury, Moon, Mars

Secondary Planetary Influence: Moon, Sun, Mercury

This day is one of mixed fortunes. If you are seeking to purchase land for agricultural reasons, the day is very auspicious. You may find yourself with a headache and an upset stomach during the early hours. This may be due in part to a family incident that causes you concern. Try to keep your temper, and take rest when needed. You may feel anxiety about finances; if you find a need to borrow capital, you find yourself humiliated and somewhat insulted. It is best to postpone financial dealings and to spend some time in the company of a good friend. You are also likely to miss your train or bus and arrive at your office late. Once you arrive there, work is heavy and tedious, and it is difficult to maintain any kind of peace of mind.

For those engaged in the stock exchange, today is a bad day. Your judgment will be unsound, and great losses can be suffered. Shares that you feel inclined to buy turn about completely by the end of the session, and you find yourself making only marginal gains. For those who trade in agricultural produce, this is somewhat a better day. Those who deal in heavy machinery, agricultural implements, and articles of luxury are also likely to have a busy day.

For those who favor the track, today is not particularly favorable. Do not bet on hunches. If you must gamble, take a tip from a short, redheaded or brickfaced, and somewhat unattractive person. But make sure that you bet only a small amount because substantial gains are not to be found under these aspects.

Your lucky numbers for the day are 1, 4; and 8. The number 8 is significant. The only lucky period is from 2 to 4 P.M.

50

Primary Planetary Influence: Mercury, Moon, Venus

Secondary Planetary Influence: Sun, Mercury, Venus

If you have secret dreams or hopes, today is most favorable for their achievement, and people who share your ideas will profit. The day begins on a fine note, and you wake up fresh and bubbling with energy. A great deal of luck is in the offing. Discuss financial matters with a partner, and take his or her advice. This is a good day for purchases. You may find private correspondence tedious and the mail somewhat heavy, though this is a lucky day for writers. This is a good day to tidy up your study and work area by going through old correspondence and throwing away things that are no longer needed. You will find your appetite good and your meals quite enjoyable.

When you arrive at your office or place of business, you are in an optimistic frame of mind.

For the stock exchange fraternity, the day is extremely lucky. The market appears somewhat bullish; shipping, synthetics, and other blue chips are in the limelight. If you hold a bullish position, now is the time to sell and walk away with a decent profit. This is not, however, a day to follow hunches but rather the advice of your broker or analyst. This is a good time for moneylenders, though those who trade in oil will experience an unusually unpredictable slowdown in prices.

For those who favor the racetrack, this day is an unusually lucky one. It is most likely that you will earn good dividends, especially by betting on white horses or on horses on whose forehead there is a crescent moon. Take your tips from women or men of your acquaintance. Avoid the sixth and seventh races, which could prove disastrous.

The evening hours are peaceful.

Lucky numbers for the day are 3, 5, and 8. The number 5 is most significant. Practically the entire day is fortuitous.

51

Primary Planetary Influence: Mercury, Moon, Mercury

Secondary Planetary Influence: Mercury, Venus, Mars

This should prove to be a day of great financial gains. You feel elated over the recovery of some long-standing debts. The morning is fine and bright, for you are in a very happy mood.

★

This day is suitable for the purchase or sale of luxury items. Young persons of your acquaintance are likely to pay you a visit, and you feel happy and cheerful in their company. The mail is somewhat heavy, and you are forced to write a great many letters. Someone may approach you to buy a luxury article, but be extremely careful, because what is offered may not be worth its price. You will enjoy your breakfast, and arrive at your office or place of business in an optimistic frame of mind.

For those who favor the stock exchange, this is a good day, as profits are likely to reach beyond expectations. Synthetics and transportation companies are extremely active. This is also a good day for those who deal in high-priced articles, for pawnbrokers, and for others who lend money. Those who deal in gold will also find this a very active day.

For those who favor the racetrack, this is a lucky day. It is wise to bet on colts or white horses. Do your betting in the first and third races only. If you play your hunches, you will most likely succeed.

Lucky numbers for the day are 1, 4, and 7. The number 4 is especially significant. The entire day is lucky for you.

52

Primary Planetary Influence: Mercury, Moon, Moon

Secondary Planetary Influence: Venus, Mars, Jupiter

This is a day in which you experience disappointment on all fronts. You wake up somewhat confused and entertain dreamy ideas that are reversed within the next few moments. You may find yourself waking with a headache or with a great deal of tension in and around the eyes. An important article or document may be misplaced, causing a great deal of concern and expenditure of time in searching for it. The arrival of unwelcome guests or friends can also upset your temper. Today is a good day to observe silence and to be alone.

Once you reach the office, vacation plans may be rejected by your boss, and you are likely to feel frustrated. For those who favor the stock exchange, this is a very dangerous day. Initial price trends are likely to be severely affected by adverse political news. Whatever position you hold in the market, you are advised not to enter into any fresh purchases, but simply to maintain your existing holdings. Do not sell out of panic. This is, however, a very lucky day for those who deal in luxury items, for ice cream vendors, gold and jewelry merchants, and flower and vegetable vendors. The day is also financially lucky for writers seeking new literary contracts.

As for the racetrack, this is not a day to indulge in any betting. All calculations and hunches are likely to cause great loss. It is better to simply be an observer.

Lucky numbers for the day are 1, 7, and 9. The number 1 is especially significant. Lucky times of the day are from 11 A.M. to 2 P.M.

53

Primary Planetary Influence: Mercury, Mars, Sun

Secondary Planetary Influence: Mars, Jupiter, Saturn

As the day begins, you balance your checkbook and find that cash reserves are greatly limited. Physically you feel ill at ease, and it is likely that some costly household article may be broken. You find yourself reflecting on the past, and you feel restless about the good old days and relationships that never were. As you look in the mirror, you see that you are advancing in age, and this, too, depresses you. Beware of quarrels with a partner. Try to be cheerful; pay a visit to a good friend.

Upon reaching your office, you feel depresssed and greatly under the influence of the negative morning atmosphere.

For those who favor the stock exchange, this day could prove a dangerous one. The influence of Mars on the planet Mercury, which rules decision making, could be ruinous. Hold on to previus purchases, and do not be quick to sell out. For most traders and merchants, the day is normal, and those who deal in corn and other agricultural produce may have a particularly good day.

For those who favor racing, today is not favorable either. Calculations and judgments are extremely ineffective today. While you may be tempted to place large bets, the returns are not really there. If you must gamble, however, bet on brown horses and colts. Try the second, third, and seventh races.

Lucky numbers for the day are 2, 3, and 7. The number 3 is most significant. The most auspicious times of the day are from 7 to 10 A.M. and from 6 to 10 P.M.

54

Primary Planetary Influence: Mercury, Mars, Mercury

Secondary Planetary Influence: Jupiter, Saturn, Saturn

You wake up with a bad headache and an upset stomach. You are completely out of sorts today. As far as money matters are concerned, this day is a most unfortunate one. You may be humiliated by a creditor or landlord who insists that you have not met his bills. Unwelcome friends can also make you uneasy. It is possible that you may lose some pocket money or misplace a valuable article. Refrain from doing anything rash, and especially don't lose your temper. In fact, it might be better to remain alone at home during the day as much as possible.

If you do go in to work, you may find yourself somewhat morose and pessimistic.

For those who play the stock market, today is not auspicious. Previous commitments are greatly upset, and you may find profits dwindling. In fact, it is a good day in which to simply watch transactions and not be a part of them.

For those who deal in grains and other agricultural produce, however, this could be a lucky day. Those who deal in machinery and iron goods can also have a busy time. Moneylenders may find that today is an unfortunate day, for they will receive news of some significant bad debts.

For those who favor the racetrack, this is also not a lucky day. Losses are likely to be quite heavy. Hunches and calculations go awry. If you must bet, however, try the third race, and look for a brown horse.

Lucky numbers for the day are 3, 7, and 9. The number 9 is especially significant. Lucky periods for the day are from 8 to 10 A.M. and 7 to 9 P.M.

55

Primary Planetary Influence: Venus, Mars, Venus

Secondary Planetary Influence: Saturn, Saturn, Jupiter

Today you start the day feeling restless and totally run-down as family concerns overpower your usually optimistic self. It may be that your partner is suddenly taken ill or that there has been a quarrel in the house or with a neighbor. As the day advances, you may be witness to an accident while traveling on a train or bus. This is certainly not a favorable day for any kind of travel. Your refusal to assist a close friend with a small loan is also likely to create great misunderstandings. If you suffer from hypertension, or high blood pressure, it may cause you great trouble today. Try to remain extremely calm and composed.

You will find your office work unusually heavy and tiring.

For those who favor the stock exchange, this is a day for either big losses or big profits. Synthetics and shares of companies producing textiles are likely to come into the limelight. This is a good day for shopkeepers and retailers who deal in cosmetics, ladies' articles, jewelry, and watches. Those who trade in oil and oilseed products will also have a lucky time today and can expect good profits.

Those who prefer the racetrack will find the day not as happy as expected. Gains and losses will be equal. Try the sixth race, and bet on a black horse.

Lucky numbers for the day are 3, 5, and 6. The number 6 is significant. There is no particularly lucky period.

56

Primary Planetary Influence: Venus, Mars, Mars

Secondary Planetary Influence: Saturn, Jupiter, Mars

This day is unusually unlucky from dawn until dusk. You wake up feeling somewhat tired and with a bad headache and a great deal of nervous tension left over from unpleasant incidents of the previous day. You may find yourself having petty quarrels with family members or a loved one. A child may have taken a fall or become ill, and your anxiety is increased by not receiving an expected letter. You also spend a great deal of time worrying about work that has to be done at the office. Try to remain as calm and tranquil as possible. The best way to do this is by meditation or by reading inspirational literature.

When it is time to go to work, you do so unwillingly, feeling that the working hours will be as bad as the early morning.

For those who are engaged in the stock exchange, this is a bad day. Political news or social disturbances reach the market and cause panic selling. Do not sell as others do, but hold on until positions improve. Those who are engaged in civil service, the military, agriculture, or mill work, however, find this day a good one. These persons hear good news or experience financial improvement.

For those who prefer the racetrack, this day is not at all favorable.

Lucky numbers for the day are 1, 2, and 9. The number 1 is important. The only auspicious hours are from 2 P.M. to 6 P.M., but even these are somewhat doubtful.

57

Primary Planetary Influence: Venus, Uranus, Jupiter

Secondary Planetary Influence: Saturn, Jupiter, Jupiter

This is a day during which many unexpected and fortuitous events take place. You wake up extremely cheerful and find the world full of many good things. Your cup, indeed, runs over today. If you happen to find yourself on holiday, a short side journey is indicated. Your partner will receive letters containing some very good news from his or her father, sister, or brother. During breakfast, you find yourself reaching for some sweet rolls. Today, your inclination toward meditation is stronger than ever. Follow it by reading inspirational material or spending some time alone. You may also receive good news from a friend engaged in the engineering profession.

For those involved in the stock market, the trend is likely to be very much in your favor. Engineering, iron, and steel companies are the catches of the day. Do not trade in textile or chemical shares. This is a good day for those who trade in machinery, fine articles, and cosmetics. Grains, gold, silver, and cloth are not particularly exciting now.

For those who favor the racetrack, this should prove a lucky day. Discard all handicapping methods, and play your hunch. Brown mares should do well. Try horse numer 8 in the second race with great advantage.

The lucky numbers for the day are 3, 4, and 8. Number 8 is especially important. Practically the entire day is lucky for you.

58

Primary Planetary Influence: Venus, Uranus, Saturn

Secondary Planetary Influence: Mars, Venus, Mercury

From the point of view of family matters and finances, this day is an auspicious one. You will find your outlook toward other family members bright and altered from the previous day. Unexpected luck will come to you. You wake up cheerful and do not bother about worries and anxieties. Today is not a day to lend money to anyone, no matter what their excuse. The mailman brings you cheerful news, and you are generally happy, even though you lose track of time and are likely to miss your train and arrive at your office late.

For those who favor the stock exchange, this is a good day. The market is likely to move forward and appear somewhat bullish. For those who deal in oil, this is a good day. Do not purchase any banking or investment stocks, however.

For those who favor the racetrack, this is a day in which you can recoup previous losses. Try betting on mares. Play your hunch rather than follow handicappers. Horses number 5, 6, and 8 are lucky.

Lucky numbers for the day are 2, 4, and 6. The lucky periods are from 8 to 10 A.M. and from 4 to 8 P.M.

59

Primary Planetary Influence: Venus, Uranus, Saturn

Secondary Planetary Influence: Venus, Mercury, Sun

This is not a particularly good day since the planet Saturn, the Cosmic gristmill, rules throughout. Because of this you wake up with an exaggerated sense of responsibility and anxiety. The morning is particularly gloomy, and you feel restless. A member of your family is likely to be unwell, and normal family life is disturbed. You had better take a walk and enjoy the morning hours rather than get caught up in things that you find troublesome. In fact, you do not feel like doing anything and even think of calling in sick to your place of business. Your breakfast may also be somewhat ordinary, and when you finally decide to go to work, it is with reluctance.

For those who favor the stock exchange, the day is a disaster. Price trends are so unpredictable that even your best broker finds it impossible to give you sound advice. New business should not be conducted. Definitely do not play hunches, as they could be costly.

For those who favor the racetrack, this is also not a favorable day. Both handicapping and hunches are likely to go wrong. If you bet, you are likely to lose heavily.

Your lucky numbers for the day are 3, 4, and 7, with the number 7 the most significant. The only lucky period is from 1 to 3 P.M.

60

Primary Planetary Influence: Venus, Uranus, Jupiter

Secondary Planetary Influence: Mercury, Sun, Moon

This is an especially good day for those involved in the literary trade, particularly for novelists. Inspiration is at its zenith now, and work produced will be of a very high caliber. For others, the morning is fairly good. You may find yourself appreciating the noble qualities of your partner more than ever. Be extremely careful while traveling both to and from work, as you could be involved in a minor accident. Performers find themselves inclined toward meditation and would do well to set aside some time in which to commune with the Cosmic.

Once you get to the office, work follows normal trends. You may receive a letter from an unknown person; it should not be ignored but given serious thought.

For those involved in the stock market, locomotive shares are particularly positive. Mechanics, those who deal in automotive parts, and those involved in education are especially favored. Purchase some gold coins today.

For those who favor the track, your showing will be poor. In fact, it would be far better for you to cancel your racecourse plans. All your ideas about winners go awry. You may see a horse fall down due to faulty shoeing. It's just possible that mares will win.

Lucky numbers for the day are 4, 5, and 8, especially number 5. Lucky hours are from 6 to 10 P.M.

61

Primary Planetary Influence: Venus, Jupiter, Mars

Secondary Planetary Influence: Sun, Moon, Sun

This is a very important day to set aside for communication with the Cosmic and especially for meditations concerning the health of a partner. In fact, you may see great improvements in his or her general health today. Misunderstandings and hot words, later regretted, are in the offing. You may suffer a slight injury when an object falls on your foot. An anticipated letter does not arrive, and this causes great disappointment. Meals are likely to be overcooked, and you rush off to your office feeling somewhat angry. Once there, work follows a heavy schedule, and by noon you are greatly fatigued.

For those in the market, synthetic shares are the best bet. The market trends are somewhat unpredictable today, though, so exercise great caution.

This is a good day for farmers, police personnel, jewelers, and goldsmiths. Those who deal in textiles, especially silk, will also find business highly favorable.

For those who favor the racetrack, do not bet on more than the first three races, or early earnings will be wiped out by the end of the day. Do not play more than three races. Brown horses are especially favored.

During the evening hours, you may find yourself continuing some business begun during the day.

Lucky numbers are 1, 2, and 7. The number 7 is most important. The evening hours are most favorable.

62

Primary Planetary Influence: Venus, Saturn, Mercury

Secondary Planetary Influence: Mercury, Sun, Uranus

Your dreams bring memories of a previous life or of a relative long deceased. You feel very sad and depressed upon arising. Hence, this would be a good day to start by communing with nature. You may meet good friends while out walking. This is a day for all kinds of unexpected mishaps. Your car may not operate this morning. You may even have to borrow money from a partner as your account may be overdrawn. The mail brings nothing of interest. It is a good day for straightening up your private papers, however, and for sorting out unanswered correspondence. Your appetite is not particularly good this morning.

Upon reaching the office, you may hear a strange story about a colleague.

For those in the stock market, the day is fairly good. Shares in transportation and engineering companies are especially favored. You may hear news about a split in a stock you have been holding for some time. Be careful, though, because market trends are generally erratic and deceptive. Those who are involved in trucking find this an especially good day, as do those who sell textiles retail. This day is not favorable for police or army personnel. They must be extremely vigilant in their duties.

For those who favor the racetrack, the day is a lucky one. Do not follow the advice of others, however, but use your own judgment. Selecting horses by drawing numbered lots among a group of people will bring good dividends to many of them.

Lucky numbers for the day are 3, 5, and 6. The number 3 is most important. If today is Friday, the entire day is most auspicious, and if it is Saturday, the entire day is most unlucky.

63

Primary Planetary Influence: Venus, Neptune, Mercury

Secondary Planetary Influence: Mercury, Mars, Uranus

This day is very auspicious for older persons in terms of their general outlook on life. They are likely to feel more energetic and alert than usual. They will meet friends of their own age group and will spend time in the company of others who also remember the good old days. For younger people, the day is one of delay and lack of fulfillment. Laundry and dry cleaning that have been given out will not be returned as promised. The morning meal will be somewhat ordinary and unappetizing.

Once at the office, you find you will have to work late.

For those involved in the stock exchange, the day is also not very comfortable. Sales of stocks will be made in error, for during the next few days their values will increase. If you must purchase, look to companies involved in shipping. Real estate is also a good investment. Older businessmen many find themselves having blood pressure problems. For others, the day is more or less normal.

At the racetrack, the day is lucky, but again only for seniors. If you take their advice, you will go home richer. You will sleep well and will arise refreshed.

Lucky numbers are 3, 5, and 9. The number 9 is most important. The period from 7 P.M. to 9 P.M. is dangerous, so be extremely careful.

64

Primary Planetary Influence: Moon, Jupiter, Mars

Secondary Planetary Influence: Mars, Saturn, Mercury

You wake up rather late in the morning and feel like doing absolutely nothing. You might have some complimentary remarks to make to a partner, who will be pleased with such kind behavior following a period of disagreements. Interesting news will be found in the local newspaper, though you will find the morning hours somewhat upset by unwanted telephone calls. Be especially careful in any communications and take time to reread anything you've written.

Should today be a work day, you will find yourself somewhat overwhelmed by a heavy workload that keeps you at the office late into the evening.

For stock exchange traders, the day is lucky for purchasing shares of companies involved in vegetable oils. There will be a great deal of gossip, however, and prices of stocks will swing both ways. Do not sell holdings, but wait for a better price. Today is especially lucky for those who deal in corn and in jewelry. If today is Thursday, the day will be all the more lucky.

For those who favor the track, the day is one of gain and loss. You will gain in the early races but lose afterward. Colts should be favored above all. The second and fourth races will surely bring you some luck. Because of your exhausting day, you will find yourself restless before bed.

Lucky numbers for the day are 1, 2, and 4, of which the numbers 1 and 2 are most significant. The night hours are generally favorable.

65

Primary Planetary Influence: Moon, Saturn, Mars

Secondary Planetary Influence: Mars, Mercury, Moon

Except for advances in financial affairs, the day portends a sense of sadness and fear in your daily routine. You wake up feeling somewhat sick. Perhaps the reason is worry about one of your children. Since it seems as if you can't really get things going this morning, you do practically nothing. You may find yourself having some disagreement with a family member or a neighbor. You would like to take the day off, but since you have too much work, you do not. Reluctantly, you go to the office.

For those who favor the stock exchange, today is lucky and advances are made. Engineering shares are especially favorable today. Other businesses should do well, with the exception of those involved in farming. Those who are connected with gold should be extremely cautious of theft during this day.

At the racetrack, this day is not a particularly fortuitous one. You may be tempted to play a hunch, and as a result, you may lose a great deal of money. If you must bet, however, the last two races will be more favorable than others.

Sleep will be refreshing and rewarding.

Lucky numbers for the day are 1, 8, and 9. The number 1 is most auspicious. The lucky time period is from 6 to 11 P.M.

66

Primary Planetary Influence: Moon, Venus, Mars

Secondary Planetary Influence: Mars, Neptune, Jupiter

With the exception of a great deal of mental uneasiness, this day is quite normal. You may find yourself purchasing some merchandise from a street salesperson. If you have a daughter, the day may start with her being upset with you since you won't honor her request for money. A husband or wife can also upset you unnecessarily today. Turn on the radio and find some good relaxing music, which can help change your already disturbed mood. Today you may receive a letter from someone whom you have long forgotten.

Upon reaching your place of business, you find yourself somewhat gloomy and morose.

For those involved in the stock market, the day is not a very favorable one. Calculations and judgments completely fail, and you attempt to make up for the loss in one stock by buying another. This is a day in which you can lose heavily.

Those involved in agriculture or the police department find this day particularly prosperous. Older persons involved in business will also have a good time.

It is better to forget racing today—if you bet, you will lose.

You will find yourself retiring with a great deal of restlessness; the same uneasiness with which the day began will again haunt you.

Lucky numbers for the day are 1, 2, and 6. The number 1 is most significant. The lucky period of the day is during the night hours only.

67

Primary Planetary Influence: Moon, Uranus, Mercury

Secondary Planetary Influence: Jupiter, Venus, Uranus

Today may be one of the luckiest days of your life. Monetary gains result from previous effort or sheer good luck. The day opens with cheerfulness and great mental tranquillity. Family life in the morning is indeed pleasing. You can greatly enhance your relationship with your children by making a definite commitment to attend a movie of their choice this evening. Wear as much white as possible today. You may receive a long-delayed response to a letter sent to a family member. Since it is in your best interest, immediately send a reply. Younger people should be careful crossing the streets.

You go off to your office in a bright and sunny frame of mind.

For those involved in the stock exchange, the day will prove one of windfall. Today you have "the Midas touch," and any securities you purchase do well. Dealers in machinery, spare parts, and jewelry will be especially lucky. Those involved in trucking may find themselves receiving contracts for long and prosperous journeys.

For those who favor the racetrack, the day is full of unexpected luck. Without handicapping or any calculations, any horse fancied appears to come in. The first and third races should prove especially lucky. Do not bet on the eighth race.

The entire day is very auspicious, and you will sleep soundly.

Lucky numbers for the day are 1, 3, and 6. The number 6 is especially important.

68

Primary Planetary Influence: Mars, Neptune, Mars

Secondary Planetary Influence: Mars, Neptune, Mars

Today you awaken in a philosophical frame of mind. You know that there is a divine power guiding your destiny. Because of this belief, you are kindhearted and affectionate. Today is a day for Cosmic communication and deep meditation. Spend the morning at home if at all possible, in communication with the God of your heart. If you must, engage in rearranging your private papers or reading old correspondence. A hot bath in which you can soak for some time will be especially effective. If you must go to the office, you do so in a resigned frame of mind.

Work at the office is unusually heavy, yet you will enjoy it. In fact, you may get caught up to the extent that you return home a little late in the evening.

For those who favor the stock exchange, blue-chip stocks are likely to remain somewhat stagnant. This is a day in which nothing outstanding takes place. Do not enter into new business. For police personnel, agriculturists, real estate brokers, and traders in silver and cotton, this day is a good one. This is also a favorable day for those who deal in grain and foodstuffs.

For racetrack fans, the day is quite unlucky. All selections made seem to go completely awry. Colts are likely to win, but not the ones you choose.

The evening hours are most favorable for social gatherings. Enjoy them in the company of good friends. Don't be surprised if you end up going to bed late. An interesting book may divert you until you fall asleep.

Lucky numbers for the day are 1, 4, and 6. The number 6 is the most significant and important. Lucky times of the day are from 7 to 9 A.M. and from 8 to 10 P.M.

69

Primary Planetary Influence: Sun, Mercury, Venus

Secondary Planetary Influence: Moon, Mercury, Jupiter

This should be a lucky day for you indeed as six auspicious planets are controlling your life. You rise with a tremendous sense of well-being. You are bubbling over with enthusiasm. Many good things are likely to happen during the morning hours. If you go through your financial accounts, you'll be pleasantly surprised to see that you are in a comfortable position.

Most likely, you will have an enjoyable breakfast with your partner. On the way to work, a street beggar may solicit your assistance. Do not turn away, but make some token donation.

When you arrive at your office, you are in a cheerful mood, and this enthusiasm continues throughout the day.

The stock market is rewarding today. Companies engaged in shipping and synthetics are the catches of the day. Those who are involved in retailing of jewelry or clothing will also do a fine business.

The racing fraternity will also have a happy time. Earnings can be above average, and you should bet on white horses. Races number 3, 4, and 7 will pay good dividends. Race number 7 is especially important for reaping the harvest.

You will find yourself sleeping well.

Lucky numbers for the day are 3, 4, and 7. Auspicious periods are from 3 to 7 P.M. and from 10 to 11 P.M.

70

Primary Planetary Influence: Moon, Saturn, Mars

Secondary Planetary Influence: Moon, Sun, Mars

You may find yourself somewhat unhappy today. In fact, you may not wish to get out of bed. One of your children has taken ill, which causes you anxiety. You suffer from constipation and feel generally upset. You would like to take the day off but know that there is too much work in the office to do so. Breakfast is somewhat disappointing, and you arrive at your office downhearted and discouraged. Once you are there, work is likely to be heavy and taxing.

Persons in love or newly married will find themselves spending money on their partners.

As for the stock exchange, be reticent. Price patterns offer a high likelihood of deception. Shipping and synthetic textiles are likely to jump, but it is not a good day to do any business. Hotel owners, however, find success. Real estate brokers and police personnel will find financial gains.

For those who favor the ponies, the day is very dangerous. Do not bet, but simply watch and enjoy. If you must, however, the second race may bring you some luck.

Lucky numbers for the day are 2, 4, and 5. The number 2 is especially auspicious. Lucky periods are from 7 to 9 A.M. and from 8 to 9 P.M. The time from 2 to 4 P.M. is a very bad time in which to do anything.

71

Primary Planetary Influence: Mercury, Moon, Venus

Secondary Planetary Influence: Sun, Mercury, Venus

This is an extremely lucky and happy day for you. You wake up from a highly erotic dream and desire to go back to sleep. If you have a partner living with you, these early morning hours could be spent in the enjoyment and bliss of love. The home life is unusually sweet this morning. You feel free and totally fearless. One of your neighbors may call on you, and you'll pass a good time in his or her company. This is an auspicious day for purchasing gold or fine clothes. You fancy good, tasty meals and arrive at your office expecting some pleasant surprise.

As for the stock exchange, this is a day in which to do good business. Mining stocks, textiles, and shipping companies are good catches. In fact, this is generally a favorable day for all traders and businessmen. Outstanding debts are likely to be recovered today. For moneylenders, goldsmiths, and pawnbrokers, this day is extremely fortuitous. For those engaged in retail trade, this day is good for rearranging sales displays and taking inventory.

For those who favor the track, the day is lucky. White horses should be chosen. Mares will smile in the face of Lady Luck. Play the even-numbered races only. Horses number one and three in any race are favored.

You will sleep well and find yourself greatly refreshed.

Lucky numbers for the day are 1, 3, and 4. The number 1 is most important. Your lucky time of day is from 5 to 7 A.M. and the entire evening.

72

Primary Planetary Influence: Venus, Mars, Jupiter

Secondary Planetary Influence: Mars, Mars, Mercury

You wake up this morning, after a sleepless and restless night, feeling somewhat sad. No doubt you're thinking about the heavy load of work that awaits you in your place of business. The radio brings depressing news as well. While you do not wish to work today, you know that you must. Why not take a long walk outdoors before heading off to the office? Even the mailman brings you bad news. This is not a day in which to write any important letters. Your breakfast is uneventful, and you go off to your office down in spirit.

As for the stock exchange, this is not a particularly favorable period. Gains in one stock will be offset by losses in another. Today is not the day to follow your hunches. Those who drive vehicles should be especially careful. Today is favorable, though, for transportation companies, real estate brokers, and farmers. If you wish to borrow money, do it now, as you may receive a more favorable rate than expected.

As for the racecourse fraternity, this is not a day for betting. The entire day is not favorable, and you will find yourself somewhat restless upon retiring.

Lucky numbers for the day are 2, 4, and 8. The number 2 is most important of all. There are no lucky periods today.

73

Primary Planetary Influence: Sun, Sun, Uranus

Secondary Planetary Influence: Sun, Uranus, Saturn

You wake up very early in the morning from a dream state in which memories of a previous life have trickled through. As this day is controlled by the planet Uranus, ruler of the unexpected, await for good things to happen that have not been planned. The morning hours may be spent in the company of offspring, listening to good music. Your partner will be in a jovial mood. There's a great deal of sunshine all around. Mail will be especially heavy today. You go off to your place of business in a cheerful frame of mind.

As for the stock market, the day is bullish. Automobile and transportation company shares shoot up without apparent reason. Those who are involved in railway companies find themselves especially favored. They may receive good news about a government-approved increase in their income. Public officials will also feel rather elated today. They are likely to be called upon by their superiors for consultations.

At the racetrack, the day is favorable. You might select a horse by simply drawing lots. This would be much more favorable than relying on calculations. Colts are especially favored. Your pockets will jingle as you return home.

Lucky numbers for the day are 1, 3, and 7. The number 7 is most important. Lucky times are during the morning hours and from 5 to 7 P.M. You will find yourself having a restful sleep.

74

Primary Planetary Influence: Moon, Mercury, Mars

Secondary Planetary Influence: Moon, Saturn, Sun

You wake up determined to enjoy this day. The morning hours are spent in the company of your partner and children. If you have recently bought some new clothing, today is the day to start wearing it. A humorous friend will visit you, and you will enjoy exchanging ideas. If you have been thinking of a partnership or strong financial interest, today is the day to pursue it. Write a few letters that you have delayed taking care of. You may receive a letter from an unexpected quarter. Meals will generally be to your satisfaction, and you will go off to your office, in your new clothing, with a cheerful mind.

As for the stock exchange, however, the winds of fortune are definitely blowing against you. Shipping and oil shares may be favorable, but the day as a whole is not auspicious for doing any business. Those involved in retailing of cutlery, soap, and drugs will find themselves very busy but should guard against theft. In fact, today they may discover hitherto undetected theft by an employee.

Unfortunately, fortunes at the racetrack are difficult to predict. If you must, stake on white colts, but not visiting the track at all is the best bet.

You will sleep extremely well this evening.

Lucky numbers for the day are 1, 6, and 7. The number 6 is especially important for you. The luckiest daily period is from 11 A.M. to 12 P.M.

75

Primary Planetary Influence: Moon, Venus, Saturn

Secondary Planetary Influence: Mars, Mercury, Moon

Though bright things present themselves to you today, you will shun them quickly. You still have not recovered from the negativity of the previous day, which is greatly disturbing your peace of mind. You may awaken with a toothache and generally feel out of sorts. In fact, you may wish to return to bed and simply be by yourself. Otherwise, the day should proceed quite normally. If possible, take a cold shower when you get up, which will help to invigorate you and wash away the "blahs." You will have little appetite today and not enjoy food. Spend some time in the company of your children, and inquire about their academic studies.

When it is time to leave for the office, you do so reluctantly.

Do not dabble in the stock exchange. If you are pressured into purchasing, look at shares in synthetics and chemicals. For businessmen the day is normal. Be very cautious, though, as you will be presented with a confidence scheme that, if you swallow the bait, could cost you a great deal of money.

Racetrack fans will find this day somewhat auspicious. Play your hunches as far as possible, and note with interest brown and white horses. Listen to tips from women and children. The first race is likely to prove profitable, but do not stake on the last three races.

You will not sleep especially well.

Lucky numbers for the day are 1, 2, and 3. The number 1 is especially important. Lucky hours of the day are from 6 to 9 P.M.

76

Primary Planetary Influence: Venus, Mercury, Saturn

Secondary Planetary Influence: Moon, Mars, Saturn

You awaken this morning exhausted due to overindulgence in sex last night. You are somewhat dazed and out of sorts. Even a glass of hot milk and a cold shower do not seem to help you feel better. Neighbors are likely to bring you unusual news regarding family members, and the mailman disappoints you by not bringing expected letters. This is, however, a lucky day for poets and writers. Whatever they write will be greatly appreciated. If you have planned a journey, postpone it. You should also avoid swimming. If you have been planning to see your physician, do so today. Your partner is somewhat concerned by your silence, so reassure him or her that you are, indeed, all right.

On the stock exchange, conditions are quite unremarkable. Price patterns remain consistent throughout the day. Hold on to your previous acquisitions, and do not purchase any new interests. Do not follow the advice of your analyst or broker as his judgment is likely to fail.

Real estate brokers and grain merchants, however, find this day very lucky.

For those who favor the ponies, the day is one of mingled fortune. Most likely you will win the first few races and lose in the last ones. If you must bet, bet on brown colts. Do not play after the third race.

You will sleep well tonight.

Lucky numbers for the day are 5, 7, and 9. The number 7 is most significant. Lucky times are from 8 P.M. to 10 P.M. The time period of 7 A.M. to 9 A.M. is a very unlucky period indeed.

77

Primary Planetary Influence: Sun, Neptune, Jupiter

Secondary Planetary Influence: Saturn, Saturn, Venus

You wake up somewhat cheerful and in a meditative frame of mind. Today is a good day to visit senior family members. You may wish to bring them flowers as a surprise. Spend some time reading inspirational material, and make a donation when solicited by one less fortunate than yourself. It is also possible that someone in your family will take ill suddenly. Do not be particularly concerned, though, as the illness is not of great significance. You may also have some regrettable words with a partner over articles that he or she purchased the day before. You will likely receive a letter from a relative requesting a reply by return mail. You go off to your office somewhat cheerful.

As for the stock exchange, shares in steel seem especially favored. Take advantage of this situation to buy in.

For those who visit the racetrack, Lady Luck seems somewhat uninterested. All judgments go wrong, and you're likely to lose heavily. It would be far better for you to abstain from betting.

You may find yourself somewhat restless upon retiring.

Lucky numbers are 1, 3, and 8. The number 8 is most auspicious. Lucky times of the day are from 1 to 3 P.M. and during the evening hours.

78

Primary Planetary Influence: Mercury, Moon, Mercury

Secondary Planetary Influence: Venus, Moon, Venus

This is an extremely lucky day for family and finances. Someone who has been ill for a long time will begin to feel better. The morning hours are lucky for whatever you wish to do. Long-standing worries pass away, and you will spend happy moments with your partner and children. If today is a holiday, why not go for a picnic or walk alongside the seashore? You feel financially at ease and are likely to spend your pocket money on luxury items. A letter comes in the mail that sets you thinking.

As for the stock market, this is a good day. Textile shares are likely to move upward. Those involved in the retail sale of textiles, jewelry, or gold will do especially good business. Astrologers and other occult practitioners, who make a living guiding others, will also find themselves especially busy.

At the racetrack, this is indeed a lucky day. Bet your hunches as much as possible. You will go home with your pockets jingling.

You will sleep well.

Lucky numbers for the day are 1, 3, and 5. The number 1 is most important. Almost the entire day is auspicious.

79

Primary Planetary Influence: Venus, Mars, Mercury

Secondary Planetary Influence: Venus, Mars, Mercury

Today the primary and secondary planets all work in your behalf. You may feel a little indisposed, but the morning hours are generally positive. Your partner may request cash to do the week's shopping, which makes you feel somewhat uncomfortable. Today is a day in which to write long-overdue letters. Try to reschedule your working period. Unwelcome friends may pay you a visit; if they do, cut them short. You may also wish to turn on the radio this morning and listen to some good classical music.

You go off to your office in good spirits and expect a positive day.

For those who favor the stock exchange, the day is favorable. Locomotive and automobile shares come to the fore. Real estate brokers and farmers will also do well.

For racing fans, the day is a mixed bag. You will take some profits home if you bet on brown horses. Mares are likely to win. Do not play the last four races.

You will sleep well.

Lucky numbers for the day are 2, 3, and 5. The number 3 is most auspicious. Lucky times of the day are from 8 A.M. to 11 A.M. The entire evening and the night hours are unfavorable.

80

Primary Planetary Influence: Saturn, Jupiter, Mars

Secondary Planetary Influence: Venus, Sun, Saturn

This morning you wake up feeling unusually optimistic. If you have been planning something for some time, you will find it coming to fruition today. Go ahead with your plans. Morning hours are especially favorable for poets and writers, as the muses will inspire them greatly. You may feel an inclination toward meditation, or you may wish to read some inspirational books. In fact, you may wish to take the day off. If so, why not do it? You may find your home filled with relatives and friends, and this too is very positive.

For the stock exchange fraternity, the day is quite normal, with nothing special to record. In fact, it is better to refrain from doing any business at all. You might wish to go through your holdings and unload some shares at a good profit. Automobile companies will be a good buy today. For most other businessmen, the day can be somewhat dull. Only a few customers will appear, and they will look rather than purchase. Retail dealers in fine women's clothing or cosmetics, however, will find themselves having a busy day.

At the racetrack, gains and losses are likely to be equal. It is better not to bet heavy sums on horses today.

Lucky numbers for the day are 1, 8, and 9. The number 8 is especially significant. Lucky times are only in the morning hours.

81

Primary Planetary Influence: Venus, Sun, Jupiter

Secondary Planetary Influence: Mars, Venus, Jupiter

You awaken this morning with a feeling of great anxiety concerning your work at the office. Once you get there, however, you find that your anxiety was misplaced. There is no cause for worry and fretting. You may find your earlier behavior strange. It may be better to read a good book and to laugh away your blues. Imaginary worries are always far worse than those of the real kind. You may receive a few letters that will cheer you up somewhat. You will not enjoy your meals because you feel slightly ill.

For those who favor the stock exchange, the day is without luster. Market actions are likely to be dull, and you may feel inclined to ignore items that are offered. Truck owners, real estate brokers, and farmers should see good returns today.

Bettors at the track will have an uneventful day. White colts are especially favored. Try the first three races, and go home with whatever profits you have.

You may find your sleep is somewhat disturbed.

Lucky numbers for the day are 2 and 5. The number 5 is especially important. Lucky daily times are from 1 to 3 P.M. and during the night hours.

82

Primary Planetary Influence: Venus, Mercury, Moon

Secondary Planetary Influence: Venus, Mars, Moon

This day is extremely fortunate from a financial point of view. If you have plans in mind, go ahead with them. You arise early, quite hale and hearty. Family life in particular is unusually cheerful. You find yourself in a playful mood, and you may tease your partner just to enjoy his or her response. Don't be surprised if some door-to-door salesman upsets you. Don't purchase anything offered as you are likely to be deceived. If you feel like it, why not enjoy a hot tub and soak? Mail received will be rather ordinary. Breakfast will be enjoyed, and you go off to your office in a cheerful mood.

For those who engage in the stock market, the day is fine. You are advised to make hay while the sun shines. Invest in transportation companies, automobile companies, and steel manufacturing. Shopkeepers in general will have many customers. Contractors and physicians will also be very busy.

For those who favor the ponies, today may yield a bumper crop of profits. Try the last three races especially. White mares are likely to win. Play your hunches rather than following the suggestions of handicappers and astrological predictions (except those of Zolar!).

Your sleep will be unusually restful.

Lucky numbers for the day are 1, 2, and 5. The number 1 is especially significant. Auspicious periods are during the early evening hours and from 9 to 10 P.M.

83

Primary Planetary Influence: Venus, Moon, Mercury

Secondary Planetary Influence: Moon, Moon, Sun

Lucky, indeed, is the person who has chosen this number. You wake up in an optimistic frame of mind as you have heard good news from your office regarding a promotion or transfer. The date is set for a long-delayed marriage, or a daughter or sister receives a proposal. You feel relieved of any anxiety, and the influence of the Moon will make you dreamy about your future life. This is an auspicious day for buying costly articles that are needed for the home.

For those who favor the stock exchange, this day is extremely lucky. Casual deals in any security connected with shipping will bring good dividends within a short period of time. Hotel owners, cloth merchants, and those selling jewelry or gold will also do good business today. Public officials will feel extremely favored today.

For racecourse fans, the day is unusually lucky. Luck will guide your money if played on a hunch. Do not rely on systems such as mathematics, handicapping, or astrology (except this one!). Horses running in the first race are especially favorable.

You will sleep well and have pleasant dreams.

Lucky numbers for the day are 1, 8, and 9. The number 9 is more important than the others. Lucky hours of the day are from 5 to 9 P.M.

84

Primary Planetary Influence: Venus, Mars, Sun

Secondary Planetary Influence: Sun, Mercury, Venus

You arise early, in good spirits and a cheerful frame of mind. The day is bright, and you are bubbling over with enthusiasm. You feel financially at ease, and the day is auspicious for entering into contracts. If you hold public office or are the chairman of some institution, you will receive an honorable mention of some kind. Important problems can be discussed at your bidding. Your home life is quite

★

congenial, and you feel proud about your son's progress in his studies. Make your partner happy by buying him or her an article of clothing. Meals will be especially tasty today.

For those who favor the stock exchange, this day is extremely lucky. Do some big business. The market is going to rise within a few weeks. Especially favored are shares in steel or automobile manufacturing. For other businessmen, the day is very fine. Real estate brokers and those who deal in automobiles or spare parts will have a busy time. The morning hours will be very lucky for them.

Those who favor the racetrack will also find the day very lucky. Persons born during the month of March are likely to have more luck than others. Play your hunch and bet on colts especially. The first three races are extraordinarily favorable.

You will sleep well and arise refreshed.

Lucky numbers for the day are 3, 5, and 7. The number 7 is the most auspicious. Lucky hours of the day are from 7 to 11 A.M. and during the evening period.

85

Primary Planetary Influence: Mercury, Uranus, Jupiter

Secondary Planetary Influence: Jupiter, Saturn, Saturn

You may arise feeling unwell because of a toothache or a problem with your bones. The morning hours will be gloomy and lack joy. Go out for a long walk or go shopping. You may hear bad news about a friend's relative. Take a warm bath and relax. The dark clouds of anxiety will begin to melt tomorrow. This is not a good day for answering correspondence. Rather, you should remain as aloof as possible and observe silence. If you have decided to go on a trip, drop the idea. Since your appetite will not be good today, you may wish to refrain from eating during most of the daytime hours.

For those who favor the stock market, this day is dangerous. Prices are extremely deceptive. Those that are rising quickly may fall equally fast. Do not be tempted to buy. In fact, it is better to remain away from the stock exchange today. For most people engaged in business, the day is unfortunate. They will lack customers. Persons dealing in oil products, however, will find themselves lucky.

For racecourse fans, the only tip that can be given is to stay away from the track. Anyone who attends and bets today will surely suffer heavy losses.

Your sleep is likely to be disturbed.

Lucky numbers for the day are 1, 6, and 7. The number 7 is most important of all. All day and evening hours are inauspicious.

86

Primary Planetary Influence: Mercury, Moon, Moon

Secondary Planetary Influence: Venus, Mars, Jupiter

Today is full of sunshine and merrymaking. You wake up in an unusually cheerful mood. Most likely, guests departed yesterday, and you now feel free to do anything you wish. For writers, this is an exceptionally good day. You are likely to be very productive. Family life is unusually cheerful. Lunar aspects make you lucky. Your imagination also plays a strong role today. You may receive a letter of great importance. Do not reply to it today, however, but wait until you feel so inclined. Your breakfast is satisfying, and you go off to your office in a cheerful mood.

For those of the stock exchange fraternity, this is a banner day. Prices are likely to rise to great heights. Shipping stocks are the catch of the day. Follow the advice of your broker or analyst. For other businessmen, too, this day should prove very lucky. Those involved in musical instruments, cutlery, cloth, and diamond sales will find this day particularly favorable. Truck owners and those who deal in spare parts will find that sales are off.

As far as the racetrack is concerned, nothing can be predicted. The influence here is so tricky that you will change your bet and then repent. Better not to bet at all.

You will sleep well.

Lucky numbers for the day are 1, 4, and 5. The number 1 is most important. Lucky times are from 5 to 7 P.M.

87

Primary Planetary Influence: Venus, Mars, Mars

Secondary Planetary Influence: Saturn, Jupiter, Mars

This is a very unlucky day for you. You arise in the morning with a heavy heart indeed. You find yourself in an uncomfortable situation, and you know no way of escaping. You feel indisposed physically, mentally, and spiritually. You might try to amuse yourself by reading a light book or listening to the radio. A partner may take ill, which causes you additional worry. Financially, this is a very poor day indeed. You will not be able to meet some of your outstanding bills. You may wish to ask a friend for a small loan. Your appetite will be poor, and you go to the office in a despondent frame of mind.

For stock exchange fans, this day is a lackluster one. It is better not to do any business at all. Prices of shares are likely to remain stagnant. Automobile and engineering companies are likely to come into the limelight, however. For other businessmen, this day is not very auspicious either. Sales are scanty. In fact, the only good business is in oil-related products.

For racetrack fans, this day is not a lucky one. Heavy losses are indicated. It is better to stay home. If you are inclined to play at all, stake on the first two races only.

You will have a disturbed sleep.

Lucky numbers for the day are 2, 4, and 6. The number 6 is most important. The whole of the day is unlucky.

88

Primary Planetary Influence: Venus, Uranus, Jupiter

Secondary Planetary Influence: Saturn, Jupiter, Jupiter

You wake up this morning in fine spirits, wanting to enjoy all the thrill and pleasure of life. Most likely you will hear good news of a promotion or other change of work. You'll find yourself inclined toward charity, and you'll be the possessor of noble thoughts. Purchase some clothes or toys for a junior member of your family. This is a good day to rearrange your room and sort out correspondence. Meals will be sumptuous, and you will arrive at your office in a most positive frame of mind.

For stock exchange followers, the day is normal. This is not a day for making any large purchases. During the closing hours of trading, there may be a great deal of activity in synthetic shares. These are not for you, though. Soap manufacturers and perfumers will do a very good business.

For those who favor the ponies, this day is quite good. Place your bets on black horses. Play the second and third race. It will be far better to use your reasoned judgment rather than play a hunch.

Unfortunately, you will have a disturbed sleep tonight.

Lucky numbers for the day are 1, 6, and 9. The number 6 is especially auspicious. Lucky times are from 4 to 7 P.M.

89

Primary Planetary Influence: Moon, Jupiter, Mars

Secondary Planetary Influence: Mars, Saturn, Mercury

You arise this morning pondering over humiliations you received yesterday. You are likely to behave somewhat strangely toward your partner and children. It is possible that some unwelcome friend or neighbor will pay you a visit. Do not think about the past, but try to enter into the future with optimism; otherwise your home life will be unpleasant. Your partner will make demands that will upset you more than usual. You may also spend some frustrating moments looking for a misplaced article or letter, but someone is likely to repay a loan. It may be wise to go for a long walk by yourself before heading off to the office.

Once you get to your office, you find yourself somewhat depressed.

As for the stock exchange, this is a day of hectic activity. Prices are likely to swing both ways. Chemical and engineering stocks are good catches today. Persons dealing in gold and silver will find this an eventful time.

Those who favor the racecourse will find this day one of windfalls. Such lucky days do not come often, so stake large amounts on your hunches and go home with your pockets full. Do not play the last two races, however.

Unfortunately, your sleep may be somewhat disturbed.

Lucky numbers for the day are 1, 2, and 4. The number 1 is most auspicious. Lucky periods are during the morning hours.

90

Primary Planetary Influence: Moon, Mercury, Saturn

Secondary Planetary Influence: Mercury, Venus, Mars

The day may be a difficult one. You wake after a good sleep and feel happy and comfortable. However, as the day progesses, you feel more and more uneasy. There's nothing thrilling in or outside the house. Try to read a light book to pass the time. This is a good day for writers, artists, musicians, and young people. You may enjoy the morning in the company of friends. Mail will be normal and uneventful, and you go off to the office in a positive spirit.

For those who favor the stock exchange, this is a dull day. Nothing moves in the market now. Do not expect to sell, but sit tight on previous holdings. There may be some unexpected flutter during the closing hours, but this should simply be observed; do not participate. Businessmen will have generally good sales. This is especially true for merchants, those who sell books and stationery items, and dealers in scientific instruments.

For racecourse fans, the day is an uneventful one. A gain in one race will be wiped out by losses in another. If you must bet, place your money on brown horses and colts. Try the seventh race.

You will sleep well.

Lucky numbers for the day are 7, 8, and 9. The number 7 is the most important.

91

Primary Planetary Influence: Moon, Mercury, Saturn

Secondary Planetary Influence: Venus, Mars, Jupiter

This is an extremely lucky day financially. Someone is likely to repay a loan. You may feel inclined to rearrange your work space at home. If you go in the early morning hours, you are likely to make a purchase of a much-needed household item at a very reasonable price. You may be visited by some friends and pass a happy time in their company. You feel hungry and desire to try something new. Today is also a good time to wear new clothes that were recently purchased. Time spent with a partner or children during the early morning hours is unusually happy.

You get to your office on time and find the work load light.

For those involved in the stock exchange, this day is extremely lucky during the first hour of trading. Synthetics and shipping shares are the catches of the day. Automobile shares are also in the limelight. Today you can make money if you move quickly.

For racecourse fans, this day is also auspicious. Brown and white horses are likely to win. Try the first and third races. Do not bet anything during the last three races.

Your sleep will be sound and refreshing.

Lucky numbers for the day are 1, 3, and 6. The number 1 is most auspicious. Lucky times of the day are during the morning hours.

92

Primary Planetary Influence: Moon, Mercury, Jupiter

Secondary Planetary Influence: Mars, Jupiter, Saturn

Today you rise with a sense of being overburdened. You are sad and depressed because your wishes of yesterday have not been fulfilled. You may have been unnecessarily insulted and humliated, which adds to your general discomfort. Try to find some silence and time for meditation. This will bring you peace of mind. You may wish to go out for a long walk by yourself. Do not think about what happened yesterday or this morning, but try to commune with nature. Come home, take a hot bath, and prepare for your office hours.

For those who are engaged in the stock market, this day is extremely lucky. The market is generally bullish; textile and synthetic companies are likely to be in the limelight. For other businessmen, the day is quite normal, with nothing special to record.

For racetrack fans, the day is unpredictable. If you were born in January or September, the day may prove lucky. Persons born in December, though, should stay away from the racetrack, as they are likely to lose heavily.

The entire day is normal. You'll have a somewhat disturbed sleep, unfortunately.

Lucky numbers for the day are 4, 8, and 9. The number 4 is most important.

93

Primary Planetary Influence: Jupiter, Saturn, Saturn

Secondary Planetary Influence: Sun, Neptune, Mars

This day is a good one for senior citizens. Someone who has been ill for a long time will begin to feel better. The elderly are likely to meet friends or relatives today. This is a good day to share inspirational ideas with them. This is a fairly pleasant day for others, too. You will have a relatively happy morning and will enjoy life generally. Today is a good day for reading inspirational literature or listening to

fine music. Writers, unfortunately, will be somewhat disappointed to
see that their manuscripts are returned by magazine editors or book
publishers. This is a good day for persons born on a Saturday or in the
month of June.

. For those who favor the stock exchange, however, the day proves
most unlucky. It is almost impossible to predict the trends of the
market. While blue-chip stocks show fair strength, steel and engineering shares seem the best buy. Generally speaking, though, this is not a
good day in which to make investments.

For other business persons, the day is also gloomy. There may be
sales tax trouble and harassment by government officials. Only merchants who are involved in oil or oil-related products do well.

For racetrack fans, the day is most unlucky. If any horses were to
be successful, they would be black ones. Do not bet after the fourth
race, however. Try your luck in the third and fourth, and stop while
you are ahead. Do not place large stakes today as you may not get the
returns you desire.

You will sleep normally and arise feeling rested.

Lucky numbers for the day are 3, 6, and 8. The number 8 is
especially significant.

94

Primary Planetary Influence: Sun, Neptune, Mercury

Secondary Planetary Influence: Saturn, Saturn, Venus

Although the primary planets are auspicious, the seondary planets
cast evil shadows everywhere you look. Your home life is likely to be
disturbed, and you wake up feeling somewhat depressed and vexed.
Perhaps you have to face someone this morning whom you do not
wish to see. This person may demand repayment of a loan. Be polite
and simply ask him or her to wait for another few days. You may find
your father in fine spirits, or you may receive a communication from
him. This is a good day to turn inward through meditation. Remain
calm and composed. You have little appetite and go to the office
oppressed by groundless fear.

For those who favor the stock exchange, the day will prove to be
lucky. Blue chips and chemical shares are likely to rise. Generally,
business will be somewhat bullish. For other businessmen, however,
the day is rather routine. Persons dealing in oil, oilseeds, and related

★

products will have good sales. Older persons in business will also find events in their favor.

This is not a good day for the racetrack. All selections and hunches go wrong, and you are likely to lose heavily. If you must play, play only one or two races and bet on black horses only.

Sleep may be disturbed and restless.

Lucky numbers for the day are 3, 5, and 6. The number 6 is most auspicious. No part of the day is particularly favorable.

95

Primary Planetary Influence: Venus, Mars, Jupiter

Secondary Planetary Influence: Venus, Sun, Saturn

Today you finally find release from a great fear that you have long been harboring. You will find yourself lighthearted and happy during the morning. Your humor may spill over so that you find yourself teasing your partner. A close relative will send you a letter of importance. Go out for a walk during the early hours, and perhaps visit a local vegetable market. Bring home some fruit or flowers. This is a good morning in which to enjoy the company of your children. If you have brought home office work to finish, you are not likely to conclude it. When the time comes to go to work, though, you will do so and still remain quite cheerful.

For stock exchange investors, the day is very dull. Prices are likely to remain stagnant. Synthetic shares may be the only catch of the day. For other businessmen, the day is generally normal. This is a good day for accounting and income tax work. Real estate brokers, police, and farmers will find this day particularly profitable.

Racetrack fans will win and lose exactly the same amounts. This being so, you may wish to simply observe and not bet at all.

You will sleep well and awaken refreshed.

Lucky numbers for the day at 3, 7, and 9. The number 9 is the most auspicious. Lucky hours are from 9 to 11 A.M. and from 7 to 8 P.M.

96

Primary Planetary Influence: Venus, Venus, Jupiter

Secondary Planetary Influence: Venus, Sun, Saturn

Today you awaken with a cheerful mind and feel hale and hearty. The day is quite normal, and you have nothing that you must do during the morning hours. Because of this, you may simply wish to read the morning paper, where you will find important news, or an entertaining book. If you have some old correspondence or a diary you are keeping, pay attention to it this morning. You are also likely to feel very optimistic in regard to your financial affairs. You may wish to call on an elderly person to inquire about his or her health. You will have a good appetite and enjoy your breakfast. You will reach your office in a relatively good frame of mind.

At the stock exchange, the day is especially lucky for women. Business transacted by a female broker or in the name of a female partner will be fruitful. Transportation and synthetic companies are especially favorable. For other businessmen, the day is generally lucky. Sales will be above average and for persons dealing in perfumes, cosmetics, and women's garments, this will be an extremely good day. For musicians, dancers, and writers, this day is also very auspicious because of the strong placement of the planet Venus.

For racetrack fans, the day is quite favorable. Profits will be small but sure. Bet on black mares, and play the last three races. This is generally a good day indeed.

You will get to bed late but will sleep soundly.

Lucky numbers for the day are 2, 4, and 5. The number 5 is most important. Lucky times are during the evening hours only.

97

Primary Planetary Influence: Mars, Neptune, Moon

Secondary Planetary Influence: Sun, Mercury, Venus

Senior citizens are likely to feel uncomfortable today and may take ill. But this will not prove dangerous, and a natural physician such as a chiropractor can be consulted. For others, the day is fine and bright. Morning hours can be spent in the company of old friends. If you have been planning a journey in the immediate future, proceed with your plans. Appetite will be abnormal during the early hours, and you may find yourself overeating. You will go to your office in a good mood.

For those involved in the stock exchange, the day is quite sound. Today is a good day for long-term investments. Transactions will yield very good profits in the long run. Long-established companies engaged in shipping are an especially good buy. The day is also auspicious for manufacturers of women's clothing, dealers in cosmetics, and goldsmiths. This is also an especially good day for gamblers.

For the racecourse fraternity, the day is quite good. Older horses are most likely to win, especially brown horses. Bet on even races only.

You are likely to be kept up somewhat late, but you sleep normally.

Auspicious numbers for the day are 1, 3, and 9. The number 9 is more favorable than the others. The lucky period is during the night hours only.

98

Primary Planetary Influence: Venus, Mercury, Venus

Secondary Planetary Influence: Mercury, Moon, Mercury

This is an extremely lucky day for both finances and family affairs. You arise in the morning from a sweet and inspiring dream. You are likely to be very busy during the morning hours and may find yourself in the company of persons you know only casually. For those involved in the literary profession, this is a very fine day; you will find your output very prolific. Your standard of writing will be high, and your inspiration will run second only to your productivity. You are likely to receive a letter from a relative who is far away. Morning television and the daily newspaper will be of interest.

For stock exchange traders, this day should produce a great windfall. Good profits are to be had. Shipping, synthetics, and chemical shares come to the fore. For other businessmen, the day is also happy. Speculators in silver and cotton are likely to be elated over their profits. The day is one for doing big business. It is also a good day for importing goods from another country.

For racecourse fans, the day is unusually lucky. The lunar influence brings and attracts luck in a most extraordinary way. Bet on white mares as much as possible. Even-numbered races prove the most auspicious.

You will sleep soundly.

Lucky numbers for the day are 1, 2, and 3. The number 1 is most significant. The entire day is auspicious.

99

Primary Planetary Influence: Venus, Mars, Moon

Secondary Planetary Influence: Venus, Mercury, Jupiter

This is a very lucky day for those occupying government positions or those engaged in education. Special work and ability is likely to be appreciated. If today happens to be Thursday, these aspects will be even more powerful. For others, the day is quite happy and cheerful. This is a better day for women than it is for men. If one is about to deliver a child, it is likely to be a son. You feel proud of your personality and try to look your best by wearing new clothing. This is also a good day for a long walk. Take your children with you, and buy them some toys or candy. Today is not a day for writing letters or answering correspondence. You will enjoy breakfast and go off to your office quite cheerfully.

For stock exchange traders, the day is also quite favorable. Established blue-chip companies are especially of interest; steel and textile organizations are particularly strong. These are to be purchased for long-term holding, however, and not for a quick profit. For other businessmen the day is quite normal and good. This is not a day in which you will be bothered by income tax or sales tax anxieties. For those individuals who are especially religious, the day promises to be a good one. God will favor their efforts more than usual.

For those who favor the racetrack, the day is also a good one. Good money can be earned. The third and fifth races are especially lucky. Older horses are the best to pick.

You will probably keep late hours and sleep well.

Lucky numbers for the day are 1, 7, and 8. The number 7 is most significant. The morning hours and 7 to 10 P.M. are especially lucky periods.

100

Primary Planetary Influence: Mercury, Uranus, Saturn

Secondary Planetary Influence: Saturn, Sun, Jupiter

Today is likely to be confusing. You arise in the morning to face serious problems that have been bothering you for a long time. Do not worry too much, though. All will be well in the near future. While you may feel physically unwell, mentally you're still on top of things. A neighbor may cause you some concern, so just try to be as polite as possible, and avoid a direct confrontation. As the day suggests a possibility of physical injury, be extremely cautious while traveling by bus or by train. It may be better for you not to drive your own car today. Expected letters will not arrive today, and your morning meal will not give you the satisfaction you are seeking. You will go to your office worried.

For those engaged in the stock market, the day is erratic and unprofitable. There are likely to be great swings in both directions. Only transportation and automobile shares are safe to purchase. In fact, it is a good day to take a holiday from the exchange. For other businessmen, too, the day is most unfavorable. Sales will be below expectations. Only those speculating in oil will find strong returns.

For racetrack fans, the day is most unpredictable. It is wisest to stake very little. If you must bet, try colts, and do not bet on the first two races. You may possibly win in the fourth race.

You may find your sleep somewhat disturbed.

Lucky numbers for the day are 4, 5, and 8. The number 4 is the most significant. The entire day is inauspicious.

101

Primary Planetary Influence: Mercury, Uranus, Saturn

Secondary Planetary Influence: Saturn, Jupiter, Saturn

Today you wake up unusually tired because you stayed up late last night. You feel somewhat drowsy and uneasy and consequently desire to do nothing during the morning. Try to occupy yourself by arranging correspondence or cleaning your room. You read some unusual item in the newspapers. For older persons, however, the day is quite good. For those who are religious, much of this day can be spent in reading inspirational literature. Sudden strange events and happenings will take place today because of the influence of Uranus. Electrical appliances may go out of order. The morning meal is disappointing, and you go off to your office reluctantly.

At the stock exchange, the day is bad. It is better not to be involved at all. Prices rise and fall against expectations, and you feel exceptionally concerned. For other businessmen, the day is also not very favorable. This is a day during which you are likely to be served with notices from income tax offices or sales tax departments. Do not ignore them, though, as inaction will only result in further harassment and legal expenses.

For racetrack fans, the day is also unfavorable. Calculations and study of horses go awry. If you must gamble at all, play your hunches. Try betting on black horses. The fourth or sixth race will prove lucky.

Your sleep will probably be disturbed.

Lucky numbers for the day are 1, 4, and 6. The number 6 is most important. The entire day is unfavorable.

102

Primary Planetary Influence: Moon, Saturn, Jupiter

Secondary Planetary Influence: Neptune, Moon, Venus

You wake up quite cheerful and write a great many letters. For musicians, writers, and painters, this is a lucky day indeed. You will find yourself much in demand. It is likely that you will spend much of your time at home doing nothing. You may be visited by friends, in whose company you will spend some enjoyable time. Your appetite is unusually good, and you go off to your office in a cheerful frame of mind.

For the stock exchange fraternity, this is a lucky day. Markets are likely to rise, especially shares in synthetics or shipping. Today is a day for bullish investments. For other businessmen, the day is also quite encouraging. Those who lend money or deal in gold, silver, or luxury items are likely to fare much better than others. The price of silver is most likely to shoot up; take full advantage of this increase by taking a strong position.

You will sleep well.

For those who favor the ponies, the day is quite lucky. Most auspicious is betting on dark-colored horses. The first and sixth races should prove unusually lucky. Play your hunch or follow the advice of older persons. For women, this day is particularly well aspected. Card-players will also be lucky throughout the day.

Your lucky numbers for the day are 1, 4, and 6. Number 4 is especially significant. The time period of 3 to 7 P.M. is particularly auspicious.

103

Primary Planetary Influence: Mercury, Moon, Jupiter

Secondary Planetary Influence: Venus, Sun, Saturn

You awake early in the morning from a happy and symbolic dream. The morning hours are fine and quite lively. This day is suitable for the purchase of household articles. Most likely you will receive a letter from an old friend requesting monetary help; do not refuse it. It is possible that you are in a religous mode and would find great solace in meditation; enter into it with deep concentration and devotion. Your morning meal is likely to be tasty, and you go off to your office in a good frame of mind.

For businessmen, the day is prosperous. Almost all shopkeepers will have heavy sales. Many businessmen will find themselves free from income tax or sales tax anxieties. Today is a good day to donate property or income to charity.

For those who are involved in the stock exchange, this day is extremely lucky, as it is for those who favor the racetrack. Small amounts should be bet on many races, rather than staking a big amount on a single race. White mares are likely to win. The third and fifth races should prove particularly lucky.

You will have a sound and restful sleep.

The lucky numbers for the day are 3, 4, and 5. Of these, the number 5 is especially significant. The evening hours are luckier than the rest of the day.

104

Primary Planetary Influence: Venus, Uranus, Saturn

Secondary Planetary Influence: Venus, Mars, Sun

Some strange incidents are likely to occur today in your family. Something that is said in humor is likely to create a storm of misunderstanding. It is far better for you to observe silence, at least during the morning hours. You may try to find a misplaced document or article, without success. The morning hours are likely to be gloomy and uncomfortable. If today is a holiday, do not go for an outing. The anger of a partner seems likely to spoil your good intentions. As a result,

★

your appetite is poor, and you go off to your office in a gloomy and dismal mood. Those involved in the police department may find superiors applauding their efforts.

For stock exchange members, the day is quite unpredictable. Engineering shares seem somewhat profitable. Automobile and locomotive shares are of special interest. Those involved in public transportation find it a good day.

At the racetrack, the day appears to be a gloomy one. Expectations and judgments go awry, and you are likely to lose heavily. If you wish to risk your money anyway, bet on white mares and play the fifth and eighth races.

The lucky numbers for the day are 5, 6, and 8. The number 8 is the most important. The entire day is inauspicious.

105

Primary Planetary Influence: Mercury, Mars, Sun
Secondary Planetary Influence: Mercury, Neptune, Sun

The influence of the three secondary planets will have more power than ever over your life today. You are likely to receive an encouraging letter from your father or an older member of the family. The atmosphere in your home is quite cheerful. You are likely to share with your family a strange incident you witnessed yesterday. You are more interested in your meals than in anything else. Perhaps your partner can prepare a dish that will indeed delight you. As the day advances, it becomes more auspicious. You find yourself in a positive philosophical mood.

For the stock exchange fraternity, the day is very encouraging. Today is a good day to sell long-standing holdings at a decent profit. Moneylenders will find themselves successful. For cardplayers and persons staking money on numbers, the day is very auspicious. The evening hours are very positive, and you should enjoy them.

At the racetrack, the day is very lucky. Male horses are most likely to win. Place your bets on older horses. Brown horses are sure to pay you good dividends. Play your hunch rather than follow mathematical calculations or recommendations from an astrologer. You will go home quite cheerful.

You will sleep well.

Lucky numbers are 2, 3, and 7. The number 2 is most important. The 6 to 9 P.M. period is an auspicious time.

106

Primary Planetary Influence: Venus, Mercury, Moon

Secondary Planetary Influence: Venus, Mars, Moon

This day is extremely lucky for you from a financial viewpoint. If you have any deals in hand, go ahead with them. You wake up in the morning hours feeling quite hale and hardy. Your family life is cheerful, and you may find yourself in a playful mood in which you tease your partner. A door-to-door salesman is likely to upset you. No matter what happens, do not purchase anything from him, as you will likely be deceived. You may wish to take a long bath. You will receive a letter.

For those who trade on the stock exchange, the day is fine. You are advised to make hay while the sun shines. Transportation, automobile, and steel shares are promising. For other businessmen, the day is also quite lucky. Shopkeepers will have many customers. Contractors and doctors will also do well.

Those who favor the ponies will reap a bumper crop of profits. Try the last three races. White mares are likely to win. Play your hunch instead of using mathematical calculations or the recommendations of any psychics (other than Zolar!).

You will find yourself sleeping soundly and restfully.

Lucky numbers for the day are 1, 2, and 5. The number 1 is most significant. Auspicious times are in the evening from 9 to 10 P.M.

107

Primary Planetary Influence: Mars, Neptune, Mercury

Secondary Planetary Influence: Jupiter, Venus, Moon

This day begins with you waking from a funny but symbolic dream. You wake up almost laughing out loud. Unfortunately, though, this is an inauspicious day for you. You will postpone or cancel an engagement scheduled for the morning hours. During most of the day you will find yourself somewhat sad and depressed. Do not lend money to anyone, as repayment will be delayed. During this day you will be left alone, but unwelcome jokes from friends can greatly disturb you. Your appetite will be poor, and you will not enjoy your meals.

During business or office hours you will come face to face with a number of problems you find gravely disturbing. It will be to your advantage to postpone any new business deals or to reconsider old proposals. If you are in the civil service, you will find this day a tough one as the pressure of work is great. From 2 P.M. onward you feel somewhat relieved from the worries of the morning and begin to feel more positive. You are likely to enjoy your evening hours with family members at home. There is a great possibility of an old or unusually religious person visiting you. Some of your time in the evening will be spent searching for a misplaced article or papers. Most likely you will feel sentimental toward children and will spend time with them in love and affection. Your home will assume a happy aspect during the evening period. Some financial good luck is in store for you. You may secure a gift from a friend. If you are religious, your meditation will assume great depth today, and your prayers will be granted. You will find yourself having a peaceful and undisturbed sleep.

Lucky numbers for the day are 1, 6, and 8. The lucky hours are from 10 A.M. to 3 P.M. and from 5 P.M. to 6 P.M. Any deals, proposals, or contracts made during these periods should prove very successful.

108

Primary Planetary Influence: Mercury, Jupiter, Mercury

Secondary Planetary Influence: Jupiter, Mars, Venus

This is a day when the goddess of love visits you with a smiling face. Today is a day to do something big. Morning hours are likely to be exceptionally favorable and lucky. You could make your partner happy by buying him or her some new clothes. Elderly persons from a partner's family are likely to visit you. Today you find yourself drawing inward and becoming a bit meditative. Use this time to commune with the Cosmic. Office work will be somewhat normal, with nothing special to record.

For those involved in the stock exchange, this should prove a lucky day. Now is the time to purchase shares in textiles. If you have a bullish position, you might wish to unload at least three-quarters of your holdings, which will yield you a good profit indeed. This is an especially good day for moneylenders and pawnbrokers. Overdue loans advanced by them are likely to be recovered in full, with interest. This is a day for those who deal in silver, and there is the possibility that they will reap great gains.

For the racecourse fraternity, the atmosphere is expensive and unpredictable. Take a good deal of money with you, because you are not likely to win. Brown and white horses will do better than others. Horse number 3 in the fifth race will also bring you a good dividend.

During the evening hours you will be somewhat more relaxed and will sleep well.

Lucky numbers for the day are 3, 5, and 7. The number 7 is the most significant. The luckiest period is during the morning time.

2.
Solar/Lunar Guides

★

★
Solar/Lunar Polarities

Your horoscope will tell you in which houses your Sun and Moon lie.

Sun in Aries

Aries in general have good memories, make fine teachers, and are natural leaders. They are inclined to mental depression, often lasting a couple of days, and are impulsive.

Moon in Aries. Quarrelsomeness: must learn self-government; misrepresentation in order to gain own way; artistic skill.

Moon in Taurus. Intuition; imagination; spirituality; exactness in thought and work; slows the impulsive Aries nature—restlessness is curbed.

Moon in Gemini. Friendlier; more feeling; more finesse and ease of expression and articulation; love of harmony in both color and music.

Moon in Cancer. Brings out the sexual side very strongly and gives full force to the ideal side of marriage; milder of voice; apt to turn to writing rather than to speaking; intensifies the social and religious trend of Aries.

Moon in Leo. Increase of ability to harmonize socially, but not of mental brilliance; bigotry and fanaticism; love of mystery and desire to press views on others.

Moon in Virgo. Curiousity about all young children, animals, and growing plants; leans to the study of biology and spiritual sciences such as astrology or numerology; males have the same intutitive sensitity as females; great strength and vigor.

Moon in Libra. Vivid but judicial thought processes—action may be delayed until a problem is weighed in the balance; Sun in Aries with the Moon in Libra places the Earth between both lights, giving the native remarkable analytical capacity and a sense of social justice; good judgment, free from personal prejudices; love of originality, dignity, and elegance.

Moon in Scorpio. Energy and perseverance; desire for great freedom; more practical than it is ordinarily the nature of Aries to be.

Moon in Sagittarius. Not a good combination: overimpulsive, aggressive, dogmatic, and often illogical; quick and ill-governed temper; a mixture of commercial desire and selfishness—rarely successful or happy; liable to intemperance because of intensity. In childhood this temperament should be reasoned with calmly—not punished, but trained for a practical life.

Moon in Capricorn. Positiveness; force; determination; a money-loving but seldom economical disposition; very sarcastic in an argument.

Moon in Aquarius. Idealizer of the beauty and harmony of home life; a good parent and friend; sometimes inclined to intemperance in food and drink.

Moon in Pisces. Capable of mastering any mechanical art; sensitive; often quarrelsome; generally unsuccessful in financial matters; failure to get proper remuneration for exercise of capabilities.

Sun in Taurus

Taurus people are noted for their exactness and persistence in mental endeavors. They often need assistance and are seldom capable of great financial plans. In order to be happy, they strongly require affection from one of the opposite sex.

Moon in Aries. Gives a very intense, vivid, and energetic quality to the cautious, scientific Taurus mentality; inventiveness and the ability to demonstrate ideas.

Moon in Taurus. When the Moon is in the same sign as the Sun, the New Moon has great influence. This gives Taurus an unusual, intense sympathy; constructive imagination, capable of learning a number of trades; frequently a leaning toward horticulture.

Moon in Gemini. In the Gemini nature, the forces of culture are dominant, resulting in more sociability and a greater love of beauty than is common to Taureans.

Moon in Cancer. Attraction to home life; love of elegance; heightened emotion and tenderness; conscious of money and inclined to be selfish in all things except home affairs. In childhood they need much tenderness and sympathetic understanding, as they are very sensitive.

Moon in Leo. A severe mixture of reasoning, stubbornness, and ambitious orthodoxy that, while capable, goes to extremes in both habits and opinions; a love of food that should be controlled.

Moon in Virgo. A tendency to ward self-aggrandizement, exactness in every detail, and power; analytical judgment; successful in scientific professions; seldom in sympathy with the methods of the past; generally discredits the unexamined work of others; in many ways breaks new territory in seach of adventrue.

Moon in Libra. Intuitive first opinions, logical later ones; suited to take a place in the legal or political world; often missing elements of sentiment and regard for the weak or misinformed; expect all people to understand ideas and conditions as well as they do themselves.

Moon in Scorpio. An intense executive manner; integrity and cooperative power; an independent nature, diverting the scientific bent of Taurus along mechanical and industrial lines.

Moon in Sagittarius. The elements of imaginative and constructive science as applied to commerical matters are intensified, making for economic ability; a quick and fiery temper that needs to cultivate and exercise calmness when under stress; strong and deep affections.

Moon in Capricorn. An inclination toward emotional anger and stubborn insistence upon every personal right; the positive, determined, self-controlled pursuit of its own desires. Proper education in manners and training in youth is essential.

Moon in Aquarius. Social polish; personal elegance; diplomacy; desire to impress others; vanity; keen sense sense of taste and smell; fussy as to food. The Sun and Moon both in fixed signs gives a tendency toward inflexibility that should be tempered in its negative applications and cultivated in constructive expression.

Moon in Pisces. A love of art and a vivid imagination; constructive skill; a tendency to dabble in too many things, turning from one to the other, with a lack of stability. These temperaments should strive for stick-to-itiveness.

★

Sun in Gemini

Geminis have kind natures and are graceful in their activities. They are often inclinded toward literary and legal vocations and have an elegance of expression.

Moon in Aries. Freedom loving—generous in granting rights to others; often radical, shunning conventional rules of action; political, legal, and teaching ability; when women, good mothers; not physically strong.

Moon in Taurus. Idealistic; delicacy of expression; drawn to the study of scientific and reflective subjects; good teachers, doctors, botanists; they succeed in any study that interests them; a well-governed, determined, and brave will.

Moon in Gemini. A peculiar combination of good nature, wit, and kindness, mixed with a dreamy, imaginative,and sensuous love of art and beauty; interested in the occult and similar studies. Need to give more attention to economy in order to insure success.

Moon in Cancer. The Gemini nature with the Moon in Cancer is relatively unaffected by planets in other parts of the horoscope. There is an added intensity of affection and an idealistic softness and sweetness in this manifestion. It gives ability for expression.

Moon in Leo. A capacity for deep friendship and intense religious feelings; wide-ranging imagination, with poetic energies. The intuitive reception of truth differs widely from the reflective and scientific—the first is particularly characteristic of this nature. The world perceived is large or small, good, bad, or indifferent, just as one makes its, takes it, or expects it.

Moon in Virgo. Intensification of both parental and sexual love; musical or verbal talents; full of fun; tends toward sarcasm; able to take on the responsibilities of government.

Moon in Libra. A dual nature: capacity for great friendship, kindness, and philanthropy, while on the other hand, possessed of conscious dignity, self-control, and force; spirituality and considerable occult power; keen insight, particulary with regard to the natures and needs of others.

Moon in Scorpio. Stronger and more dynamic than usual for Gemini; capacity for tenderness and delicacy in friendship, combined with skill in positive execution.

Moon in Sagittarius. Lives as much for others as for the self; admirable capacity for tenderness toward family and sometimes a visionary nature full of hypothetical schemes, perhaps more excitable than is favorable for the development of a successful character.

Moon in Capricorn. Commerical instincts, financial judgment; brilliant business ideas; a need for early training to guard against a surplus of visionary enthusiasm; more distrustful of others than most Geminis; a tendency toward egotism; a disposition to waste time.

Moon in Aquarius. A decided dispostion toward agriculture, gardening, and botany; a high degree of intellectual ability, with the stability of Aquarius.

Moon in Pisces. One of the most powerful combinations in the Gemini nativity: elegance; a natural friendliness; on the other hand, a lack of the calm and poise that enable one to grasp benefits from surrounding conditions. Should study ethics, justice, natural law, and practical arts, such as architecture, to fit them for a vocation both useful and remunerative.

Sun in Cancer

Devotion to family life is dominant in Cancers. They are also sensitive and inclined to nervous conditions.

Moon in Aries: Ambition but without sufficient tenacity of purpose and concentration to gain the end sought.

Moon in Taurus: A strong inclination toward construction or building; a love of mechanical arts; sensitive to the forcefulness of others— lacks aggression sometimes even for self-defense. Should be governed by kindness during childhood.

Moon in Gemini: Periodicity of habit; deep emotions, capacity for close friendships and intense devotion; love of children and life; interest in all that is beautiful, spiritual, and ennobling; a sensitivity that needs protection—this nature must cultivate and develop self-reliance and caution.

Moon in Cancer: A bright and active outlook; generally sensitive, dislike of long analytical tasks; preference for matters of common and general interest; a tendency to have a vague conception of deep subjects and a disposition to shun them because of the study required in their mastery.

★

Moon in Leo: Gives a humanitarian view of marriage, a broad nature, a wide range of harmonic vision, an incentive toward the cultivation of moral and spiritual power.

Moon in Virgo: Intensification of emotions, especialy toward mate and kindred; a vivid conception of beauty; love of the mysterious and of weird, strange, and profound ideas; limited intellectual power; love of travel; appreciation of elegance in movement and in form; apt to be critical about art, out of intuition rather than study.

Moon in Libra: Powerful emotions, intensification of benevolent and aspiring thoughts and feelings; a ruling personality, with control, firmness, and willpower in situations requiring a well-rounded character; often author or judges.

Moon in Scorpio: An attraction to progressive industry and the application of production and organization; an intense desire for justice and personal liberty; in childhood, self-willed, quick-tempered, suffering under restraint—this condition should be governed with much kindness.

Moon in Sagittarius: Acutely methodical; a capacity for idealistic and forceful plans, stronger financial and economic interests than usual in Cancer; a desire to give offspring a grand start in the world; a resistance to the idea of foregoing the pleasures in life merely to attain wealth or position.

Moon in Capricorn: A strong inclination toward original thought in enterprise and generally a sense of idealism and grandeur; impelled onward to social excellence and virtue; pleasure in a beautiful home life.

Moon in Aquarius. A wider view of personal life and destiny than normal in Cancer; direct and frank; a love of home and friends.

Moon in Pisces. A deeply affectionate nature; brilliantly intuitive and spiritual; a talent for mechanical and constructive work in art; keen senses; an ability to interpret symbolically; strong perceptions; great power of bodily expression.

Sun in Leo

Leos are characterized by mental harmony, and warm, sunny, and genial natures. They are endowed with great vitality, which is often used persuasively. In business they are urgent rather than aggressive and aspire to power through eloquence and vigor. They mature late and should therefore cultivate calmness.

Moon in Aries. Apt to be stubborn and extremely rigid in demands. Prefer vocations in one of the professions, such as law or medicine; an oversensitive nervous system.

Moon in Taurus. An inclination to influence morals and ethics; good physicians; fine orators, expressing power and elegance; a wide range of imagination, but usually of an egotistic type, with the self as the center of all activity.

Moon in Gemini. Ambition for culture and great achievements; an intense desire for personal freedom; methodical, with a desire to be orderly in their own way and to have others accept that order as absolute.

Moon in Cancer. This combination is not an easy one to handle and frequently gives poor results. A strong chart is needed to give the mentality and body the amount of will and dynamic energy necessary to a complete and powerful character.

Moon in Leo. A practical, artistic, and graceful imagination, with vividness and convincing power; marked independence, but capable of strong attractions to those who hold like views; often bigoted.

Moon in Virgo. A need to shape life's actions according to a definite plan that will provide security; a strong social nature, distinct love of family, home, and country; often criticized for being virtuous but unsuccessful.

Moon in Libra. An element of mysticism and love of the occult; disposition to make much of every little personal incident; suited in many ways to religious teaching and poetic interpretation—giving vivid descriptions of matters of which only a moderate amount of evidence is obtainable.

Moon in Scorpio. Not a favorable combination for a Leo, but does not detract from the sign's innate power: ability to lead; full of energy; able to mold others to their will; intellectual independence, with little respect for dogmatic rules.

Moon in Sagittarius. Makes the Leo more aggressive, scheming, and economical and, in many instances, severe; added imaginative power; when extremely angry, a tendency toward irrational action; tends toward hasty generalizations rather than attention to details; more training is required along practical lines than is usual for a Leo.

Moon in Capricorn. Wide-ranging commercial ability; extremely social nature, not opposed to using friendship as a way to success; often very exacting and demanding, favoring their own methods.

Moon in Aquarius. Love of luxury; a rather unstable and ungovernable temper; an excessive love of food; needs to cultivate persistence,

96 SOLAR/LUNAR GUIDE

directness, and orderliness, so that nervous energy does not interfere with insight into the real needs.

Moon in Pisces. A very fine and appreciative sense of the artistic and beautiful; great imaginative power; mechanical ability.

Sun in Virgo

Virgos often develop into publicists, politicians, and shrewd businessmen. When they succeed, they are very forceful and have the ability to utilize the energies of others for their own advantage.

Moon in Aries. Fine mental power and intellectual ability; orderly and systematic; inclined to think that no action can be performed well except by strict method; a mirthful sense; native good humor—even sarcastic remarks are good-natured; a wit in constant play.

Moon in Taurus. A complex mixture with a decided liking for the natural sciences; foresight and intuition; a love of home life; strong will and business ability.

Moon in Gemini. Culture; elegance of expression and a delightful manner; suited to vocations that call for friendship and enthusiasm; fastidious in matters of appearance.

Moon in Cancer. An affectionate nature with great sensitivity, even to the point of jealousy; lack of confidence; deep attachment to home life and family; economical in business.

Moon in Leo. An inclination to religiosity that may even lead to melancholia; an ability to comprehend harmonies of music and color; acute sense of taste and smell; wise early training needed to offset any morbidity of temper or of thought.

Moon in Virgo. Strong love of home life, kindred, country, or the place of birth; extremely sensitive to the thoughts, feelings, and general conditions of those with whom they are in company; should choose companions carefully.

Moon in Libra. A very complex mixture of domestic inclinations; artistic imagination; mathematical power; genial egotism; capacity for self-government and control of the emotions; agreeable companions; successful as authors or investigators.

Moon in Scorpio. Integrity; conscientious persistence; insistent upon personal rights and disposed to enforce them.

Moon in Sagittarius. A dynamic combination: financial selfishness and love of gain; a capacity to achieve and enjoy the pleasures of ownership; verbal directness that often causes them to appear harsh.

Moon in Capricorn. When well endowed, capable of extensive commercial undertakings, especially when experience has been gained. This combination of energies gives the power to recognize chances for commercial gain with intuitive quickness.

Moon in Aquarius. Magnetic power; an ability to formulate practical concepts and use mechanical forces; a good humor that wins more cooperation than would result from demands; a desire for tender home relations.

Moon in Pisces. Drawn toward mechanical work, with facility for theatrical vocations; seldom has brilliance, but often displays a fondness for the superficial and elegant; often attracted to the stage.

Sun in Libra

The dominating characteristics of Libras are a tendency to rulership, pride, and ambition, as well as extreme conservativism and worship of the law. Seldom are they affected by others' opinions or desires, instead acting according to their own choices. Many Libras become soldiers—they love power but find it difficult to obey others of higher rank.

Moon in Aries. Definite and useful imaginative ability, with clear concepts of method; brilliance in perception; a regularity of application that is the foundation of great accomplishments.

Moon in Taurus. Usually Libra is positive, dogmatic, certain, and logical, but not sensitive. This combination produces a sensitivity, inspiration, foresight, and psychological power, often with an admirable grandeur of purpose.

Moon in Gemini. Quick to act; kindly temper; modifying the more rigid and persistent Libra strains; it gives mental clarity and pliability in bodily movement. In oratory, in government of the masses through thought and feeling, in power to influence the rules of social conduct, few natures excel more than this one.

Moon in Cancer. Vivid paternal feelings, more delicate and intense maternal feelings; love of home surroundings is increased; a desire for quiet, usually lacking in Libra; in some a desire to enter business life with definite ambitions and plans for commercial success.

Moon in Leo. An understanding of delicate and refined ideas and strong moral forces; a love of the classics, of music, and of all that symbolizes or interprets the mysteries of the ages; will study the

★

personal rights of the individual and seek to harmonize these with the forces of progress along lines of stability.

Moon in Virgo. A deep love of family and children that will stand firm through any adversity, no matter how severe; a delicacy and sincerity of expression that is very attractive; great social control, blended with will and determination.

Moon in Libra. A tendency toward rampant egotism and self-adulation; an unconscious or semiconscious grasping at others' rights; on the other hand, keen perceptions and mathematical ability; artistic leanings realized with grace, precision, and eagerness.

Moon in Scorpio. Implacable leaders who demand to be followed, they brook no laziness, condone no laggards; they build great plans and will struggle hard to effect them; often considered severe, they believe in justice and will grant to others any rights that have been determined or earned.

Moon in Sagittarius. Always practical, grasping results, utilizing opportunities, calculating costs, and evaluating products; thorough planners, difficult to overcome, they seldom fail to gain success and often win wide recognition.

Moon in Capricorn. An imaginative business nature, leading to speculative habits; mathematical power and a fondness for building schemes of great importance; if mentally well endowed, will combine original methods with just determinations.

Moon in Aquarius. Inclined to be drawn to psychic activity; remarkable psychometric powers, not to be confused with intuition and foresight.

Moon in Pisces. Interest in mathematics, mechanical arts, and exactness; love of color and of elegance in forms; modified egotism.

Sun in Scorpio

This nature is the most markedly dynamic of all, is earnest, wholehearted, and persistent in the production of things to satisfy daily needs. Scorpio has been much maligned and unfairly discredited by most astrologers. They demand freedom and will struggle for their liberty, perhaps causing resentment from those passed on the way.

Moon in Aries. There is forcefulness and perseverance in this combination. In handling a child of this nature, parents or guardians need to maintain deep and sympathetic understanding of their sensitive natures. There is often resistance (not stubbornness) with later a restless determination to accomplish definite aims and purposes. This nature needs constructive training.

Moon in Taurus. Practical and capable of doing excellent work; when highly organized, evinces a marked desire to gain power and influence, as well as competence in gratifying this ambition.

Moon in Gemini. The effect of this combination is variable, depending on the position of the rest of the planets. Generally, increased expressive ability; vivid and fluent language; extended imaginative power.

Moon in Cancer. A beneficial combination—calmer, more constant, and in many ways more expressive than usual for Scorpio; capable of giving more happiness and a greater sense of security to the mate through words and acts.

Moon in Leo. A sense of humanitarianism and social interrelations; strong religious sentiments and concern for society; more sympathetic than common in Scorpio.

Moon in Virgo. Love of home; an intense desire for comfort and plenty of rich food; increased patriotic sense that may lead to self-adulation and an egotistic manner of speaking.

Moon in Libra. Strong ambition; firmness and perseverance in industry; willful; a dominating individuality; a keen sense of values; not inclined toward metaphysical subjects, as they are too positive to respond with the necessary sensitivity.

Moon in Scorpio. Inclined to be fretful; dislikes restraint and is disturbed by any interruption of plans; dislikes being dictated to, but likes suggestions and ideas for improvement.

Moon in Sagittarius. A keen business interest, with appreciation of values and insight into the opportune relationship between times and places leading to successful ventures; needs calm advice rather than arbitrary government and should be given freedom of action.

Moon in Capricorn. Executive power; ambitious for gain and accumulation; often evinces persistence and aggression without the logical foresight to make them successful.

Moon in Aquarius. This combination has a beneficial effect on the individual: tenderness, love of home, sweetness of temper, and moderation; a degree of ambition and desire for self-satisfaction, with increased appetites—a love of feasting and of social pleasures.

Moon in Pisces. A clear and intense conception of artistic merit in practical affairs; capacity for regularity and exactitude; remarkable mathematical power shown in methods of calculation; frequently become accountants.

Sun in Sagittarius

The predominant characteristic of Sagittarians is their ability to defend both themselves and others. They are also skillful in accumulating wealth and are cautious and brave, always prepared to meet emergencies.

Moon in Aries. Impulsive, energetic, and eccentric; directive ability as well as executive power. Nothing is slow or sluggish under this influence, but there is sufficient reserve to keep all plans and movements secret.

Moon in Taurus. Practical; imaginative, with a keen perception of coming trends; judgment is sensitive and quick, not easily changed; often considered stubborn because of the intensity of opinions.

Moon in Gemini. Congeniality, gracefulness, and love of culture added to an otherwise practical nature, with more than ordinary bluntness of speech and action. Less cautious and defensive than most Sagittarians; often attracted to the commerce.

Moon in Cancer. Increased expression of parental tenderness; attraction to a romantic idea of married life; should not act hastily in matters involving the emotions; needs to guard the temper, as emotional outbursts can cause distrust and misery.

Moon in Leo. A bundle of contradictions, often blamed for unintentially hurting others, when forced to defend themselves. Changefulness and various moods are difficult to describe; uncompromising when injured, although kindness is generally present.

Moon in Virgo. Love of home and family life; conservative in politics; patriotic; an underlying desire to establish and protect wealth and investments.

Moon in Libra. Great ambition, firmness, and perseverance; a calm force of an executive nature and pride in carrying out all plans. The physical body is generally a powerful one.

Moon in Scorpio. A strong sense of justice and desire for personal liberty; powerful persevering energy; capacity for continued effort to a successful end in any line; ability to resist disease and to heal quickly.

Moon in Sagittarius. Regularity in work; aptitude for mental arithmetic; interested in orderly business methods; a morbid fear of failure;

should be trained in some vocation that will secure the future; should guard against any tendency toward miserliness or despondency over finance.

Moon in Capricorn. This combination tends to capacity for industry. The nature so endowed often attempts to use personal willpower in order to avoid the necessity of physical labor. It projects impulsiveness and forcefulness.

Moon in Aquarius. The dominantly defensive nature of Sagittarius modified by a calmer and less aggressive temperament; inclined toward intemperate habits of eating, especially of highly seasoned foods, and to excessive drinking—tendencies to guard against.

• **Moon in Pisces.** A quick temper and quarrelsome disposition that need restraining; artistic and mathematical ability; with a degree of secondary executive ability; needs a great deal of rest.

Sun in Capricorn

Capricorns have great reserves of power. When highly charged, they are full of forceful fire—destructive and revengeful when attacked; when badgered, sarcastic. They are rigid in their judgment and usually happy in marriage.

Moon in Aries. Ability for management—the true executive, one able to attend to all main issues, while the details are assigned to others; good bosses, as they have the intelligence to allow assistants to work things out in their own way.

Moon in Taurus. A combination of executive and scientific ability in commerce; relatively imaginative in business; tender at home; often become engineers, railroaders, or are involved in naval and marine construction.

Moon in Gemini. A beneficial combination that gives the severe Capricorn nature a congeniality that it needs to bridge over many rough places in life; added gracefulness, with a clearer sense of artistic beauty.

Moon in Cancer. A strong love of home comforts; increased tendency toward cautiousness; sensitive, gracious, and congenial.

Moon in Leo: This combination produces a changeable nature that can tend toward extremes of kindness and severity; inclined to be dogmatic; forceful in support or opposition and seldom neutral in any matter that bears, directly or indirectly, upon its interests.

Moon in Virgo. A true homemaker, who finds much enjoyment in the home, especially if it is enlivened by children; often deeply interested in public education and civil reform.

Moon in Libra. Self-controlled; characterized by dignity, stability, and seriousness; capable of high attainment, leadership in the affairs of life, and a mature sensitiveness to the dominant demands of others.

Moon in Scorpio. A deep sense of justice and of personal responsibility; imaginative, facile, and consistent expression; self-controlled; a trait much needed by Capricorn.

Moon in Sagittarius. Characterized by severity, haste, and defensiveness; will seldom compromise opinions and will contest a doubtful point rather than modify a belief; in executive positions, essentially commercial and conscious of money.

Moon in Capricorn. Inclined to worry and subject to depression and periods of despondency; should guard against egotistical impulses and try to gain self-control; often a good accountant and capable of carrying out the orders of others.

Moon in Aquarius. Much depends on other planetary influences. With Venus in Capricorn, a love of children; with Jupiter, tends to be egotistical. With the other planets, it follows patterns of the entire horoscope.

Moon in Pisces. Generally a practical person, but not always one of a high order; sometimes attracted to military matters and to the love of sports; love of display and of personal ease in home affairs.

Sun in Aquarius

Aquarians are susceptible to a wide range of desires, because of their impressionable mental faculties, and are sensitive to and easily understand the needs of others. They show good taste in their surroundings, particularly in all that pertains to the home and its comforts.

Moon in Aries. Verbal facility; love of music, rhythms, and poetry; rather detached view of home conditions; enjoys association with friends and neighbors.

Moon in Taurus. This combination is sensitive and nervous; inclined to be impressed by the auras of those around them; a tendency toward pessimistic reserve, sometimes drawn to clairvoyant and other psychic professions.

Moon in Gemini. Grace, ease, and tenderness; value and highly praise friends; in home life, genial and affectionate, but not as constant as might be desired; often attracted to the theatrical profession.

Moon in Cancer. Dramatic and intense, with an imaginative reaction to events; great constancy in friendship; no wide range of ambition or desire for attainment higher than necessary.

Moon in Leo. This combination produces higher motives and more direct incentives to activity, avoiding the despondency into which the Aquarian is apt to drift; demonstrates hopefulness, good cheer, artistic ambition, foresight, and security.

Moon in Virgo. This is not a favorable location for the Moon, for it tends to draw the native too closely into the realm of physical sensation and sexuality. These natives need to school themselves against drifting along the path of temptation. They should guard against intemperance in all ways.

Moon in Libra. Can be positive and decisive, but when opportunity permits delay, they will procrastinate; fairly intuitive; disposed to generalize and avoid specific statements; a tendency toward melancholia when things go wrong.

Moon in Scorpio. Strong mechanical skills, without inventive power; likely to be changeable about opinions, which often interfere with the accomplishment of desires.

Moon in Sagittarius. A beneficial influence when governed by reason and a calm sense of procedure; this endowment gives directness, executive power, caution, and persistence in matters of importance; excitable and irascible under moderate provocation; needs self-government and favorable planetary aspects to express character at its best.

Moon in Capricorn. Judicious and forceful commercial abilities and a sense of freedom not usual in Aquarians; vividly expressive; controlled impulsiveness that gives power for success; a love of masses and generalities; should seek exactness and accuracy.

Moon in Aquarius. Generally is very sensitive and more than usually intuitive; confiding toward friends; given to suffer greatly from disappointment; magnifies small injuries into large ones; an intensely religious, domestic, and patriotic disposition.

Moon in Pisces. Capabilities in art criticism, mechanical drawing, and engraving; interest in natural phenomena; pride in personal appearance and in the ability to execute tasks successfully; in the main, selfish, particularly in small affairs.

★

Sun in Pisces

Those born in Pisces have a natural aptitude for the arts, particularly those characterized by symbolism, beauty, and elements of form; may also be successful in many of the mechanical trades; alert perceptions and the ability to memorize anything of interest.

Moon in Aries. Increased artistic and mechanical abilities, with greater directive capacity, more force in application, and more satisfactory practical results; when highly developed, mathematical ability and literary tastes are assisted by fluent verbal expression.

Moon in Taurus. Often has a deep interest in higher forms of mechanics and mathematics, frequently leading to the study of architecture, engineering, construction work, or, if opportunities in these areas are lacking, to practices of the manual branches of these disciplines and of analytical chemistry; more spiritual and romantic marriages.

Moon in Gemini. A technical education along some practical, commercial line is always best for persons with this endowment. An inclination toward portraiture, landscape painting, or caricature by itself does not bring financial success to people of this somewhat flighty temperament. These people enjoy social contacts. They are well informed about painting.

Moon in Cancer. Constancy and tenderness in the affections, qualities beneficial to home life; not endowed with the ability for scientific research or prolonged educational study, so should be careful to avoid waste of time and energy.

Moon in Leo. Inclined to erratic methods, conflicting views, and excessive emotion; should avoid building castles in the air and seek a pratical view in all essential matters—looking at the world as it really is; an occupation that stimulates is necessary for happiness.

Moon in Virgo. Calmness; a feeling of security; home and family interests; spiritual force; a more analytical habit of mind, with a desire for the practical application of perceptive ideas.

Moon in Libra. Often an unsatisfied, unsteady, and variable mental state; less material; nervous; more pride, perseverance, and positiveness when in good health.

Moon in Scorpio. Directness, industry, and forcefulness; a disposition to direct others in life or in industry; a keen insight into the use of mechanical instruments, aiding in the understanding of the laws of physics and their application.

Moon in Sagittarius. This influence is not harmonious. It is necessary for one born with this combination to learn to master the self in all ways. All extremes, haste, and irrational expression should be avoided.

Moon in Capricorn. Energy and forcefulness, making the choice of vocation wide: one of a practical type is preferred, generally leading to moderate success.

Moon in Aquarius. This mentality needs more dignity, persistence, executive force, and aggressiveness. Likely to be extreme and variable in marital matters and self-government and to practice constancy, with a real impulse toward filial love rather than marriage or partnership.

Moon in Pisces. Pisces is the home of the Moon, which exerts a powerful influence in this region: a love of all that is strange, weird, and phenomenal, giving wide-ranging interests in decorative arts and artistic home surroundings.

---★---

Judgments Drawn from the Moon

Following is a list of ancient aphorisms, the origins of which are lost in time, concerning one's birth or dreams during a particular phase of the Moon. To use this list one must consult an almanac or calendar for the current year or the year of one's birth, unless Mom or Granny has a very good memory!

Each lunar month begins with the New Moon (Sun/Moon conjunction) and lasts for twenty-eight to thirty days, when the next New Moon appears.

Days of the Month

1. A child born within twenty-one hours after the New Moon will be fortunate and live to a good old age; whatever is dreamed on this day will be fortunate and pleasant to the dreamer; various undertakings will succeed on it, particularly mental enterprises and well-timed innovations.
2. This day is favorable to scientific discoveries, mystic and mysterious revelations, and the discovery of things lost or hidden. The child born on this day will thrive, but dreams on this day are not to be depended upon.
3. This day is favorable to generation and to productions generally, whether physical or mental. A child born on this day will be fortunate through persons in power, and all dreams will prove true.
4. This day is unlucky, but favorable to unjust and tyrannical undertakings. Persons falling ill rarely recover, and dreams will be ineffectual.
5. This day is favorable for the initiation of a good enterprise, and dreams will be tolerably trustworthy; a child born on this day will be vain and deceitful.
6. This day is one of pride and is propitious to conspiracies and revolts. Its dreams will not come to pass immediately, and the child born upon it will not live long.
7. A day of religious undertakings, prayers, and spiritual success. Keep secret your dreams on this day. If you fall ill, you will

soon recover; the child born today will have long life but many troubles.

8. This is a day of expiatory sacrifice. Its dreams will come to pass; the business begun on it will prosper, and anything lost will be found.

9. This day differs little from the former. It is one of blessing for children, and the child born thereon will acquire great riches and honor.

10. Here is a fatal day, but it is good for the beginning of a journey, for marriage, and for engagements in business. Those who fall sick on it will rarely recover. The child born thereon will be religious and of an engaging form and manner; if a female, she will possess great wisdom and learning.

11. Dreams on this day are fortunate and visions deceptive; it gives health, longevity, and common sense to children born on it, but those who fall sick will seldom recover.

12. This day is favorable to prophecy and to important magical operations. Its dreams will quickly be proved true.

13. An unlucky day and fatal number. Favors asked on this day will, however, be granted.

14. The angel Cassiel of the hierarchy of Uriel governs this day. What was lost yesterday may be found, but the sickness that befalls a person on this day is likely to prove mortal.

15. A day of exile and reprobation, but good for dealing in merchandise. The child born on this day will have bad manners and be unfortunate.

16. The child born on this day will be foolish; it is an unlucky day to marry or to begin any kind of business.

17. A day of salvation for the good and of destruction for the wicked; a dangerous day, if it falls upon a Saturday. The child born on this day will be valiant but will suffer hardships; if a female, she will be chaste, industrious, and respected and live to a great age.

18. According to one ancient interpretation, this day is dangerous, and the child born on it will be dishonest, but according to another account, it is a day of conjugal affection and virtuous life.

19. A beneficent or unfortunate day for the great ones of the world. Dreams on this day will be vain and untrue; the child born on it will grow up healthy and strong but will be selfish and ungentle in disposition.

★

20. A day propitious to divine revelations. The child born on it will be fortunate, of a cheerful countenance, religious, and much beloved. Any kind of business begun on this day will be unfortunate.

21. A day of danger to mind and reason. The child born on it will be of an ungovernable temper, forsake his friends, wander in a foreign land, and be unhappy throughout life. It is a good day for marriage, and all business begun on it will be successful.

22. A day of trial, sorrow, and serious misfortune. The child born on it will be wicked, coming to an untimely end after many dangers. This day threatens everything with disappointment and crosses, and those who fall sick on it seldom recover.

23. A day of preference in worldly advancement and tenderness; the child born on it will be rich and greatly esteemed. Any dreams had on this day are certain to come true.

24. This day is favorable for dreams, and the child born on it will be of a sweet and amiable disposition.

25. This day is bad for dreams, and those who fall sick on it are in great danger. The child born on this day will be its parents' delight but will not live to any great age.

26. This day is good for dreams, but children born on it will experience many hardships, though they may turn out happily.

27. A most unfortunate day for seeking anything that is lost, but a child born on it will make a great stir in the world, as statesman, soldier, physician, or clergyman.

28. A day of strength and rescue. A child born before noon on this day will live to be a rich and truly good man, but if born after that hour, he may be dissipated or worthless.

29. A day of miscarriage and failure in all things. Today's dreams are unworthy of any attention, as their predictions will never be fulfilled.

Table of the Days of the Moon for the Interpretation of Dreams and Visions

The first day of the Moon is that of the New Moon, when the Moon is new in the morning. But when the New Moon arrives in one of the evening hours, the first day is counted from the morning after. The lunar month has sometimes twenty-nine days and sometimes thirty, including the period in which the Moon can't be seen. Consult a calendar that shows the Moon phases before referring to the following.

First Day. Dreams are fortunate.

Second Day. That which you have dreamed contains no truth.

Third Day. The dream is without consequence.

Fourth Day. Dreams are fortunate, and you may look for their fulfillment.

Fifth Day. They are entirely futile, and nothing can follow from them.

Sixth Day. Be very careful to tell your dream to no one.

Seventh Day. Keep your dream in mind, because there is truth in it.

Eighth Day. Something will follow from your dreaming: It has a purpose.

Ninth Day. You will see a result at once.

Tenth Day. The dream will be true and will joyfully come to pass.

Eleventh Day. The realization of the dream will be with you in four days.

Twelfth Day. You will have cause to remember your dream, because it will be realized by its opposite.

Thirteenth Day. That which you dream will be true, without question.

Fourteenth Day. It will happen, but long after.

Fifteenth Day. The realization will be with you in thirty days.

Luna.

Sixteenth Day. That which you have dreamed will come to pass.

Seventeenth Day. Tell no one until the third day thereafter.

Eighteenth Day. Be careful: The dream is likely to be made void.

Nineteenth Day. Keep the dream in your mind: You will have joy in the heart because of it.

Twentieth Day. You will assuredly see the result in four days' time.

Twenty-first Day. Put no trust in the dream, for nothing will come of it.

Twenty-second Day. Be patient for a few days only, and you shall see what you shall see.

Twenty-third Day. The dream will be fulfilled in three days.

Twenty-fourth Day. It will bring you much satisfaction.

Twenty-fifth Day. It will come to pass in eight or nine days.

Twenty-sixth Day. Take heed: This dream is important to you.

Twenty-seventh Day. Great contentment will follow this dream.

Twenty-eighth Day. It is true and will come to pass with joy.

Twenty-ninth Day. Rest assured: The dream is true.

Thirtieth Day. It will come to pass on the same morning.

Moon Tables

Many followers of astrology plan their actions according to the swift tempo of the Moon. The Moon makes a complete trip around the zodiac in less than a month, remaining only about two and a half days in each sign. Knowing where the moon is placed each hour of the day can enable you to plan your activities in advance.

The time of the Moon's entry into a sign varies each year, but its influence will be the same on all born under the sign, regardless of their birth dates. Below is a summary of the possible positive and negative effects of the Moon on each sign, followed by a timetable of its entry into the signs. Some persons are more strongly influenced by the Moon's vibration than by the Sun's, depending upon the position of these planets in their horoscopes. In order to ascertain which of these two planets has the stronger influence on your life, compare the daily horoscope for your Sun sign with the predictions below.

Aries

Favorable. For beginning new enterprises dealing with engineers, soldiers, and managers; handling metals, tools, and firearms; getting protection; collecting money; purchasing precious stones; hiring employees and servants.

Unfavorable. For treatments or operations on the head, face, eyes, and teeth; adjusting misunderstandings; beginning lawsuits; money matters; long-term loans; marriage and love affairs; all matters requiring stability.

Taurus

Favorable. For dealing with professional people; dancing, singing, and purchasing clothes and luxuries; visiting and short journeys; sports; painting and decorating; love affairs; home duties; purchasing ornaments and luxuries; dealing with the arts; social activities; amusements; those in power of government; renting a house; destroying pests; educational matters; dental work.

Unfavorable. For starting on a long journey; ocean trips; speed; treatment and operations to the neck, throat, and lower jaw; secret affairs; legacies or inheritances; short-term loans; all things that require a quick turnover.

Gemini

Favorable. For slaughtering animals; business; transportation; advertising; publishing; lectures; agreements; writing; studies; destroying pests; dealing with neighbors, brothers, and sisters; moving; short journeys; health examinations; excursions; dancing; all things that require dexterity.

Unfavorable. For real estate transactions; employment; entering into partnership; deciding important matters other than those relating to communication; construction; gardening; love affairs; marriage; treatments or operations to the arms, shoulders, or hands.

Cancer

Favorable. For domestic life and home duties; getting advice; lawsuits; purchasing or disposing of furniture; collecting money; fishing; sea and land voyages; meetings; romance; all things that require a quick resolution and improve appearances.

Unfavorable. For making loans of objects or money; building; business in general; treatments and operations to the breast, stomach, lungs, and liver; nuptials.

Leo

Favorable. For ceremonies and honors; employment; long-term loans; investments; digging foundations; dental work; gardening; love affairs.

Unfavorable. For treatments and operations to the back, ribs, heart, and spine; purchasing animals; starting out on a journey; partnerships; moving.

Virgo

Favorable. For employment; business and money matters; conferences; farming; slaughtering animals; investigations; destroying pests; professional work; meetings; correspondence and short journeys; dealing with inferiors; hiring servants.

Unfavorable. For marriage; love affairs; traveling on the water; construction work; building homes; treatments to the appendix and intestines.

Libra

Favorable. For love affairs; marriages; journeys; social activities; visiting; transportation and flying; dealing with the public; collecting money; making peace; home duties; adjusting misunderstandings; advertising; arts.

Unfavorable. For technical studies; traveling on the water; moving; construction; handling of tools; fire; steel and iron; dealing with enemies; treatments connected with operations.

Scorpio

Favorable. For chemistry; technical studies; experiments; investigations; legacies; inheritances and all things pertaining to estates; renting a house; your home duties; all things having to do with metals and liquids.

Unfavorable. For starting on a journey or traveling on land; starting new business ventures; money matters; lawsuits; marriage; treatments and operations.

Sagittarius

Favorable. For beginning new enterprises and legal affairs; purchasing precious stones; mountain climbing; sports; starting on long journeys; hunting; joining lodges, churches, and societies; adjusting misunderstandings and disputes; contacting religious people; partnership; business.

Unfavorable. For handling of metals; digging the soil; treatments and operations; false rumors; secret affairs.

Capricorn

Favorable: For collecting money; dealing with government; industries; employment; construction; building; leadership; slaughtering animals; home duties; real estate; purchasing materials; business in general; starting work that requires a long time to finish; deep studies; professional work.

Unfavorable. For beginning a lawsuit; medical treatments or operations; dental work; marriage; romance; dealing with those in authority; money matters.

Aquarius

Favorable. For construction; railroads; electricity; motors; radio; meetings and friendship; debates and lectures; flying; slaughtering animals; all things original and unconventional; radical changes; antiques; renting a house.

Unfavorable. For making loans; starting work that requires a long time; borrowing money; dealing with superiors; love affairs; operations and treatments on the legs and ankles.

Pisces

Favorable. For visiting instutitions; making peace; dealing with the police; mysteries; art; amusement; lawsuits; improving personal appearance; home duties; traveling; farming; loaning of money; love affairs; marriage.

Unfavorable. For handling metals; new enterprises; endowments; foundations; treatments and operations to the feet, toes, and nerves; things requiring speed; hiring employees; going before the public.

Four-Year Timetable

Note: The time of the Moon's entry into the signs of the zodiac is calculated according to Eastern Standard Time. For Central Time, subtract one hour; for Mountain Time, subtract two hours; and for Pacific Time, subtract three hours. During Daylight Savings Time, subtract one hour from all calculations.

JANUARY 1987		FEBRUARY 1987	
1. Aquarius	6:54 A.M.	1. Aries	9:10 P.M.
2. Aquarius		2. Aries	
3. Pisces	7:37 P.M.	3. Aries	
4. Pisces		4. Taurus	3:54 A.M.
5. Aries	11:52 A.M.	5. Taurus	
6. Aries		6. Gemini	2:24 P.M.
7. Taurus	8:14 P.M.	7. Gemini	
8. Taurus		8. Gemini	
9. Gemini	7:40 P.M.	9. Cancer	2:56 A.M.
10. Gemini		10. Cancer	
11. Gemini		11. Leo	3:22 P.M.
12. Cancer	8:19 P.M.	12. Leo	
13. Cancer		13. Leo	
14. Cancer		14. Virgo	2:27 A.M.
15. Leo	8:46 A.M.	15. Virgo	
16. Leo		16. Libra	11:45 A.M.
17. Virgo	8:16 P.M.	17. Libra	
18. Virgo		18. Scorpio	7:05 P.M.
19. Virgo		19. Scorpio	
20. Libra	6:10 A.M.	20. Scorpio	
21. Libra		21. Sagittarius	12:10 A.M.
22. Scorpio	1:31 P.M.	22. Sagittarius	
23. Scorpio		23. Capricorn	2:58 A.M.
24. Sagittarius	5:36 P.M.	24. Capricorn	
25. Sagittarius		25. Aquarius	4:09 A.M.
26. Capricorn	6:43 P.M.	26. Aquarius	
27. Capricorn		27. Pisces	5:08 A.M.
28. Aquarius	6:18 P.M.	28. Pisces	
29. Aquarius			
30. Pisces	6:25 P.M.		
31. Pisces			

MARCH 1987		APRIL 1987	
1. Aries	7:38 P.M.	1. Taurus	
2. Aries		2. Gemini	7:17 P.M.
3. Taurus	1:12 P.M.	3. Gemini	
4. Taurus		4. Cancer	6:34 P.M.
5. Gemini	10:27 P.M.	5. Cancer	
6. Gemini		6. Cancer	
7. Gemini		7. Leo	7:05 P.M.
8. Cancer	10:25 A.M.	8. Leo	
9. Cancer		9. Virgo	6:29 P.M.
10. Leo	10:55 P.M.	10. Virgo	
11. Leo		11. Virgo	
12. Leo		12. Libra	3:06 A.M.
13. Virgo	9:56 P.M.	13. Libra	
14. Virgo		14. Scorpio	8:41 A.M.
15. Libra	6:35 P.M.	15. Scorpio	
16. Libra		16. Sagittarius	12:02 P.M.
17. Libra		17. Sagittarius	
18. Scorpio	12:58 A.M.	18. Capricorn	2:22 P.M.
19. Scorpio		19. Capricorn	
20. Sagittarius	5:33 A.M.	20. Aquarius	4:46 P.M.
21. Sagittarius		21. Aquarius	
22. Capricorn	8:49 A.M.	22. Pisces	8:03 P.M.
23. Capricorn		23. Pisces	
24. Aquarius	11:19 A.M.	24. Pisces	
25. Aquarius		25. Aries	12:41 A.M.
26. Pisces	1:47 P.M.	26. Aries	
27. Pisces		27. Taurus	7:07 P.M.
28. Aries	5:13 A.M.	28. Taurus	
29. Aries		29. Gemini	3:44 P.M.
30. Taurus	10:47 P.M.	30. Gemini	
31. Taurus			

MAY 1987		JUNE 1987	
1. Gemini		1. Leo	
2. Cancer	2:40 A.M.	2. Leo	
3. Cancer		3. Virgo	10:57 A.M.
4. Leo	3:07 P.M.	4. Virgo	
5. Leo		5. Libra	9:25 P.M.
6. Leo		6. Libra	
7. Virgo	3:08 A.M.	7. Libra	
8. Virgo		8. Scorpio	4:07 A.M.
9. Libra	12:30 P.M.	9. Scorpio	
10. Libra		10. Sagittarius	6:54 A.M.
11. Scorpio	5:10 P.M.	11. Sagittarius	
12. Scorpio		12. Capricorn	7:06 P.M.
13. Sagittarius	8:42 P.M.	13. Capricorn	
14. Sagittarius		14. Aquarius	6:46 A.M.
15. Capricorn	9:37 P.M.	15. Aquarius	
16. Capricorn		16. Pisces	7:55 A.M.
17. Aquarius	10:43 P.M.	17. Pisces	
18. Aquarius		18. Aries	11:57 A.M.
19. Aquarius		19. Aries	
20. Pisces	1:25 A.M.	20. Taurus	7:10 P.M.
21. Pisces		21. Taurus	
22. Aries	6:24 A.M.	22. Taurus	
23. Aries		23. Gemini	4:55 A.M.
24. Taurus	1:40 P.M.	24. Gemini	
25. Taurus		25. Cancer	4:23 P.M.
26. Gemini	10:56 P.M.	26. Cancer	
27. Gemini		27. Leo	4:53 A.M.
28. Gemini		28. Leo	
29. Cancer	10:00 A.M.	29. Leo	
30. Cancer		30. Virgo	
31. Leo	10:26 P.M.		

JULY 1987		AUGUST 1987	
1. Virgo		1. Scorpio	8:10 P.M.
2. Virgo		2. Scorpio	
3. Libra	4:55 A.M.	3. Scorpio	
4. Libra		4. Sagittarius	1:48 A.M.
5. Scorpio	1:04 P.M.	5. Sagittarius	
6. Scorpio		6. Capricorn	3:52 A.M.
7. Sagittarius	5:06 P.M.	7. Capricorn	
8. Sagittarius		8. Aquarius	3:38 A.M.
9. Capricorn	5:44 P.M.	9. Aquarius	
10. Capricorn		10. Pisces	3:02 A.M.
11. Aquarius	4:50 P.M.	11. Pisces	
12. Aquarius		12. Aries	4:10 A.M.
13. Pisces	4:37 P.M.	13. Aries	
14. Pisces		14. Taurus	8:39 A.M.
15. Aries	7:01 P.M.	15. Taurus	
16. Aries		16. Gemini	5:00 P.M.
17. Aries		17. Gemini	
18. Taurus	1:05 A.M.	18. Gemini	
19. Taurus		19. Cancer	4:20 A.M.
20. Gemini	10:33 A.M.	20. Cancer	
21. Gemini		21. Leo	4:59 P.M.
22. Cancer	10:14 P.M.	22. Leo	
23. Cancer		23. Leo	
24. Cancer		24. Virgo	5:24 A.M.
25. Leo	10:51 A.M.	25. Virgo	
26. Leo		26. Libra	4:36 P.M.
27. Virgo	11:26 P.M.	27. Libra	
28. Virgo		28. Libra	
29. Virgo		29. Scorpio	1:50 A.M.
30. Libra	11:00 A.M.	30. Scorpio	
31. Libra		31. Sagittarius	8:25 A.M.

SEPTEMBER 1987		OCTOBER 1987	
1. Sagittarius		1. Aquarius	8:52 P.M.
2. Capricorn	12:05 P.M.	2. Aquarius	
3. Capricorn		3. Pisces	10:40 P.M.
4. Aquarius	1:22 P.M.	4. Pisces	
5. Aquarius		5. Pisces	
6. Pisces	1:38 P.M.	6. Aries	12:36 A.M.
7. Pisces		7. Aries	
8. Aries	2:35 P.M.	8. Taurus	3:58 A.M.
9. Aries		9. Taurus	
10. Taurus	5:58 P.M.	10. Gemini	10:04 A.M.
11. Taurus		11. Gemini	
12. Taurus		12. Cancer	7:32 P.M.
13. Gemini	12:55 A.M.	13. Cancer	
14. Gemini		14. Cancer	
15. Cancer	11:23 A.M.	15. Leo	7:35 A.M.
16. Cancer		16. Leo	
17. Leo	11:51 P.M.	17. Virgo	8:07 P.M.
18. Leo		18. Virgo	
19. Leo		19. Virgo	
20. Virgo	12:14 P.M.	20. Libra	6:51 A.M.
21. Virgo		21. Libra	
22. Libra	10:59 P.M.	22. Scorpio	2:42 P.M.
23. Libra		23. Scorpio	
24. Libra		24. Sagittarius	7:58 P.M.
25. Scorpio	7:31 A.M.	25. Sagittarius	
26. Scorpio		26. Capricorn	11:34 P.M.
27. Sagittarius	1:50 P.M.	27. Capricorn	
28. Sagittarius		28. Aquarius	2:28 A.M.
29. Capricorn	6:09 P.M.	29. Aquarius	
30. Capricorn		30. Pisces	5:20 A.M.
		31. Pisces	

NOVEMBER 1987		DECEMBER 1987	
1. Pisces		1. Taurus	8:06 P.M.
2. Aries	8:41 A.M.	2. Taurus	
3. Aries		3. Taurus	
4. Taurus	1:03 P.M.	4. Gemini	3:14 A.M.
5. Taurus		5. Gemini	
6. Gemini	7:17 P.M.	6. Cancer	12:21 P.M.
7. Gemini		7. Cancer	
8. Gemini		8. Leo	11:41 P.M.
9. Cancer	4:11 A.M.	9. Leo	
10. Cancer		10. Leo	
11. Leo	3:46 P.M.	11. Virgo	12:31 P.M.
12. Leo		12. Virgo	
13. Leo		13. Virgo	
14. Virgo	4:30 A.M.	14. Libra	12:41 A.M.
15. Virgo		15. Libra	
16. Libra	3:49 P.M.	16. Scorpio	10:42 A.M.
17. Libra		17. Scorpio	
18. Scorpio	11:48 P.M.	18. Sagittarius	2:34 P.M.
19. Scorpio		19. Sagittarius	
20. Sagittarius	4:17 A.M.	20. Capricorn	4:08 P.M.
21. Sagittarius		21. Capricorn	
22. Sagittarius		22. Aquarius	4:21 P.M.
23. Capricorn	6:33 A.M.	23. Aquarius	
24. Capricorn		24. Pisces	5:11 P.M.
25. Aquarius	8:14 A.M.	25. Pisces	
26. Aquarius		26. Aries	8:06 P.M.
27. Pisces	10:41 A.M.	27. Aries	
28. Pisces		28. Aries	
29. Aries	2:37 P.M.	29. Taurus	1:37 A.M.
30. Aries		30. Taurus	
		31. Gemini	9:30 A.M.

JANUARY 1988		FEBRUARY 1988	
1. Gemini		1. Leo	1:07 P.M.
2. Cancer	7:17 P.M.	2. Leo	
3. Cancer		3. Leo	
4. Cancer		4. Virgo	1:55 A.M.
5. Leo	6:48 A.M.	5. Virgo	
6. Leo		6. Libra	2:37 P.M.
7. Virgo	7:36 P.M.	7. Libra	
8. Virgo		8. Libra	
9. Virgo		8. Libra	
10. Libra	8:18 A.M.	9. Scorpio	1:43 A.M.
11. Libra		10. Scorpio	
12. Scorpio	6:40 P.M.	11. Sagittarius	9:37 A.M.
13. Scorpio		12. Sagittarius	
14. Scorpio		13. Capricorn	1:37 P.M.
15. Sagittarius	12:59 A.M.	14. Capricorn	
16. Sagittarius		15. Aquarius	2:26 P.M.
17. Capricorn	3:16 A.M.	16. Aquarius	
18. Capricorn		17. Pisces	1:45 P.M.
19. Aquarius	3:03 A.M.	18. Pisces	
20. Aquarius		19. Aries	1:36 P.M.
21. Pisces	2:28 A.M.	20. Aries	
22. Pisces		21. Taurus	3:51 P.M.
23. Aries	3:32 A.M.	22. Taurus	
24. Aries		23. Gemini	9:43 P.M.
25. Taurus	7:37 A.M.	24. Gemini	
26. Taurus		25. Gemini	
27. Gemini	3:03 P.M.	26. Cancer	7:13 A.M.
28. Gemini		27. Cancer	
29. Gemini		28. Leo	7:13 P.M.
30. Cancer	1:12 A.M.	29. Leo	
31. Cancer			

MARCH 1988		APRIL 1988	
1. Leo		1. Libra	3:06 A.M.
2. Virgo	8:07 A.M.	2. Libra	
3. Virgo		3. Scorpio	1:27 P.M.
4. Libra	8:33 P.M.	4. Scorpio	
5. Libra		5. Sagittarius	9:30 P.M.
6. Libra		6. Sagittarius	
7. Scorpio	7:28 A.M.	7. Sagittarius	
8. Scorpio		8. Capricorn	3:20 A.M.
9. Sagittarius	4:00 P.M.	9. Capricorn	
10. Sagittarius		10. Aquarius	7:11 A.M.
11. Capricorn	9:32 A.M.	11. Aquarius	
12. Capricorn		12. Pisces	9:25 A.M.
13. Capricorn		13. Pisces	
14. Aquarius	12:09 A.M.	14. Aries	10:47 A.M.
15. Aquarius		15. Aries	
16. Pisces	12:43 A.M.	16. Taurus	12:32 P.M.
17. Pisces		17. Taurus	
18. Aries	12:46 A.M.	18. Gemini	4:11 P.M.
19. Aries		19. Gemini	
20. Taurus	2:06 A.M.	20. Cancer	11:05 P.M.
21. Taurus		21. Cancer	
22. Gemini	6:22 A.M.	22. Cancer	
23. Gemini		23. Leo	10:35 A.M.
24. Cancer	2:28 P.M.	24. Leo	
25. Cancer		25. Virgo	10:17 P.M.
26. Leo	1:55 A.M.	26. Virgo	
27. Leo		27. Virgo	
28. Leo		28. Libra	10:38 A.M.
29. Virgo	2:50 P.M.	29. Libra	
30. Virgo		30. Scorpio	8:40 P.M.
31. Virgo			

MAY 1988		JUNE 1988	
1. Scorpio		1. Capricorn	3:59 P.M.
2. Scorpio		2. Capricorn	
3. Sagittarius	3:53 A.M.	3. Aquarius	6:35 P.M.
4. Sagittarius		4. Aquarius	
5. Capricorn	8:55 A.M.	5. Pisces	9:01 A.M.
6. Capricorn		6. Pisces	
7. Aquarius	12:38 P.M.	7. Aries	12:05 A.M.
8. Aquarius		8. Aries	
9. Pisces	3:40 P.M.	9. Aries	
10. Pisces		10. Taurus	4:03 A.M.
11. Aries	6:24 P.M.	11. Taurus	
12. Aries		12. Gemini	9:15 P.M.
13. Taurus	9:23 P.M.	13. Gemini	
14. Taurus		14. Cancer	4:20 P.M.
15. Taurus		15. Cancer	
16. Gemini	1:32 A.M.	16. Cancer	
17. Gemini		17. Leo	1:58 A.M.
18. Cancer	8:06 A.M.	18. Leo	
19. Cancer		19. Virgo	2:04 P.M.
20. Leo	5:52 P.M.	20. Virgo	
21. Leo		21. Virgo	
22. Leo		22. Libra	2:58 A.M.
23. Virgo	6:13 A.M.	23. Libra	
24. Virgo		24. Scorpio	1:59 P.M.
25. Libra	6:50 P.M.	25. Scorpio	
26. Libra		26. Sagittarius	9:19 P.M.
27. Libra		27. Sagittarius	
28. Scorpio	5:07 A.M.	28. Sagittarius	
29. Scorpio		29. Capricorn	1:01 A.M.
30. Sagittarius	11:58 A.M.	30. Capricorn	
31. Sagittarius			

123

JULY 1988		AUGUST 1988	
1. Aquarius	2:30 A.M.	1. Aries	12:54 P.M.
2. Aquarius		2. Aries	
3. Pisces	3:34 A.M.	3. Taurus	3:25 P.M.
4. Pisces		4. Taurus	
5. Aries	5:38 A.M.	5. Gemini	8:44 A.M.
6. Aries		6. Gemini	
7. Taurus	9:28 A.M.	7. Gemini	
8. Taurus		8. Cancer	4:53 A.M.
9. Gemini	3:17 P.M.	9. Cancer	
10. Gemini		10. Leo	3:27 P.M.
11. Cancer	11:09 P.M.	11. Leo	
12. Cancer		12. Leo	
13. Leo	9:12 A.M.	13. Virgo	3:47 A.M.
14. Leo		14. Virgo	
15. Leo		15. Libra	4:53 P.M.
16. Virgo	9:18 A.M.	16. Libra	
17. Virgo		17. Libra	
18. Virgo		18. Scorpio	5:13 A.M.
19. Libra	10:23 P.M.	19. Scorpio	
20. Libra		20. Sagittarius	2:56 P.M.
21. Scorpio	9:14 P.M.	21. Sagittarius	
22. Scorpio		22. Capricorn	9:50 P.M.
23. Scorpio		23. Capricorn	
24. Sagittarius	6:43 P.M.	24. Aquarius	11:06 P.M.
25. Sagittarius		25. Aquarius	
26. Capricorn	11:08 A.M.	26. Pisces	11:02 P.M.
27. Capricorn		27. Pisces	
28. Aquarius	12:26 P.M.	28. Aries	10:30 P.M.
29. Aquarius		29. Aries	
30. Pisces	12:24 P.M.	30. Taurus	11:23 P.M.
31. Pisces		31. Taurus	

SEPTEMBER 1988		OCTOBER 1988	
1. Taurus		1. Cancer	5:39 P.M.
2. Gemini	3:12 A.M.	2. Cancer	
3. Gemini		3. Cancer	
4. Cancer	10:38 P.M.	4. Leo	3:32 A.M.
5. Cancer		5. Leo	
6. Leo	9:15 P.M.	6. Virgo	4:02 P.M.
7. Leo		7. Virgo	
8. Leo		8. Virgo	
9. Virgo	9:49 A.M.	9. Libra	5:04 A.M.
10. Virgo		10. Libra	
11. Libra	10:52 P.M.	11. Scorpio	4:59 P.M.
12. Libra		12. Scorpio	
13. Libra		13. Scorpio	
14. Scorpio	11:08 A.M.	14. Sagittarius	2:59 A.M.
15. Scorpio		15. Sagittarius	
16. Sagittarius	9:26 P.M.	16. Capricorn	10:45 A.M.
17. Sagittarius		17. Capricorn	
18. Sagittarius		18. Aquarius	4:06 P.M.
19. Capricorn	4:46 A.M.	19. Aquarius	
20. Capricorn		20. Pisces	6:59 P.M.
21. Aquarius	8:44 A.M.	21. Pisces	
22. Aquarius		22. Aries	8:00 P.M.
23. Pisces	9:52 A.M.	23. Aries	
24. Pisces		24. Taurus	8:23 A.M.
25. Aries	9:30 A.M.	25. Taurus	
26. Aries		26. Gemini	9:56 P.M.
27. Taurus	9:30 A.M.	27. Gemini	
28. Taurus		28. Gemini	
29. Gemini	11:44 A.M.	29. Cancer	2:29 A.M.
30. Gemini		30. Cancer	
		31. Leo	11:04 A.M.

NOVEMBER 1988

1. Leo
2. Virgo   11:03 P.M.
3. Virgo
4. Virgo
5. Libra   12:05 P.M.
6. Libra
7. Scorpio   11:47 P.M.
8. Scorpio
9. Scorpio
10. Sagittarius   9:06 A.M.
11. Sagittarius
12. Capricorn   4:13 P.M.
13. Capricorn
14. Aquarius   9:37 P.M.
15. Aquarius
16. Aquarius
17. Pisces   1:35 A.M.
18. Pisces
19. Aries   4:13 A.M.
20. Aries
21. Taurus   6:03 A.M.
22. Taurus
23. Gemini   8:13 A.M.
24. Gemini
25. Cancer   12:20 P.M.
26. Cancer
27. Leo   7:53 P.M.
28. Leo
29. Leo
30. Virgo   7:00 A.M.

DECEMBER 1988

1. Virgo
2. Libra   7:57 P.M.
3. Libra
4. Libra
5. Scorpio   7:52 A.M.
6. Scorpio
7. Sagittarius   4:56 P.M.
8. Sagittarius
9. Capricorn   11:08 P.M.
10. Capricorn
11. Capricorn
12. Aquarius   3:26 A.M.
13. Aquarius
14. Pisces   6:54 A.M.
15. Pisces
16. Aries   11:04 A.M.
17. Aries
18. Taurus   1:12 P.M.
19. Taurus
20. Gemini   4:44 P.M.
21. Gemini
22. Cancer   9:36 P.M.
23. Cancer
24. Leo   4:58 A.M.
25. Leo
26. Leo
27. Virgo   3:28 P.M.
28. Virgo
29. Virgo
30. Libra   4:10 A.M.
31. Libra

JANUARY 1989		FEBRUARY 1989	
1. Scorpio	4:35 P.M.	1. Sagittarius	
2. Scorpio		2. Capricorn	6:31 P.M.
3. Scorpio		3. Capricorn	
4. Sagittarius	2:12 A.M.	4. Aquarius	9:52 P.M.
5. Sagittarius		5. Aquarius	
6. Capricorn	8:15 A.M.	6. Aquarius	
7. Capricorn		7. Pisces	10:53 P.M.
8. Aquarius	11:31 A.M.	8. Pisces	
9. Aquarius		9. Aries	11:19 P.M.
10. Pisces	1:32 P.M.	10. Aries	
11. Pisces		11. Taurus	12:46 A.M.
12. Aries	3:36 P.M.	12. Taurus	
13. Aries		13. Gemini	4:23 A.M.
14. Taurus	6:37 P.M.	14. Gemini	
15. Taurus		15. Cancer	10:41 A.M.
16. Gemini	10:57 P.M.	16. Cancer	
17. Gemini		17. Leo	7:34 P.M.
18. Gemini		18. Leo	
19. Cancer	4:58 A.M.	19. Leo	
20. Cancer		20. Virgo	6:35 A.M.
21. Leo	1:03 P.M.	21. Virgo	
22. Leo		22. Libra	7:06 P.M.
23. Virgo	11:33 P.M.	23. Libra	
24. Virgo		24. Libra	
25. Libra	12:02 P.M.	25. Scorpio	7:58 A.M.
26. Libra		26. Scorpio	
27. Libra		27. Sagittarius	7:30 P.M.
28. Libra		28. Sagittarius	
29. Scorpio	12:50 A.M.		
30. Scorpio			
31. Sagittarius	11:31 P.M.		

MARCH 1989		APRIL 1989	
1. Sagittarius		1. Aquarius	
2. Capricorn	3:59 A.M.	2. Pisces	8:38 P.M.
3. Capricorn		3. Pisces	
4. Aquarius	8:37 A.M.	4. Aries	8:52 P.M.
5. Aquarius		5. Aries	
6. Pisces	9:59 A.M.	6. Taurus	8:08 P.M.
7. Pisces		7. Taurus	
8. Aries	9:37 A.M.	8. Gemini	8:32 P.M.
9. Aries		9. Gemini	
10. Taurus	9:26 A.M.	10. Cancer	11:59 P.M.
11. Taurus		11. Cancer	
12. Gemini	11:17 A.M.	12. Cancer	
13. Gemini		13. Leo	7:32 A.M.
14. Cancer	4:28 P.M.	14. Leo	
15. Cancer		15. Virgo	6:40 P.M.
16. Cancer		16. Virgo	
17. Leo	1:14 A.M.	17. Virgo	
18. Leo		18. Libra	7:32 P.M.
19. Virgo	12:40 P.M.	19. Libra	
20. Virgo		20. Libra	
21. Virgo		21. Scorpio	8:14 P.M.
22. Libra	1:25 A.M.	22. Scorpio	
23. Libra		23. Sagittarius	7:39 P.M.
24. Scorpio	2:11 P.M.	24. Sagittarius	
25. Scorpio		25. Capricorn	5:16 P.M.
26. Scorpio		26. Capricorn	
27. Sagittarius	1:55 A.M.	27. Capricorn	
28. Sagittarius		28. Aquarius	12:34 A.M.
29. Capricorn	11:26 A.M.	29. Aquarius	
30. Capricorn		30. Pisces	5:04 A.M.
31. Aquarius	5:46 P.M.		

MAY 1989		JUNE 1989	
1. Pisces		1. Taurus	
2. Aries	6:51 A.M.	2. Gemini	5:03 P.M.
3. Aries		3. Gemini	
4. Taurus	6:56 A.M.	4. Cancer	7:18 P.M.
5. Taurus		5. Cancer	
6. Gemini	7:04 P.M.	6. Cancer	
7. Gemini		7. Leo	12:29 A.M.
8. Cancer	9:20 A.M.	8. Leo	
9. Cancer		9. Virgo	9:30 A.M.
10. Leo	3:24 P.M.	10. Virgo	
11. Leo		11. Libra	9:32 P.M.
12. Virgo	1:31 A.M.	12. Libra	
13. Virgo		13. Libra	
14. Virgo		14. Scorpio	10:12 P.M.
15. Libra	2:08 P.M.	15. Scorpio	
16. Libra		16. Sagittarius	9:13 P.M.
17. Scorpio	2:48 A.M.	17. Sagittarius	
18. Scorpio		18. Sagittarius	
19. Sagittarius	1:53 P.M.	19. Capricorn	5:42 A.M.
20. Sagittarius		20. Capricorn	
21. Sagittarius		21. Aquarius	11:58 A.M.
22. Capricorn	10:55 P.M.	22. Aquarius	
23. Capricorn		23. Pisces	4:37 P.M.
24. Aquarius	6:02 A.M.	24. Pisces	
25. Aquarius		25. Aries	8:07 P.M.
26. Pisces	11:14 A.M.	26. Aries	
27. Pisces		27. Taurus	10:46 P.M.
28. Aries	2:26 P.M.	28. Taurus	
29. Aries		29. Taurus	
30. Aries		30. Gemini	1:09 P.M.
31. Taurus	4:10 P.M.		

JULY 1989		AUGUST 1989	
1. Gemini		1. Leo	
2. Cancer	4:20 A.M.	2. Leo	
3. Cancer		3. Virgo	2:20 A.M.
4. Leo	9:38 A.M.	4. Virgo	
5. Leo		5. Libra	1:29 P.M.
6. Virgo	6:05 P.M.	6. Libra	
7. Virgo		7. Libra	
8. Virgo		8. Scorpio	2:06 A.M.
9. Libra	5:31 A.M.	9. Scorpio	
10. Libra		10. Sagittarius	2:03 P.M.
11. Scorpio	5:10 P.M.	11. Sagittarius	
12. Scorpio		12. Capricorn	11:17 P.M.
13. Scorpio		13. Capricorn	
14. Sagittarius	5:32 A.M.	14. Aquarius	5:00 A.M.
15. Sagittarius		15. Aquarius	
16. Capricorn	2:02 P.M.	16. Pisces	7:46 P.M.
17. Capricorn		17. Pisces	
18. Aquarius	7:36 P.M.	18. Aries	9:00 A.M.
19. Aquarius		19. Aries	
20. Pisces	11:08 P.M.	20. Taurus	9:11 A.M.
21. Pisces		21. Taurus	
22. Pisces		22. Gemini	12:40 P.M.
23. Aries	1:41 A.M.	23. Gemini	
24. Aries		24. Gemini	
25. Taurus	4:11 A.M.	25. Cancer	5:14 P.M.
26. Taurus		26. Cancer	
27. Gemini	7:16 P.M.	27. Cancer	
28. Gemini		28. Leo	12:12 A.M.
29. Cancer	11:33 A.M.	29. Leo	
30. Cancer		30. Virgo	9:30 A.M.
31. Leo	5:42 P.M.	31. Virgo	

SEPTEMBER 1989		OCTOBER 1989	
1. Libra	8:48 P.M.	1. Scorpio	3:54 P.M.
2. Libra		2. Scorpio	
3. Libra		3. Scorpio	
4. Scorpio	9:24 A.M.	4. Sagittarius	4:30 A.M.
5. Scorpio		5. Sagittarius	
6. Sagittarius	9:52 P.M.	6. Capricorn	3:46 P.M.
7. Sagittarius		7. Capricorn	
8. Sagittarius		8. Capricorn	
9. Capricorn	8:14 A.M.	9. Aquarius	12:07 A.M.
10. Capricorn		10. Aquarius	
11. Aquarius	3:03 P.M.	11. Pisces	4:38 A.M.
12. Aquarius		12. Pisces	
13. Pisces	6:08 P.M.	13. Aries	5:42 A.M.
14. Pisces		14. Aries	
15. Aries	6:39 P.M.	15. Taurus	4:53 A.M.
16. Aries		16. Taurus	
17. Taurus	6:23 P.M.	17. Gemini	4:20 A.M.
18. Taurus		18. Gemini	
19. Gemini	7:17 P.M.	19. Cancer	6:10 A.M.
20. Gemini		20. Cancer	
21. Cancer	10:51 P.M.	21. Leo	11:48 A.M.
22. Cancer		22. Leo	
23. Leo	5:45 A.M.	23. Virgo	9:16 P.M.
24. Leo		24. Virgo	
25. Leo		25. Virgo	
26. Virgo	3:33 P.M.	26. Libra	9:12 A.M.
27. Virgo		27. Libra	
28. Virgo		28. Scorpio	9:57 A.M.
29. Libra	3:16 A.M.	29. Scorpio	
30. Libra		30. Scorpio	
		31. Sagittarius	10:24 A.M.

NOVEMBER 1989		DECEMBER 1989	
1. Sagittarius		1. Capricorn	
2. Capricorn	9:47 P.M.	2. Aquarius	12:43 P.M.
3. Capricorn		3. Aquarius	
4. Capricorn		4. Pisces	7:49 P.M.
5. Aquarius	7:10 P.M.	5. Pisces	
6. Aquarius		6. Aries	12:12 A.M.
7. Pisces	1:26 P.M.	7. Aries	
8. Pisces		8. Taurus	2:00 A.M.
9. Aries	4:09 P.M.	9. Taurus	
10. Aries		10. Gemini	2:16 A.M.
11. Taurus	4:10 P.M.	11. Gemini	
12. Taurus		12. Cancer	2:50 A.M.
13. Gemini	3:20 P.M.	13. Cancer	
14. Gemini		14. Cancer	
15. Cancer	3:52 P.M.	15. Leo	5:42 A.M.
16. Cancer		16. Leo	
17. Leo	7:46 P.M.	17. Virgo	12:20 P.M.
18. Leo		18. Virgo	
19. Leo		19. Libra	10:46 P.M.
20. Virgo	3:55 A.M.	20. Libra	
21. Virgo		21. Libra	
22. Libra	3:26 P.M.	22. Scorpio	11:19 A.M.
23. Libra		23. Scorpio	
24. Libra		24. Sagittarius	11:38 P.M.
25. Scorpio	4:14 A.M.	25. Sagittarius	
26. Scorpio		26. Sagittarius	
27. Sagittarius	4:31 P.M.	27. Capricorn	11:11 A.M.
28. Sagittarius		28. Capricorn	
29. Sagittarius		29. Aquarius	6:39 P.M.
30. Capricorn	3:27 A.M.	30. Aquarius	
		31. Aquarius	

JANUARY 1990		FEBRUARY 1990	
1. Pisces	1:11 A.M.	1. Taurus	2:28 P.M.
2. Pisces		2. Taurus	
3. Aries	5:57 A.M.	3. Gemini	5:13 P.M.
4. Aries		4. Gemini	
5. Taurus	9:05 A.M.	5. Cancer	8:28 P.M.
6. Taurus		6. Cancer	
7. Gemini	11:02 A.M.	7. Cancer	
8. Gemini		8. Leo	12:52 A.M.
9. Cancer	12:53 P.M.	9. Leo	
10. Cancer		10. Virgo	7:14 P.M.
11. Leo	4:03 P.M.	11. Virgo	
12. Leo		12. Libra	4:10 P.M.
13. Virgo	9:58 P.M.	13. Libra	
14. Virgo		14. Libra	
15. Virgo		15. Scorpio	3:35 A.M.
16. Libra	7:18 P.M.	16. Scorpio	
17. Libra		17. Sagittarius	4:08 P.M.
18. Scorpio	7:17 P.M.	18. Sagittarius	
19. Scorpio		19. Sagittarius	
20. Scorpio		20. Capricorn	3:31 A.M.
21. Sagittarius	7:45 P.M.	21. Capricorn	
22. Sagittarius		22. Aquarius	11:53 A.M.
23. Capricorn	6:28 P.M.	23. Aquarius	
24. Capricorn		24. Pisces	4:50 P.M.
25. Capricorn		25. Pisces	
26. Aquarius	2:26 A.M.	26. Aries	7:17 P.M.
27. Aquarius		27. Aries	
28. Pisces	7:52 P.M.	28. Taurus	8:44 P.M.
29. Pisces			
30. Aries	11:35 A.M.		

MARCH 1990		APRIL 1990	
1. Taurus		1. Cancer	7:51 P.M.
2. Gemini	10:38 P.M.	2. Cancer	
3. Gemini		3. Leo	12:51 P.M.
4. Gemini		4. Leo	
5. Cancer	2:03 A.M.	5. Virgo	8:42 P.M.
6. Cancer		6. Virgo	
7. Leo	7:25 P.M.	7. Virgo	
8. Leo		8. Libra	6:45 A.M.
9. Virgo	2:48 P.M.	9. Libra	
10. Virgo		10. Scorpio	6:18 P.M.
11. Virgo		11. Scorpio	
12. Libra	12:10 A.M.	12. Sagittarius	6:49 A.M.
13. Libra		13. Sagittarius	
14. Scorpio	11:26 A.M.	14. Sagittarius	
15. Scorpio		15. Capricorn	7:16 P.M.
16. Sagittarius	11:57 P.M.	16. Capricorn	
17. Sagittarius		17. Capricorn	
18. Sagittarius		18. Aquarius	5:53 A.M.
19. Capricorn	12:02 P.M.	19. Aquarius	
20. Capricorn		20. Pisces	12:58 P.M.
21. Aquarius	9:32 P.M.	21. Pisces	
22. Aquarius		22. Aries	3:59 P.M.
23. Aquarius		23. Aries	
24. Pisces	3:09 A.M.	24. Taurus	4:04 P.M.
25. Pisces		25. Taurus	
26. Aries	5:16 A.M.	26. Gemini	3:13 P.M.
27. Aries		27. Gemini	
28. Taurus	5:27 A.M.	28. Cancer	3:40 P.M.
29. Taurus		29. Cancer	
30. Gemini	5:43 A.M.	30. Leo	7:09 P.M.
31. Gemini			

MAY 1990			JUNE 1990	
1. Leo			1. Libra	6:32 P.M.
2. Leo			2. Libra	
3. Virgo	2:19 A.M.		3. Libra	
4. Virgo			4. Scorpio	6:22 A.M.
5. Libra	12:29 P.M.		5. Scorpio	
6. Libra			6. Sagittarius	7:00 P.M.
7. Libra			7. Sagittarius	
8. Scorpio	12:23 A.M.		8. Sagittarius	
9. Scorpio			9. Capricorn	7:13 A.M.
10. Sagittarius	12:57 P.M.		10. Capricorn	
11. Sagittarius			11. Aquarius	6:10 P.M.
12. Sagitarius			12. Aquarius	
13. Capricorn	1:22 A.M.		13. Aquarius	
14. Capricorn			14. Pisces	3:01 A.M.
15. Aquarius	12:31 P.M.		15. Pisces	
16. Aquarius			16. Aries	8:56 A.M.
17. Pisces	8:55 P.M.		17. Aries	
18. Pisces			18. Taurus	11:44 A.M.
19. Aries	1:32 A.M.		19. Taurus	
20. Aries			20. Gemini	12:15 P.M.
21. Aries			21. Gemini	
22. Taurus	2:43 A.M.		22. Cancer	12:10 P.M.
23. Taurus			23. Cancer	
24. Gemini	2:01 A.M.		24. Leo	1:26 P.M.
25. Gemini			25. Leo	
26. Cancer	1:35 A.M.		26. Virgo	5:43 P.M.
27. Cancer			27. Virgo	
28. Leo	3:30 A.M.		28. Virgo	
29. Leo			29. Libra	1:48 A.M.
30. Virgo	10:09 A.M.		30. Libra	
31. Virgo				

JULY 1990		AUGUST 1990	
1. Scorpio	1:02 P.M.	1. Sagittarius	
2. Scorpio		2. Capricorn	9:09 P.M.
3. Scorpio		3. Capricorn	
4. Sagittarius	1:36 A.M.	4. Capricorn	
5. Sagittarius		5. Aquarius	7:20 P.M.
6. Capricorn	1:40 P.M.	6. Aquarius	
7. Capricorn		7. Pisces	2:55 P.M.
8. Capricorn		8. Pisces	
9. Aquarius	12:07 A.M.	9. Aries	8:14 P.M.
10. Aquarius		10. Aries	
11. Pisces	8:30 A.M.	11. Taurus	11:56 P.M.
12. Pisces		12. Taurus	
13. Aries	2:37 P.M.	13. Taurus	
14. Aries		14. Gemini	2:42 A.M.
15. Taurus	6:30 P.M.	15. Gemini	
16. Taurus		16. Cancer	5:13 A.M.
17. Gemini	8:33 P.M.	17. Cancer	
18. Gemini		18. Leo	8:12 A.M.
19. Cancer	9:45 P.M.	19. Leo	
20. Cancer		20. Virgo	12:34 P.M.
21. Leo	11:30 P.M.	21. Virgo	
22. Leo		22. Libra	7:17 P.M.
23. Leo		23. Libra	
24. Virgo	3:18 A.M.	24. Scorpio	4:57 A.M.
25. Virgo		25. Scorpio	
26. Libra	10:19 A.M.	26. Scorpio	
27. Libra		27. Sagittarius	4:58 P.M.
28. Scorpio	8:40 P.M.	28. Sagittarius	
29. Scorpio		29. Sagittarius	
30. Scorpio		30. Capricorn	5:24 A.M.
31. Sagittarius	9:01 A.M.	31. Capricorn	

SEPTEMBER 1990		OCTOBER 1990	
1. Aquarius	3:52 P.M.	1. Pisces	8:43 A.M.
2. Aquarius		2. Pisces	
3. Pisces	11:06 P.M.	3. Aries	12:43 P.M.
4. Pisces		4. Aries	
5. Pisces		5. Taurus	2:07 P.M.
6. Aries	3:24 A.M.	6. Taurus	
7. Aries		7. Gemini	2:48 P.M.
8. Taurus	5:56 A.M.	8. Gemini	
9. Taurus		9. Cancer	4:30 P.M.
10. Gemini	8:06 A.M.	10. Cancer	
11. Gemini		11. Leo	8:17 P.M.
12. Cancer	10:54 A.M.	12. Leo	
13. Cancer		13. Leo	
14. Leo	2:53 P.M.	14. Virgo	2:21 A.M.
15. Leo		15. Virgo	
16. Virgo	8:19 P.M.	16. Libra	10:27 P.M.
17. Virgo		17. Libra	
18. Virgo		18. Scorpio	8:25 P.M.
19. Libra	3:35 A.M.	19. Scorpio	
20. Libra		20. Scorpio	
21. Scorpio	1:07 P.M.	21. Sagittarius	8:10 A.M.
22. Scorpio		22. Sagittarius	
23. Scorpio		23. Capricorn	9:04 P.M.
24. Sagittarius	12:53 A.M.	24. Capricorn	
25. Sagittarius		25. Capricorn	
26. Capricorn	1:37 P.M.	26. Aquarius	9:15 A.M.
27. Capricorn		27. Aquarius	
28. Aquarius	12:55 A.M.	28. Pisces	6:23 P.M.
29. Aquarius		29. Pisces	
30. Aquarius		30. Aries	11:15 P.M.
		31. Aries	

NOVEMBER 1990		DECEMBER 1990	
1. Aries		1. Gemini	11:23 A.M.
2. Taurus	12:32 A.M.	2. Gemini	
3. Taurus		3. Cancer	10:28 A.M.
4. Gemini	12:07 A.M.	4. Cancer	
5. Gemini		5. Leo	11:01 A.M.
6. Cancer	12:07 A.M.	6. Leo	
7. Cancer		7. Virgo	2:40 P.M.
8. Leo	2:25 A.M.	8. Virgo	
9. Leo		9. Libra	10:01 P.M.
10. Virgo	7:49 P.M.	10. Libra	
11. Virgo		11. Libra	
12. Libra	4:09 P.M.	12. Scorpio	8:28 A.M.
13. Libra		13. Scorpio	
14. Libra		14. Sagittarius	8:45 P.M.
15. Scorpio	2:40 A.M.	15. Sagittarius	
16. Scorpio		16. Sagittarius	
17. Sagittarius	2:40 P.M.	17. Capricorn	9:36 A.M.
18. Sagittarius		18. Capricorn	
19. Sagittarius		19. Aquarius	9:00 P.M.
20. Capricorn	3:32 A.M.	20. Aquarius	
21. Capricorn		21. Aquarius	
22. Aquarius	4:08 P.M.	22. Pisces	8:49 A.M.
23. Aquarius		23. Pisces	
24. Aquarius		24. Aries	4:46 A.M.
25. Pisces	2:33 A.M.	25. Aries	
26. Pisces		26. Taurus	9:10 P.M.
27. Aries	9:07 A.M.	27. Taurus	
28. Aries		28. Gemini	10:27 P.M.
29. Taurus	11:38 A.M.	29. Gemini	
30. Taurus		30. Cancer	10:03 P.M.
		31. Cancer	

JANUARY 1991		FEBRUARY 1991	
1. Leo	9:55 P.M.	1. Virgo	
2. Leo		2. Libra	3:03 P.M.
3. Virgo	11:58 P.M.	3. Libra	
4. Virgo		4. Scorpio	11:02 P.M.
5. Virgo		5. Scorpio	
6. Libra	5:34 A.M.	6. Scorpio	
7. Libra		7. Sagittarius	10:24 A.M.
8. Scorpio	3:00 P.M.	8. Sagittarius	
9. Scorpio		9. Capricorn	11:17 P.M.
10. Scorpio		10. Capricorn	
11. Sagittarius	3:07 A.M.	11. Capricorn	
12. Sagittarius		12. Aquarius	11:17 A.M.
13. Capricorn	4:01 P.M.	13. Aquarius	
14. Capricorn		14. Pisces	9:01 P.M.
15. Capricorn		15. Pisces	
16. Aquarius	4:05 A.M.	16. Pisces	
17. Aquarius		17. Aries	4:12 A.M.
18. Pisces	2:24 P.M.	18. Aries	
19. Pisces		19. Taurus	9:25 A.M.
20. Aries	10:28 P.M.	20. Taurus	
21. Aries		21. Gemini	1:11 P.M.
22. Aries		22. Gemini	
23. Taurus	4:02 A.M.	23. Cancer	3:57 P.M.
24. Taurus		24. Cancer	
25. Gemini	7:07 P.M.	25. Leo	6:13 P.M.
26. Gemini		26. Leo	
27. Cancer	8:24 A.M.	27. Virgo	8:51 P.M.
28. Cancer		28. Virgo	
29. Leo	9:04 A.M.		
30. Leo			
31. Virgo	10:45 A.M.		

MARCH 1991		APRIL 1991	
1. Virgo		1. Scorpio	
2. Libra	1:04 A.M.	2. Scorpio	
3. Libra		3. Sagittarius	3:00 A.M.
4. Scorpio	8:09 A.M.	4. Sagittarius	
5. Scorpio		5. Capricorn	3:21 P.M.
6. Sagittarius	6:36 P.M.	6. Capricorn	
7. Sagittarius		7. Capricorn	
8. Sagittarius		8. Aquarius	4:00 A.M.
9. Capricorn	7:15 P.M.	9. Aquarius	
10. Capricorn		10. Pisces	2:18 P.M.
11. Aquarius	7:32 P.M.	11. Pisces	
12. Aquarius		12. Aries	8:50 P.M.
13. Aquarius		13. Aries	
14. Pisces	5:12 A.M.	14. Aries	
15. Pisces		15. Taurus	12:06 A.M.
16. Aries	11:38 A.M.	16. Taurus	
17. Aries		17. Gemini	1:42 A.M.
18. Taurus	3:41 P.M.	18. Gemini	
19. Taurus		19. Cancer	3:18 A.M.
20. Gemini	6:38 P.M.	20. Cancer	
21. Gemini		21. Leo	6:05 A.M.
22. Cancer	9:28 P.M.	22. Leo	
23. Cancer		23. Virgo	10:30 A.M.
24. Cancer		24. Virgo	
25. Leo	12:44 A.M.	25. Libra	4:37 P.M.
26. Leo		26. Libra	
27. Virgo	4:42 A.M.	27. Scorpio	12:35 A.M.
28. Virgo		28. Scorpio	
29. Libra	9:50 A.M.	29. Sagittarius	10:43 A.M.
30. Libra		30. Sagittarius	
31. Scorpio	5:02 P.M.		

MAY 1991		JUNE 1991	
1. Sagittarius		1. Aquarius	6:43 P.M.
2. Capricorn	10:55 P.M.	2. Aquarius	
3. Capricorn		3. Aquarius	
4. Capricorn		4. Pisces	6:37 P.M.
5. Aquarius	11:52 A.M.	5. Pisces	
6. Aquarius		6. Aries	3:26 P.M.
7. Pisces	11:05 P.M.	7. Aries	
8. Pisces		8. Taurus	8:13 P.M.
9. Pisces		9. Taurus	
10. Aries	6:35 A.M.	10. Gemini	9:37 A.M.
11. Aries		11. Gemini	
12. Taurus	10:08 A.M.	12. Cancer	9:17 P.M.
13. Taurus		13. Cancer	
14. Gemini	11:03 A.M.	14. Leo	9:11 A.M.
15. Gemini		15. Leo	
16. Cancer	11:15 A.M.	16. Virgo	11:04 P.M.
17. Cancer		17. Virgo	
18. Leo	12:31 P.M.	18. Virgo	
19. Leo		19. Libra	4:02 A.M.
20. Virgo	4:01 P.M.	20. Libra	
21. Virgo		21. Scorpio	12:19 P.M.
22. Libra		22. Scorpio	
23. Libra		23. Sagittarius	11:17 P.M.
24. Libra		24. Sagittarius	
25. Scorpio	6:42 A.M.	25. Sagittarius	
26. Scorpio		26. Capricorn	11:50 A.M.
27. Sagittarius	5:22 P.M.	27. Capricorn	
28. Sagittarius		28. Capricorn	
29. Sagittarius		29. Aquarius	12:48 A.M.
30. Capricorn	5:41 A.M.	30. Aquarius	
31. Capricorn			

JULY 1991		AUGUST 1991	
1. Pisces	12:52 P.M.	1. Aries	
2. Pisces		2. Taurus	11:33 A.M.
3. Aries	11:34 P.M.	3. Taurus	
4. Aries		4. Gemini	3:55 P.M.
5. Aries		5. Gemini	
6. Taurus	4:53 A.M.	6. Cancer	5:48 P.M.
7. Taurus		7. Cancer	
8. Gemini	7:43 P.M.	8. Leo	5:10 P.M.
9. Gemini		9. Leo	
10. Cancer	8:04 A.M.	10. Virgo	6:36 P.M.
11. Cancer		11. Virgo	
12. Leo	7:36 A.M.	12. Libra	8:53 P.M.
13. Leo		13. Libra	
14. Virgo	8:13 A.M.	14. Libra	
15. Virgo		15. Scorpio	2:35 A.M.
16. Libra	11:35 A.M.	16. Scorpio	
17. Libra		17. Sagittarius	12:12 P.M.
18. Scorpio	6:42 P.M.	18. Sagittarius	
19. Scorpio		19. Sagittarius	
20. Scorpio		20. Capricorn	12:35 A.M.
21. Sagittarius	5:17 A.M.	21. Capricorn	
22. Sagittarius		22. Aquarius	1:28 P.M.
23. Capricorn	5:56 P.M.	23. Aquarius	
24. Capricorn		24. Aquarius	
25. Capricorn		25. Pisces	12:52 A.M.
26. Aquarius	5:50 A.M.	26. Pisces	
27. Aquarius		27. Aries	10:02 A.M.
28. Pisces	6:36 P.M.	28. Aries	
29. Pisces		29. Taurus	5:01 P.M.
30. Pisces		30. Taurus	
31. Aries	4:21 A.M.	31. Gemini	10:03 P.M.

SEPTEMBER 1991		OCTOBER 1991	
1. Gemini		1. Cancer	
2. Gemini		2. Leo	9:59 A.M.
3. Cancer	1:20 A.M.	3. Leo	
4. Cancer		4. Virgo	12:45 P.M.
5. Leo	3:14 A.M.	5. Virgo	
6. Leo		6. Libra	4:01 P.M.
7. Virgo	4:36 A.M.	7. Libra	
8. Virgo		8. Scorpio	9:01 P.M.
9. Libra	6:52 A.M.	9. Scorpio	
10. Libra		10. Scorpio	
11. Scorpio	11:43 A.M.	11. Sagittarius	4:59 A.M.
12. Scorpio		12. Sagittarius	
13. Sagittarius	8:15 P.M.	13. Capricorn	4:11 P.M.
14. Sagittarius		14. Capricorn	
15. Sagittarius		15. Capricorn	
16. Capricorn	8:05 A.M.	16. Aquarius	5:05 A.M.
17. Capricorn		17. Aquarius	
18. Aquarius	8:59 P.M.	18. Pisces	4:54 A.M.
19. Aquarius		19. Pisces	
20. Aquarius		20. Pisces	
21. Pisces	8:21 A.M.	21. Aries	1:34 A.M.
22. Pisces		22. Aries	
23. Aries	4:57 P.M.	23. Taurus	6:56 A.M.
24. Aries		24. Taurus	
25. Taurus	11:00 P.M.	25. Gemini	10:10 A.M.
26. Taurus		26. Gemini	
27. Taurus		27. Cancer	12:38 P.M.
28. Gemini	3:26 A.M.	28. Cancer	
29. Gemini		29. Leo	3:21 P.M.
30. Cancer	6:59 A.M.	30. Leo	
		31. Virgo	6:48 P.M.

NOVEMBER 1991		DECEMBER 1991	
1. Virgo		1. Libra	
2. Libra	11:13 P.M.	2. Scorpio	11:34 P.M.
3. Libra		3. Scorpio	
4. Libra		4. Sagittarius	8:33 P.M.
5. Scorpio	5:10 A.M.	5. Sagittarius	
6. Scorpio		6. Sagittarius	
7. Sagittarius	1:22 P.M.	7. Capricorn	7:42 P.M.
8. Sagittarius		8. Capricorn	
9. Sagittarius		9. Aquarius	8:28 P.M.
10. Capricorn	12:17 A.M.	10. Aquarius	
11. Capricorn		11. Aquarius	
12. Aquarius	1:07 P.M.	12. Pisces	9:20 A.M.
13. Aquarius		13. Pisces	
14. Aquarius		14. Aries	8:07 P.M.
15. Pisces	1:34 A.M.	15. Aries	
16. Pisces		16. Aries	
17. Aries	11:09 A.M.	17. Taurus	3:11 A.M.
18. Aries		18. Taurus	
19. Taurus	4:50 P.M.	19. Gemini	6:22 A.M.
20. Taurus		20. Gemini	
21. Gemini	7:23 P.M.	21. Cancer	6:55 P.M.
22. Gemini		22. Cancer	
23. Cancer	8:26 P.M.	23. Leo	6:39 A.M.
24. Cancer		24. Leo	
25. Leo	9:38 P.M.	25. Virgo	7:25 P.M.
26. Leo		26. Virgo	
27. Leo		27. Libra	10:38 P.M.
28. Virgo	12:13 A.M.	28. Libra	
29. Virgo		29. Scorpio	5:04 P.M.
30. Libra	4:48 A.M.	30. Scorpio	
		31. Scorpio	

3.
The Secrets of
Spiritual Power
★

How to Develop Your ESP through Witchcraft, Magic, and Sorcery

In the traditional greeting of witches everywhere:

BLESSED BE!

In the following section you will receive instructions in the development of psycho-mental power that were originally distributed as correspondence lessons by the Academy of Mystic Arts, which I founded in 1972.

Thousands of students throughout the United States and other parts of the world paid hundreds of dollars to receive these teachings, which are now yours for the cost of this book. And the lessons are the same as those sent by mail.

At first I hesitated to make this material available in this way. After meditation, however, I concluded that now, as the Piscean Age is ending, was the time to make public many of the techniques that have been kept secret.

An astrological age begins when the vernal equinox enters an astrological sign. It lasts about 2,000 years.

According to mystical tradition, each age commences with the birth and appearance of a great master, an avatar, who is its herald. In the Piscean Age, this master was Jesus Christ.

The Age of Pisces was ruled by the planet Neptune, which gave rise to organized religion with all its ritual and dogma. This was the age of the monk and the monastery, and since Pisces rules Cosmic consciousness through isolation and withdrawal, these were the methods by which one had to find the Path.

Today, however, the Age of Aquarius is almost upon us. Ruled not by Neptune but by Uranus, planet of individuation and universal consciousness through sharing and love (Uranus is the higher vibration of the planet Venus), it is a time in which that which was hidden must now be made known.

And so it was that I concluded that it was my sacred charge to make known in this way many of the secret techniques I had discovered during my own search for the Truth.

Do not let the brevity or simplicity of this first lesson fool you. Remember that you are just beginning to use powers that have been asleep for your entire life. Just as an athlete begins training slowly and for short periods of time, so must you follow this same pattern in our work together.

Now, until you go on to the next lesson, I ask that you follow with care these instructions that will unite you with us and place you under our protection against ill happenings caused by others.

On the *evening* of the first Thursday following the purchase of this book, specifically from the hour of 7:30 P.M. until 12 P.M. on Friday, take this page, a small bowl of water, an ashtray, an envelope, and some matches to a room in which you can be *alone*. Dip the first finger of your left hand into the water and trace the "XP" and the "Triangle" that appears in the illustration on page 192 in the center of your forehead. As you do this, read aloud (in a soft voice that only you can hear) these words: "With this Sacred Act, I, of my own free will and spirit, do herewith call upon the Council of Seven to bring me Light, Life, and Love. I with them and they with me, forever and ever, blessed be!" After saying these words aloud, copy this page in your own handwriting or make a photocopy, and fold it seven times, then burn it completely. As you watch it burn, you will feel our presence develop. Carefully place the ashes in an envelope, and place it under your pillow when you go to sleep, removing it the next day and scattering the ashes outdoors. Be sure to read these instructions again before carrying them out, and be prepared to feel us join with you.

Lesson 1

You who read this have elected to seek a path trodden by the chosen few. In this and the lessons that follow you will receive instruction in matter formerly reserved for distribution only in the coven, or circle of thirteen witches, which by tradition meets only when the Moon, or Mother Goddess, is "right" in the heavens.

You will be asked to keep many of the things that you will learn to yourself and never to mention them to the uninitiated, remembering that throughout the centuries over nine million of your brethren have met their deaths because of their beliefs. Remember, too, the words of the Great Master who said, "Neither cast ye pearls before swine." Those who have not ear to hear shall never hear, therefore speak not to them of the things that follow.

The Antiquity of the Craft

In the beginning of time itself there arose a protohuman animal who stood above others of his clan in the acquisition of food and other life-giving substances. To him was given the great honor of guiding the self-preservation of the tribe. It was his wisdom, coupled with the belief that all things have a "spiritual essence," that gave rise to animism.

Primitive man hovered in fear before the awesome display of nature's elements of wind, rain, and the fire of lightning. In order to calm these forces, there arose a belief in "spirits" who lived within people and responded to the right word or ritual, known only by the tribe shaman or magician. So, too, everything that existed, both animate and inanimate, was thought to contain a living spirit who was either pleased or displeased by one's presence.

If one tripped on a stone, it was not his own clumsiness but rather the work of the spirit living in the stone. In time, certain spirits were found to exercise greater power than others, and to these was given the classification "Gods," or "what is evoked."

To perpetuate the worship of such special deities, a priesthood and mystery was created based on the myth of the goddess or god. The very word *mystery* comes from the ancient Greek word *mystērion,* meaning "to be silent" or "keeping silent." Thus, the first requisite of the Craft was nonbetrayal of its mysteries. Next, each candidate was initiated into the mysteries of the cult and underwent an experience that you, too, will have later on in your studies.

The Myth of Osiris formed the basis of the Egyptian mysteries, the beginning of the modern witch cult. It recounts that Geb (earth) and Nut (sky) united and gave birth to Osiris, who ruled over the land and was the first king of Egypt. His evil brother Set, jealous of his many accomplishments, ambushed and slew him and cast his body into the

★

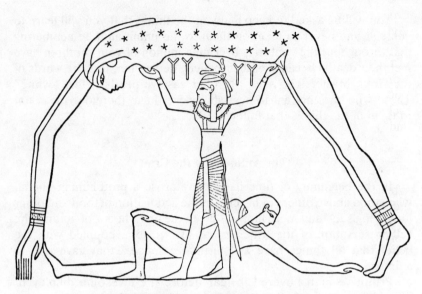

The Egyptian gods of the earth,
the air, and the heavenly vault

Nile, after cutting it into many pieces. His two sisters Isis and Nephtys bewailed his loss until eventually Isis found his body and by means of magic power reconstituted it and infused life into it once again. In appreciation for the life given by Isis, Osiris married her, and she gave birth to Horus. Osiris then departed to the other world, where he became Lord of Eternity. All departed souls must therefore come before Osiris for judgment.

In accordance with the Osiris legend, every ancient initiation consisted of a ceremony in which the candidate was sybolically put to death and reborn. As a result of this gnosis, or spiritual insight, the candidate emerged with superior knowledge and often was given a new name to indicate his rebirth.

With the rise of Christianity, believers in the mystery religions were persecuted and driven into hiding, but their traditions were kept alive by the faithful. In Persia, in the sixth century B.C., they considered themselves practitioners of the Great Art, and these followers of the mystic Zoroaster, or Zarathustra, came to be known as magi, from which the word *magic* comes. These same priests, according to the New Testament, attended the birth of the child Jesus.

In ancient Rome, those who practiced the magical art through evocation of the spirits came to be called sorcerers, or those who divined through the casting of lots.

In Anglo-Saxon England, those people who possessed knowledge of the occult, or hidden things, were called "wicca," or "wise." This word later evolved into the word *witch,* signifying a female practitioner of the arts. The male counterpart came to be called a "warlock," derived from the word *warloga,* originally meaning "traitor" and later evolving to mean "enemy, devil, magician."

In medieval England, these individuals, when evoking spirits of the deceased, were called necromancers.

When magic was used for beneficial purposes it was said to be White; when used for evil it was called Black. One must look at the individual acts themselves, however, in order to distinguish one type of magic from the other, for often anything that is in any way different from the beliefs of the majority is thought to be evil and therefore "black."

Further Instructions

In this and in each lesson to follow, you will receive an exercise intended to quicken and awaken the master or psychic self lying dormant within you. We ask that you keep these instructions in inviolate secrecy, never speaking of them in public.

Practice each exercise at least *once* daily for a period of ten days. Then rest for a period of three days. It is most important that these instructions be followed.

Exercise 1

Find a comfortable chair in a quiet room, and begin to relax by closing your eyes. Close your mouth, and breathe in and out slowly through your nose. After you have relaxed and as you breathe in, mentally count to eight. Hold your breath for a count of four. Exhale for another count of eight. Rest for four counts. Repeat.

After practicing the above for a few minutes, instead of mentally counting, accompany each *incoming* breath with the sound "RAaaaaaaaa." Accompany each *outgoing* breath with the sound "MAaaaaaaaa." One cannot live without breath. With its proper control, you will be preparing to attain the health, love, and position you seek.

Practice this exercise at least fifteen minutes each day, preferably before retiring in the evening.

★

Lesson 2

In the last lesson we introduced you to the antiquity of our Order and the meaning of the mysteries. In this one, we continue in the same vein.

Entering the Mystery

When an individual decides to become a part of a cult, sect, or secret society, many things rightly go through his mind as to what benefits he will derive from his membership. In the past, and even today, people unite for many of the same reasons that led their fore-fathers to seek the mysteries. Some of these reasons are misguided, and some simply inadequate.

To begin with, many seek to learn magic, or the Great Art, in order to obtain happiness, health, or peace of mind. But often they do not realize that for anything of value to be acquired, it must be worked for and earned, and these shortsighted individuals quickly leave the mysteries and seek success elsewhere.

Still others unite for educational reasons, seeking merely to en-hance their intellectual knowledge of people, places, and things. There is nothing wrong with this group, yet they, too, miss the mark.

Others seek happiness for purely carnal reasons, believing that the mysteries will offer them unlimited sexual freedom to do what they please, whenever they please. These, too, fail in their search for the Book of Shadows—the handwritten book containing the rituals of the great.

Last but not least, there exist those rare individuals who some-where deep inside themselves have a desire to become a part of something that they may not yet understand or even know exists, yet they seek oneness. Only this group is destined to succeed in the end.

Therefore, we may say that witchcraft as a mystery means many things to many people, and thus its pursuit, and membership in its cult, is as broad or as narrow as humanity itself. While offering a system of religious or mystical allegory through its use of symbols to convey great truths, it becomes personal to the extent that people see in it what they desire to see. As a candidate participates in a ritual, it is a drama or play based on themes derived from and directed out of the universal mind. In this way, withcraft has been called a Cosmic religion. Since the initiate emerges from his studies with knowledge unobtainable elsewhere, it is a gnosis.

Three Stages of a Mystery: Preparation, Probation, Initiation

In ancient times, each candidate who desired admission to the mysteries was first subjected to a series of tests to determine his or her worthiness to receive the mystical teachings. According to a very ancient tradition of the Great White Brotherhood, each would-be initiate was required to learn the meaning of four sacred verbs believed to contain in their understanding the ultimate success or failure of the candidate. We give these to you as they were given to us.

To Will. "To will" means that you have determined once and for all to change your mind and your manner of thinking in order to find greater prosperity. "To will" means also that despite any circumstances that may tend to prevent you from doing so, you *will* continue in your studies until you achieve success.

To Know. "To know" means that you have selected for your teachers those persons who have in their possession the keys to the wisdom you seek. How can you be sure that you have selected the right teacher? By the lectures themselves, by the exercises, and by the way you yourself feel about these studies.

To Dare. "To dare" means that you possess the courage to study things that are not generally known and that may require you to change your thinking.

To Be Silent. "To be silent" means that all we have said thus far has been as a whisper heard by and for you alone. This is perhaps the most important command of the four!

In the Egyptian mysteries, each candidate was required to read the following confession before Maat, Goddess of Truth. As it represents one of the first of its kind, we present it for you to ponder. The original papyrus from which it has been translated still rests within the British Museum.

Homage to thee, O thou great God, thou lord of the two Maat goddesses! I have come to thee, O my Lord, and I have made myself to come hither that I may behold thy beauties. I know thee, and I know thy name, and I know the names of the two and

forty gods who live with thee in this Hall of Matti. . . . Verily I
have come to thee, and I have brought Maat unto thee, and I have
destroyed wickedness.

I have not done evil to mankind.
I have not committed theft, murder, nor robbed with violence.
I have not made light the bushel.
I have not uttered falsehood or vile words.
I have not carried off food by force.
I have not lost my temper and become angry.
I have invaded no man's land.
I have not pried into matters to make mischief.
I have not made my speech to burn with anger.
I have not made myself deaf unto the words of right and truth.
I have not made another person to weep.
I have not multiplied my speech beyond what should be said.
I have not polluted running water nor laid waste the lands which
    have been ploughed.
I have never uttered curses against the king.
I have not exalted my speech.
I have not increased by wealth save through my own posses-
    sions.
I have not uttered curses against that which belongeth to God
    and is with me.

I am pure. I am pure. I am pure.

My purity is the purity of the Divinity of the Holy Temple.

Therefore let not evil befall me either in this land or in this Hall
of Maat, because I know the names of the gods who are therein.

Further Instructions

In the last session we introduced you to the use of certain psycho-
physiological exercises that have been used throughout the ages to
develop the psychic body and psychic centers. Do not pass off these
exercises as unnecessary to your advancement or you will find yourself in the position of the man who had never operated a car before
and won one as a prize. Upon receiving the keys, he unlocked the car
door and threw them away, wondering "how to get the damn thing
started"!

Exercise 2

Continue to practice the breathing exercise taught in the last lesson.

The ancients discovered that the power to concentrate the mind is related to the ability to hold one's vision on a single spot or object. This and the next few exercises will develop this important ability.

Obtain a piece of white paper and a pen or pencil. Draw a triangle, as illustrated, and place in the center a single dot.

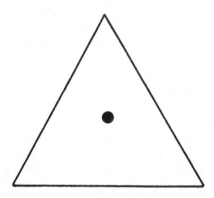

Fix your attention on the dot, and see how long you can hold your gaze without blinking or turning away. Try to hold your gaze for at least five minutes. At first your eyes may water, and your mind will want to turn away. Continue to practice, and you will find success.

Next, continue to gaze at the dot and try to literally move it toward each of the three corners of the triangle. For many, especially those whose vision has been impaired, the entire experiment can be accomplished by closing the eyes and mentally performing the experiment. Some students will find themselves capable of having a second dot appear within the triangle. This exciting experiment will help to strengthen your senses and start to unleash the power of the subconscious mind.

Try this exercise at least twice daily, using a fresh piece of paper each time.

★

Lesson 3

In the last lesson we introduced you to the Confession of Maat as an example of the type of confession used in the mysteries since their inception. A confession, together with a vow of secrecy, is found in all of the original mysteries and today's counterparts, including the witch cult.

From their earliest stages, mystery cults have employed baptism and lustration, as well as vows of secrecy and confession, in their initiatory rites. Subjecting a candidate to the four elements, especially water and fire, was believed to give the initiate ultimate power over these same universal forces. Emergence in or sprinkling with water has persisted down to the present day in the services of our churches. From a psychological viewpoint, it is believed that baptism produces in the candidate a feeling of well-being that results from the recognition, on an unconscious level, of a return to the womb or to the original watery state from which all mankind emerged.

In addition to baptism, the sacrifice of such animals as white lambs, rams, and pigs was commonplace. Often the blood of the animal was either drunk or poured over the candidate in the belief that such an act would transfer the strength of the animal to the initiate.

Besides sacrifices during the probationary period, the mysteries often required fasting, maiming, tattooing, long pilgrimages, or large contributions of wealth. The following instructions given to a would-be initiate have been handed down to us by a master in the mysteries of Isis:

> She will break the ice and descend into the river in winter; thrice a morning she will bathe in the Tiber and lave her tumid head in its very depths. Then with bleeding knees she will creep, naked and shivering, over the whole length of the Campus Martius.

Having passed through a period of probation and preparation, each candidate's worthiness for admission into a cult was reevaluated, and a final decision was reached by those in charge. Should the decision of the masters be in the candidate's favor, he or she was advised when and where to present himself or herself for initiation. At the time and place specified, each candidate was subjected to varieties of physical and psychological stimulation including expectancy, whirling dances, contemplation of sacred objects, and inhalation of incense and various fumes. Together with mental suggestion and hypnosis, these often produced in the initiate hallucinations of actual communion and union with the deity.

The following is an account of an actual initiation into the cult of Isis that took place within the Great Pyramid in Egypt.

The Pastophore [priest] has by now led the postulant to the end of the gallery of the Arcana and opens a door giving access to another long narrow vault, at the end of which roars a blazing furnace.

At this the postulant trembles. "Where am I going now?" he wonders half aloud. "It's an inescapable fate—it's death!"

"Son of Earth," says the Pastrophore, "death itself frightens the imperfect only. If you are afraid, what are you doing here? Look at me; once I, too, passed through those flames as if they were a garden of roses."

Encouraged by the Magus' kindly smile, the postulant, reassured, steps forward while behind him the door is closed on the gallery of the Arcana. Reflection reminds him that the teaching he has just received would be useless to a man about to die. He does not know how this new ordeal will end; but had he foreseen how the others would end? As he approaches the barrier of fire, his confidence increases, the danger diminishes in his eyes. The furnace is nothing more than an optical illusion created by small piles of resinous wood arranged on iron grills between which is traced a path. He goes eagerly forward, for he thinks he has come through the ordeal; but suddenly the unforeseen happens. In front of him the vaulted passageway ends abruptly at a stagnant pool, whose broad, still surface covers unknown depths. Behind him a cascade of oil falls from the opened ceiling and leaps into flames; the furnace is a real furnace now.

Penned between this curtain of flame and the sheet of water, which may conceal a trap, he has to judge the lesser danger. He enters the dark water and walks carefully down a slippery slope. With each step the water level seems to rise—it reaches his chest; it goes higher—his shoulders; one more step and the water will close over his head. But the light from the furnace shows him that he has reached the middle of the lake. Further on, the slope begins to rise again, and at the water's edge on the opposite bank a flight of steps leads to a platform surrounded on three sides by a lofty arcade. On the wall at the end is a brass doorway that seems divided into two by a narrow, twisted column sculptured with a lion's jaws, which holds a large metal ring.

This door is closed. The postulant, soaked to the skin and shivering, with difficulty mounts the stairs. On reaching the platform he is surprised to find himself walking on a floor of hollow-sounding metal. He stops outside the door to get his bearings. Beyond the water the reflection from the furnace dims and then is extinguished. Darkness reigns again under these unknown vaults; the silence is filled with dread: he can go forward, how retreat?

But listen—mysterious words are heard in that empty gloom: "If you stop," says this voice,"you will perish. Behind you is death; before you salvation."

One can imagine the anxiety of the poor postulant. Driven by terror, trembling in the darkness, he feels round the sculptures on the brazen doorway, trying to discover the secret mechanism that will make it open. The ring he saw just now in the lion's jaws, representing a serpent with its tail in its mouth—could it be a sort of knocker to be lifted and let fall on the sonorous metal of the door? He has barely seized it in his hands when by a mechanical trick the metal floor collapses under him, and he is left suspended over a gaping pit.

This ordeal had the appearance of great danger, for the postulant might loose his grip; but the Magi foresaw the possibility. The depths over which the metal floor opened were divided by several lengths of cloth stretched horizontally one above the other; this simple precaution was enough to lessen any fall, and besides, several Pastrophores were hidden there, waiting to catch the postulant in their arms. But if he did not fall, the metal floor was immediately raised again and screwed back in its original position. When the postulant felt his feet touch ground again, the brazen door opened before him. The leader of an escort of twelve Neocores (guardians of the sanctuary) bandaged his eyes and led him by torchlight along the final galleries leading from the Sphinx to the Great Pyramid.

Thus ends all that can be said of this initiation at this time.

Exercise 3

Obtain a candle, a holder, and matches, and retire to a room that can easily be darkened.

After relaxing for a few moments, light the candle, and extinguish other lights in the room.

Begin to center your gaze and attention on the area, or "aura," surrounding the flame. As you gaze at this area, mentally will the aura of the flame to turn red. Do this by thinking, "Red, red, red." After the color red is noted, try the same thing with the color blue. Proceed to the color green, and then yellow. Now continue with other colors.

Be sure to try this experiment at least once daily for ten days.

Lesson 4

In the last lesson we discussed the initiation of a candidate into the mysteries and presented an eyewitness account of an initiation that took place into the mysteries of Isis in the Great Pyramind of Egypt.

Though the rise of Christianity caused the Craft to take the practice of its rites underground in order to avoid persecution, Christianity nonetheless borrowed much from the cult. The names of the days of the week are taken from the ancient belief in their astrological influence by the various planets. Sunday, is, of course, named after the Sun; Monday, after the Moon; Tuesday, after the planet Mars, called Tyr by the Norsemen; Wednesday, after the god Mercury, called Wotan; Thursday, after the god Thor, or Jupiter; Friday, after Venus, or Freia; and Saturday, after Saturn.

Among other examples, in Italy the healing springs of the god Apollo were rededicated to St. Apollinaris, and 25 December the Pagan Mithraic birth of the Sun, was designated as the birthday of the Christ, who was in actuality born in the spring.

Mention must also be made of the influence of the Crusades on the development of magic. Returning from the East, many crusaders carried with them books unknown in Europe that dealt with such subjects as demons, spirits, and other forms of magic. So, too, many carried with them strange tales of men who possessed powers not known or accepted in Europe before Franz Mesmer, who is credited with the discovery of hypnotism.

Unusual though it may seem, witchcraft was not considered a danger to Christianity until A.D. 1137, when the first proclamation appeared mentioning the influence of witches. In 1437 and 1445, Pope Eugene IV issued papal bulls (church decrees) commanding punishment of witches who caused bad weather. These bulls are interesting in that they establish the ability of the Craft to influence weather. In 1484 the papal order *Summis Desiderantes* appeared, causing the execution of scores of thousands of witches.

Initially, membership in the Order was limited solely to initiated families and their children. As the influence of Christianity began to fail, due chiefly to corruption among the clergy, the less well educated sought to return to their old beliefs. Since women occupied the lowest position in the society of the time, they were in the first to reunite with the Craft. Next came those who had seen the influence of the cult while away on the Crusades or those into whose hands books on magic had fallen. Finally, new recruits were found among those who had been helped in one way or another by members of the cult.

Among the prerequisites for membership in the Order was the requirement that the would-be initiate freely consent to becoming a witch. So, too, each was required to deny the Catholic faith. Lastly, attendance was required at the Sabbath, together with actual initiation into the mysteries.

Since the Order then, as today, was essentially a secret organization, you may wonder how it is we know what took place within its confines. One way is through evidence revealed at the various witch trials. Though sometimes doubtful, since given under the threat and pain of torture, these trial records provide much of what is known today about the early workings and organization of the ancient mysteries.

In speaking of these trials, we must note the possibility that many who confessed were simply neurotics who delighted in their own fancies and who sincerely believed in their ability to do all kinds of evil. Thus, we find statements like that of Jane Bosden, who "confessed freely and without torture and continued constant in it in the midst of the flames in which she burnt."

Attempting to bolster a faltering Christianity, these trials, directed by the clergy, were preoccupied with sex, in the belief that the cult was a phallic one, that its practices were essentially orgiastic, and that its sole purpose was to increase or reverse fecundity. What better example of witchcraft could be found than the failure of one's crops, the inability of one's herd to produce milk, or the lack of one's issue?

From its inception, the cult was always connected in some way with the keeping of animals. In the Egyptian mysteries, animals were united with human form and thought of as gods. This was accomplished through the high priest wearing animal masks or horns that were believed to convey the strength (particularly masculine strength) and characteristics of the animal to the wearer. Of the various animals associated with the Order during the early period, the horned god remains foremost. A painting of a horned dancer on the wall of a cave in Ariege, France, has been dated approximately 8000 B.C.

In Mesopotamia, the number of horns indicated the importance of the god. In the New Testament book of Revelation, we find reference to a Seven Horned Lamb. (The significance of the various numbers will be explained later on in your studies.) The demon of early Christianity, Eukidon, possessed horns, tails, and hooves. The Egyptian god and goddess, Osiris and Isis, wore horns of fertility, as did the satyric Greek god Pan.

At first the interest of the early church in the horned god was a casual one. However, as time went on, and more and more reports were gathered that attested to the appearance of the "beast" at the ceremonies of the witches, Christianity began to take more of an interest.

In the seventh century the Archbishop of Canterbury issued an injunction prohibiting sacrifice to devils and eating and drinking in heathen temples. In time the concept of the horned god evolved into the belief in a superior being, personifying evil, who was believed to appear at every meeting of the Craft to instruct them in their evil practices. In the next lesson, we will tell you more about this Devil, or Satan, as he is also called.

In addition to the horned god, small animals, especially black cats, have always been associated with the Wicca folk. The animals, orginally the totem or badge of a particular clan or tribe, were used for divination purposes or predicting the future. Since they were often found near members of the Order, the belief arose in the ability of the Prince of Darkness to transform himself into any form or appearance in order to seduce followers away from the church. The idea of a personal spirit, sometimes called a genius, is a very ancient one. Plato tells of the demon that often prompted Socrates not to do a particular thing. Of the sage Pythagoras it was written that he conversed with an eagle.

At the various trials the names given to such small animals, also called familiars, included angel, little master, imp, fury, maumet, and nigget. Among the types of animals represented were rats, butterflies, wasps, toads, and of course cats.

From the actual records of the Order we have learned that the initiates generally divided their familiars into two classes: domestic and divining.

The *divining* familiar was a special animal given to the witch by the Devil, along with instructions as to how to use the animal in order to obtain information about the future and other matters. In 1615, the following was written concerning the use of familiars:

> That there are witches who keep familiars, which are little imps in the form of toads, and give them to eat a mess of milk and flour and give them the first morsel, and they do not dare absent themselves from the house without asking leave, and they must say how long they will be absent, as three or four days, and if they (the familiars) say that it is too much, those who keep them dare not make the journey or go against their will.

One adherent, Gentien le Clerc, declared that he had more trust in his familiar than in God, that there was more profit in it than in God, and that he gained nothing by looking to God, whereas his familiar always brought him something.

The animal could also be a large creature such as a horse, stag, or large bird. The words used to conjure up a response from the familiar always included the use of the secret name of the god or goddess of the cult.

The *domestic* familiar was always a small animal that could be kept within the confines of the house. The geographic distribution of such traditions suggests that the origin of the habit was in Scandinavia, Finland, or Lapland. It was believed that such a crature was fed by the owner on food into which a drop of the witch's blood had been mixed. The feeding of the familiar constituted a ritual that may account for the belief in imps.

The familiar could be bought and sold or given as a gift.

> One good wife Weed gave her a white cat, telling her that if she would deny God, and affirm the same by her blood, then whomsoever she cursed and sent that cat unto, they should die shortly after (1646).

There are also instances in which the familiar was inherited from another witch. Another method of finding a familiar was to recite a prayer to the god or goddess and then to take the first animal that appeared thereafter.

Exercise 4

Continuing with the development of your ability to concentrate, try the following.

Obtain a small shallow bowl, a wooden match or toothpick, and a glass of water, and go to a quiet room.

Fill the bowl with water, and float the stick on the surface.

Place one hand on each side of the bowl, palms facing toward the bowl.

Now, while being careful not to blow on the stick, try to cause it to move by concentrating and fixing your attention on its end.

First, cause it to move *away from you* by concentrating your attention and pushing the match away, then to the *right,* and then to the *left*.

Try this experiment once daily for ten days as originally instructed.

Lesson 5

In the last lesson we discussed the use of familiars by members of the Craft. It should be pointed out that we of the twentieth century are often too quick to dismiss the beliefs of the past as being mere superstition, with little basis in fact. The important thing to remember always is that it is not so much why we believe a particular thing but rather what happens to us as a result of having a particular belief. Long before the discovery by science of what is called hypnotism, few accepted the ancient teaching that each of us possess more than one mind. Now it is generally accepted that the working of the unconscious mind is far more important than that of the conscious mind. This is because the former is the master-servant that accepts each and every idea fed to it by the conscious mind. By programming your thinking as taught in this course of instruction, you will be able to make maximum use of this other mind.

At this stage of our lessons, we must stop and clarify a subject that has been greatly misunderstood throughout the ages, namely, the concept of Satan or the Devil.

Although most members of the Christian faith believe the Devil is their religion's particular possession, its origin is found in the more remote past.

In the Old Testament, Satan is mentioned only three times. In Zechariah 3:1–2: "Then he showed me Joshua the high priest standing before the angel of the Lord, and Satan standing at his right hand to accuse him. And the Lord said to Satan, 'The Lord rebuke you, O Satan! The Lord who has chosen Jerusalem rebuke you!'" In Job 1–2, Satan is presented as the tempter and adversary of God, plying for the soul of his servant Job. In 1 Chronicles 21:1, Satan appears as the tempter of David. All of these passages are considered by scholars to be from the postexilic period and dated later than 539 B.C. This means that the concept of Satan did not stem from the period during which the Jews were held in captivity by the Egyptians. Rather, current scholars believe that the idea of a force of evil equal to God was derived from the contact with members of the Zoroastrian faith, which had its origin in Persia, the same religion that gave us magic.

The Zoroastrian religion, based on the teachings of Zoroaster, holds that *two* gods, Ahura Mazda (also known as Ormazd), the leader of the "host of light" and the source of all good, and Angra Mainya (also known as Ahriman), the spirit of darkness and source of all evil, constantly battle for control of the world and all its manifestations, and that in the end, Ormazd, the god of good, will win and defeat the god of evil.

This concept, when it came into Judaism, led to the creation of Satan, patterned after Ahriman—a creature who stood in direct opposition to God and who sought to frustrate the purposes of both man and God. An important distinction, though, is the fact that for the Jews, Satan (the Hebrew word literally means "adversary" or "accuser") was always inferior to God, not equal as in the Zoroastrian religion.

With the rise of Christianity, Satan was transformed into the Devil (a Greek word meaning "slanderer") and was defined by the church at the Council of Toledo in A.D. 447.

The real truth concerning the Devil, however, is something that you as a member of our Order have now been privileged to receive.

The Devil as understood by Christianity is merely a misunder-

★

standing based on ignorance of the true nature of Wicca and its traditional association with horned gods and priests.

When during the medieval period Christians happened to stumble upon meetings of our Order, which were usually held outdoors and at night, they often saw a creature with horns dancing around the fire. What they saw was not a superhuman being at all, but merely the high priest portraying the god as has been done for centuries. Due to the teaching of the church, however, that the Devil was a real, existing being, these observers allowed their imagination to convince them that they hd actually seen the Devil. When they went back to their priest and reported what they had seen, he in turn encouraged their imagination by convincing them they had seen Satan himself. (Remember, too, that most people in this period could neither read nor write and thus did not know why the church came to believe in the Devil.) So it was that the idea arose of the existence of the Devil as "god of the witches."

The next item for discussion is the idea of a pact wth the Devil. As we described in a previous lesson, one of the requirements of membership in the mysteries was that of initiation. Those outside believed that witches had signed a pact with the Devil in which they had promised to give their soul in return for a period of prosperity, usually seven years. Nothing could actually be further from the truth.

While the cult has always required that the initiate sign an agreement to support and not to betray its secrets, this agreement has nothing to do with the soul of the would-be witch!

Once again, the high priest, as representative of the god of the coven, might ask for a pledge of loyalty, much in the same way that a modern priest requests a restatement of faith though the reciting of the Apostles' Creed. This pledge, however, during the early period in our history, was seldom written because few persons could read and write. Once again we see how a mistaken idea can create a great misconception in the minds of those who do not understand.

Exercise 5

To continue the development of your power to concentrate, try the following at least once daily.

Collect a group of small items, such as a pencil, a comb, a button, a bottle cap, some paper clips, and similar objects, and take them to a quiet room in which you have placed a comfortable chair.

★

Pick up each item in turn, hold it in your hand, and carefully study the way it appears. Carefully note any scratches, dents, the color, the texture—everything about it.

Now close your eyes, relax your body, and try to picture in your mind exactly how the item looks. See every detail of the item, and try to hold this picture as long as you can.

After doing this with each item, close your eyes once again, and try to picture every item you have seen, one after the other.

Remember that these practices will enable you to become all you wish to be. Do not pass by these exercises. They will build within you something of great value.

Lesson 6

In this lesson we depart momentarily from our discussion of the workings of our Order throughout history to present to you the technique of psychic and divine meditation as it is taught and practiced in the East.

We ask, as we have done in the past, that you keep these instructions in inviolate secrecy, remembering that to do so is to serve our Order and its masters!

In the East, long before the advent of modern communication, such as telephone or radio, the masters often had occasion to transmit information from one branch of the Great White Brotherhood to another. When the passage of this information could not be achieved by ordinary messenger, or when the latter was too slow, the Masters employed the use of what is now called extrasensory perception. Let us assure you that there is nothing "extrasensory" about this strange ability, for its origin lies within the mind of man and a special group of psychic transformers called the chakras. These psychic centers correspond to many of the glands of the endocrine system and can be awakened through the type of exercises you have been doing.

Sometimes these centers are awakened before they are mature through an accident or the use of drugs. When this happens, a psychic experience may occur to a person before he is emotionally ready, resulting in a nervous breakdown or similar disorder. Therefore, the Council of Elders who guide us ask that you do not use any type of drugs while practicing these exercises. To do so would be much like lighting a match to find the origin of a gas leak. Our path has been likened to the edge of a razor; be careful, lest you cut yourself!

For thousands of years, the masters who have preceded us have taught that each one of us has two minds, not one. These two minds, the conscious and the unconscious, are connected in a special way that allows information to pass back and forth. All that you have ever seen, heard, or experienced is placed in special files within the unconscious mind and held there until you wish to withdraw it.

The conscious mind is the intellect, our reasoning part. It is this mind that receives perceptions through the five senses: taste, touch, sight, sound, and smell.

Sometimes these perceptions do not register on the conscious mind, and we are unaware that we have experienced something at the time that the event takes place. Much later, something else may happen that makes us remember a past experience, causing the information we had forgotten to reappear, seemingly like magic. When this happens, we think we have received some special knowledge from a source other than ourselves.

The unconscious mind is the center of control for the organs in the body and the seat of the memory and dreams; it is the connecting link between our mind and the universal, or Cosmic, mind. Through the practice of exercises such as those you have been receiving, both minds are brought into harmony, and we become one with the purpose of the universe. This sense of oneness is the real goal behind all mystic disciplines, including alchemy, religion, and yoga.

The occult masters were very quick to discover that when we lower the influence of the conscious mind and its sense perceptions, we raise the influence of the unconscious mind. Thus, we must find a means whereby this can be done each day. In the next few pages, you will find such a method.

Exercise 6: Instructions in the Contact with the Universal Mind

Before attempting to contact the universal mind, wash your hands and face, and dry them on a towel that has not yet been used. Pour yourself a small glass of clean water, slightly chilled, and take it to a room that can be slightly darkened and in which you have placed a comfortable chair. If you have some incense, you may wish to light it.

★

While standing in front of your easy chair, take the water glass in both hands, and hold it in front of your chest, a little above the navel. Now close your eyes, take a deep breath, and hold it as long as you can. Then slowly exhale. Repeat until you have taken seven breaths, slowly exhaling each in turn.

With your eyes still closed, drink the water, place the glass on a table, and sit down in the chair.

Place your body in a comfortable position, with both hands resting in your lap. Close your eyes once again, and relax a few moments by practicing the breathing exercise you were taught in the very first lesson. After a few minutes, begin to picture in your mind each part of your body.

Begin by picturing your right foot as it actually appears. When you have pictured it in your mind's eye, order it to relax, while imagining that a steam or mist is passing out of it as steam passes out of a kettle.

After relaxing your right foot in this way, go to the left foot. Then back to the right ankle, then the left ankle, and so on. After you have relaxed both legs, relax your stomach, then your lower back, then your chest, then your upper back and shoulders. Then your right hand, your left hand, your right arm, your left arm. Then your neck, your face, and last, the very top of your head.

Once you have succeeded in relaxing your entire body by picturing each part in turn, seeing the steam pass out, and ordering it to relax, imagine that your entire body is asleep (and it will be).

Now, in your mind's eye, picture in the distance a blue light, and see it come closer and closer, until it touches your forehead. After the light touches you, see it move away from you, very slowly. Next imagine a yellow light. See it come toward you, again very slowly, until it, too, touches your forehead. Feel this light move away from you. Now picture a white light in the same manner.

After you have visualized these lights in turn, try to picture yourself sitting in the chair exactly as you would look if you were looking at yourself in a mirror. At this point, *stop.* Allow your mind to receive whatever impressions may come to you. In the next lesson, we will take you further in this technique.

Try to spend at least fifteen minutes each day in the practice of this exercise. If you can develop the habit of meditating each day at the same time, you will find the best results. This exercise can also be practiced while lying in bed prior to going to sleep. In fact, if you practice it each evening, you will find that you will sleep unusually soundly and may receive a special dream experience.

Lesson 7

This lesson continues the presentation of the technique of divine meditation. We must, however, take a few moments to explain the difference between two terms—*silence* and *meditation*—as they are often confused.

Entering the Silence

After you have succeeded in completely relaxing your body and mind as instructed in the last lesson, you will sometimes feel that you are drifting with no single thought uppermost. When this happens, various pictures and images—possibly even some words—may come to you as if from a great distance.

It is interesting how we immediately assume that such information comes from outside ourselves rather than from within our own consciousness. We least of all wish to give ourselves credit for possessing a most amazing faculty, which enables us to overcome ordinary time/space considerations.

When we receive such impressions as these, we are reaching out to the masters. Deep within the boundaries of our unconscious mind there is a small entrance through which each person can enter into the light of universal consciousness. By passing through this narrow entrance daily, we become greater and eventually possess the pearl of great price.

When we enter into the silence, we open ourselves up to receive other ideas and impressions as they exist in unseen regions. Many times, the things that are sensed or seen result from certain needs we may have to fulfill in order to advance in this lifetime. In other words, often we are brought experiences in order that we might grow and evolve in spirit.

In the silence, we become like radios able to tune in on many stations and receive various broadcasts. Such a state is essentially passive and brings us much information that we could not ordinarily obtain.

Let Us Meditate

Meditation, unlike silence, requires that we consciously *fix our attention* upon a given image or idea and, through concentration and visualization, will into being that which we desire.

When one meditates, he passes far beyond the object of attention to the essence behind that object. In a sense one passes both through and to the object at the same time. From this world of ideas, we enter into the world of the gods and begin to create out of the unseen that which we wish to bring into the seen. We actually begin to create in the material world through our thoughts alone.

So, too, in meditation one can reach out to join with and contact other minds, no matter where they may be located. Later on in this work you will learn how to do this while asleep as well.

In conclusion, the primary difference between silence and meditation is that one is *passive* and the other *active*. In the former we open ourselves up and receive. In the latter we concentrate our attention and direct it where we wish. Both abilities must be mastered, though; they will enable you to direct your life as you wish.

The ancient masters who were our forefathers discovered long ago that there is a connection between the psychic nature of man and the nervous system. The connecting links or transformers, called chakras in the Indian system, were later associated with the endocrine glands.

As each of your psychic centers is awakened through the exercises that accompany each lesson you receive, they begin to give off a sound that can be heard and identified. The regular practice of meditation on these sounds has been found to further stimulate and awaken them. Later on in your studies you will learn which of these glands is associated with each of the aspects of your psychic life. For the present, however, we ask that you practice a very important exercise called in the Indian Yoga system *anahata nadam* or the "sound of no instrument."

Exercise 7

Sit on the floor, cross-legged and erect, facing a chair or low table on which you can rest your elbows without bending forward. Practice rhythmic breathing through both nostrils for at least five minutes. Then do the following.

While resting on your elbows on the table, press your thumbs tightly on the prominence in front of the hole in each ear, thereby closing off any sound. Close your eyes with your index fingers, and rest the other fingers on your forehead. With your eyes closed, fix your attention on the point between your eyebrows, and keep your inward gaze fixed there. Mentally chant "om," but make no sound or movement of the tongue. Continuing to hold your hands as directed, listen intently within the *right* ear, where the flow of Cosmic energy is greatest. Concentrate on whichever sound is loudest but on only *one* sound at a time. As other sounds come to the fore, listen in turn to each. Don't forget to continue to fix your attention at the point between the eyebrows. *Note:* If you are left-handed, the sound may seem louder in your left ear. Some of the sounds you may hear are as follows.

NADAM

Om Nadam: a rolling sound like a mighty sea

Cin Nadam: hum of bees, rainfall, whistling sounds, high frequency

Cincin Nadam: a waterfall

Ghanta Nadam: sound of a distant bell ringing

Sankha Nadam: sound of a conch shell

Tantri Vina: nasal sound, humming sound of a bass fiddle

Tala Nadam: sound of a small snare drum

Venu Nadam: flute sound

Mridamga: bass drum

Bheri Nadam: echoing sound

Megha Nadam: roll of distant thunder

Try to hear each sound in turn, but fix your attention on the sound that emerges first.

Lesson 8

In the last lesson we presented a technique that will do more to develop the psychic nature than you may now realize. You see, it is the nature of the mind that that upon which we daily direct our thought to is what we become. By this we mean simply that during each and every moment of each and every day you are becoming something by simply thinking along certain lines. This indeed is the only true secret behind all the mystical teachings of the ages. Remember this, dear novice, as long as you continue your search for Light, Love, and Life.

Besides those mystics who sought to seek out and join with the mystery religions, there have always been those who preferred to study by themselves. Individuals in this group came in time to be called magicians and sorcerers.

Magic, like any other religion, has certain principles upon which it is based; these must be mastered by ever novice. In this and the next few lessons we will introduce this ancient and much misunderstood art.

While magic differs greatly from modern religion, it stems from the same source and like religion consists of two parts—a ritual and a doctrine. Ritual is nothing more than ceremony that is performed by followers of the religion. The doctrine, or dogma, is simply the beliefs upon which the rituals are based.

In most religions, each person has a special relationship with the supreme God or gods. This relationship is usually one in which God or the gods are approached by prayer, by which one humbly asks or begs for divine assistance.

In magic, however, it is not God that is dealt with but rather less important spiritual beings who are believed to exist as helpers or assistants in carrying out God's plan. The magician does not ask that these holy personages assist him, but orders or demands that they do so. He does this ever believing that they cannot refuse to aid him since he has been given power over them by God himself.

His power comes simply from knowing the right words or right rituals that cause the spiritual forces to do his bidding. Once armed with this special knowledge (the kind of special teachings you are now receiving), the magician is given unlimited power.

In Christianity and Judaism, the name of God was kept a secret in the belief that if you knew the name you would then have power to compel God to do your bidding. Because of this tradition, the word *Jehovah* was never written out in the ancient Jewish manuscripts.

If this idea seems strange to you, call someone's name as he walks away from you: you will find that he stops and turns toward you. In that very instant, you exhibited "power" over him, did you not?

To the ancients, all things that exist have a spiritual as well as a material essence. The only difference between a living thing and that which appears not to live is a difference in Spirit. So, too, those beings that are given greater mobility, including the opportunity for self-consciousness, contain another substance called "Soul." Man is a creature having both Soul and Spirit.

So, too, it is the nature of this Spirit and of this Soul that it transcends all people and all things. Since it is everywhere present, in all things and all people at the same time, one can contact another person through it—which is what advanced brothers and sisters are able to do.

While magic describes in a general way the ability to cause certain things to come about, it has been further divided into two types— Black and White. But magic *by itself* is neither good nor evil. Like electricity, which can be used to light a house or produce heat or take a life, magic itself ever stands neutral.

The ancients believed in both God *and* magic, which they considered to have been taught to man by God. Of the various laws upon which their doctrine was based, two laws, the Law of Sympathy and the Law of Imitation, stand out.

The *Law of Sympathy* states that a mysterious or spiritual link exists between any thing in the world *and any one or more of its parts,* for example, a tree and its leaves. This is merely a restatement of the general belief in the Oneness of the universe discussed above. It is further divided into two rules, the Rule of Parts and the Rule of Contagion. The *Rule of Parts* says that even though something is no longer connected with something else (such as a leaf of a tree), one can affect the tree by affecting the leaf. In primitive magic or voodoo as practiced in the Caribbean islands, one sometimes hears stories of someone being affected by magic that consists of taking a lock of the person's hair and performing magical ceremonies over it.

The *Rule of Contagion* states that an article that is found close to a person, such as a ring that is worn or a favorite pin or watch, in time forms a connection with that person. One can influence someone by stealing this type of object and performing magic on it.

The *Law of Imitation,* like the Law of Sympathy, says that because of this connection one can cause the spirits to imitate certain acts and thereby produce certain phenomena. For instance, an ancient ceremony to produce rain consisted of pouring water over an unclothed virgin.

If these early beliefs seem hard for you to accept, let us pause to look at our own religions. In most, we have a minister or priest who we believe has certain spiritual power because of his relationship to God. We might even use a sacred medal upon which the picture of certain saints has been engraved in order to keep us from harm. These practices suggest that even today we think in terms of the spiritual nature of the universe. The difference, however, is that we are usually not aware of the true meaning behind many of our beliefs.

Exercise 8

Retire to the room in which you practice these exercises, and take a comfortable seat. Close your eyes, and relax your body as you have been taught. After you have rested for a while, arise, and obtain a picture of a friend or relative whom you have not seen for some time.

Return to your chair, and spend a few minutes looking at the face of the person whose picture you are holding. Now close your eyes, once again relax your body, and try to "see" that person exactly as he appeared in the picture. Try to picture each and every detail.

Practice this at least once daily.

Lesson 9

In the previous lesson we began our discussion of the nature of magic and introduced you to some of its very basic principles. One thing we hope you will come to realize is that what one person considers magical may *not* be at all once we understand how something is done. By this we mean that often we think that someone has certain mystical power because of some special dispensation from the Cosmic rather than as the result of special training and practice, such as you are now receiving. What we are suggesting is very simple; anyone, including yourself, can become a master if he will work to become one. In fact, it is our utmost desire that each and every one of you now reading these words be enabled to obtain all that you may wish in this lifetime, including good health, prosperity, and above all, peace of Spirit. It is to all this that the masters have dedicated themselves.

As we concluded the last lesson, we had explained that behind the practice of magic stands a belief in the Oneness of all that exists. It is only because of this Oneness that magic can work at all.

In the ancient works on ritual magic that have come down to us, the preparation of the magician or sorcerer is discussed at great length. The sorcerer must have great strength of mind so as not to be dissuaded from the object of his work: the evocation of those spirits that will do his bidding. His purpose and will must be unshakable, and he must be prepared to face even the fires of hell! Many of the rituals advocate a period of chasitity or lack of association with members of

★

the opposite sex. Why this requirement should be imposed will be explained later. Often the requirement of a period of fasting is also stated, to bring about purity of body. This last element has been found to be a part of almost all religions, although very few today are aware of its purpose. Those who have investigated fasting under scientific conditions have found that it affects both the mind and the body. Metaphysically speaking, fasting causes the spiritual body to separate from the physical and thus pass further out into the astral planes. Later you will learn the various techniques of projecting the astral or psychic body.

Besides the magician's personal self-preparation, everything else that is to be used during the ceremony of evocation must be made by himself. This includes such clothing as robes, hats, and slippers and all the ritual instruments.

At one time the magician's vestment was to be made from linen woven by a virgin, symbol of purity. His slippers and head covering were to be made of white lambskin. On his hat were to be inscribed the four Hebrew names of God: Jehovah, Adonay, Eloy, and Gibor.

The ritual implements that were required are listed below, but the modern reader may use equivalents. All had to bear the names of the various angels whose assistance is required in order that the magician might succeed in this endeavor.

Two knives. The first, with a black handle, is used for cutting and forming magic circles. The second, with a white handle, is used for all other operations.

Sword.

Wands. Of hazel-wood branches or offshoots. This must be cut and trimmed on the day and in the hour of the sun, but inscribed with magical characters on the hour and day of Mercury. Another magical text advises to use wood from trees that have never borne fruit.

Dagger.

Needle or lancet.

Pen. Prepared from the quill of a male goose.

Ink. Made from vitriol, gum arabic, and gall nuts.

Candles. Must be made from fresh wax.

Silk. Usually red in color and covered with symbols drawn in the blood taken from pigeons, using the quill from a male goose.

Circles. Made from parchment that has not been used for any other purpose.

In all of the above, a primary requirement is that the magician obtain each object from its original source so that he can be assured of its purity. For instance, in the case of the circles, the magician must even kill the sheep or goat from whose skin the parchment is to be taken. The kid must be placed on a block with the throat turned upward. The throat must be struck with a single blow during which time the magician must pronounce the name of the spirit later to be invoked. The animal must die on the first blow and must be skinned while the following invocation is read.

Adiram, Dalmay, Lauday, Tetragrammation, Anereton, and all ye holy angels of God, be ye here and deign to impart virtue into this skin, that it may be properly conserved, and that all things thereon written may attain their perfection.

The skin is to be stretched and salted with special salt that has itself been blessed. The skin is to be placed in the sun for one day and then placed into quicklime until it begins to peel. It is to be peeled with the use of another special knife, cleansed, stretched upon a board of new wood, and left to dry. Once dry, the skin is to be removed from the board, blessed, fumigated, and preserved for further use. It is also said that it must not have been seen by women, for it will then lose its power.

It should be pointed out at this time that, for the most part, those who performed the raising of spirits were men, thus the statements in regard to women. In this sense, sorcery may be viewed as the counterpart to witchcraft, which is one of the reasons we include it in this study. The witch, usually a woman, works in a group in order to bring about her magic. The magician, usually a man, works alone in order to obtain his desired ends. In each case, the state of their minds is similar. They both share a certain purpose and dedication to make their will the will of the universe! Whether or not they succeed in their efforts depends on many things, but especially their own idea as to whether or not they will succeed. You see, it is not so much what we say as what we do not say! Emerson, the great American philosopher, sug-

★

gested that what we are speaks so loudly that no one can hear what we are saying. By this he meant to suggest that the inner and not the outer man is the real master of us all. It is this inner man who speaks to us in our moments of silence and meditation; it is this man whom we invoke in prayer or through the ceremonies such as we are now considering.

As you go on in this work, you will come face to face with this great understanding: that we are only an idea away from greatness, wealth, prosperity, health, and peace of mind. It is only a question of our acceptance of that which we know but have forgotten. When we are able to do this at will, we are indeed masters.

Exercise 9

By now, you have begun to realize that you have certain mental abilities of which you were probably not aware. In order to demonstrate to yourself the nature of these abilities, we ask that you do the following.

When you next find yourself seated behind someone, as in the theater or on a bus, you are to direct your gaze and attention toward the nape of his neck. With your vision centered on this spot, send your thoughts to the person as follows: "You feel me looking at you. You feel me looking at you. Turn around and look at me."

Continue to direct your vision and thoughts in this manner. After a short time, the person you have been concentrating upon will turn and look at you.

Should you be seated in front of this person, concentrate on that spot between the two eyes, in the center of the forehead. Again, send your thoughts so that the person will look up from what he is doing and look at you.

When you have succeeded in making this person look at you, practice on others. See if you can make them scratch their nose, straighten their tie, smooth their hair, or perform some similar action.

Lesson 10

In this lesson we continue our discussion of magic and its influence. Once the magician has succeeded in preparing all his equipment as instructed by these most ancient rituals, he is ready to wait for that very special moment in time to begin his work of evocation. You see, not each and every day is right for the work of magic. One must wait for the various planets and signs to be correctly placed in the heavens. So, too, the magician must himself feel that he is ready before undertaking so serious a task as the raising of spirits.

Once the appointed day or evening has arrived, the magician retires to his private quarters, taking with him the materials necessary. In some cases, the rituals also require that he take along a young boy, a number of companions, or perhaps just a faithful dog. These assistants are sometimes needed to help carry the various tools and instruments.

When the exact moment has arrived, the magician dresses in the required vestments and begins the ceremony. Since he long ago decided which spirit (of as many as seventy-two different ones) he wished to evoke, he takes care to wear the appropriate seal or insignia of the spirit before commencing the ritual.

The ancient manuscripts, such as the Key of Solomon, which give us our knowledge of these things, state the belief that the King of Israel captured the seventy-two spirits, those emissaries of the gods we spoke of in the last lesson, and locked them up in a brass vessel, and cast them into a deep lake. Supposedly the Babylonians stumbled upon the jug and, thinking that it contained a great treasure, broke open the seal and let loose the spirits. Of course, Solomon in all his wisdom had taken care to leave behind special rituals for those magicians who wish to make these spirits do their bidding.

When we speak of spirits, of course, we are referring to the belief in the existence of spiritual entities that can be seen visibly and that have an actual existence and being.

According to some sources, each spirit takes the form of a human-animal creature possessing very definite and particular characteristics. For instance, one very famous spirit is called Baal. He appears with a human head, or with the head of a toad or cat, or with all three at once. Another spirit, Valefor, appears as a many-headed lion. Still others appear in human form but astride or riding upon various animals. Examples of these are Beleth, who rides a pale horse and is preceded by many musicians; Saleos, who rides on a crocodile; and Ashtaroth, who rides on a dragon.

In each case, a specific description of the spirit is given together with mention of his particular skill. Should you wish to find out certain special secrets, you must contact one spirit, whereas should you want other information or services, another spirit would be required.

Because of this, the workings of magic require very exact and precise techniques, formulas, and actions. There is nothing left to chance. Just as one cannot make water without combining two atoms of hydrogen with one atom of oxygen, so one cannot bring about particular magical happenings without following a formula.

The ancients thought, just as Zolar does, that nothing in the universe ever occurred by chance. Each and every moment expresses the working of a particular law. Much of what you currently think has occurred by accident may not have happened that way. Rather, there may indeed be a definite plan in which, very much like a great play, we are all actors and actresses playing roles about which really know very little.

In Indian philosophy the word *maya,* meaning "illusion," is used to describe this unusual reality. This does not mean, as many have thought, that the things we see do not have existence, but rather that *this* existence is not the ultimate existence.

We need and require a new orientation. We need something that tells us who we are, where we are, and where are we going. This is the need of all mankind, of all races, of all people everywhere. It is only because this need cannot be filled by organized religion that many have left the faiths of their fathers in favor of new ideas (or old ones such as Wicca.)

So, too, these ancient rituals seem to be telling us that what we call God may not be the personal, humanlike being we have conceived.

Does this idea shock you? If God is a power rather than a person, would it not explain why some of us are able to use "him" while others are unable to do so? Would it not explain why some people appear to prosper while others find only misfortune? Why some people are ill and others are healthy? Why some find love and others only hate?

You see, what we are suggesting is only an idea and nothing more. It is a very grand idea, and one in which many of the masters have found great peace and sublime wisdom. For it is their belief that each one of us need only be plugged in to the source of all power in order to be turned on.

It is the purpose of these lessons to show you the technique of becoming one with the Cosmos. This is the only secret of the ages, the pearl of great price, spoken of in the New Testament. This is why

Wicca has always existed throughout the ages. This is why our Order was founded. And this is why you must continue in your studies.

The masters have dedicated themselves and their lives in this incarnation to bring forth their teachings as a spark in the darkened room. This spark must be struck, kindled, and fanned until it burns brightly and constantly. It is your task to aid us in this effort. This is why you came to us.

Exercise 10

In order that you might experience for yourself the evocation of a spirit, we ask that you perform the following each day for seven days.

Obtain a clear glass without any marking, a table, a chair, and a darkened room. Fill the glass with cold water, and hold it in both hands in front of your stomach near the solar plexus. While holding

Seal of the spirit Barbuelis.
"Sigillo e caratteri per coercizione ed obbedienza"
"Baba cuci hiebu ziadhi elenehet na vena via achya salna"

★

the glass in this position, take seven deep breaths, holding each one as long as you can and slowly exhaling each one in turn.

After seven breaths, place your glass in the center of the seal of the spirit Barbuelis (on page 180). While gazing into the glass, read the following aloud three times. "Baba cuci hiebu ziadhi elenehet na vena via achya salna."

Contine to gaze into the center of the glass, trying not to blink your eyes until you see a white mist beginning to appear. When it does, quietly ask any question, and continue to gaze into the glass. Don't be afraid if you feel yourself "falling into the glass." This is part of the process of constructing what is called an astral tube, which will allow you to "see" with your mind's eye. You should begin to mentally "hear" an answer to your question.

Lesson 11

In the last exercise we introduced you to a very ancient technique for contacting the so-called spiritual beings that are believed by many to inhabit our Cosmos. If you did not find success and actually "hear" an answer to your question in the practice of this exercise, continue each day and the success that you seek will come to you.

Besides the belief in magic that we present to you, there is yet another topic that the masters feel must be discussed at this time: the question of life after death.

To the ancients, there was never any doubt that what we call life is not limited to a single incarnation but continues to be born, to die, to exist in the world of the spirit, and to be reborn again. In this way, we all evolve toward the Godhead, or whatever name you choose to give to the Master of the Universe.

In discussing magic, we must mention the very ancient art of necromancy, which is the magical means of "raising the dead" in order to gain information of the spirit world, to foresee coming events (of which the spirits are believed to have prior knowledge), or to influence things in the material world.

In many of these ancient ceremonies, the blood of an animal recently sacrificed was required in order to bring about the conditions necessary to ensure that the ceremony would work. Of course, the belief that blood contains magical properties is a very old one that has persisted down to the present day, with some religious sects prohibiting blood transfusions. This belief probably came about because a person who lost a great deal of blood often died: Thus blood contained the essence of life.

Variations of these ceremonies require that the magician take his assistant to the churchyard or tomb where the deceased is buried exactly at midnight, for the ceremony must be performed between the hours of midnight and one in the morning.

In order to raise the spirit, the grave had first to be opened or a hole made so that access to the naked body could be found. Once the magician drew and consecrated his magic circle, in which he must stay while performing the spell, while his assistant held a consecrated torch, he turned himself to the four points of the compass, and then touched the dead body three times with the magical wand, repeating:

> By the virtue of the Holy Resurrection and the torments of the dammed, I conjure and exorcise thee, Spirit of [name of deceased] to answer my liege demands, being obedient unto these sacred ceremonies, on pain of everlasting torment and distress . . . Berald, Beroald, Balbin, Gab, Gabor, Agaba.
> Arise, arise, I charge and command thee.

At this point, the ghost or apparition would become visible, and the magician could put any question he wished to it.

Still other ceremonies, it was believed, would enable the magician to physically raise the body of the dead upright, so that it actually stood before him. The magician was cautioned not to step outside his magical circle lest the spirit be able to seize and destroy him.

From these very ancient beliefs come the beginnings of modern spiritualism, a religion that believes that it is possible for a living person to communicate with a deceased friend or relative through another "sensitive" person called a medium.

Modern spiritualist churches insist that they have the power to contact the deceased who are existing somewhere and that these deceased are the angels or guardians referred to in the Scriptures. They further state that these beings are anxious to help those of us on the earthly plane through their greater wisdom and understanding.

What can be said of the mediums of these churches? To begin with,

★

if you have never attended such a church or visited such a person, we suggest that you do so. However, make sure that you take with you only a minimal amount of cash and a maximum of common horse sense.

To say that these persons can indeed make contact with a departed member of one's family is to jump feet first into a commonplace error of which we are all guilty: the error of thinking ourselves limited human beings. Because the medium brings us knowledge, we think it has come from a source outside of ourselves rather than from within ourselves. In other words, the things we are told by this person are probably things that we ourselves know but that we have forgotten for whatever reason.

The explanation as to what takes place during the mediums' seance most likely lies in the area of extrasensory percention, or ESP. If a mind can transmit a thought, why can it not pick up the thoughts (even though they may be forgotten) from deep within the mind of another? By now, many of you have already experienced and shown to yourselves that such things do exist.

Exercise 11

Dwell on the ideas summarized in the lesson, and try the following.

Go to a quiet room. Relax your body and mind as you have been taught. After you have rested and relaxed, try to picture in your mind's eye the face of a loved one or close friend who has departed. When you have succeeded in clearly seeing this face or whole being, mentally ask the question, "Are you existing somewhere? Is there really a place after death in which we can meet?"

After you have asked this question, continue to relax and wait for an answer.

Try this for no more than half an hour each day until you find some degree of success.

Lesson 12

In the previous lesson we turned our attention to a discussion of the beliefs in a life after death and the fact that each individual continues his existence, ever evolving toward the Godhead.

We now turn our attention to a very important subject that is greatly misunderstood: the subject of memory. Why do we remember some things and forget others? What is the purpose of memory? Are there different types of memory? These are all questions that you may have wondered about.

The masters have spent many lifetimes in seeking answers to these questions. To begin with, let us tell you that without memory our life would be very different indeed. No learning would be possible. In fact, you could not even be recognized or respond to another's calling of your name if you didn't remember your name.

Many psychologists feel that all knowledge may just be recall and that anything that can't be remembered has never really been learned. There are others who feel that many times, even though we can't recall something, we can recognize it if we see it! Memory, then, cannot just be recall.

But what is the purpose of this thing we call memory, and why do we remember at all? Memory lives in our unconscious. When we remember, we somehow open the door to this other part of ourselves and pull out information on anything we may wish. We do not have to stop and think about remembering; we just remember.

But we have all experienced times when for some reason we could not reach in and pull out what we desired. What happened then? It could be that for some reason we actually closed the door to our memory, or rather some part of us closed that door. This can happen for many reasons, among them the fact that remembering sometimes causes us pain. How many times have you remembered when someone hurt you or when something happened that was not pleasure but pain? When the hurt becomes so great that we cannot stand to remember, something deep within our minds allows us to forget.

On other occasions, we do not remember because we did not take the time to put what we wanted to remember into our minds in such a form that we could extract it easily. In order to remember, we must train ourselves to do just that.

But there other kinds of memory—for instance, the memory of another life, of being someone else. Somewhere deep within our minds lies a record of everything we have done in our former lives: not one life, not this life, but *all* our lives over endless centuries.

Right now there is a great deal of research being conducted by psychologists into the possibility that everyone might actually remember having lived before. Many masters actually know who they

were and what they did in many of their previous lives. This knowledge comes, naturally, to many as they advance along our path of
Wicca; it may actually aid them in understanding why they live as they
do and the real meaning of many experiences that come to them. On
the other hand, it may very well be that knowledge of a previous life
carries with it certain pain and suffering. Not all of us have lived good
lives. Many of us committed some error or perhaps an actual crime
against our fellowman or society. For these things we suffered, perhaps died, or were put to death by society. All life is not bliss. There
must be times of sorrow.

So what we are suggesting to you is that there are reasons why we
remember and why we don't. The master within us knows who we are,
who we have been, and who we will become. There is no hiding from
these three since they are all one.

Each one of us has some special task or job he must accomplish in
this lifetime if he is to advance and make genuine progress in the next
life. We are born to live this special life and to do that special something. The problem is that most of us never really understand what it is
we must do! Things would be so much easier for all of us if each
understood his or her place in this lifetime and worked toward that
understanding. To know would give us a real sense of belonging and
being a part of the great wholeness of life without fear of not fitting in,
a feeling that many of us have as we travel along this path.

Memory proves its mastery of us by providing us with a means to
grow. Thus, if the nature of every moment is growth, then the nature of
memory itself be likewise. To grow means to enlarge or go forward. If
we are not growing in this way, we are not making progress. If we are
not making progress, then we are not fulfilling the reason for our being
here in the first place. We are born to know and to grow. To do
otherwise is a failure to ourselves and to our creator. We must use this
thing called memory. We must give it an ample opportunity to work for
us, to guide us toward the things we need. If we allow it to so work, it
will work for us.

Exercise 12

Following is an ancient exercise used by the masters to develop a
near-photographic memory. Practice it each day. Each evening when
you are relaxed and ready to go to sleep, close your eyes, breathe as
you have been taught, and begin to see in your mind's eye exactly what

you did just before you retired for the evening. Mentally, begin to see each event, *going backward* to the first moment of your rising in the morning. Certain events will be remembered more easily than others. When you come to these, ask yourself why you have remembered them and what particular lesson is to be learned. Practice each and every night without fail.

Lesson 13

In the last lesson we began a discussion of the importance of developing the ability to remember. This ability is not a physical one but is a very important part of the thing that we call the mind or Soul. To use this ability is to use a part of us that is spiritual in nature and absolutely not limited by our physical world.

When we say it is not limited by the physical world, we mean to suggest that its real nature is one of Spirit. Since memory is a spiritual thing, it must be used wisely and well.

For instance, if you wish to change your life tomorrow, you must forget your life as it was yesterday. You must forget all the hurts, the pain, the sorrow that came to you in the past. You must dismiss these things from your mind and begin to mold yourself into the new, happy person you really want to be.

What we are suggesting here is not easy to do at all. It means that you must give up in order to gain. The nature of the universe is one in which something must always be given in order to gain something else. Let us repeat this very important law again. "In order to gain something new, you must give up something old!"

This means that if you really wish to change your life, to become happier, to get a better job, and to enjoy better health and all the wonderful things Wicca stands for, you must give up your old times. No one can go forward and look backward at the same time!

Now perhaps this idea of giving up old ideas is something you would like to do but feel that you can't. You might have tried to change your life many times but failed in the attempts. Maybe you really wanted to get a new job, get into another field in which you could earn more money. Perhaps you are not happy in your home life and have considered doing something to change this situation. If all these thoughts are yours, then why have you not changed? The answer, brothers and sisters, is simply because you continue to look backward.

Yes, you look back and remember, but you remember only the wrong. Don't you really want to be happy? Wouldn't you really like to wake up with a smile instead of a frown? Wouldn't you like to feel that each day is something special and that you can make of it what you wish? Certainly you want all these things. How do you get them?

The solution is the same as the problem: Simply remember, but remember *only the good*. At first, this will seem quite difficult to do. You will try each day to think of one good thought, one good idea, and one good feeling that came to you the same day or the day before. At first, there will be a war within yourself. Every time you think of the good, the bad will appear to remind you of itself. But you will win out if you continue steadfast in this effort to change yourself and your life.

You should also know that the masters were once ordinary people, too. They had the same troubles, the same problems, the same difficulties. But they did something about these things—they began to change themselves. While you can't change every person and every thing outside of yourself, you can change how you feel about these people and things. This is where true mysticism comes into the picture. Wicca gives you the ability to step out of yourself in order to really see what is taking place.

If you desire to become a master—and certainly you must or you wouldn't be working toward this goal—you must begin right now to do as they do and begin to change your thoughts. We are not suggesting that you completely forget every instance of pain that has ever taken place in your life. This would be too much to ask of any person. We are simply suggesting to you that you should dwell on only the good, so as not to limit your growth. Do you think for one minute that a mighty oak tree would ever come about if it continually remembered being a small acorn?

How do we go about changing our memory? Each day set aside a few minutes, preferably in the early morning just after arising, in which to count your blessings. That's right, take a few moments in which to take an inventory of all those wonderful things that you take for granted in your life each and every day. There may be many things wrong with your life, but there are also many things right as well. For instance, when was the last time you looked up at the stars? Certainly, you can find in each day at least one thing that was beautiful, good, pleasurable, that made you feel fine, nice, and at peace with yourself. Even if you can think of only one thing that brought you happiness, concentrate on that thing. In time, as you practice this simple daily exercise, you will easily find other things that make you feel happy.

You must take both control and responsibility for each and every one of your thoughts. Why? Because they are living things!

A story is told about Jesus' disciple Peter, whom we know as the Big Fisherman. Whenever he became depressed, whenever he began to feel sorry for himself, whenever he felt rejected, he would take out his nets and begin to mend them or weave new ones. He did this one simple thing (which to us seems of little value) because his nets were known throughout the land as the very best nets made anywhere. Is there not one thing that you do best? Certainly there is. Go then and dwell on this thing. Don't let a single day go by without taking inventory. And when you take the time to do this, you will be surprised because your inventory will begin to increase, your water will turn into wine, and all the things that you really want out of life will begin to become reality. Read this lesson over at least once a day for the next week.

Exercise 13

Continuing in our development of your ability to remember what is good, try the following. Each day, for no more than half an hour, while listening to the radio or television or talking with another person, listen carefully to *exactly* what is said and mentally repeat to yourself exactly the *opposite*! For instance, suppose your daughter says, "I'm going out to play now." When you hear this you should quickly think to yourself, "You are not going to play now. You are staying in the house." This is to be thought mentally and not to be said out loud. Try this each day for ten days.

Lesson 14

You are now reaching the end of the First Degree of spiritual and psychic enlightenment. If you have followed our instructions, you have begun to build within yourself something of great value, something that no one can ever take away from you, and something worth many times more than the time and effort you have spent.

Just as a workman finishing his task should receive some reward, so should you receive the very finest that life has to offer. Certainly you have worked hard and long. You now wish to quench the great thirst that builds within you.

Before we present to you one of the highest honors we can give, and one that will take you even further along the Path, we ask that you especially consider the following words of wisdom.

By now you have come to realize that the nature of your life is one filled with great mystery. Your sleeping and waking moments contain extraordinary experiences. Should you wish to fully understand the great powers you are beginning to release in your life, you will have to spend many months and years in this search. The very nature of Wicca makes it a lifelong work.

What is the value of such a study, you rightly ask? The answer, my brothers and sisters, lies in an understanding of your own nature. Yes, that's it! Every single thing you have ever wished for that is good and beautiful already lies within, but it lies within you sleeping. The task of all mysticism, including Wicca, is simply to awaken the sleeping giant.

In the many lessons you have already read, our task has been simply to awaken you to an awareness of your inner self. This has been done through the special exercises, which actually build psycho-mental power, and the repetition of certain ideas. If you have practiced these exercises as instructed and have read the lessons at least once daily, you have made good progress. If you have not done this, stop right now! Go no further with these lessons, for you will be ill prepared for the vigorous psychic work that follows.

If you can honestly say that you have mastered all the previous lessons, we invite you to join with those who have gone beyond the first degree, to Self-Mastery.

In the pages that follow, we introduce you to the first of many sacred ceremonies you will receive. This ceremony, thousands of years old, has remained the secret possession of followers of the Craft for centuries. This lesson will introduce the practice of the ceremony.

Since first discovered, this ancient ritual has been kept in inviolate and utmost secrecy. Reveal this ceremony to no person without the permission of the masters or receive the sting of the scorpion! Do not be the first to disobey this request.

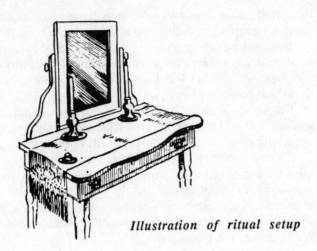

Illustration of ritual setup

A Sacred Ritual

Time. Choose one period each week during which you can perform this ritual alone and without interruption. Whatever day and hour you choose, always use that same hour and day. Once begun, never change the day and hour.

Place. Choose a particular place for this ritual. The place can be anywhere—a corner of your bedroom, a spare room, any place that is convenient and in which you can be entirely alone. As this work is secret, the place you have chosen should have a door that can be locked, preventing others from entering once you have begun. Once you have chosen this place, try to use it each time.

Instruments. Those things that are needed for the ritual include the following.

A small table. This can be of any size and of normal height.

Two candlesticks with candles. The candlesticks should be of wood or metal and can be of any shape or size. The candles should be at least six inches high.

A mirror. This should be at least twelve inches square. Place it at the back of the table or hang it directly over the table.

A small, comfortable chair. This should be placed in front of the table so that when you sit in it you can see yourself in the mirror.

A dish of water.
Matches.
A clock or watch.
Incense (optional).

Place the table, mirror, and chair in a dark part of the room. Place one candle in its holder at the left of the mirror and one at the right. Place the dish of water in front of the mirror, and have the matches ready to light the candles. Darken the room as much as you can, except for a small light that you will need for reading. If you wish to light incense to create an aura, do so.

Now you are ready to begin.

THE PROGRESS OF THE RITUAL

Step 1: The Master's Message. Sit down in the chair, before the table, and read aloud, but softly, the following words.

My Dear Novice,

I greet you from the Temple of the White Flame with the traditional greeting of our sacred Order:

BLESSED BE!

As Grand Master, I greet you and reach out to guide you in the first steps of this ancient ritual. I ask that you pledge to me your full attention, your devotion and total faith, so that you may advance and become proficient in the work of Wicca—and so that this ritual may be enlightening and illuminating to you.

Remember that there is but one Divine Power, the Sovereign Ruler and Architect of all things. Learn to worship this Light in secret and never reveal to anyone, living or "dead," the mysteries you are now to learn. To merely speak of these things to others will destroy your success in this great work.

Remember, too, that you derive your strength and force from the Heart of the White Flame, and that to abandon the many hands that guide you is to leave yourself in utter darkness.

Should you not be able to so pledge yourself, your life, and light to this work, then stop now, and destroy these words and resign from Wicca forever.

Having read this message slowly and carefully, dim the lights, sit down again in the chair, and meditate for five minutes.

Step 2: Lighting the Candles. After five minutes, light the candle at the left of the mirror. Gaze into the mirror at your own image, and say these words: "Blessed Be the White Flame that illuminates my Path."

Now light the candle at the right side of the mirror. Sit back in your chair, close enough to the table so that the light illuminates your face in the mirror. Continue to look into the mirror for seven minutes. Then repeat: "Blessed Be the White Flame that illuminates my Path."

Step 3: Drawing the Sacred Figure. Now stand up and, using your right hand, trace the sacred emblem of our Order, as shown above, on the mirror, with a crayon or something else that will show up. Mark heavily the small spot where the arrow points on the diagram. To make this spot more visible, you may wish to use a white crayon or some wax or butter. You must be able to see this point when you are sitting in your chair.

Step 4: Salutation. Step back a few feet from the table. While standing quietly, look steadily at the spot in the center of the Sacred Triangle, and repeat the following: "Hail, O Sacred Seal of the Unseen Masters." Remain standing and concentrating on the Sacred Triangle for eleven minutes. During this time, you will see it fade, disappear, and appear again. This is to be expected, so do not be frightened.

Step 5: Invocation. After eleven minutes have passed, while still standing, raise your right arm and place the point of your index finger in the center of your forehead. While holding it there, pronounce aloud the following invocation seven times. This should be memorized.

Peace, O Thou Great and Glorious One. Thou art to me both Father and Mother. I come to Thee in these moments of silence, revealing to Thee my most deep desires. Show me Thy Presence and bring to me that which I so earnestly seek.

Step 6: Be Seated. After reciting the invocation seven times, once again take your seat. When you have done so, repeat the following words softly:

Before Thee, I accept Truth and the teachings of Wicca, as the guardian of my conscience, as the principle of my life.

Step 7: Concentration. Continue to gaze into the mirror and concentrate deeply for seven minutes. Then stand up, and put out the candle on the left of the mirror, and move the other candle toward the mirror so you can still see your face clearly.

Step 8: Concentration. Remain seated and continue to concentrate on the reflection of your face for eleven minutes. Watch this reflection and see what happens, but do not be frightened.

Step 9: Conclusion. After the eleven minutes have passed, rise once more. While looking into the mirror, repeat the following phrases, which should be memorized.

Hail my brothers and sisters in Wicca, I seek and search for further Light, Love, and Life so that I may advance in my studies. I am now one with you before this sacred emblem of our Order, and with the sanction of my guardian, Mathrem. Blessed Be!

While remaining standing, put out the other candle and recite softly: "May peace profound abide between me and thee forever and ever."

Use the clock or watch to time the ceremony at first. After you have practiced for a while, you will find that this is no longer needed.

Please perform this ritual at least three times before you go on to the next lesson, which adds to the ceremony and instructs you in using it to obtain things on the spiritual and material plane.

★

Lesson 15

In this lecture we come to the end of our First-Degree studies. If you have followed our ritual instructions in the last lesson, you have begun to experience what is known as Higher Contact and that which leads toward Divine Consciousness. In time you will come to rely on the practice of this most ancient ritual as a means by which to obtain almost any just desire, and it is with this thought in mind that we proceed with this lesson.

Once again we ask you to keep our words and guidance deep within your heart. It is not well to speak of such things as these to those who do not understand who you are or who you have become through the practice of these teachings. But we assure you, you have only just begun your studies.

Perhaps at one time you thought that you could obtain many of life's blessings with a simple formula. Now, however, you know that you must study and work hard for each and every morsel that is brushed from the plates of the Immortals. This is as it should be, though, for to obtain without effort would mean that we would not appreciate what we finally receive. So continue your efforts and know that we are always with you in this great work.

Having made all the preparations we mentioned in the last lesson, you are now ready to perform the actual ceremony. We ask that you read the following through, at least once, before actually practicing it.

You will find Form Seven on the following page. (You may wish to make photocopies.) Before you begin your ceremony, you *must* fill out this form. The form is a petition to the divine forces that are evoked through the practice of the ceremony. It is through this form that you indicate why you are performing this ancient ritual. Fill it out as follows.

1. On the line in the upper left corner (which reads *Date Begun*), write the date you start your ceremony.

2. On the line in the upper right corner (which reads *Date Ended*), write nothing until you have ceased your efforts to accomplish the purpose of the ceremony.

3. At the bottom of the form, write the name of the person or persons involved in your desires. If it is yourself, write your name in the first place and the names of any others in their proper places.

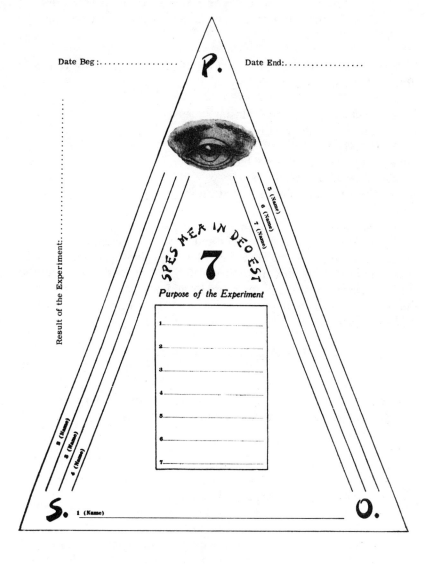

Date Beg :.................. **P.** Date End:..................

Result of the Experiment:..................

5 (Name)
6 (Name)
7 (Name)

SPES MEA IN DEO EST

7

Purpose of the Experiment

1 ....
2 ....
3 ....
4 ....
5 ....
6 ....
7 ....

2 (Name)
3 (Name)
4 (Name)

S. 1 (Name) _____ **O.**

4. In the box that appears in the center of the form, write the purpose of the ceremony, for example, "I want my boss to give me a raise," "I want my husband to be good to me," etc. Write only one purpose, for the ceremony can be directed toward only one end at a time.

Remember that in order to perform the actual ceremony you must follow these steps.

1. Reading of the Grand Master's message
2. Lighting of the candles
3. Introduction of Form Seven
4. Tracing of the Sacred Triangle
5. Affirmation
6. The period of silent concentration
7. The final invocation

Now that you clearly understand how this ceremony is to be performed, fill out Form Seven, and let us begin. You should now be standing in front of the table on which you have laid out everything you will need. The light in the room turned on, you now begin to read aloud in a soft, low voice the message of the Grand Master, which follows.

The Message of the Grand Master

Dearly Beloved Novice,
    Once again I greet you from the Temple of the White Flame with the traditional greeting of our sacred Order:

BLESSED BE!

As you now begin this ceremony, ancient as the very mountains and respected throughout the ages, I and the Council of Seven, Masters of the White Flame, stand beside you in spirit and mind. I reach my hand out to you, over the distance that separates us, and sense your devotion and trust. Always remember that there is but one great Power that guides each one of us, and that as you stand here now, you are about to come closer to this great Oneness than ever before in your life. Do not be afraid of anything that you may see and hear, for I and the

★

Council of Seven are with you now, and you are in the midst of a great company. All your brothers and sisters who have gone before you, who have traveled this same road, are with you now and will keep you from any harm. Have faith in God and your Order, trust in us who are your true friends, and that which you seek shall be yours. Blessed Be!

When you have finished reading this message from the Grand Master, turn out the main light in the room, pull your chair up to the table, and sit down. Seat yourself comfortably, but so that you can see your face in the mirror. Sit in this manner for eleven minutes, meditate upon the purpose of this ceremony, and that which you desire to come into your life. Do not let any other thoughts enter your mind except that which you desire. This is most important.

Now light the candle on your left and say: "Blessed Be the White Flame that illuminates my Path."

Sit back once again, and continue to concentrate upon your reflection in the mirror. Look into your own eyes as you concentrate on the thing that you desire more than anything else. After seven minutes have passed, light the candle on the right side, once again saying: "Blessed Be the White Flame that illuminates my Path."

After seven additional minutes have passed, take your finger and trace our sacred symbol on the mirror.

Now rise from your chair and say: "Hail, O Sacred Seal of the Unseen Masters."

Continue to remain standing for eleven minutes more, and continue to concentrate on the Sacred Triangle. After this time has passed, sit down quietly.

Once again, arise, and place the point of the first finger of your right hand in the center of your forehead. While holding it there, repeat the following seven times.

Peace, O Thou Great and Glorious One. Thou Art to me both Father and Mother. I come to Thee in these moments of silence, revealing to Thee my most deep desires. Show me Thy Presence and bring to me that which I so earnestly seek.

Now, once more take your seat, rest your mind, and repeat:

Before Thee, I accept Truth and the teachings of Wicca, as the guardian of my conscience, as the principle of my life.

Gaze into the mirror once more for seven minutes, then put out the candle on the left, saying:

> May peace profound abide between me and thee, my brothers and sisters in Wicca. I am now one with you before this sacred emblem of our Order. Blessed Be!

Now extinguish the candle on the right, and remain seated and resting for a few minutes. When you feel relaxed, turn on the lights, and put away in a secret place your candles and especially Form Seven. No one must discover or handle this form if your wishes are to become reality. Each form may be used seven times for the same request, and then a new one must be used. You may produce extra forms by photocopying the original from the book.

During the practice of this sacred ceremony many things will take place. You may hear voices; you may feel chilly and also see many strange faces in the mirror. Don't be frightened. Whatever comes to you comes because you were meant to see and experience it. Try to practice this ceremony at least once a week. It will aid and strengthen your development.

You have reached the end of the First Degree and now have completed the first step on your road to personal and spiritual advancement. Now you must rededicate yourself to go even further.

As you advance into the Second Degree, many of the great mysteries will be made known to you, and you will understand why secrecy is so important. You must believe and trust us. Only then can we help and guide you successfully.

Beginning with the next lesson, you will be instructed in such things as astral projection, psychic healing, thought projection, and many other mysteries that are known to few persons. All these things will unite to make you into the person you wish to be. Never give up this search, and know always that we are with you and want you to succeed in this work.

Lesson 16

You have now ascended into the Second Degree and will discover instructions in many secret teachings that will enable you to make positive changes in your life and to achieve and receive all those things you sincerely desire.

As you enter into this most mystical degree, you will be asked to accept principles that may at first reading appear strange or unusual.

Since the first part of this Second Degree is devoted to an in-depth study and explanation of the technique known as psychic or spiritual healing, your beloved Grand Master will now assume the role of your Class Master. It is from his lips and pen that you will receive this most sacred tradition. We ask, once more, that you keep secret the special methods that will begin to unfold in this and the lessons to follow. In this way, you will be able to build within yourself those special psycho-mental powers that can be called upon in any emergency and that are used daily by the Council of Elders.

To understand the cause and cure of that which is called disease is to come closer to an understanding of the universe and God than you ever have before. The true nature of disease is not realized even by many physicians or doctors. The value of almost all their treatment lies simply in the alleviation of pain or other symptoms of disease, rather than in the cure of the disease itself.

If you are to understand but one thing in your studies, understand this, that it is only the Cosmic that can cure or heal anything. When you or a loved one are ill, you have in some way interfered with or broken the law of life, for it is the desire of the Cosmic that each of us enjoy perfect health. This means that in some unknown way you have allowed yourself to limit the flow of health through you. The following example will make this clear.

High in the mountains there is a large and beautiful lake from which flows a river that winds its way down the mountainside until it reaches a village far below. Each year when the spring rains come, this lake fills to capacity and begins to pour its life-giving waters into the river. One spring, a group of young boys decided they would climb the mountain and see if they could build a dam across the river and thus create a swimming hole for the summer months.

Not realizing what they were doing, they succeeded in piling trees and wood across this river at one of its narrow spots, so its waters no longer flowed past that point but spilled over onto the neighboring ground. Since these boys were all quite young, they were driven from totally completing their task by a spring storm that frightened them with its thunder and lightning, so much so that they were afraid to even return to the mountain.

When the time came for the spring planting, the village farmers found that the precious water needed to make their crops grow was not available. When the crops began to die, one farmer asked why the river had disappeared and decided to climb up to the mountains to find out what had happened. Upon discovering the dam the boys had built, he simply removed the blockage, and once again the waters began to flow.

What we call health, my brothers and sisters, is very much like this river. If we allow it to flow within us, all is taken care of and we, like the crops, grow and flourish.

When we, in our ignorance, allow something to block the divine flow, illness results until we or a physician remove this blockage. All illness, then, is simply due to this one thing, the inability of the Cosmic to flow through us.

While disease make take on various forms, there is but one cause. Understand and picture this story in your mind, for it contains the secret of health and the cure of illness. Whenever you are ill, read this lesson over again.

Pay particular attention to the exercise that follows. It will teach you a technique that will begin to make you into your own physician. Study and practice it well. Someday it may even save your life.

Exercise 16

Of the various secret methods for restoring health taught by mystics throughout the world, special use of the breath is perhaps the most common. This is one reason why breath control was your first lesson.

Breath control has long been associated with the qualities of the Soul, since one begins to live with the first breath and ceases to live with the last. Learning to control and regulate the breath provides the means to gain control over that special form of energy the Indians call *prana,* or primal energy. One form of *prana* is known to us as electricity. The Yogis claim that if we can learn to control this energy within our bodies, we can control it throughout all of nature.

At least once a day, for a period of ten days, do the following: Obtain two bowls or dishes, large enough to put both your hands in. Fill one bowl with ice-cold water and the other with warm water. Take a deep breath *through your mouth,* hold it as long as you can and exhale slowly *through your nose.* Repeat this three times. Now take another breath. While holding it, place both hands within the bowl of *cold* water. Continue to hold your breath as long as you can. When you

Alchemical allegory: Soul and Spirit separated from the body

Alchemical allegory: The Soul rising towards God

have to exhale, remove your hands from the water. Repeat the same procedure with the *warm* water. When you must exhale, remove both hands from the water. Continue to practice this deep breathing and holding of the breath while alternating between the cold and warm water. After you have done this a few times, or as soon as you begin to feel strange or in any way tired, take one final breath and place the *right hand in the warm water* and the left hand in the *cold* water *at the same time*. This is important. Keep both hands in the water as long as you can, and then exhale. This completes the exercise, which will begin to release the healing energies within your hands.

Lesson 17

In the last lesson we spoke of the real nature of health and illness. One's health is like a car. When the car starts each day and takes us where we wish to go, we think nothing of it. But when this same car breaks down and ceases to run, we become angry and immediately call our local service station.

There is much to be learned in this comparison. If we take time to service our car properly, many problems that might develop later can be avoided. This kind of car maintenance is called preventative maintenance and is well known to mechanics and others who work with machines. Unfortunately, most of us do not apply this same kind of thinking to our bodies and health.

It is thought provoking, too, to realize that in China it has long been the custom to pay one's physician as long as one is well and to cease paying when one becomes ill. This is exactly the opposite of the current way of thinking in the West.

Right now, we call a physician only when we are *ill*. Why? Simply because our culture and society is so accustomed to this practice. If we take time each day to be healthy—through proper nutrition, breathing, and especially thinking—we would *not* have to take time to be ill.

No one really wants to be ill, to take time out from his job, from enjoying life, from being with his loved ones. Yet each year almost all of us find ourselves ill for at least one or two days. Why is this so?

The answer may be stated as follows. As we have *not* taken time to be well, we are forced by our bodies to take time to be ill. By forced, we mean that the life process within us causes illness to manifest itself in order to make us well. Toxins, wrong nutrition, and wrong living habits build up within us until they must be righted. When they cannot be righted, life ceases, and we pass through the Great Initiation, only to be reborn.

Mystics throughout the centuries have maintained that we all should live until the age 144. How many of us actually attain this great age? Very few, and the reason we do not is because we have not truly lived our lives correctly.

The laws of nature and God must be fulfilled. There cannot be an abridgement of these laws without suffering.

While much of our dis-ease comes from wrong living or thinking in *this* lifetime, sometimes the influence of a *previous* lifetime causes us to be born with a particular weakness. Very often people with such conditions seek the assistance of the masters so that this Karmic condition can be turned about and done away with. Of the various causes of illness, those of this category are the most difficult for you to heal, but even they can be healed with the right technique.

However, although you will learn all that is to be known about healing in these lessons, you will not be legally entitled to call yourself a physician or to extract fees for assisting another person in the recovery of his health. Also, as a healer you should never volunteer to assist another person unless he requests your assistance. Many times people will come to you, and you will notice that they are not feeling well. While you may assist them through an "absent treatment," which will be explained to you more fully in future lessons, you should not offer your services.

You must also be cautious in dealing with those who do ask, since many times people become frightened of what they do not understand and turn against those who would help them.

Exercise 17

In the last lesson, we gave you a basic exercise that would begin to release the healing energies in your body. The following exercise continues in the same vein.

While seated in a comfortable chair, with your back as straight as possible, take a deep breath *through your nose,* hold it as long as possible, and then slowly exhale through your mouth. Repeat six times.

Now take another breath and while still holding it raise both arms up over your head, with the three middle fingers of each hand held close together and the small finger and thumb extended. Move your arms around you in a circle until you find a spot in the air that creates a tingling sensation in the hands and arms.

Once you have found this spot, which is a source of psychic energy, close your eyes, and imagine this energy flowing through your arms, down into your body, and reaching your toes. When you have completed this sequence, close your hands into a tight fist and lower your arms. If you have done this correctly, you will feel this energy flowing through your body.

This exercise will continue to build the healing energy within you. In order to be able to heal others, you must have an extra amount of healing energy yourself. It is this extra energy that you will learn to transmit to others. The injunction "Physician, heal thyself" is perhaps the most important rule we could give you.

To further your self-healing at this time, we ask that you practice the following exercise as well. This exercise is to be practiced whenever possible, during the day at various odd moments or at a scheduled time.

Close your eyes and relax your body. In your mind's eye picture a blue light spinning round like a whirlpool. If you have trouble seeing this light, obtain something blue and look at the color for a while.

You *must* be able to see this light, and you *must* be able to see it in motion.

Once you have created this light, see it touching that part of your body you wish to be healed. If, for instance, you have had some trouble with your digestion, see the light swirling round over your stomach. After the light spins round for some time, see it moving away from you and disappearing into the distance.

All this is to be seen in the mind, with your eyes closed.

If you are in good health, imagine the light spinning around your entire body and especially over the center of your forehead.

Lesson 18

The previous lesson instructed you in the practice of increasing your own psychic energy through special breathing, visualization, and thought control. In this lesson we wish to give you the fundamentals of healing through the laying on of the hands. This method, known as contact healing, is one of the oldest methods known to mankind and one that even the ancient Egyptian priests known as the Kheri Hebs had knowledge of. In future lessons we will fully explain to you all that is known of other methods of healing, including the various "absent" techniques often employed by the masters. However, remember that only God can heal and that you and the masters are the instruments of the Cosmic.

When Illness Strikes a Loved One

When what we call disease first makes its appearance, take whatever steps are necessary to make your loved one comfortable. If the illness is anything more than an ordinary cold, *call your physician*. While you are waiting for him to come, or for an appointment, you may do whatever you can to help by the use of the spiritual power you have been developing through practice of the special exercises and through the assistance of the masters. By now you know that the power of God is real and that you have the ability to change the course of your life, as well as that of others, through the use of your mind.

Centuries ago, the ancients discovered that through the use of certain words, rituals, and practices the healing energy within the body can be increased. Since God is everywhere present, he is present within you and within the person you are seeking to help. When you learn to invoke this divine presence, you actually change the material or "seen" world by first changing the immaterial or "unseen" world.

Remember that since God is within you, you can use his strength, if you open yourself up and allow him to work through you. Even the master Jesus never claimed that he did anything. It was simply the Father in him that did the work. Remember this, too: Once you allow your ego or self to lead you to think that you are doing the healing, no healing will take place. Each one of us is simply an instrument.

Preparing Yourself. In order to be a fit instrument for the great work that is now to be done, you must first calm your mind so that you will be able to assist your subject. Certainly you cannot expect to bring about a healing and give peace and calmness to someone who is disturbed if you, yourself, are not possessed of this same inner calm.

Take a few minutes before beginning any treatment to relax yourself as you have been taught and to open yourself up to the healing energy that is about to flow through you. If your are in any way disturbed or if you are not feeling well or are physically tired, do not try to assist another. We cannot stress this point enough. Only if you are in good health yourself and feel at peace with yourself and your subject can you expect to bring about a change of conditions. If you do not obey this all-important rule, you may find yourself taking on the symptoms of the disease you are treating.

Preparing Your Subject. Make certain that the subject you are attempting to assist is comfortable. Begin by relaxing him. You can do this easily by speaking in a calm voice. Tell him that he will be all right and that everything will be well.

Next you must make a connection between your mind and the mind of the subject by telling him of your previous success in this work and by speaking of the nature of the mind and the fact that both of you are instruments of the Cosmic. You must tell the subject what it is that you are going to do, and you must *convince* him that, whatever happens, he will feel more relaxed and that this relaxation is the beginning of the healing process itself. Whatever you do, you must convince your subject that you *can* and *will* assist him to become well. Once you are sure that your subject is resting comfortably, begin the special Master Invocation that follows.

The Master Invocation. This is a list of five special points or steps you must memorize so that you never forget them. These steps when spoken by you, in your own words, will create a mystical union between you and your subject, enabling the healing process to take place. Do not be misled by the simplicity of each of these points, as they were discovered long ago by masters with great wisdom. If you use them well, they will serve you forever. Whenever you attempt to do any healing, you must say something in your *own* words on each of these subjects.

1. The Cosmic and the Supreme Mind will now help you through me.
2. Forget the past and any worries you may have, and place your faith in this Supreme Mind.
3. Feel courage and strength, for you will be well.
4. Now relax each part of the body as I speak of it.
5. I know all will be well: AXISCO PAS.

How do you use these steps? Once you have relaxed yourself and your subject is sitting or lying comfortably, ask him to close his eyes.

Begin to speak the invocation, slowly and in a low voice. For instance, of the first point you might say: "You know that God loves you and me very much. That is why we are together now. Since God is within both of us, his power flowing through me will now begin to help you. Through me, the power of the Supreme Mind will make you better." Now go on to the second point. Say something like this: "I want you to begin to forget the past, all the problems that you have had, and put your faith in the Supreme Mind right now. There is no need to worry about your illness at all. You will recover because you are a good person, and God loves and needs good people to carry out his work. Since the Supreme Mind is always with us, it is his will that everything be perfectly right. Do not worry, for you will be well."

Now proceed with the third, fourth, and fifth steps. Don't be afraid to repeat yourself, for this will only add to the feeling you are trying to create.

You must memorize these points of the Master Invocation. Use them each time you attempt to heal another person. Later we will present special instructions in the use of the breath and the hands.

Exercise 18

Practice the use of the Master Invocation to relax and to put to sleep a person who has difficulty relaxing. Find someone who has trouble going to sleep, and tell him you can assist him. Arrange in advance to help this person by setting a specific time and place. If possible, try to arrange this experiment a half-hour after the subject has eaten a substantial meal. After you have asked the subject to sit in a comfortable chair or to recline on a couch, ask him to close his eyes. Speak of each part of his body in turn, starting with the feet. When you have completely relaxed him as you taught yourself to do earlier, begin the Master Invocation. Go through each point in your own words. I know you will be successful with this experiment. Try it on one person at least five times.

Lesson 19

In the last lesson we introduced you to the Master Invocation, which will enable you to contact the mind of the person you are

★

seeking to assist in recovering from an illness through the use of spiritual or divine healing. No matter what school of healing you accept, be it the use of drugs, homeopathy, or chiropractic, you must by now realize that you and the physician are on but different paths leading to the same goal—the restoration of health in the subject. It matters not how this health is restored as long as it *is* restored. The honest physician will admit that his method relies on the natural forces but that he approaches them from a different basis. It may rightly be said, though, that your method goes to the cause of the problem while that of the physician too often simply treats the symptoms. In any event, both the physician and the spiritual healer should work together to bring this healing about.

It is important, too, that each subject have faith and confidence in your ability to help him. Many times it is this faith alone that makes the difference between a method that works and one that does not. By now, you know that telepathy or ESP is not a superstition but a reality. Since this is so, it is possible for your subject to pick up your thoughts through his unconscious mind and transform them into reality. Therefore, you must always hold in mind a clear image of the subject enjoying full and complete health once more. Never, under any circumstances, convey to your subject any doubt whatsoever in your ability to assist him through God's help. Any doubt that you may have will be quickly seized upon and distorted out of proportion by a subject lacking understanding.

The Use of the Eyes in Healing

It is important that you maintain a positive manner when approaching your subject, and use of your eyes is crucial to this part of a treatment. We now call to your attention the All-Seeing eye that is placed in the very top of the sacred symbol of the Order (see the illustration in Lesson 14). Throughout the ages, the eyes have been called the windows of the Soul and have been believed to convey both good and evil. In some countries, a belief in the "evil eye" continues to be widespread.

It is a generally accepted fact that the eyes can and do convey a special form of energy that can be used for healing. Since this is so, you must approach each subject with a firm gaze and look directly into his eyes or place your attention at the center of his forehead. Do not look away from your subject. Even after his eyes are closed and you are speaking the Master Invocation, continue to look directly at him.

Through this simple technique you will be able to greatly influence the healing forces.

The Use of the Hands in Healing

The Bible contains more than five hundred references to the use of the hands in healing and conveying blessings, among them Numbers 8:10; Acts 6:6, 13:3; 1 Timothy 4:4; Mark 6:5; Luke 4:40, 13:13; Mark 5:23, 16:18. So important is the use of the hand that the masters of your Order have chosen the symbol , meaning hand, to be part of their insignia. This symbol often appears in many churches, as it was long ago associated with the master Jesus. Almost anyone can learn to awaken this healing power within himself and others.

Before beginning any healing through the use of laying on of the hands, you must prepare yourself as instructed in the last lesson. You must always make certain that your hands are clean. If at all possbile you should have a bowl of water brought into the room where your subject is resting; actually wash your hands in his presence. Make sure that the water used is clear and slightly cool. Next take both hands and rub them together vigorously for a few minutes. Now have your subject close his eyes and begin the Master Invocation. When you have completed this invocation and the subject is resting, rub your hands together once again.

It is not necessary for you to *actually* touch your subject unless he or she requests it. Since the influence of the spiritual body extends beyond the physical, you have simply to move your hands within six inches or so of the physical body in order to get satisfactory results. Whenever you begin your treatment, be sure that the fingers of each hand are arranged with the little finger and thumb extending outward and the middle three fingers closed together. This causes the energy that you have invoked to flow more freely.

Begin by placing both hands, fingers extended, over the forehead of your subject. As you hold them about six inches over your subject (eyes still closed and resting), picture the healing light flowing from your subject's head toward the feet, always keeping the hands within six inches of the physical body but not actually touching it. As you make these "opening passes," continue to feel the healing energy flowing through you and into the subject and hold in mind this thought: "You are in Peace. All is well with you, and the healing power of God is near." Repeat this mentally as you continue these passes. When your passes have reached the feet of your subject, move your hands away from his body and gently shake them both as if you were shaking off water. Once you have done this, rub them together once more and begin the passes from the head to the feet once again. You may wish to continue these opening passes as many as three times. Let your feeling be your guide in this matter.

Now place your hands gently and lightly over that part of the body that is ailing or that the subject has told you is giving him pain. While holding your hands in this position, send the healing thoughts toward that particular organ or zone.

During this entire procedure, you may remain silent and simply project your energies, or you may speak your healing thoughts aloud. Once more, you must let your own intuition guide you in this matter.

The Use of the Breath in Healing

Sometimes the use of the breath along with the laying on of hands has been found to be of great value in healing. To produce warmth and especially to break up congestion, open your mouth wide, and slowly breath upon that portion of the body you wish to heal. This is especially effective if done before the laying on of hands.

As an alternative, if the subject has fever or is in pain, bring your lips together as if to kiss someone or whistle, and breathe once more. This will produce a cooling effect. Try these two ways of breathing on the back of your own hand, and you will understand our instructions more clearly.

Remember always that only the Cosmic can bring about any healing. You are only an instrument of God. If you forget this, no healing will take place. Also, for you to be successful in treating another, you must be sure that the room in which you are to work is quiet and that you will be undisturbed for at least half an hour for each treatment. If you are interrupted, your work will not be effective.

Exercise 19: The Treatment of a Headache

The next time a member of your family or a loved one complains of a headache, before he reaches for aspirin, try the following.

Prepare yourself as we have instructed. Relax your subject, and recite the Master Invocation. After making the opening passes, slowly stroke the forehead of your subject by placing both hands in the middle and slowly moving them outward. As you do this, mentally "will" your subject to relax and think to yourself: "The pain in your head is easing. You are relaxing more and more. There, now, the pain is going away. Now there is no more pain at all."

Leave the room of the subject, and allow him to rest for about ten minutes. If you have done your work well, he will fall into a deep sleep. After ten minutes have passed, quietly reenter the room and softly call the name of the subject until he awakens. Do not awaken him by creating any kind of noise or through the use of an alarm clock. If you awaken him suddenly, you will destroy all you have done.

Lesson 20

We now turn out attention to diagnosing illness through the use of the various psychic powers you have been developing. By now you know that you have a responsibility to use your inner psycho-mental powers to bring about health wherever illness is found. Up to this point in these studies we have dealt primarily with the use of healing techniques when a person is physically in your presence. In future lessons, we will present methods for treating loved ones who are absent from you.

Before you or any other healer can successfully treat another person you must know all that you can about the person, on both the physical and spiritual level. Many times an illness that appears to be physical in nature will be found to have originated from a mental disorder. To treat such an illness, you must fully understand what or who is bothering your subject and causing the illness to take place.

Make it your business to quietly talk with your subject before beginning any treatment. As you talk to this person, you will begin to receive impressions as to the real cause of the problem. You must follow your feelings as to this cause, no matter how strange it may seem.

When I was a young student of these same teachings, I heard about a woman who had lost the use of her arm as a result of a can of food falling on her wrist in the food market. The doctors could find no physical cause for her inability to move her hand and arm; the real cause was later discovered to be her guilt at having to place her aged mother in a nursing home.

Many times the Cosmic operates in strange ways to bring about the working out of the Divine Law. We are not always in a position to fully understand everything that happens in our lives on all levels. It is only the fully developed master—the person we are assisting you to become—who can truly understand all that is happening in the Cosmos. We want you to become this self-sufficient person and will do all in our power to make this happen. You must become as strong as an oak tree and be able to withstand any wind. This is why you are studying these lessons. If you do not forget this, you will be well on your way to all the happines life can bring you.

How You Can Diagnose Illness through the Feet

Many centuries ago, the masters of our Order discovered that the nervous systems caused relationships between different body parts, sometimes in a strange fashion. For instance, it was discovered that if

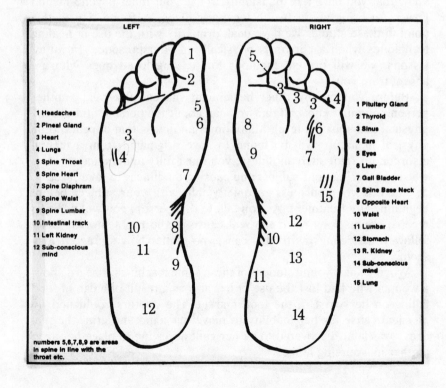

1 Headaches
2 Pineal Gland
3 Heart
4 Lungs
5 Spine Throat
6 Spine Heart
7 Spine Diaphram
8 Spine Waist
9 Spine Lumbar
10 Intestinal track
11 Left Kidney
12 Sub-conscious mind

1 Pituitary Gland
2 Thyroid
3 Sinus
4 Ears
5 Eyes
6 Liver
7 Gall Bladder
8 Spine Base Neck
9 Opposite Heart
10 Waist
11 Lumbar
12 Stomach
13 R. Kidney
14 Sub-conscious mind
15 Lung

numbers 5,6,7,8,9 are areas in spine in line with the throat etc.

★

you put pressure on certain parts of the body, other parts far away could be affected. It is with this unusual knowledge that we now instruct you in the use of the feet to determine what part of the body must be treated. It is important that we do this so you can direct your concentration toward that part of the body that *really* needs assistance, rather than give merely general treatments.

We have reproduced a drawing of your feet as they might appear if you looked at them from the bottom up. The various numbers written on them correspond to different organs in the body. This correspondence obtains for each and every human being, no matter what his sex or age may be. This means that you can also use this method on yourself to determine what problems you, too, may have. Knowledge of this special technique can make you better able to help those who request your assistance.

To use this diagnostic technique, simply ask your subject to remove both shoes. When this has been done, hold one foot at a time and *begin to press with your thumb* all around the foot and the toes. You must press hard. When you strike a tender area that causes your patient pain, you will know from the correspondence chart which organ is ailing. Make a mental note of each area that appears to be sensitive, so you can later direct your healing energies.

When you have done this with each of your subject's feet and have noted where the problems are, go back over each of the feet. This time, when you come to the sensitive area, press with your thumb while taking and holding deep breaths. Continue pressing on each area until the pain disappears. You will know when this is because your subject will tell you. When you have completed this with each foot, stop. Now begin the Master Invocation as instructed, and concentrate on the particular organ that needs to be healed.

How to Use this Method on Yourself

You can examine your own feet in the same way. As soon as you find a tender spot, press firmly with your thumb, *while holding the breath,* until the pain goes away. In this way, you will be giving yourself a healing treatment. Once you have examined and treated your own feet, relax your body as you have been instructed, and begin to send healing thoughts to the organ or organs that have been affected. You can do this easily by picturing the organ in your mind and speaking to it as follows: "OK, my heart. You have been bothering me for too long. I know that I have not treated you as I should, but you do know that I love you, and you know that the presence of God is within you, healing you and making you strong. I know that each new day you will become healthier and healthier, and that soon you will be entirely restored."

You will find that each of the various organs in the body can be talked to in this way. The stomach is perhaps the most stubborn, but this is only because it is here that we often mistreat ourselves the most by eating or drinking foods that are not of true value. In later lessons, you will learn the mystic methods for determining which foods you can and cannot eat. Remember that you are a unique being and that not all foods or liquids are right for all people.

This method of diagnosis and treatment should be used *at least once daily,* whether on another or on yourself, preferably before going to bed. This will allow the healing forces to do their work while the subject is sleeping and without interference from the material world.

Exercise 20

Practice the above technique during the coming week. Also try the following method of psychically charging water, which you will then give to your subject or which you yourself will drink.

Obtain a glass of pure spring water. Make sure the glass is as thin as possible. A crystal glass would be best. Hold the glass directly in front of your solar plexus. Take *eleven* deep breaths through the mouth, hold each as long as possible, and slowly exhale.

When you have completed this, recite *seven* times the words "Helion, Melion, Tetragrammaton." Immediately drink the contents of the glass or give it to another to drink. You should do this each evening just before going to bed, along with the foot diagnosis and treatment. Both will work together to restore natural healing in the body.

Lesson 21

In the last lesson we instructed you in the use of the feet to diagnose illness. As we pointed out, the early masters were aware of the relationship between body parts, but many modern physicians fail to take this point into consideration. If illness exists in even the smallest part of the physical body, the *entire person is ill.* Never forget this, since it holds the key to much of the work that you will receive in the lessons to follow.

Special Times for Giving Healing Treatments

Although the healing treatments we are instructing you in can be given twenty-four hours a day, any day, sometimes when the degree of success desired does not appear, special attention must be paid to

COSMIC ENERGY TIMETABLE FOR BEST HEALING

Birth Date	Sign	Treatment Month	Treatment Hours
Mar. 21–Apr. 20	Aries	Dec., Jan., Feb.	10–11 A.M.
		Mar., Apr., May	9–11 A.M.
		All other months	8–9 A.M.
Apr. 21–May 20	Taurus	Dec. through May	11 A.M.–12 P.M.
		All other months	9–10 A.M.
May 21–June 21	Gemini	Jan. through May	12–1 P.M.
		All other months	10–11 A.M.
June 22–July 22	Cancer	Dec. through May	1–2 P.M.
		All other months	11 A.M.–12 P.M.
July 23–Aug. 22	Leo	Dec. through May	2–3 P.M.
		All other months	12–2 P.M.
Aug. 23–Sept. 22	Virgo	Dec. through May	3–4 P.M.
		All other months	2–4 P.M.
Sept. 23–Oct. 22	Libra	Dec. through Aug.	3–4 P.M.
		Sept. through Nov.	2–3 P.M.
Oct. 23–Nov. 21	Scorpio	Dec. through July	4–5 P.M.
		All other months	2–3 P.M.
Nov. 22–Dec. 21	Sagittarius	Dec. through July	3–4 P.M.
		All other months	2–3 P.M.
Dec. 22–Jan. 19	Capricorn	Dec., Jan., Feb.	7–8 A.M.
		Mar., Apr., May	6–7 A.M.
		All other months	5–6 A.M.
Jan. 20–Feb. 19	Aquarius	Dec., Jan., Feb.	8–9 A.M.
		Mar., Apr., May	7–8 A.M.
		All other months	6–7 A.M.
Feb. 20–Mar. 20	Pisces	Dec., Jan., Feb.	9–10 A.M.
		Mar., Apr., May	8–9 A.M.
		All other months	7–8 A.M.

particular hours during which any treatment will be more effective. To use the following table, you must determine when your subject was born and under what astrological sign. Once you know this, you can easily consult the respective category and schedule your healing treatment for that particular time of day. Healings performed during these special times are always more effective and work more quickly.

To make certain that you fully understand the use of the Cosmic Energy table, let us cite an example. Your subject was born on July 30, and you wish to give a healing treatment during the month of June. Looking up his birth date, you find that his sign is Leo and that during the month of June treatments should be given between noon and two in the afternoon. This means that you will work during this time for best results or, on stubborn cases, throughout the entire month.

How to Charge Yourself before a Healing

Even if you are doing healings at various hours of the day, you may wish to set aside the special time indicated in the above chart for "recharging" your own psychic battery. This, too, can be done at any time, but is more effective if done during that special hour.

The Use of the Pendulum

Among the various methods of diagnosing illness used by the masters, radiesthesia, or the use of the pendulum, plays an important role.

This method was used by the ancient Hebrew, Egyptian, and Chinese mystics.

To make your own pendulum, obtain a small glass or plastic bead, or a small ring, and attach it to a piece of thread, preferably of black silk, or fishing line—it must be pliant and strong.

Once you have made your pendulum, carry it with you for a few days in order to allow your own vibrations to enter into it. At least once each day, hold it between both hands and take three deep breaths, slowly exhaling after each.

Now take your pendulum to a quiet room. While sitting in a relaxed manner, grasp the string between the first three fingers of the right hand, if you are right-handed, or the left hand, if you are left-handed.

While holding the pendulum in this manner, you will note that it may remain stationary, swing, oscillate back and forth, or gyrate or spin in both directions.

Obtain a pencil and hold the pendulum over it. You will find that it moves back and forth over the length. If you move to the right end you will find the pendulum spinning clockwise, indicating positive energy. If you move to the left end of the pencil, the pendulum will spin counterclockwise, indicating negative energy.

How to Test Food and Water. Certainly by now you know that health is something that comes from the Cosmic through many different ways. Many times people eat or drink foods or beverages that do not agree with them. This is not to say that the foods themselves are not wholesome, but rather that there is something in the food that is not in harmony with that person's vibrations.

One way to test which foods agree with you is to take each type of food, in turn, and place it on a separate plate or clean paper in front of you. Suspend the pendulum over the food, and wait for it to begin to move. Once the pendulum is moving, place your left hand between the food and the pendulum, palm downward toward the food. If the pendulum continues to move clockwise, this food is *good for you*. If the pendulum changes to a counterclockwise movement, the food is *bad for you* and should be eliminated from the diet. If it oscillates, it is neither good nor bad but "in between."

If you wish to assist others in determining what foods they should eat, have them place their left hands over the food. Remember the old saying "One man's food is another man's poison." No food or liquid is of itself "good" or "bad." But when it comes into a particular body, certain changes take place that can mean health or illness. As a healer, you must become aware of such changes.

Exercise 21

Use the following technique every day, even on days when you are not performing healing services.

While seated in a comfortable chair, with your back as straight as possible, take a deep breath *through your nose,* hold it as long as possible, and slowly exhale *through your mouth.* Repeat six times.

Now take another breath and while still holding it, raise both arms up over your head, with the middle three fingers close together and the small finger and thumb extended. Move your arms around you in a circle until you find a spot in the air that creates a tingling sensation in the hands and arms.

Once you have found this spot, which is a source of psychic energy, close your eyes, and imagine this energy flowing through your arms, down into your body, and reaching your toes. When you have completed this sequence, close your hands into a tight fist and lower your arms. If you have done this correctly, you will feel this energy flowing through your body.

Lesson 22

Recalling the last lesson, we introduced you to the use of the pendulum as a means of diagnosing illness in yourself and others. Alone the pendulum can do nothing. In your hands, though, it can be used for many things, including the answering of questions you direct to your subconscious mind. When you take the pendulum in hand, it may do any of the following.

1. Remain stationary
2. Swing or oscillate
3. Gyrate in a clockwise manner
4. Gyrate in a counterclockwise manner
5. Move in an ellipse

Each movement has a meaning that you must learn to interpret if you are to be able to use this remarkable instrument.

Testing the Pendulum

The following are just a few of the things you can determine through use of the pendulum.

Sex. If you hold the pendulum over the upturned palm of a male, the pendulum will move clockwise or swing back and forth. Over the hand of a female, the pendulum will move in a circular clockwise fashion.

Have a friend give you the signatuures of two people whose sex is unknown to you. Test them by holding the pendulum over the signature.

Judging Character from Handwriting. Place a letter or a piece of paper on which there is writing on a table in front of you, and hold the pendulum over it. Watch the pendulum to see the movement it makes. The movements can be interpreted as follows.

Gyrating perpendicularly across the writing: the highest character possible
Oscillating along the writing: generally good character
Rotating elliptically: somewhat confused mind
Revolving counterclockwise: lacking in conscience but not evil
Revolving clockwise: a thoroughly bad character

Catching Arithmetical Errors. Have someone give you two slips of paper with a column of numbers and a sum. On one slip, have the wrong sum shown. Your pendulum will gyrate clockwise over the correct calculation and counterclockwise over the wrong one.

Tell Time. Suspend the pendulum in the center of an ordinary drinking glass, so that it hangs down into the glass. Now concentrate on what time it is. The pendulum will begin to move back and forth, striking the sides of the glass the correct number of hours.

Answers to Questions. Write one question on a slip of paper, and suspend the pendulum over the paper. If the answer is yes, look for positive reaction rotation (clockwise). If the answer is no, expect a negative response (counterclockwise).

The pendulum can also be questioned "out loud" by asking whether such and such a thing is true. The pendulum will either move or cease moving at the correct response. Experiment for yourself.

Test Friendships. Place an object worn by another person next to one of your own. Suspend the pendulum between the two objects. If you and that person are in harmony, the pendulum will move back and forth between the two. If it moves away from the two objects, your friend is not a true one.

The above are just a few of the uses to which the pendulum can be directed. It has been found that best results are often obtained during the hours 7–11 A.M., 3–5 P.M., and 8–11 P.M. This is not to say, though, that you cannot use this very important tool whenever it is needed.

Using the Pendulum for Diagnosis of Illness

By now, you have no doubt understood that everything in the Cosmos exists in a state of vibration or movement. The true understanding of the various cycles of movement that govern the inner planes of spiritual being will be revealed more fully as you enter into the higher degrees of our teachings.

When it comes to illness, any disease begins as a change in the molecular structure of the various nerves and cells concerned. The pendulum is invaluable in measuring this change in vibrations. This is not to say that one cannot give general healing treatments without a knowledge of the nature of the illness; but to be a healer of the highest order, the energy must be channeled to the particular organs or nerves affected.

If you wish to use your pendulum to pinpoint a particular area in which illness is manifesting itself (or is about to appear), simply try one of the following methods.

1. Seat your patient in front of you. Take your pendulum in your right hand, if you are right-handed, or in your left hand, if you are left-handed. Let the pendulum begin to gyrate, and then take the index finger (the first finger) of the hand not holding the pendulum, and touch the various parts of the body, one at a time.

When you reach a part of the body that is "out of tune," the pendulum will change its movement from gyration to oscillation. When this happens, make a mental note of that particular organ, for you will want to treat it as we direct you in the lessons to come.

2. Refer to the diagram of the hand appearing in the illustration. Have your subject remove any rings from his *left* hand and wash it. Then have your subject turn the hand palm upward. Move your pendulum over the various points, which correspond to parts of the body as shown in the diagram. Clockwise movement indicates good health

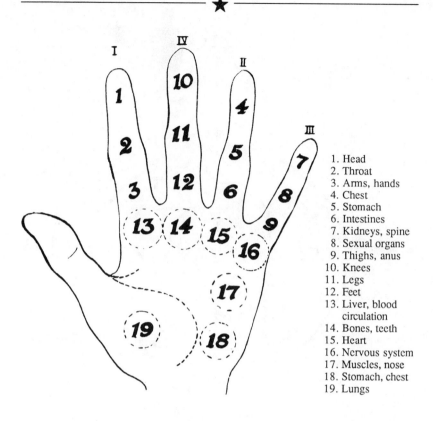

1. Head
2. Throat
3. Arms, hands
4. Chest
5. Stomach
6. Intestines
7. Kidneys, spine
8. Sexual organs
9. Thighs, anus
10. Knees
11. Legs
12. Feet
13. Liver, blood
    circulation
14. Bones, teeth
15. Heart
16. Nervous system
17. Muscles, nose
18. Stomach, chest
19. Lungs

and counterclockwise movement, illness. If you wish to analyze your own vibrations, place your left hand, palm downward, on paper. Trace with a pencil the outline of your hand. Once you have done this, use your pendulum in the same way as discussed previously.

3. Use the diagram in the circular illustration, being sure that you have aligned it along the actual north-south axis. Holding the *right* hand of your subject in your *left* hand, suspend your pendulum over the center of the diagram. After a few minutes the pendulum will begin to move, its direction indicating the part of the body affected.

If you wish to make a diagnosis for someone who is not able to come to you in person, request a sample of his clothing, preferably something that has been worn next to the skin or an object that he carries or wears, such as a watch or lighter.

Place this object in the middle of the diagram, and perform the

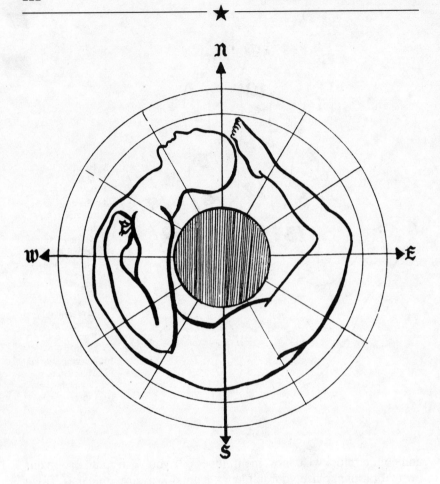

same testing. A similar diagnosis can be made from the sole of the foot, following the diagram you received with lesson 20.

Remember that what you think to be the cause of illness may not be so. You should allow the pendulum to do its job. For example, a person might come to you with a bad complexion. You may think that his problem is with his skin, but you may discover that the problem is in the intestines. Never allow the human part of yourself to interfere with the work of the Cosmic.

Whenever people come to you for assistance, help them as best you can. The fact that they have come to you is an indication that you *can* assist them.

★

Lesson 23

Continuing in our search for renewed health and healing, this lesson will present the techniques for the release of healing forces from the breath.

If you remember our very first exercise together, we introduced you to a special way of breathing. In India and Tibet, the use of the breath to bring about many so-called miracles is well established. In these countries it is believed that through control of the breath one can, in time, gain control of the Cosmic energy. It is for this reason that many of the exercises we have presented to you request breathing in a special manner.

The ancient Indian Yogis were the first to discover that there is a direct relationship between a person's breathing and his health and mental ability. They discovered that when a person inhaled and held the breath for certain periods of time, a special energy was drawn out of the breath and absorbed by the nervous system. It is this very same energy that governs all life in the Cosmos. These same teachers named this special force *prana* and called the special techniques for controlling this energy *pranayama*.

If we stop to think for a moment, we know that these most ancient teachings are correct. When we have what is called a cold and find ourselves unable to breathe properly, do we not also find ourselves tired and without energy? So, too, when we are nervous and upset, our hearts beat quickly and our breath moves in and out, almost out of control. People who are unusually calm and relaxed breathe slowly and without any effort whatsoever. Also animals that live to the greatest age breathe the slowest and have the slowest heartbeat. Don't you want to live a full, rich life? Certainly you do! So you see that it is more than just important that we learn all there is to be known about the control of the breath, not just for our own sake, but in order to help others as well.

Exercise 23

To begin to understand what proper breathing can do, try the following exercise each day—upon rising, at midday, and before retiring. Practice *ten* times at each period of the day.

Ascertain your heartbeat by placing your fingers over your pulse (found on the inside of the wrist of either hand). Count with your pulse beat until it is firmly fixed in your mind. This beat is then the basis for your special breathing.

Sit in a posture so that your back is straight. Close your *right* nostril with your left forefinger, and breathe in through the *left* nostril for six counts. Hold your breath for three counts, and then exhale through the *right* nostril for six counts. Rest three counts.

Now inhale through the *right* nostril for six counts, hold the breath for three counts, and exhale through the *left* for six counts. Rest three counts. This completes one cycle.

In other words, you are to breathe *in* through one side of your nose and *out* through the other, then *in* through that side and *out* through the other.

Each day add five cycles until a total of forty cycles is reached.

If you practice this exercise as instructed every day, you will soon feel building within you a strange feeling of peace and quiet. You will also find that you do not catch cold as easily and that your memory begins to improve. This is just one of the many ways to use the breath.

Every cell of the body is a blending of positive and negative energy. For the most part the foods and liquids we drink and the earth on which we talk provide the *negative energy* forces. It is our breathing that provides the *positive energy*. When an imbalance of positive and negative forces arises *anywhere* in the body, that which we call illness or disease comes about.

While for the most part our foods provide all the negative force we need, we can also increase this energy aspect through breath control. Bring the five fingertips of both hands together, without the palms touching. Now take a deep breath and exhale all the air out of the lungs, while continuing to hold your fingers in this same position. Continue to hold your breath out as long as you can. When you have to take another breath, *separate* your fingers. Repeat this exercise *seven* times.

Whenever you feel a cold coming on, repeat this exercise a few times each hour, and you will find that you do not catch the cold. A lack of negative energy often occurs when there is congestion in the body in the form of mucus.

Positive energy keeps us active and is often needed when we are nervous or unusually tired. One way to gain positive energy is through charging water, as we instructed you in a previous lesson. Another way to recharge your own batteries is by practicing the following exercise.

Take your thumb and first two fingers of the right hand and place them in the hollow of your neck in the back of your head to the left of your spinal cord. While holding these three fingers there, take a deep breath and hold it as long as possible, slowly exhaling only when you can hold your breath no longer. As you repeat this exercise a few times, mentally imagine this energy flowing from your fingers into your neck and down your spine. Make certain that you use your *right* hand only.

Whenever you feel tired or nervous, take a few minutes to practice this exercise. It can also be used when you feel tired and have to drive for some distance. Simply pull off the road, repeat the exercise a few times, and begin your journey again.

This exercise works because the *right* hand, especially the thumb and first two fingers, gives off *positive* energy. The *left* hand, especially the thumb and first two fingers, gives off *negative* energy. If you are left-handed, these patterns may be reversed.

Be sure to try these important exercises, as in the next lesson we will instruct you in how to transmit this healing energy to another person. Whenever you are in doubt as to which type of energy may be lacking in your own body or in that of another, give both treatments. Always give a positive treatment first. Wait at least seven minutes, and then follow with a negative treatment. There is no way you can give yourself or another person too much of either energy, so you have no need to worry. Any extra energy will be given off through the hands.

Another method to determine which treatment is needed is as follows. Have the patient sit in a comfortable chair. Take his right hand in yours as if shaking hands. Close your eyes very tightly, and wait until you begin to see some faint lights in your eyes. This will take two or three minutes. The lights will appear hazy, all over the inside of your eyelids. Usually only one color is seen, though it is possible to see a different color in each eye. The meaning of these colors is as follows: Orange, red, purple—positive treatments must be given. Blue, green, yellow—negative treatments are needed. White light—both positive and negative treatments.

Try this exercise with a friend or member of the family. After using it a few times, you will be able to tell how much energy is needed by the brightness of the colors. The next lesson will give you complete instructions for using these techniques on others.

A repeated word of caution: Never attempt any kind of healing treatment unless you feel well yourself. To do otherwise will put strain on your own health and may result in your taking on the illness you are attempting to cure.

Lesson 24

In the previous lesson we introduced techniques for determining what illness your subject may be suffering from. Remember that according to the ancient teachings, there is but one disease—ignorance. When we violate the laws of God and Nature, we are subjected to the power behind these laws. God does not single us out and inflict a particular illness on us. We do not need God to do this, for in most cases, we do it ourselves.

How many times have you eaten or drunk something that you know does not agree with you? Or perhaps you were advised by a physician to give up smoking but have failed to do it. On the other hand, you may find that when you fail to drink a certain amount of water, you do not feel well, and yet you continue to disregard these things.

We are suggesting that many times we are responsible for whether or not we find true health. The trouble is that we just do not take the time to be healthy. Unfortunately, the only time most of us consult a physician is when we are in the midst of illness. Why? Just as we take time to change the oil in our automobiles and lubricate the various moving parts, so must we pay attention to our bodies in order to bring them good health. Take time to be healthy, and you will find good health.

Our discussion cannot be complete without mention of another important point—right thinking. Never allow yourself to become upset immediately before or after eating a meal. If you do, you will interfere with the natural flow of digestive juices and upset the delicate balance in your system. If you are upset, do not eat! It is better to miss a meal or two than to take food into the system when the system is not properly prepared for digestion.

In our temples in the Orient, it is the practice of the brothers to make each meal a time during which they reflect on the many blessings they have received from the Cosmic. They do this by refraining from any conversation and listening to the reading of various scriptures and truths. While you may not be able to do this, you can refrain from thinking of anything of a negative nature that might adversely affect your disposition. Also try the following method of obtaining energy and serenity before a meal.

Once you have prepared your food and placed it before you and have made certain that your hands are clean, rub your two hands together for a few minutes. Place them palms *downward* over your food, a few inches from the plate. While holding your hands in this position, take a deep breath and see in your mind the psychic energy flowing from your hands downard to your food. Repeat this a few times while saying to yourself, "This which I bless now blesses me." If you do this at each meal you will find that greater nourishment is derived.

In the last lesson we spoke of how you can use this very same psychic energy to heal others. When you first approach a subject, always speak in positive tones of health and well-being, remembering the use of the Master Invocation.

After taking the hands of your subject, mentally order him or her to relax. Once you have begun to see the various colored lights and have determined which type of energy is lacking, you are ready to begin giving the healing treatment to the subject.

Refer to the illustration on the next page. Assume the position as shown in position 1. Place your hands on each of the patient's wrists, and wrap your knees around the patient. Now instruct the patient to close his eyes. Take a deep breath and feel the energy flowing from you into the subject. Once you have done this a few times, assume position 2 by standing behind your subject and placing the fingertips of each hand on the temples. Take deep breaths, hold them as long as you can, and envision the healing forces flowing from your hands through the head of the patient and down through the spine.

Now assume position 3. Stand to the right side of your subject, and place your *right* hand on his forehead and the *left* hand on the back of the neck. Again, do your breathing, and feel the healing flowing through you and into your subject. In position 4, simply reverse position 3. Stand on the left side of the patient, and place your *left* hand on the forehead and the right hand on the neck. Again, you must feel the healing energy flowing through you.

In position 5, both hands are placed on the shoulders of the subject, and the healing energy is directed down the two sides of the body. In this step, imagine the energy actually flowing downward until it reaches the very tips of the toes of your subject.

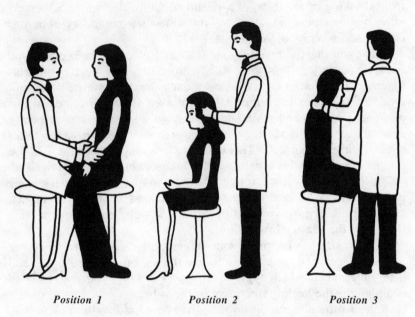

Position 1   Position 2   Position 3

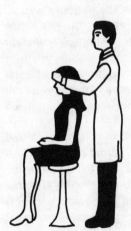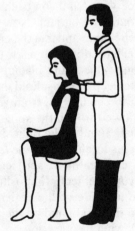

Position 4   Position 5   Position 6

In position 6, the left hand of the healer is placed on the throat of the subject while the right hand is moved very slowly down the spine. You must continue to feel the healing energy flowing from you through the entire process. When you feel it lessening, begin to take deep breaths once more.

Finally, move behind the patient once more, placing your fingertips of the right hand on the right side of the spine, in line with whatever organ you wish to treat. For example, if you wish to treat the heart of your patient, stand on his right side, in back of him, and place the fingertips of the right hand over the part of the back corresponding to the heart. Now direct the healing energies to that organ.

After you have completed this entire treatment, which can take as much as twenty minutes or more, the subject should feel relaxed. You may wish to instruct him or her to lie down and sleep for a short time. If the patient does not feel more relaxed, more at ease, and generally at peace, you have not followed our instructions correctly.

Do not allow anything—such as an alarm clock or telephone—to awaken the patient suddenly or you will undo the results of your treatment. This is very important. In fact, we recommend that each brother and sister studying these lessons learn to awaken without the use of an alarm clock. Simply give yourself suggestions the night before as to the time you wish to arise, and you will awaken.

How often should these treatments be given? The answer is that your effectiveness as a healer is limited only by your practice of these lessons. As you progress and develop your own psychic abilities, you will find that you can bring about success much more quickly. Certainly your first treatment should bring a certain amount of peace and relaxation to your subject. Remember, too, that your effectiveness will be colored by the actions of your subject. If he continues to do those things that brought about the illness in the first place, you are not likely to find much success. Always follow your inner voice when it comes to what you say to your subject. If you feel that there is a particular thing that he or she should do to make the healing permanent, then do not hesitate to tell him so. Finally, you must practice these techniques over and over until you become a master of them. "Physician, heal thyself" is more than just a spiritual injunction. It contains a great wisdom that you must begin to apply in your own life.

Lesson 25

In the last few lessons we have shared with you instructions that have been the possession of the secret brotherhoods and orders in all parts of the world. If you have truly applied these teachings in your own life, you by now know how effective they can be in alleviating pain and illness. Throughout all the teachings you have received thus far runs a continuous thread of ageless wisdom, namely, that it is the power of our minds that brings disease and that it is this same power that brings healing.

While we have given you specific techniques to be used in the physical presence of a sister or brother in need, there is yet another, wondrous method that we have not yet discussed.

While learning the First Degree of knowledge, you came to understand that there are few limits to the workings of a mind attuned to the Cosmos. You no doubt amazed yourself by discovering that you *do* have the ability to move objects, cause others to turn and look your way, and to bring about health where illness existed. In the lessons to come you will be taught and will master still greater mysteries, including the art of leaving the physical body and traveling to other planes of being.

But before leaving the field of healing, we must present those techniques that the masters have found most useful in the practice of healing at a distance, or "absent healing," as it is commonly called.

There are times in the life of each of us when it is difficult to determine exactly what our effect has been in a particular instance in which we sought to bring healing to another. Consider the following hypothetical story. You are out walking and a friend who knows of your good work comes up to you and asks that you offer healing prayers for her sister-in-law who has been ill with the flu. You promise to do so that evening but in the course of the day totally forget your promise. The next day you meet this same person, who thanks you for your help and tells you that her sister-in-law has made an amazing recovery, *thanks to you.*

In this instance you apparently "did nothing" that you "know of" to assist in bringing about a healing. How then did this healing take place? The answer is that many times it is merely your thought that you will pray for the healing of another that begins to set off the healing energies and direct them toward the person needing them.

★

If we consider the facts that our guides in spirit are always with us and that our minds are always part of the great Cosmic Mind, then certainly any thought we think at any time becomes a living force. This is important. It means that often simply by thinking of health and connecting this thought with one who is ill, you can and many times do bring about healing.

To understand why this comes about, we should look to your earlier lessons. If the mind of one person can send thoughts to another, causing him to turn around, does this not prove that what is called ESP (extrasensory perception) is a real thing? Certainly it does.

In fact, it may surprise you to know that among professional healers such as Oral Roberts (United States) and Harry Edwards (England), the vast majority of healing instances they participate in are conducted in the absence of the physical body of the patient. According to Reverend Edwards, his absent healing ministry has a success factor of about 80 percent. This means that about eight people out of ten who write to him for healing assistance are healed in various degrees.

Each of us has a great Cosmic responsibility to offer prayers for our absent sisters and brothers when such prayers are requested. This also means that if the right techniques are followed, we can bring about a great deal of health and well-being without incurring the hostility of our friends and families who know little of what we are doing when we enter our sanctums. This is why absent healing is so important and why we are taking all this time to explain fully the techniques at work.

Before commencing with a discussion of these techniques, one final comment must be made. It has been found over the years that sometimes a person finds little success in contact healing but for some reason is able to use absent healing with an amazing degree of success. Why this is so appears to lie in the fact that some persons feel ill at ease when they come into the presence of another person. Perhaps they lack a certain self-confidence. In absent healing, one need not even know where the other person lives or have met him at all in order to be successful.

There are few genuine mystical secrets to making absent healing work. One has simply to learn the art of tuning in to the great Cosmic supply and allowing this to broadcast out to the sister or brother in need of assistance. Do the following exercise to begin to be effective in this way.

Exercise 25

First, set aside a time each day in which to do your healing work. Try, if at all possible, to make this the same time each day, and conduct your healing from the same room. Make sure, too, that during this time you will remain undisturbed and that nothing or no one will interrupt your important work.

Second, try to obtain a point of contact with your absent subject by obtaining an article of his clothing (a small piece cut from a sock, tie, or underclothes has been found most effective) or a piece of jewelry, such as a ring that has been worn for some time. If a request for healing comes to you through the mail, the letter itself might serve this requirement, but only if it is handwritten.

Third, a recent photograph of the person to be treated is an important part of making this contact. A recent photo contains better emanations, which will allow you to tune in on the person shown in the picture. This picture need not be a large one. Any small snapshot will serve the purpose.

When you have obtained these objects, it is important that the subject know you have begun to work in his behalf. If the request for healing comes to you through the mail, be sure to acknowledge the letter and advise the person writing that you have begun to offer prayers for his healing. It is also helpful if you can receive periodic reports as to the condition of the subject, which will better allow you to concentrate your efforts.

Once you have gathered together the articles mentioned above and have selected a time in which to begin, simply retire to your sanctum and begin to relax, as you have been taught. After you are completely relaxed, take the object you have received from your subject, and hold it in your *left* hand. Now take the photograph in your *right hand* or place it in front of you. Begin to focus all your attention on the photo, especially on the forehead of the subject. While centering your gaze there, begin to think thoughts such as, "You are beginning to relax. The healing that you seek is reaching out to you. God and the masters, through me, are healing your [name the part of the body to be healed]. You feel the presence of the Cosmic and the Unseen Masters. All will be well." You must continue to think these thoughts while looking at the photograph. You may even wish to repeat the Master Invocation, if you feel that this would be helpful. Concentrate as hard as you can. You may even wish to speak these things in a soft voice as if the

★

subject were actually before you. Continue this for no more than a half-hour, and under no conditions speak of what you are doing to another living person.

To practice absent healing, take the daily newspaper and look for someone in need. Concentrate as taught above to assist him. Perhaps he has lost a job or had an accident. Seek no material reward, for you will be blessed by the Cosmic.

Lesson 26

With this and the next few lessons we come to the end of our discussion of some of the master techniques for psychic and divine healing. Of course, no series of lessons in this or any aspect of psychic work can ever be considered complete. While we can share with you many of the secrets that we have received and tested throughout the centuries, we cannot judge how far you, our disciple, can carry these techniques. In India there is a saying that the disciple should stand on his master's shoulders. This means that you must not only master these special teachings but become better at their use than we are. In this way, each master brings greater light to the Path than he who goes before. Never forget this all-important goal.

By now you have had an opportunity to practice the absent healing techniques we gave you in the last lesson.

In this lesson we wish to speak with you about the nature of color as a means of changing one's health. The ancient masters and those who have gone before us all taught that great wisdom lies in the recognition of each person as a total spiritual being. This means simply that *everything about you* tells who you really are. By everything we mean the way you dress, the food you eat, the kind of house you live in, the kind of car you drive, your preference for a particular food. What we are concerned with now, though, is the subject of color.

From the beginning of time, mankind associated certain colors with peace and tranquillity and others with war and excitement. The ability to see certain colors has even been projected into our modern society. For example, in many areas the color green is used to indicate "Go" on traffic lights while the color red always indicates "Stop." Why is this so? Why were these two colors chosen from all the rest?

The subject of color and why one chooses one color over another contains great mystical secrets. For many centuries the masters of your Order have taught that the origin of all colors lies in what is called the human aura. While you will learn a great deal about this mysterious subject in lessons to come, it is sufficient to say here that there exists a magnetic field or energy pattern around everything that exists. This energy field can actually be seen, by those who have developed their psychic abilities, as various bands of color. This means that color is given off by the electrons and atoms that move about within the human body. While this ability to see the aura can be developed, very few come by it naturally. At one time, this ability was more common, for we have such expressions as "seeing red" or being "green with envy" in many languages. Perhaps, by now, you have even discovered that sometimes when you look at another person you are able to see a faint tint or colored light surrounding him. This is not always visible but can be seen under certain circumstances and special lighting. Usually only a single color is seen at one time, but it is possible to see more than one color and various blendings as well. Following is a brief description of what these various colors mean.

Red. This color represents the body, earth, force, vigor, and energy. It means health, strength, and strong natural emotions such as friendship and love. The best shade of red is almost a crimson or rose. This indicates a pure love. When this color becomes muddy or dark, it indicates a high temper and nervousness. Anger is indicated by this dark red covered with black spots or flashes. Scarlet red means that the person is conceited. Pink means immaturity. Red is associated with the nerves and blood.

Orange. This is the color of the Sun and means intellectual things. This is the color that seems to surround scientists, intellectuals, and teachers. This color usually accompanies those who are thoughtful and considerate of others. Too much orange often means trouble with the kidneys or with a partnership or marriage.

Yellow. Golden yellow indicates health and well-being. Happy, friendly, positive, optimistic—these characteristics come with this color. When the yellow becomes ruddy, the person becomes timid. People with red hair tend to feel inferior and to constantly doubt their ability to perform. Generally, the brighter the yellow, the better.

Green. Since it corresponds to the color of the earth, especially if it has a dash of blue, green means peace and healing. Love of nature, peace, the outdoors, calmness—these qualities correspond to this color. If the color becomes blue-green, the person becomes more helpful and trustworthy. If the color tends toward yellow, deceit may come to the fore. This is especially true of the combination of slate (gray) and green. When a dull green is found, the person usually has a certain amount of tact and diplomacy.

Blue. This is the color of the sky, spirit, contemplation, prayer, and heaven. The very highest form of religious feeling is represented by a beautiful clear violet tint. When the color is very pale, it indicates that the person is struggling toward maturity. The middle blue or aqua means that the person will work harder and get more done. When a person is ruled by religious fear rather than by genuine faith, the color blue-gray will often appear.

Indigo and Violet. These colors often appear in the lives of those who are seeking a path or cause with which to associate themselves. Those with a great deal of purple will tend to be somewhat overbearing; often heart trouble and stomach trouble will follow them. A deep purple comes to those who are very involved in the ceremony of religion and not the genuine mystical life.

Brown. This color, like the earth, stands for material things. This indicates a desire for material things and sometimes indicates greed and avarice.

Gray. Fear, depression, and lack of courage come to those who dwell on this color.

Black. Hatred, malice, gloom, depression, and limitation comes with this color.

White. This is the color of the masters, the Christ, and the Cosmic.

We can use our special knowledge of colors to determine another person's path in life and, by choosing to associate with one or more of them, affect our own lives, health, and well-being.

If you have been very nervous recently or know of someone who is always complaining of nerves, look at the colors you (or he) are wearing or have around you. If you are wearing a great deal of red or sleeping in a room that has a great deal of red, you will actually cause your condition to get worse, since red also means fire or that which is hot. The same thing is true of the foods you are eating. If you are using a great deal of spices, also coffee and tea, you are actually *making yourself ill.* The way to change these conditions is to begin to change your colors to those of the green family. This may even mean painting your bedroom green, throwing out some clothes (be sure to give them to someone in need), and totally changing your diet to include more green vegetables. If you have recently tried to heal someone who is nervous but have found little success, look to the colors with which he surrounds himself.

Let us give another example. Suppose you know someone who thinks too much and is always getting himself into difficulty. Look to the colors he chooses. In this case you would recommend a change to the blue family, which is of the nature of feeling rather than pure thought. The color indigo, especially, would do much to change this person.

Why are we telling you these things? Simply because we have found them to be true. If you will look to the colors in your own life, you will be amazed at how true this great secret really is. In the case of a young child who is always getting into trouble, one can have him paint with only those colors that bring about peace and thoughtfulness. By also dressing him in these same shades and coloring his room accordingly, miraculous changes will be found to take place.

If in your own life, you have not been able to make any recent gains on the material plane, perhaps it is because you have neglected the browns. Once again, look to the colors around you. If you do not have enough of a particular color, begin to put it into your life. Think, act, and meditate on the color that best represents what you wish to be. Even do all your mental painting in that one color alone. At first, you will find this difficult to do. Go back to the candle exercise in lesson 3. This will help you to *think* a particular color. For the next ten days, think, act, and breathe colors. Also try the following exercise.

Exercise 26

For fifteen minutes each day, preferably at the same time, enter into your meditation, and completely relax your body. In your mind's eye, picture a beautiful temple with a large wooden door. As you open and enter through this door, you see an altar upon which is placed the symbol of our Order. To the side of this symbol are placed two candles, one on each side. Now being to see the candles in each of the various colors. See them become red, and feel the red. Change this color to orange. Feel the orange. Do this until you have gone through each of the colors. When you have trouble feeling a particular color, know that this is lacking in your life and work extra hard to develop it.

Lesson 27

We hope that you have had the opportunity to apply the special knowledge of the hidden influence surrounding colors and their usage in your own life. It is our intention that each lesson you receive have some practical as well as mystical application. We want you to be able to apply these teachings in your day-to-day activity. Only in this way can you truly become the master of life you have always wished to be.

Since we are soon to come to the end of this particular phase of our instructions in healing, it is only fitting that we give you all the knowledge we have acquired over the centuries in regard to this most important subject. For instance, along the lines of our previous discussion, it might interest you to know that *every time you think you project a certain color.* This means, then, that by training ourselves to think and actually become certain colors, we are actually able to change our vibrations (a subject that will be explained in depth in future lessons) and thus our awareness and perception of the worlds around us.

This principle of changing our vibrations through color is of great importance, since it has been discovered that certain illnesses seem to thrive on a particular color or vibration. A number of years ago, a few of the masters set out to prove that this was so. They did this by selecting a person who knew nothing of their efforts and mentally surrounding that person with one particular color each day for a period of seven days. They did this by mentally seeing the person surrounded with a red, blue, green, or yellow light, almost as if the person were actually covered by this light. First, they imagined this light surrounding themselves, and when they could see and feel it, they projected it toward the other person. It was found that after a period of weeks and months, those receiving the projected lights had remarkable changes come into their life. In some cases, an actual physical healing occurred; in others, there were decided gains in material areas, such as new jobs, promotions, and unexpected money; in others, romantic involvements.

The important thing to note here is that these things occurred when there was a projection of color combined with a specific feeling of love toward the object of the projection.

To further prove that this principle of projection of colors worked, the masters conducted further experiments in which they projected the color black or gray, accompanied by thoughts of limitation and want. Within a similar period of time, the subject individuals found themselves faced with difficulty and problems on the material plane. Both thse instances demonstrate that there is a definite occult principle at work in regard to color.

The same thing has been found by some physicians and hospitals, who have proved that the color of the room in which patients are placed has a decided effect on their health and well-being.

What does all this mean? Simply that color is a force that has great occult value. Remember this well when you are called upon to assist a brother or sister in need. What color is he wearing? What colors does he have in his home? All these things are indications of his mental state.

Besides color, sound has also been found to exercise a great influence on human health and psychic development. It has been found that in large cities where there is a great amount of noise, there tend to be a large number of nervous ailments. Some experts have suggested that noise pollution is an even greater problem than air pollution, since it more directly affects the nerves.

The ancient Indian Yogis discovered that certain special vocal incantations, which they called mantras, had the ability to stimulate the various psychic centers in the body. (You were introduced to these centers in a previous lesson in which we taught you to meditate and listen to the sound given off by each of these centers.)

To chant these sounds correctly you should obtain a small pitch pipe of the kind often used by vocal instructors and singers. If this is not available, a note struck on a tuned piano will also suffice.

Each chant should be made with the full force of the voice and allowed to continue for as long as the breath will allow.

The RAAAAA Sound. This sound, pronounced "rah," is sounded on the note A above middle C. If it is sounded when one is tired, it will produce greater physical energy. Try chanting this sound the next time you feel tired and worn out. Chant it at least nine times in succession.

The MAAAAA Sound. This sound, pronounced "ma" (the sound a baby makes), if chanted the same way as "ra," will produce a feeling of comfort and being cared for.

The RAMA Sound. When the two sounds above are combined, the pituitary gland is stimulated, which leads to greater psychic powers and awareness. One should visualize a bright yellow light and chant

RARARA, MAMAMA, and the RAAAAAAA-MAAAAA, drawing the sound out as long as possible.

The AUM Sound. This sound, pronounced "oom" like the word *loom,* is best chanted on D above middle C. This sound has a great effect on the pineal gland, or "third eye," which is the center of psychic vision.

The THO Sound. This sound, when chanted, stimulates the throat center and is especially suited for any trouble with the thyroid gland. The musical note for this sound is F-sharp above middle C.

The EHM Sound. This sound, pronounced like the word *aim,* affects the thymus gland and is very helpful in cases of heart disorders. The musical note is B above middle C.

The MEH Sound. This sound, usually chanted on middle C, has a great soothing effect on the nervous system and the heart.

The EAA Sound. This sound, chanted on C above middle C, has been found to calm the mind and exerts a strange effect on water by creating ripples or small waves.

By practicing these sounds each day, you will greatly advance your psychic senses and bring healing to a troubled body or mind. Remember, too, that those sounds that bring about greater health can be used in the presence of another before or after a healing treatment.

It has also been found that if one chants the AUM sound before a period of meditation (such as you have been taught in earlier lessons), the effect of the meditation is more clear and beneficial.

Many centuries ago, a master of our Order discovered that the unconscious mind has the ability to develop its own special chant or prayer, which is exactly right for the occasion or whatever work is to be accomplished, but which has no meaning to anyone other than that particular member of the Craft.

The next time you wish to bring something about in your life, simply chant over and over whatever sounds or "make believe" words come to mind. At first this will appear to be nothing more than baby talk. The words or sounds you make up will have no meaning. However, it has been found that such chanting can work miracles. The explanation for this seems to be that the mind expresses itself in its own special language. When this language is recognized a tremendous power is released that can be called upon for the exclusive use of the person.

Because of the special nature of the material contained in this lesson, we ask that you read it over at least once each day.

Exercise 27

Before going on, try the various techniques presented in this lesson. Be sure to try the last-mentioned method of creating and releasing psychic energy.

Lesson 28

In this lesson we wish to carry you across yet another river of understanding.

We have spoken of the importance of diet in maintaining health and given you a way in which you can select the food that is right for you. You no doubt remember our discussion of the use of the pendulum and perhaps have become proficient in its use at this point in your studies. In this lesson we will discuss the importance of water.

The physical body is mostly made up of liquids, which somewhat explains the great influence of the Full Moon on criminals and those who are called mentally ill. If you have ever looked at the Full Moon on a clear night, you, too, have probably felt the great power it releases. In a later lesson, we will instruct you in using the various phases of the Moon to obtain many wonderful things.

You most likely know that the Moon has a great influence over the ocean tides, easily causing thousands of pounds of water to be lifted and cast about. In brief, the Moon is able to do this since water has a particular blend of atoms and molecules (the small particles of energy that make up all things) that easily respond to energy, especially psychic energy.

In an earlier lesson, we instructed you in a method of charging water through the use of the breath. If you recall, we then told you that this water could be taken either by yourself, or given to another, and that it would have a special healing effect when used in this way. In some of the older manuscripts, this specially charged water is called the Elixir of Life. Credit is usually given to a master known as Le Comte de Cagliostro for the use of a special ritual whereby water was charged in this special way.

Following is the ritual of this great master as it is recorded in our archives.

On the first night of the Full Moon and for six nights there-after, at the hour of midnight, obtain a glass of the finest crystal available, fill it with virgin spring water, and while facing the Full Moon, place both hands around the glass, and hold it high above your head. While holding the glass in that position, recite *seven* times the words "Helion, Melion, Tetragrammaton."

Now take the glass and hold it directly in front of the solar plexus. Take *eleven* deep breaths through the mouth, hold each as long as possible, and slowly exhale.

Once more hold the glass above the head while facing the full moon and recite the following: "Uriel, Seraph, Josatta, Ablatti, Agla, Caila, I pray and conjure thee by the Four words which God uttered with his Mouth unto His servant Moses—Josat, Ablati, Agla, Caila—and ask that thy Peace shall enter into this thy Saliva of the Moon. So may it be."

Immediately drink the contents of the glass or give it to a loved one, and retire for the night. If you have followed these instructions correctly, you will receive a spirit visitation during your sleeping state and will awaken feeling refreshed and re-newed.

From the above ritual, you can see that water is of great impor-tance. In ancient times, the masters would frequently evoke the gods of water; thus there exists a mystical reason for having water in our sanctums or places of meditation. Some masters have claimed that if one places a small bowl of water near the side of the bed while one sleeps, the vibration of the water will greatly aid psychic develop-ment. Each evening fill a bowl with fresh water. Before going to sleep, dip the fingers of the right hand into the water, and trace the symbol of our Order on your forehead.

Besides the use of water in various rituals, water has been found to contain great healing powers. If you or someone you wish to help is suffering from pain in a particular part of the body, do the following.

Immediately before going to sleep, obtain a cloth (preferably of a flannel material) and completely saturate it with clear, cold water. Do not wring the cloth out, but be sure to leave a certain amount of moisture. Take the cloth and wrap it around the part that has been bothering you or another and use some small safety pins to keep it in place. Now obtain another cloth or towel, and wrap it around the damp cloth. Fix this in place with a pin or tie it in some way. When this has been done, retire for the night but only after making sure that you have sufficient covers.

If these instructions are followed, the healing power contained in the water will be released during the night while you or your patient sleeps. This technique has been found to be of great value in the case of sprains and stiff necks and arms. Some members of the Order report that it also works well in the case of a sore throat.

To make the most of this healing method, repeat the technique for *three* days in a row, then rest for three days. If you combine this method with proper concentration and breathing, as you have been taught, you will find that you can bring healing to many parts of your body. Remember, too, to charge and drink the water each night. This will work from the inside while the water packs work from the outside.

While we are speaking of the drinking of water, mention should be made of the fact that as a whole we all tend to drink too much coffee and tea and not enough pure, clear water. Do not be afraid to drink all the water you wish. Some have also found it of value to drink a cup of warm water, each morning, before breakfast. This has the effect of flushing out the system and aiding the digestion.

Besides using water as we have instructed above, just being near an ocean, a lake, or a brook has great value in restoring lost psychic energy. Water that moves tends to increase the flow of energy, while that which is still brings about greater peace and relaxation. Try the following.

Exercise 28

Obtain a bowl of clear water. The bowl should be about five inches deep and about ten inches in diameter. Place the bowl on a table and pull up a comfortable chair. Turn off all the lights in the room, and begin to chant the sound EA (sounded in the word *create*), the "E" on the note C and the "A" on the note A. Chant three times. Rest. Chant five times. Rest. Chant seven times. Rest. If you have done this correctly, the room will be filled with ozone and the fragrance of flowers. You will also feel a sense of greater intensity in the vibrations present there.

Lesson 29

We have now come to the end of the first half of the Second Degree. Before going on to the second half, which will begin instructions in the development and projection of the so-called astral body, there are a few final statements to be made in regard to health and illness. It is my wish that you do not become just another person who can heal, but the very best in your field. Just as my personal master was adept in healing, as was his master, too, so must you, following in my footsteps, become great at this ancient art.

In fact, as you advance in your studies, a time will surely come when others around you will begin to seek out your wisdom and understanding. They will come to you because you are a truly great person and have a reputation for being a genuine occult master. We are working so hard in order to prepare you for this time. When others come to you they will carry with them many of the same burdens that you brought when you first entered our Order. Many will be sick. Many will need love. Many will be in financial need. You must be able to help these people help themselves. How can you do this? First, you can share with them your wisdom. Second, you can make certain that they study this series of lessons. Both these things must be done.

As you attempt to help others, you will also find that those who are ill in body are always ill in mind or have been ill in mind. There are no exceptions to this great law, and it is this that I wish to discuss with you in this lesson.

A few lessons ago we suggested that unless you eat properly, health can never be restored. The same thing is true of thinking. The ancients had a saying: "Mens sana in corpore sano," a healthy mind in a healthy body. But what does this really mean?

By now you have reached a point in these studies in which you have proved to yourself the power of your own mind. Stop to think. You have been able to cause material things to move. You have been able to project and receive thoughts. You have been able to tune in to the Cosmic energy. And now you are even learning to master that thing called illness. If you stop to look back to when you first began this book, would you have imagined that such things as these were possible?

No one really knows what the connection is between the mind and body. Scientists have discovered that various mental diseases, which for countless centuries have placed poor souls in institutions, can in some cases be completely cured by changing the chemistry of the blood. And what is blood manufactured from but the food you eat?

The picture is more complex than this, though. While improper eating can cause a certain mental illness to arise, a mental illness can also cause improper eating. When we become mentally upset, we are actually drawn to eat the wrong foods in an attempt to fulfill the needs of the mind. We do this because we do not really understand what is happening to us. In order to be free from this tyranny we must stop and examine our habits. Let me give you a practical example. If you have a problem losing weight, the following exercise will enable you to take off pounds quickly and easily.

Exercise for Losing Weight

Most people who have a weight problem simply eat too much. They eat all the time, although many times they are not aware that they are doing so. To break this chain, every time you feel hungry, take out the food you want to eat, and place it in front of you. Now take a copy of our sacred logo and hold it in your right hand, if that is the hand you eat with, or your left, if that is the case. Look at the food. Look at the center of the sacred emblem, and mentally ask the question, "Why am I eating this?" Continue to stare at the center of your card while asking this question over and over again. If you truly *need* the food, your mind will tell you so. If you are eating for some other reason your mind will tell you so, too. And your hunger will vanish! People have lost ten to fifty pounds, quickly and easily, by just doing this!

There is a strange circular relationship between the demands of the mind and those of the body. You must understand this completely if you are to be a truly great healer. When the body is not happy, the mind seeks to make up for the lack of fulfillment. When the mind is not complete, the body is pushed to do the same thing. Unless a balance is always maintained between the body and the mind, good health can never be found. In an earlier lesson, we instructed you in the use of the pendulum to find out exactly which foods you should or should not eat. Now you must do the same thing with your mind, for unless you find peace within yourself, you will never find peace in anything outside of yourself. This is the great law. It has always been. It will always be so.

★

When you come upon a case in which all your efforts to bring about a healing of the body fail, you must take the person into your sanctum and begin to talk to him as follows. You must ask him why he thinks he has not gotten well. While he may not wish to tell you the truth, his unconscious mind does know the answer. You must continue to question, to probe, not in a harsh way but in the way of a loving mother or father. The person who sits before you is your child—and yourself! Be gentle. Be kind, and after some time you will hear the person tell you the truth. And what will this be? You will find that this person has created the illness *through incorrect thinking*! He may be in the midst of a bad marriage. She may be worrying about her husband, a child, a member of the family. He may be very angry about someone or something, never able to express this emotion until this very moment. She may have had a fight with someone and never forgiven him. Any one or all of these thoughts can in time actually cause a physical illness.

You may be interested to know that in almost every case of cancer, the most difficult of all diseases to cure, the person is in a state of supreme anxiety and frustration. This continues to build within the mind of the person until the connection between the brain and the mind within the cells is short-circuited. When this happens, all the energy toward expansion, which has been blocked, is directed into the cells, which begin to wildly duplicate and expand, without control—this is cancer! Relieve this inability to expand, and the condition disappears. If the cancer has spread too far, those cells no longer under the control of the brain must be removed, leaving only those that are yet connected with the mind.

In the case of heart disease, the inability to give or receive love is always present. In the ancient Egyptian texts, it was suggested that after death the heart of each person was weighed in the presence of the gods. By this they meant that it was examined to see if it was true and worthy. If it was found lacking, it was believed that the dead could not pass on to heaven. Everyone who has had a heart attack must learn to rebuild his heart through love. This may mean forgiveness. This may mean getting out of a bad marriage. This may mean leaving one's family or giving up a job that is not right. If this is not done in time, a second heart attack usually comes about. Heart attacks are warnings that one is not right with himself and with his God. Restore the balance, and health returns.

If you, reading these words, have suffered from either of these diseases, look back in your own life and see if I have not told the truth. Be honest with yourself this one time, even if you have to shed a few tears over the past.

Finally, let me suggest that even accidents appear to be caused by the mind in order to punish the body. In this case, a battle is going on for control of the soul. The mind wants one thing, the body something else. To win out, the mind causes an accident to take place.

Whenever you come upon a person who has had many accidents, you must ask him about his life *before* the accidents took place. Within his thoughts and emotions you will find the reason for each of the accidents. Remove the wrong idea and the accidents will cease.

Now that we have shared with you some very deep thoughts, let us conclude with a final comment. Remember that the master Jesus said a physician must first heal himself *before* he attempts to assist others. There are far too many blind leading the blind. It is your task to crusade for the Truth, not what people think is so but what really is.

Exercise 29

If you are treating a person who you believe is not telling you the truth in regard to what is causing the illness, think of the question you wish answered. Relax. Close your eyes while in the presence of this friend, and ask him the question once again out loud. When he answers, repeat his answer mentally. If his answer is true, you will see a tiny speck of light within your eyelids, almost like a star. If the answer is false, no light will be seen. Practice this on a number of people for ten days until it works each time.

Lesson 30

With this lesson we come to the end of the of the first half of the Second Degree. For many weeks and months now you have studied and, hopefully, acquired secrets that have long been possessed by mystics all over the world. In presenting and sharing these teachings with you we have sought to accomplish one thing: to give you our wisdom and experience in these matters. Why have we done this?

Throughout the centuries mankind has sought to understand the miracle of that which is called life. Countless philosophies have been spawned, and, wherever two or more were gathered together in the name of Truth, the topic of health and healing has come to the fore. In presenting these instructions to you it has been my personal wish that you master them in order to be free from the chains of illness. It is indeed difficult for one to seek the spiritual path if the body is ailing. So, too, as a crusader for truth, it is your task to do all that is in your power to bring others the same understandings that you yourself have acquired.

As we bring this first half of the Second Degree to an end, it is important that I share with you some final understandings in regard to this matter. Just as my master long ago gave me his understanding, so now do I give you mine. Remember always that whenever a healing takes place, it is not your will but the will of the Cosmic that has brought this miracle about. Though man will come close to the creation of life, never will he be able to strike the infinite spark. Just as the very creation of life represents an expression of divine love, so in the finality a healing represents a similar expression.

But one thing you must know. There are times when, although it may appear to you that a healilng should take place, still it will not come about. One of the greatest frustrations of the would-be healer is the first loss of a life. Many times I have sat in my own sanctum and questioned why it was that the Cosmic did not answer my plea. As you advance in these teachings, you will come to understand that everything that happens in the universe is part of the divine plan. This means that when a person recovers from an illness it is meant that he or she should so recover. If you are not able to somehow find and increase the divine light glowing within each individual, this, too, must be accepted as part of the divine plan.

In the case of the loss of a loved one's life, one must truly realize how little and frail is this thing called a human being. Indeed there are times when, in order to fulfill the Cosmic scheme, the life of a young person seems to have been pointlessly snuffed out. It has always been the teaching of Wicca that life is a continuum. There is no real beginning. There is no real end. Viewed in this way, the coming and going of an illness, of an adversity, or even of that which is called life is to be understood as if one were viewing a motion picture film. Just as the film can be advanced *forward* in the projector, so can it be stopped or moved *backward,* too. While we can see one particular frame and understand its expression of life, it requires divine wisdom to see those frames to come or to truly understand those that have already been.

When you fail to bring a healing about, remember that you have not failed. Also remember that God and the masters have not failed, either. Many times, in order to work out the divine plan, an illness must take place. Just as a growing child can outgrow a suit of clothing, so does a growing soul sometimes outgrow its body. When this happens a new body must be provided and the only way in which this can be done is through that which we call transition or death. Since transition is always the movement from one plane or state of being to another plane, it should be a moment of rejoicing and not one of sadness.

Unfortunately, the vast majority of humans do not know these things that are now being revealed to you. But I tell you this, you have lived before and you will live again!

When healing, you must always work in conjunction with medical science. Never, never think yourself superior to the laws of nature. In fact, never think yourself superior to another person. Remember that the same Divine Master who created the illness created the physician and healing as well. If an individual finds relief through other healing processes, even if you do not agree with the therapy he is using, you must nonetheless let him travel his own path. You know now that you can assist such an individual through what is called absent healing. There is no need for you to make physical contact with this individual. Rather, you must simply become one with the Cosmic and release the thought that a healing will take place.

Finally, I wish to leave you with these enduring ideas. First, you are one with God and Nature. The same laws that govern the universe govern your life. But just as the fish swimming in the ocean knows not where the water is to be found, so do you, not having become truly conscious, sense the Oneness. For you to become a true master healer, you must become one with that which you are. Forget the ego; forget the self. Just as a handful of salt dissolves and spreads throughout the infinite ocean, so must you dissolve and spread yourself into the continuity of selflessness. To the extent that you become more and more aware of this Oneness, to that extent your skill in healing will become truly renowned. Finally, ask no monetary rewards when you have assisted a brother or sister. As the great master Jesus did, always instruct them to tell no one of your help. Just as the stars in the heavens do nothing to advertise their magnitude, so must you continue to maintain the stillness, the silence, the peace profound. In the next lesson we begin instructions in the art of that which has been called the projection of the astral body.

Exercise 30

For this last exercise in this particular phase of your work, we ask you to enter a room in which you are able to feel the light and warmth of the Sun. Place a chair in such a position that the light of the Sun will be reflected on it. Sit down, relax your body, and gaze toward the Sun with eyes closed. When you become relaxed and are able to sense the warmth of the Sun, begin to imagine that the energy of the Sun is totally encompassing you, spinning round and round, starting with your feet and moving toward your head. As this light and energy of the Sun swirls round and round you, it carries you upward from your chair. Imagine yourself actually floating up from your chair and out in the direction of the Sun. As you come closer and closer to the Sun, which you see now in your mind's eye, its warmth and healing rays totally penetrate your being. Now imagine yourself actually entering into the center of the Sun. At the moment of Oneness, when your consciousness reaches the very center of the universe, healing takes place. If you have been troubled with an illness that has persisted for some time, use this exercise daily for at least seven days.

Lesson 31

With this lesson, we present material that has long been suppressed and kept secret by the occult masters and avatars all over the world. We refer to the techniques for releasing and projecting what has been called the "double," the "psychic," or the "astral" body. Since it is our desire to present to you all that is known about this subject, it will be necessary for you to spend many weeks and months in the development of this art. Why? Simply because we wish you to become free.

If we take a few minutes to look back from whence we have come, you will find that our purpose in all these lessons has been to enable you to become independent from all but your own will. Our initial discussions and exercises, if understood and faithfully carried out, have begun to develop within you a strange sense of security and profound peace. For instance, you have long ago proved to yourself that you have the ability to influence others through the use of your mind. In recent lessons, you also learned that even illness can be overcome in ways you most likely never imagined.

All these things have as their intention one goal—to make you free. Free from what? Free from ignorance, from want, from poor health, from unhappiness. All that you wish in life can be yours if you will study and faithfully follow our instructions.

When we talk of projection of the psychic body, we have begun to enter an area that is probably the least known of all the mysteries. This is so because the very nature of astral projection is such that one cannot read about it in books and lessons. Rather it must be experienced. And this is our intention in these lessons: to give you just that: the experience of a genuine astral projection. But we cannot leave you here. We must also give you the hows and whys of this ancient art of soul travel.

Let us begin our journey by telling you that astral projection is among the very oldest of occult arts. Going back into ancient times, we find countless references to the fact that among the powers of the masters is found the *ability to leave the physical body at will*. Even organized religion accepts the belief that there is a spiritual form of some kind existing within the physical body. Also, most religions teach that at death this spiritual form is somehow separated from the physical body. While some religions further believe that this spiritual form passes into different planes of being, still others maintain that such an exit marks the end of all life.

It is important to stress, at this point, that we know that life does indeed continue after that which has been called death takes place. We know this to be true (just as you will, too) because we have left the physical body while it is still alive and have traveled to some of the other planes. Thus we know that within every being there exists an exact duplicate of the physical body, made up of divine energy and light. It is this double that has been called the astral body. But let us explain still further.

Modern science teaches that everything that exists in the material world is made up of two things, matter and energy. Imagine that you have before you a wooden table. Touch this table with your fingers. Feel how hard it is. Now put your ear to it. You will hear no sound, nor does the table move to show any signs of life. Now, imagine yourself standing before a giant tree. You touch the tree and find the same hardness, yet you know the tree is alive because it has grown and continues growing. The difference between the tree and the table is that the tree still has the form of energy we call life.

If we had a special kind of microscope that would allow us to look deep within the table, we would find that some kind of energy still exists there, even though it cannot be seen by the eyes. This special kind of energy was long ago called an atom, meaning the smallest kind of energy. Science says that everything that exists begins with atoms, and this includes the human being as well.

Carrying our example still further, we find that when we look at the human body there is matter and there is energy, too. In fact, some of the energy we have is derived from the intake of other matter, that is, the food and liquids we eat and drink, the air we consume. Indeed, every human is a self-contained power generator that actually throws off excess energy. In the previous lessons you have learned how you can use this excess energy to help yourself or another. But while most people don't even know about this special energy, it exists all around us and can, under special circumstances, be measured and actually seen.

What does all this have to do with the astral body? Simply this: *All the so-called "psychic" senses, including the astral body, are nothing more than energy counterparts of physical forms.* By this we mean that if we could separate our physical eyes from the energy that surrounds them and enables them to work, this energy is the psychic sense of sight. Thus, if we can learn to separate this *unseen* energy from its material form (which *can* be seen) we can immediately enter into these other planes. So, too, when the psychic healing takes place, you have not healed the body but have healed the energy that makes up the body.

In the case of the astral body, it is nothing more than the sum total of all the nerve energy existing in the physical body. This is why we have stressed the importance of a healthy body together with a healthy mind.

When an astral or psychic projection does take place, the *greater part* of the energy we have referred to is somehow separated *momentarily* from its physical form. We say the greater part since in a state of projection the psychic body is always connected with the physical body by a special cord (about which you will learn more in later lessons). We say momentarily for if the disconnection was permanent, the death of the physical body would result.

Do you understand what we are saying? Have we made ourselves clear? As we want you to understand the truth regarding these matters, let us give you one more example. Imagine that you have a portable radio, the kind that works on batteries. The battery is the energy. As long as it is placed within the radio and working, the radio works. If you remove the battery, the radio becomes dead. Place the battery within another radio and that one comes alive. Such is the nature of life and death. When you truly understand these things, as you will when you have finished this degree, you gain great freedom and even greater wisdom.

Perhaps the most interesting understanding of the psychic body is that of the ancient Egyptians. Conceiving of the human personality as made up of various elements, they had something called the "Ka," which was not the soul of each person, but rather its *vehicle*. In hieroglyphic representations, the "Ka" is depicted as as winged bird, usually hovering over the mummy (the deceased's physical body.) They further believed that this "Ka" could travel independently of the physical body and after death even return to visit the physical body.

In Tibet, the death of one of the lamas (high priests) is celebrated in a way that sheds light on our discussion. It is their belif that death (the permanent separation of the physical and psychic bodies) does not occur at once but over many days. During this time, the lama will perform certain rituals and magical practices intended to make this transition from one plane to the next an easy one. You will eventually learn more of these special rituals and how you can aid one who has passed on (or is about to do so.) We should also mention that the practice of saying prayers or holding masses for the dead comes from this ancient understanding, although modern religions have long ago lost or forgotten the true understanding of these things. Also, mention should be made of our preference for the use of the word *transition* to *death*. We prefer to use this word since we know that nothing that exists in the universe ever dies or can be destroyed.

Exercise 31

In order to become aware of the psychic energy that surrounds the physical body, we ask that you try the following exercise once each day for the next week. This exercise has been found to strengthen and increase the energy needed to enable you to make successful projections at will. Take a glass of cold water into a room that has been darkened. While sitting in a comfortable chair, place both hands around the glass, and place it in your lap so you can look down into it. Take a deep breath. While holding it as long as possible, gaze into the glass. After repeating this a few times, you should begin to see a violet or blue mist around the glass and your hands. Practice this once each night until this mist is seen. Once you see it, continue to concentrate, along with the deep breathing, until you can make the mist increase and grow brighter.

Lesson 32

In the last lesson we presented the basic understandings of the phenomenon of astral projection and what the so-called psychic body really is.

While *conscious* projection of the astral body is somewhat rare, every living person has experienced the *unconscious* phenomenon to some extent. Every night during sleep, the psychic body moves out of coincidence to some degree in order to recharge the nervous system with Cosmic energy. The energy that is brought into the body through this means is absolutely necessary to good health and mental wellbeing. It is for this reason that we become unusually nervous if we are unable to sleep. Coffee works to fuse together to a greater degree the physical and the astral, so that sleep does not take place.

As a result of your ability to fully relax, an ability that you have been increasing through the use of these techniques, you should in time be able to actually *decrease* your sleep requirement. It is generally said that one requires less sleep when older, although it is not usually explained why this is so. The reason is that as we grow older the astral is permitted greater freedom of movement as the adhesion between it and the energy in the physical body decreases naturally with the aging process.

As we have suggested, two kinds of projection take place: spontaneous (involuntary) and experimental (voluntary). Below are some of the forms these projections take.

Flying Dreams. Have you ever gone to sleep and dreamed that you were flying upward through the air? The dream might be so vivid that you actually feel the rush of the wind past you. In fact, you might even see the tops of roofs or the ground far below. As you soar higher and higher, you begin to feel as light as a balloon and unusually free and limitless. If you have had this kind of experience, you have projected your astral body.

Falling Dreams. Have you ever dreamed that you were falling through the air? You have no awareness of how you reached such a great height but simply find yourself moving toward the earth, faster and faster, until you crash. Most likely you awoke from your dream before the actual crach took place. With this kind of dream experience, most persons awake suddenly, often frightened and disturbed. If you have had this kind of dream, you have had an astral projection.

Repercussion. You are most likely lying on your back. You are just about to fall asleep. You feel yourself floating upward. Suddenly, your entire body jerks as if hit by something, and you awaken somewhat disturbed and frightened. This experience is caused by the sudden return of the psychic body into the physical body and is one of the most common projection experiences.

Seeing Yourself Asleep. You have fallen asleep and dream that you can see yourself in the bed sleeping. This kind of dream, although difficult to remember, often accompanies a projection. In fact, it is one of the first steps in the voluntary control of astral projection.

Bumping into Another Person. You are walking down a street, not really paying any attention to where you are doing or what you are doing. Suddenly, accidentally, you walk into another person and feel for an instant that some part of you has "gone right through" that person. This, too, is due to a temporary jarring loose of the astral body.

Continuous Motion Aftereffect. Most likely you have been riding in a bus or car for a number of hours (sometimes even flying in a plane.) Your trip ends, and you get out of the vehicle but continue to feel as if you are still moving forward. This is due to the astral form being somewhat dislodged from the physical as a result of the vibrations that are generated by the bouncing of the physical body for long periods of time. This is, perhaps, one of the most common experiences, though little known for what it is.

Fainting or Passing Out. You feel yourself becoming weaker and weaker. Your mind begins to spin. You feel yourself passing out of the

★

body. You lose consciousness and fall to the ground. Again, you have projected the astral body.

Spinning and Making Yourself Dizzy. You probably did this when you were a young child. You turn yourself around and around until you become dizzy and fall to the floor. As you spin around, it is as if you are floating out of yourself. This, too, is yet another way to cause the astral to separate from the physical. In fact, spinning around until starting to become dizzy was one of the techniques to develop the psychic powers used by the mystics and seers in ancient times and is still practiced by such groups as the whirling dervishes today. If you are not a young person, though, we suggest that you try this with great care and make sure that you stop spinning before you actually pass out.

The experience of one or more of the above should be sufficient to convince you of the reality of astral projection. Remember, though, that in these instances, you did not have conscious control of the experience. It is the ability to make a projection happen at will that distinguishes a true master from someone who has simply read about this unusual phenomenon. In the next lesson, we will continue our discussion of the use and theory of astral projection. Until that time, we ask that you try the following.

Exercise 32

Find a comfortable chair in a darkened room. Remove your shoes and any tight clothing. Totally relax yourself, as you have already been taught, by concentrating on each part of the body in turn and relaxing it. When you are sure that you are completely relaxed, take a deep breath and hold it as long as you can. Now exhale this breath *through the mouth.* As you do so, say the word *ra,* and use your willpower to push out the astral form from the physical body.

If you have done this correctly, you will actually feel yourself moving out of the physical body. Or you may see something move out and stand in front of you. Try this experiment once or twice each day.

★

Lesson 33

In the last lesson we gave you the first step in projecting the so-called astral body. We say "so-called" because the astral body is not really "starlike" at all. Rather, it is composed of atoms and molecules just like everything else that exists in the Cosmos. In many ways it duplicates the physical body; hence it is sometimes called the "double."

Just as we do not usually "know" our physical bodies, so is the genuine nature of the astral being little understood and appreciated. It is through this vehicle that much that has been called psychic takes place. Therefore, it is of the greatest importance that we come to realize its great power in our lives and learn to use it to our full advantage.

For the most part we seldom allude to the existence of this other self. Since we are so overwhelmed by the physical side of our existence, we fail to comprehend the need for another side. This is why the lessons you are receiving are so important. They feed your inner being in a special sort of way with a kind of food unavailable anywhere else. Also, this is why you must remain faithful to these studies, for they promise to reward you with all the happiness and peace of mind you are seeking.

If you tried the last exercise, your experience could have been one of the following.

No Projection at All. This can be due to the fact that the physical body was too tired. You would feel very sleepy or perhaps actually went to sleep while practicing. Solution: Do not practice when you are tired.

Tingling or Cold Numbness in the Hands or Legs. This means that you did not fully relax all parts of the body before breathing in the special way instructed. Therefore you awakened only the hands and feet of the astral. Solution: Spend more time relaxing yourself thoroughly before beginning the breathing exercise.

Feeling of Being Only Slightly Outside the Physical Body. In this case you did not move out far enough. Fear or newness caused the astral to draw back into the physical. Solution: Read this lesson over and over again. Push yourself out with greater effort.

Partial Success in Seeming to Leave the Physical Body. Here you would have received some impressions, but again the astral did not move far enough away from the physical body. Solution: More practice.

Beginning to Leave the Physical Body but Suddenly Returning with a Mental Shock. Here the element of fear or a feeling of coldness caused the astral to return too suddenly, thereby actually causing the physical body to jolt.

Total Success in Moving the Astral Body Out and Away from the Physical.

The Nature of and Reason for Fear

By now you can see that your failure to find success in the last exercise can be due to essentially one of two causes: fear or lack of practice. Let us speak of the former first.

When we fear something we are saying to ourselves that there exists something we do not understand and that we believe this something is harmful. What is wrong with this kind of thinking? Simply this: While it is true that in astral projection we come face to face with something new, an experience that promises what appears to be a brand-new adventure, the fact that we do not consciously know what is happening (or likely to happen) does not preclude our knowing in another kind of way.

By this we mean to suggest that the phenomenon of leaving and entering the physical body has been taking place for millions of years, and you, yourself, have been experiencing it each and every sleeping night of your life. If you recall the first lesson in which we spoke of the many daily occurrences that are related to the phenomenon of astral projection, we mentioned at least a few in your own experience. You have been leaving and entering the physical body as long as you have lived, but you did not consciously know this to be so.

The key word is *know*. When we say "know" we mean actually "experience." Just as you did not believe that one mind could actually project and receive thoughts, or that you could heal yourself or another, or that there exists a whole other world within you, so did you not realize what actually happens each and every night you sleep. But now through the help of your Order, you can experience it for yourself.

What will you discover? First, that the astral self is totally free to travel anywhere you will it to. Second, that by leaving the body as we instruct in these lessons you do not cause the death of the physical body, since the physical body lives only because of the nightly astral travel. Third, that to use and practice this technique is to become free of the limitations of the physical world.

So, you see, fear really has little to do with the experience of astral projection. We should only fear that which cannot be explained or understood. This is not the case with the experience at hand, though, for the techniques of projecting the astral body have been taught and practiced for centuries.

In the finality always be sure to distinguish between caution and fear. The former makes sense, such as in guarding against being burned by touching a hot pot without a holder. Fear is when you refuse to cook ever again. This is foolish and shows ignorance rather than knowledge.

Exercise 33

Try the following experiment at least three times. Just before retiring for the evening, but not when you are especially tired, take a shower, and leave yourself slightly damp. Sit in a comfortable chair with a high back so you can rest your head, or lie on a bed or couch. Thoroughly relax yourself as you have been taught, and begin taking *seven* deep breaths, exhaling each as slowly as possible. When you have finished breathing, close your eyes and picture another room in your house that you know well. See and feel yourself standing there. See all the details, the colors. When you actually feel that you are there, try to see yourself sitting in the chair or lying on the bed. See yourself exactly as you would appear if someone held up a mirror in front of you. Continue to practice each night, seeing yourself in the same room and recalling every detail. If you wish you can also try seeing and feeling the room of a distant friend.

Lesson 34

In the last lesson, we presented instructions as to how you can begin to visualize yourself in another place and begin to actually feel yourself there. Continue practicing this very important exercise. When practicing, some students have found it helpful to picture themselves standing before a particular object of art or picture of a person whom they know very well. You will find greater success if you work

★

with a place that is familiar to you and that you have visited many times.

If you are having difficulty with this exercise, alternate projecting your consciousness with actually getting up and physically walking into the room to which you wish to project.

If you are practicing after retiring in the evening, you may wish to get up from your bed and walk to the room into which you are projecting. When you do so, be sure to look at exactly how the room appears. Note how dark or light it is and where the furniture is placed. See everything as it actually is. Then return to your bed, relax yourself, and begin once again to project yourself to this place.

We cannot say enough about the desire and will to succeed in these lessons. Unlike many of the other studies you have had or many that will follow, astral projection requires an intense effort on your part. You must wish to leave your body and return if you are to find success.

Dreams and the Dream Control Method

While we have taken a number of pages to discuss the occult significance of sleep and exactly what happens each evening as you "die" and are "born again" in the physical body, we have not as yet entered into a discussion as to exactly what happens when you dream.

As you no doubt know, dreams have long been held to reveal the past, present, and future. But exactly where do dreams originate, and how can we use them to master the art of astral projection?

When we sleep, the other part of us, the master or higher self, often indulges in the acting out of those things that we have been unable to do while in the waking state. For instance, have you ever gone to bed slightly hungry and dreamed you were eating something? This is a most commonplace occurrence.

Besides dreams that serve as fulfillments of wishes, there are also dreams that come about as a result of the release of ideas that have been locked in the unconscious mind for various reasons. For example, suppose you dream of acting out a certain scene over and over again. You know that this action does not originate in this lifetime. What you may not know is that this particular dream is a carryover from previous lives. Yes, it is possible to dream of something or someone whom you knew in another lifetime. Such a dream often contains the seeds of something that you should come to grips with in order to advance in this lifetime.

How to Remember Your Dreams

While every person dreams every night, many of us do not remember our dreams. To do this you must program yourself just before
going to sleep, thinking thoughts such as, "I will remember my
dreams. I will awaken after each dream is concluded and will be able
to recall all that has taken place." It has also been found helpful to
keep near your bed a small writing pad and pencil, to jot down any
impressions that may come to you right after they have taken place. In
other words, you can train yourself to remember more of your dream
life by simply causing yourself to do so. Once again, you must practice
in order to become a master.

But besides remembering the dreams that normally flow to us, it
has been found possible to actually program our dreams in such a way
that our unconscious mind works for us while we sleep. It is this latter
technique we are concerned with here.

Once again, the imagination and the technique of visualization, a
technique you are becoming quite proficient in by now, must be
employed. Just as you have probably allowed yourself to imagine
various things while daydreaming, so now you must actually program
yourself to dream a particular dream. Following is the dream we wish
you to program.

Exercise 34

Have you ever gone to an office building or store in which there is
an elevator? If you have, you will remember standing in front of the
door with other people, seeing the door open, going inside and pushing the button, seeing the door close, and feeling the elevator begin to
rise upward. After a certain passage of time, you reached your floor,
the door opened, and you stepped out. This is exactly the dream we
wish you to recreate in your mind, but with one difference: In your
dream you are the only passenger, and after entering the elevator, you
lie down on the floor on your back. You feel yourself going to sleep;
you feel the elevator rising upward and upward, higher and higher.
When you reach your stop, you get up from the floor of the elevator
and step outside.

You must begin to practice this exact dream every night. You must
see yourself wearing the same clothes, going into the same elevator.
See the color of the elevator; push the same button; feel the elevator
rise and carry you upward. It is imperative that you use exactly the

same dream over and over again. If you vary the dream in any way, you will reduce the effectiveness of this very important technique. Once you have succeeded in moving out of the elevator, travel wherever you will. Return to the elevator, lie down on the floor, and when the elevator reaches the ground floor, you will awaken naturally. Be sure to practice this technique. We want you to be successful in this work more than anything else.

Try to arrange your sleeping quarters so that you can be undisturbed and free from any sudden noise or anything that will jar the astral back into the physical. Avoid the use of an alarm clock. Use a clock radio if you must, or better still, train yourself to awaken naturally by giveing yourself the suggestion the night before.

In conclusion, there is no shortcut to developing the psychic abilities. Trees that grow fast, like the willow, have shallow roots and are easily blown down when the first strong wind comes along. The oak, though, grows ever so slowly and has deep roots; while it may bend during a storm, it is rarely blown over.

One's psychic ability must become like the oak tree, well grounded.

Omnia tempus revelat.

4.
Fortune-telling with Cards

★

The History of Cards

From time immemorial there has been a universal curisoity as to what the future has in store. It is human nature to want to know what tomorrow and the future in general may bring.

Beyond the portals of today, Destiny holds the secret of love, health, wealth, travel, and marriage; happiness with sweethearts, husgands, or wives; success, fame, fortune, and inheritances. From ancient times, a deck of playing cards has seemed to hold the answers to these interesting questions of life.

A deck of ordinary playing cards has come to mean a great many things. The almost endless mathematical combinations that are possible is nothing short of a mystery. In the past among certain people a deck of cards was considered the "instrument of the Devil." This was partly because in the frontier days, before there were many books, newspapers, or other diversions, men amused themselves with various games played with cards and gambling often led to gunplay in those rough days when most men carried a gun for protection. However, gambling did not originate with playing cards. Men used to gamble on many events, on the weather, for example, or the successful outcome of a venture.

Fortune-telling with playing cards is no more evil than some other practices in vogue today. One may read evil into anything. If we look back into history, we will learn further interesting things about cards.

Discoveries show that many generations of ancients used some form of playing cards for amusement or divination. Various forms of playing cards closely resembling those of today, it has been discovered, were used by the ancient Celtic races. The gypsies of central Russia also devised a set of playing cards that were later used in clairvoyance and in divining the future. The fame of the gypsies' predictions spread to Greece and the Roman Empire. A set of simple "cards" fashioned in stone were used by the ancient Egyptians. The Chaldeans used a series of "cards" molded from clay to designate certain things that they saw in the stars.

It remained for some of the early Christians to give the cards a special meaning or reason for being. Formerly there was only one suit to a deck of cards. Their representations were as follows.

Ace represents One or All: One God, One Universe.
Two Spot represents God (Father) and Son.
Three Spot represents God (Father), Son, and Holy Ghost.
Four Spot represents the four corners of the earth.
Five Spot represents God in the midst of the world.
Six Spot represents the number of days it took for God to create the world.
Seven Spot represents mystery or the day of rest.
Eight Spot represents the seven planets and the Moon.
Nine Spot represents the major constellations in the sky.
Ten Spot represents the completed universe of ten planets and satellites.

And then, in honor of the nation, the Royal House was represented by

The Jack: the court servant
The Queen: the female ruler of the nation
The King: the male ruler of the nation

As time marched on, the various suits were added to the deck of cards, each of which corresponded to certain ideals dear to the hearts of the inventors.

The modern deck of playing cards contains four suits corresponding to the four seasons of the year. Twelve face cards represent the twelve journeys of the Sun or months of the year. There are fifty-two cards in a deck, denoting the number of weeks in the year, and 365 spots, representing the number of days in the year.

There are many other symbolical mysteries in a deck of cards that space does not permit me to indicate here. Suffice it to know that the deck of cards was scientifically conceived. The only evil that can be connected with them is the use to which man in his ignorance puts them.

For many generations past, it has been a well-known fact that a person who could tell fortunes by any method has had a good deal of popularity and entertainment from this ability. Various systems of fortune-telling have come down to us from the past, many of them long since forgotten, but the pleasure of card reading has survived. Even today there are thousands of people who are strongly interested in this diversion, either because they actually believe in such predictions, as the ancients did, or because they are interested for entertainment. At any rate it is always interesting to have your fortune told.

★
The Karma System

Using Thirty-two Cards

This system of card reading is known as the Karma System of Fortune-telling with Ordinary Playing Cards and is perhaps the simplest system known. On a large sheet of paper or cardboard, draw twelve squares and number them as shown on the following page.

The numbers in these squares represent days or weeks or months. Fortunes told with this system are supposed to happen within twelve months. If a person wants the numbers to represent weeks, he should state this at the beginning of the layout; likewise, if the person wishes it to represent days or months.

As you gain practice with this system, you will automatically memorize these spaces and numbers so that you will not need the chart of squares before you.

You now take a deck of ordinary cards and remove all of the two, three, four, five, and six spots and lay them to one side. You will now have left in your deck the Aces, Kings, Queens, Jacks, Tens, Nines, Eights, and Sevens.

Hand the deck of cards to your client, and ask him or her to shuffle the cards thoroughly and at the same time to make a silent wish. If you are telling your own fortune, shuffle them yourself and make a silent wish. For simplicity we will suppose that you are telling your own fortune. After thoroughly shuffling and wishing, cut the cards in three piles. Place them so that the motion of cutting the cards will be toward you. Now turn up the three piles, and count the spots on the upturned cards. Jacks count 20, Queens count 25, and Kings count 30. The total of these three cards will be your "lucky number" for the day, the week, or the month, as the case may be. If the nine of Hearts turns up, you will get your wish immediately. If you do not cut the card, you will find out later when you will get your wish, if at all.

Put the three piles back together, and shuffle them until "hunch" tells you to stop. Remember that a Seven Spot is an indicator card and

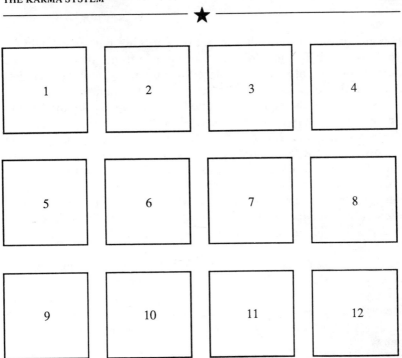

must never be put in any of the squares on your chart. When you have finished shuffling, hold the deck in your right hand, backs up. Start dealing them off one at a time, laying them on the table before you, face up. Continue to deal them off one at a time until a Seven Spot turns up. This is you indicator card. Now take the very next card, and lay it face up in Square 1 on your chart. Proceed until you come to another Seven Spot, and lay the card following that in Square 2 on your chart. When you have gone through the deck, pick it up and shuffle it again until another hunch tells you to stop, and go through the same process with the Seven Spots again. Continue this process until all of the squares on your chart are filled with cards.

Note that if two Seven Spots turn up next to each other, that drawing is "killed." Replace the two Seven Spots in the deck (not together), and proceed to the next Seven Spot. Do not use the card following a double Seven. Ordinarily you will go through the deck three times to fill all the spaces in your chart—but if you have several double Sevens you may have to go through the deck several more times before you have all the squares filled. A double seven shows that

★

you did not shuffle enough—or that the cards are not placed right for your particular fortune. You will not be able to get them out of the deck until they are properly placed according to your destiny. Remember, do not place a Seven Spot in any of the squares.

When all of the squares are filled, you are ready for the second operation, which is very simple indeed. Shuffle the deck until you get the feeling that you should stop. Then deal off the cards one by one in the order that they come from the top of the deck, and place one card over each of the cards already on your chart. You may lay them crosswise or partially overlapped so that you can still see what card is underneath. Start in the upper left-hand corner at Square 1, and cover each of the twelve cards in this manner with one card each. The cards that you have left in your hand you may lay aside, for you will not need them anymore.

In this second operation you may place the seven spots on the chart if they show up. You are finished with them as indicator cards, since you are dealing those top cards onto your chart from the deck in the order that they are in. Once you have covered each of the twelve cards, you are now ready to begin your translation. Refer to the list below.

Meaning of the Cards

Below are listed the literal meanings of the various cards in the four suits. You will combine meanings and balance them according to what cards appear together in any of the squares on your chart. You will soon learn how to read the cards after you have them laid out.

HEARTS

Ace. Always pertains to home affairs. The card over it or under it will denote the nature of the home affairs.

King. Thoughts of, influence of, or association with an elderly or middle-aged man of medium-light complexion, possibly bald-headed or partly gray-haired.

Queen. Thoughts of, influence of, or association with a medium-light-complexioned lady. The part played by the lady will be indicated by the other cards in the square with her.

Jack. Thoughts of, influence of, or association with a medium-light-complexioned young man. If a red card is in the same square with him, it is favorable; if a black card, it is unfavorable.

Ten. Always denotes a brilliant future. Hopes, ambitions, and plans. If accompanied by a red card, there will be no interference with these plans. If accompanied by a black card, some delays in realizing ambitions.

Nine. This is the Wish Card. If it shows up anywhere, the wish made while shuffling the cards will come true but will be controlled by the card appearing with it in the square. Also, it will come true within the number of days, weeks, or months indicated by the number of the square in which it appears. If in the second square, it will come to fruition in two days, weeks, or months.

Eight. Denotes love, affection, sympathy, consolation, and favors from other people. It will be tempered or influenced by the card with it in the square.

Seven. Denotes a very pleasant surprise. If a face card appears with it in the square, you may describe the person the favor comes from. If some other card appears with it, you will be surprised to hear a particular piece of news, the nature of which will be indicated by the card.

DIAMONDS

Ace. Always pertains to a letter or message that is to be received. The other card in the square with it denotes the nature of the letter or message. If a face card appears with it, the letter or message will come from a person fitting that description.

King. Thoughts of, influence of, or association with a very light-complexioned or possibly a gray-haired, middle-aged, or elderly gentleman.

Queen. Thoughts of, influence of, or association with a light blonde lady. The card appearing with it denotes the nature of this association.

Jack. Thoughts of, influence of, or association with a very blond young man. If with a red card, good results. If with a black card, disappointing results.

Ten. Big money is denoted by the Ten of Diamonds. Ease or difficulty in obtaining it will be shown by the accompanying card in the square. If a red card, ease; if a black card, difficulty.

Nine. Indicates inheritance or receipt of extra money aside from the regular source of income. If a red card is with it, the amount will be quite large; if a black card is with it, the amount will be small or there may be some trouble over it. If a face card is with it, the money comes through the influence of a person who fits the description of the card.

Eight. Receipt of money owing or a gift of a small amount of money. If a face card is with it, the money comes from a person who fits the description of that card.

Seven. Receipt of a surprise present. If with a face card, it means the renewal of an old friendship that will be pleasing.

CLUBS

Ace. Denotes a marriage or news of a marriage that is reasonably close. If it appears with a card that fits your description, it may be you or some member of your family who will marry.

King. Thoughts of, influence of, or association with a middle-aged, medium-dark gentleman. The card appearing with it in the square denotes the way he will show up in your fortune.

Queen. Thoughts of, influence of, or association with a medium-brunette lady. If with a red card, it is favorable; if with a black card, it is unfavorable.

Jack. Thoughts of, influence of, or association with a medium-dark young man. Nature of the association is indicated by the card in the square with it.

Ten. Usually denotes business worry. If with a red card, the worry will not last long. If with a black card, the worry may continue for some time.

Nine. This card has no special meaning of its own. It only means "for sure." It intensifies the meaning of the card appearing in the square with it. If a face card is with it, you will definitely meet that particular person.

Eight. Anxiety. You feel uncertain and somewhat anxious about something, probably in business or working conditions.

Seven. Denotes a slight delay in some plans. The nature of these plans will be revealed by the card appearing with it in the square.

SPADES

Ace. Signifies trouble, slander, gossip, and intrigues. If a red card is in the square with it, these will not amount to much. If a black card is with it, it will annoy you for quite some time.

King. Thoughts of, influence of, or association with a rather dark-complexioned middle-aged or elderly gentleman.

Queen. Thoughts of, influence of, or association with a brunette lady. If with a red card, results are favorable. If with a black card, the results will be unsatisfactory.

Jack. Thoughts of, influence of, or association with a very dark-complexioned young man; he will likely have brown eyes, black hair, and ruddy skin. The nature of the association will be revealed by the card in the square with it.

Ten. This card denotes news of death or very severe illness. If a red card is with it, the news will not affect you much—it will be someone distant in your affections. If a black card goes with it, the news comes from a relative or close friend.

Nine. Reverses in personal affairs or worries in business. If with a red card, they will not be serious. If with a black card, they will continue for a time.

Eight. Aggressive actions or threats. Nothing necessarily serious, mostly persistent annoyances to your peace of mind. If with a red card, they will soon be over. If with a black card, you will be annoyed for some time.

Seven. Disappointment in some plans. If with a red card, they will eventually materialize even though delayed. If with a black card, you might as well abandon the idea for the present and concentrate on something else.

After a little practice you will memorize what each card indicates and will not have to refer to the above lists.

Most people who are interested in fortune-telling with cards are inclined to be mediums. While laying out the cards for a friend or any other person who wishes you to read the cards for them, if you feel impelled to add something more to what the cards mean, be sure to add these impressions to the fortune, for often to a psychically inclined person the cards act as a "concentration point," through which information of a valuable nature can come.

After you have looked up all the meanings of the cards in the square, take notice of the layout, which is also a clue to interpretation of the fortune. Two face cards that appear together in a square indicate a brother and sister if they are both of the same suit; a wife and husband, if opposite suits. Two Queens mean sisters or companions or partners. Two Jacks mean brothers, pals, or partners. King and Jack means father and son or possibly partners.

After you have analyzed the meaning of each of the cards that are on top and can be seen in the different squares, flip through the entire pile of cards in each position. What you are looking for is whether the *same card* appears in the *same position* in two adjacent squares, for example, the Jack appearing as the bottom card in Square 1 and also in Square 2.

The meanings of cards of the same denomination when beside each other are as follows.

Aces. Change of place, which could be either residence or business. If two black ones, the change is unfavorable. If a black and a red one, the change is doubtful and must be given careful thought and consideration.

Kings. You will be conversing or having some dealing with an officer of the law.

Queens. You will have a pleasant new friendship that will be very inspiring to you. If both Queens are black, the friend will be dark-skinned. If red Queens, the friend will be medium-complexioned.

Jacks. You will change your affections from one person to another. Denotes a change in close associations. If both Jacks are red, the change will be permanent; if black, the change will be temporary. If they alternate red and black, the change will keep you in an uncertain attitude.

Tens. Change of times. By this is meant change in conditions and environment around you. If both are red, the change will be most successful. If they are both black, the change will not prove satisfactory, and you are advised to prevent it. If alternate in color, the change will be satisfactory.

Nines. A change in business is about to take place. If they are both black, it will be necessary for you to keep close watch on business conditions to prevent complications in the changes that are coming. If they are both red, the change will be satisfactory but not necessarily beneficial.

Eights. You are to take a trip into another state. If both are red, the trip will prove to be both pleasant and profitable. If both are black, the trip will be attended with delays, disappointments, and uncertain conditions. If the colors alternate, the trip will be pleasant but not necessarily profitable.

Sevens. A series of sudden developments, all of them of a minor nature, will change some of your personal plans. These changes come as a surprise. If both are red, the changes are for the best. If they are both black, the changes will delay you somewhat, and you are advised to be reluctant in entertaining such changes. If the colors alternate, the changes will cause about the same results as your original plans.

The next thing that you will look for in this layout is the number of face cards showing. If there are six or more face cards showing, you are going to be in a crowd of people very soon. It may be a party, dance, lecture, or a similar event at which large crowds of people gather. If all of the Queens are showing, the crowd will be equally divided as to males and females. If one or two Queens are missing, the crowd will be mostly of men. If all of the Queens are showing and one or more Kings are missing, the crowd will be mostly women.

You will not count the number of Hearts showing in the layout. If there are six or more Hearts showing, you will have a goodly amount of love and affection throughout the coming days, weeks, or months, according to whatever time you have set for this fortune to cover.

Next count the number of Diamonds. If there are six or more Diamonds showing, you will handle a great deal of money during the time covered by the fortune.

Last count the number of Spades showing. If there are six or more Spades showing, you will be much concerned about your domestic life during the time covered by the fortune.

Example of a Fortune

An imaginary layout is outlined below. Lay the cards out as indicated, and follow the interpretation of this sample fortune closely, so that you will become familiar with the translating of the cards. Remember that the cards on the bottom are the most important ones.

Some people adopt an unreasonable and fantastic approach to their fortunes. They lay out the cards, ask to have the future of the next few days foretold, and wish for a million dollars. This, of course, is ridiculous, and the person having his fortune told must be instructed not to wish for impossible things but for reasonable things that could happen to him if Fate sees fit. The cards will tell if he is to get that particular wish or not. If one isn't serious or reasonable, he should not have his fortune told.

In Square 1 put the Eight of Diamonds. On top of it lay the Queen of Clubs.
In Square 2 put the Ten of Clubs. On top of it put the Ace of Diamonds.

In Square 3 put the Ten of Diamonds. On top of it put the King of Clubs.

In Square 4 put the Queen of Diamonds. On top of it put the King of Spades.

In Square 5 put the Ten of Hearts. On top of it put the Seven of Diamonds.

In Square 6 put the Eight of Hearts. On top of it put the Jack of Spades.

In Square 7 put the Nine of Spades. On top of it put the Jack of Hearts.

In Square 8 put the Ace of Clubs. On top of it put the Queen of Spades.

In Square 9 put the Jack of Diamonds. On top of it put the Ace of Spades.

In Square 10 put the Nine of Clubs. On top of it put the Queen of Hearts.

In Square 11 put the Ace of Hearts. On top of it put the Seven of Hearts.

In Square 12 put the Nine of Hearts. On top of it put the Nine of Diamonds.

We are now ready to begin the translating of the cards. Starting with *Square 1,* begin the reading in this manner.

There is a dark lady, probably a medium brunette, through whose influence you are to receive a small amount of money. The money may come from her or it may come through her influence; at any rate, in receiving this money you will have some association with this brunette lady. Since this is in Square 1, it will occur within one day, one week, or one month.

Square 2. The Ace of Diamonds means that you are to receive within two days, weeks, or months a letter containing a great deal of information about business worries that the writer is deeply concerned about. The letter probably comes from a close friend or relative, at any rate, someone close enough that his business worry would concern you. Notice if on the bottom of each side of the Ten of Clubs there is a red card—this indicates that the person's business worries will not last long. (If there should be any black cards surrounding the Ten of Clubs on the bottom, the worries of the person in whom you are interested will not be overcome soon).

Square 3. Through the influence of a medium-dark, elderly, or middle-aged gentleman, you are to receive a rather large sum of money. This is to come within three days, weeks, or months.

Square 4. There are two face cards in this square. Within four days, weeks, or months, you are to have some pleasant association with a rather dark middle-aged gentleman and his gray-haired wife. The nature of this association is not shown; however, it will probably be a reasonably pleasant association since there is a red card beside the Queen on the bottom.

Square 5. The Seven of Diamonds on top of the Ten of Hearts indicates that within five days, weeks, or months you will be in receipt of a gift or assistance will agreeably affect your future. Denotes a very encouraging outlook for your future since there is a red card on every side of the Ten of Hearts on the bottom.

Square 6 is the Jack of Spades on top of the Eight of Hearts. This denotes that you are to have close association with a dark-complexioned young man who is very much in love with someone. He will tell you all about it. (If the person having her fortune told happens to be a young unmarried lady in love with a dark, handsome young man, this square would mean something important is to happen within six days, weeks, or months.)

Square 7. The Jack of Hearts is on top of the Nine of Spades so a medium-light young man of your acquaintance is going to have some reverses or troubles in his personal affairs and may come to you for consolation. You may tell him that his troubles are not as serious as they seem, because there is a majority of red cards surrounding the Nine of Spades on the bottom.

Square 8 shows that a very dark brunette lady of your acquaintance is going to get married within eight days, weeks, or months. On the top and bottom side of the Ace of Clubs (marriage) there is a red card; therefore the marriage will be quite satisfactory, but the black card to the left side of the Ace of Clubs indicates that there will occasionally be differences of opinion.

Square 9. The Ace of Spades on top of the Jack of Diamonds denotes that a rather light-complexioned young male friend is to get mixed up in some slander, gossip, and confusion that will worry him very much, and you will hear all about it. He should not take this too seriously, for above him on the bottom is a red card and beside him is the Nine of Clubs, which is not a bad card. Therefore he will get out of his troubles without too much difficulty.

Square 10 in this layout does not indicate anything of importance.

We can merely say that within ten days, weeks, or months there will definitely be some pleasant association with a medium-light lady, which looks beneficial since there are all red cards surrounding the Nine of Clubs.

Square 11 is interesting. The Seven of Hearts on top of the Ace of Hearts indicates that a very pleasant surprise of some sort is coming into the home. The surprise may come from a stranger, or it may come from some member of the family. It is impossible to say where it comes from, but the important part is that it comes directly to your door or right into your home. And this, of course, will occur within eleven days, weeks, or months since these cards happen to be in Square 11.

Square 12 is very interesting. When you shuffled the cards and made a wish at the beginning of the fortune, you must have wished something about money or inheritance. This square indicates that you are going to get your wish within twelve days, weeks, or months. It also indicates that about the same time that you get your wish, you will also receive a gift of money, an inheritance, or extra money from a source other than your regular income.

Note that if Nine of Hearts had not shown up in this layout, it would have meant that you are not to get your wish very soon. But if the Wish Card (Nine of Hearts) does show up, you must not tell your wish to a living soul until it materializes.

Now that we have finished analyzing the meanings of the individual squares, we will look at how the cards are placed beside each other, starting with the bottom layer. We find that there are two Tens beside each other in the top row on the bottom; therefore you are going to have a change of the conditions surrounding you. The cards are alternate colors, so the change will be satisfactory.

Now we refer to the layer of cards on top. We find two Kings together on the top row. This indicates that you will be having some dealings or conversation with a policeman, judge, attorney, justice of the peace, or some other person connected with the law. It doesn't mean that there is any special trouble in store, but that you will have some dealings with him that will likely be important but not serious. If all black cards were around these Kings on the top row, it would be likely that you would have some dispute or quarrel that might result in your consulting an officer of the law. But in this layout there is a red Jack below one of the Kings and a red Ace to the left of one of the Kings. Therefore we can say that it will likely just be a friendly conversation.

On the second row we find two Jacks next to each other on the top layer. This denotes that you are going to change your affections from someone you are now very fond of to another person. Since the Jacks are alternate colors the change will be to your present best friend. If both Jacks were red it would perhaps be to a person of approximately the same complexion as your present lover or friend. If both Jacks were black, it would mean the same, but when the colors alternate, the change will be to a person opposite in description to your present lover or friend.

The two Nines on top of each other in Square 12 do not have any special meaning—they must be either parallel or perpendicular to each other. There are no other cards on the chart of the same denomination next to another so we are finished with this aspect of the interpretation.

We now count the number of Hearts on both the top and bottom layers. There are seven Hearts showing on the chart. This means that your life will be blessed with a reasonable amount of love and affection in the time that the fortune covers, either in days, weeks, or months.

Now we count the Diamonds. There are seven Diamonds on the chart. This means that for the duration of the fortune you will handle a considerable amount of money.

Now count the Clubs. There are only five Clubs; therefore your mind will not be taken up with business as much as with other things of life for the duration of your fortune.

Last count the Spades. There are only five Spades, so you will not be giving any special time or thought to your domestic affairs for the time covered by your fortune. You will merely follow your regular domestic routine.

We will now count the face cards. There are nine face cards on the chart. The four Queens are there, but two Kings are missing, therefore forthcoming gatherings will consist mostly of women.

This completes this section of the fortune. You may now gather up all of the cards, and lay your chart to one side in preparation for the next layout, which is very simple.

★

How to Tell What Is
Going to Happen Tomorrow

In this layout you will also need a chart at first. Later you will memorize it and may discard it.

On a piece of cardboard draw five squares, approximately four inches long and three inches wide. Arrange them as shown on the following page.

Square A represents the time around breakfast, or from approximately 6 A.M. to 9:30 A.M.

Square B represents the time before lunchtime, or from approximately 9:30 A.M. until noon.

Square C represents the afternoon, or from approximately noon to 3:30 P.M.

Square D represents the time before supper, or from approximately 3:30 P.M. until 6:30 P.M.

Square E represents the evening hours, or from approximately 6:30 P.M. to 10:30 P.M.

When you have this chart drawn, you may enter the hours in the various squares, which will be easier than referring to this list. After some practice you will automatically memorize the hours covered by each of the squares.

We are now ready for the next simple procedure. By learning each step thoroughly as you go along, you will find that telling fortunes is very simple and accurate.

Lay the part of the deck of cards aside that you used in the first layout. Pick up the part of the deck that you discarded when you began the fortune. The part of the deck that you will be using now has all of the two, three, four, five, and six cards in it, but does not contain any of the cards, you formerly used.

Shuffle the cards thoroughly. Then lay them on the table in front of you in a fan shape, with their faces down. Draw or choose five cards at random from them, and lay them in the squares on your chart in this manner:

Place the first card you choose in Square A, face up. Place the second card you choose, face up, in Square B. Place the third chosen card in Square C; place the fourth chosen card in Square D—all of

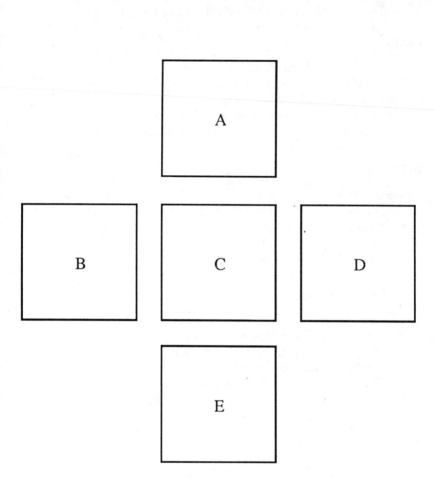

them face up. Now place the fifth chosen card in Square E, face down. The idea of placing this last card face down is just to create a bit of suspense about how the day will terminate after you see what is going to happen for every other part of the day. When you have looked up the cards for the other portions of the day, you may turn the card in Square E up to see what the evening hours have in store for you.

Meanings of the Cards in this Layout

HEARTS

Two Spot: A medium-blond young man
Three Spot: A medium-light elderly man
Four Spot: A medium-light lady
Five Spot: Love. Affection. Good news. Happy frame of mind
Six Spot: Favors or a gift from a close friend or one of the family

DIAMONDS

Two Spot: Very good news by letter, telephone, or messenger.
Three Spot: You will do some shopping or spend money.
Four Spot: You will be paid or will receive money.
Five Spot: You will sign papers or make a promise.
Six Spot: You will make an important discovery or find a lost
    article.

CLUBS

Two Spot: A medium-dark young man
Three Spot: A medium-dark elderly man
Four Spot: A medium-brunette lady
Five Spot: A favorable proposition
Six Spot: Opportunity to take a favorable trip

SPADES

Two Spot: Disappointment in personal plans
Three Spot: Loss of money or other valuables through carelessness
Four Spot: Extra expenses. You will have to spend money.
Five Spot: You will hear a sickness or a minor accident.
Six Spot: You will feel irritable or cross and be impatient and
    restless.

Sample Fortune

For this example, lay the cards in the squares as follows so that you
may see them in front of you and follow the interpretation carefully.

In Square A, place the Four of Spades.
In Square B, place the Six of Hearts.
In Square C, place the Two of Hearts.
In Square D, place the Five of Diamonds.
In Square E, place the Two of Clubs, face down.

This sample layout is supposed to be the cards you have chosen after they have been shuffled, as instructed previously.

We now begin the translation of this layout. Start with Square A, at the top. Between 6 A.M. and 9:30 A.M., you will have to pay out some money that you probably had not figured on. You may feel impelled to say something disagreeable—this may leave a "bad taste" in your mouth so early in the morning, but it will not be important. (This elaboration is an example of the kinds of hunches or impressions you might get while reading a fortune.)

Then between 9:30 A.M. and noon, according to Square B, you will have some favors conferred upon you by close friends or relatives, which will make you very happy indeed.

In Square C, it says that between noon and 3:30 P.M. you will meet or have some dealings or association with a medium-light man. The cards on either side are red, which is good; therefore we will say that the association will be agreeable. If they had been black, the association would not have amounted to much.

In Square D, we find that between 3:30 P.M. and 6:30 P.M. you will be concerned about some papers or documents or possibly that you will make some agreements or promises that will have favorable results since there is a red card to the left of it.

Now turn the card in Square E face up, which in this example would be the Two of Clubs. This denotes that after supper or between 6:30 and 10:30 P.M. you will be with a medium-dark young man. If the one who is having the fortune told is a young lady, she may be told that this dark, handsome young man will take her somewhere or that she will have the opportunity to have a date with him. But if the person having his fortune told is a man, then he can be told that he will have the company of a young lady during the evening. In either case, the association will be pleasant because there is a red card above it.

Now we count the red cards and discover that there are more red cards than there are black cards. The day, therefore, will be a fortunate day for you, and you can safely go ahead and carry out any plans you might have.

If there had been a majority of black cards, the day would be rather unfavorable, and you should postpone important plans until another time.

If all of the cards are red, it will be a most successful day to push every interest and get as much accomplished as possible.

If all the cards are black, it will be a rather unsettled day, and you should be careful to avoid accidents—guard your health and do not take any risks.

If there is a majority of Hearts, you will feel romantic during the day.

If there is a majority of Diamonds, you will be very much concerned about your home or personal affairs.

If there should be two of one suit and two of another suit, your thought and time will be equally divided between the two during the day.

With only a little practice, you will be able to read these cards easily and rapidly. Remember to include your hunches.

How to Answer Questions with Cards

Almost everyone who has his fortune told will have several questions come to mind that may be suggested by some of the things in the fortune. It is very easy to answer questions with this system of fortune-telling cards.

When answering questions, you will remove all of the face cards from the deck and lay them to one side.

To begin with, you must translate the person's question into a form that can be answered "Yes" or "No." Almost any question that may come to a person's mind can be worded in such a manner that it can be answered by "Yes" or "No."

The person asking the question must shuffle the cards thoroughly and while shuffling them must silently ask the question and keep his mind on that question.

After you have shuffled the number cards and asked the question, you will begin dealing the cards off from the back and turning them face up, four at a time. If an Ace does not appear with the first four cards dealt off, lay them to one side and deal off four more. When the first Ace appears, lay the four cards in front of you side by side on the table face up. Continue until all four Aces are on the table in front of you. Now count the number of black cards, including the Aces. Then count the number of red cards, including the Aces. If there is a larger number of black cards the answer is "No." If there is a larger number of red cards the answer is "Yes."

Go through the same laying-out process for each question.

As to how long you or anyone else should shuffle the cards, "conscience" should be your guide. You will have a "certain feeling" when you have shuffled them enough. Follow this feeling. Keep on shuffling them until something inside of you tells you that you have shuffled them sufficiently; then lay them out according to the above directions. This "inner feeling" is what one may call the Voice of Fate assuring you that you have shuffled them enough and that the cards are now in the right position to answer your questions accurately. When you have finished shuffling them, if you have a feeling that the deck should be cut once, twice, or three times, do so—for this cutting may be necessary to get the cards in the proper position to the Aces to accurately answer your question.

You will perhaps by now realize that the secret of telling fortunes by the Karma System is not in the cards themselves, but is instead in their positions according to the Karma interpretations. The cards are placed in their proper positions according to Fate. The value of this system is also enhanced by adding to the regular interpretations any "hunches" or "impressions" that you may receive as you go along in the process of interpreting the cards.

No one should tell his fortune by cards nor have his fortune told with the cards more than once every twenty-four hours! If you tell your fortune or have it told more than once in twenty-four hours, the fortunes will conflict. Two readings within twenty-four hours will neutralize the indications of both. You have not then had your fortune told at all but have been merely playing with the cards and cannot take what they tell you seriously.

Many people like to "run the cards" a second time, just to see if they will tell them the same thing again. This is an acknowledgment of disbelief, which is resented by Karma. Be satisfied with the first layout, take it seriously, and you will be surprised at the accuracy of the predictions, provided you have followed the instructions correctly.

★

How to Find Initials of Future Husband or Wife

This is a feature of fortune-telling with cards that many young people are very interested in. Many persons want to learn if they will marry again. First the questioner should ask the cards if he or she will marry or remarry. If the answer is "No," it will be useless to proceed. If the answer is "Yes," he or she may proceed to find the initials of the next husband or wife.

The Alphabet in the Cards

There are always two cards that represent each letter of the alphabet, a "blond" and a "brunette, or red and black." A list of the letters and corresponding cards follows.

A. Ace of Hearts or Spades
B. Two of Hearts or Spades
C. Three of Hearts or Spades
D. Four of Hearts or Spades
E. Five of Hearts or Spades
F. Six of Hearts or Spades
G. Seven of Hearts or Spades
H. Eight of Hearts or Spades
I. Nine of Hearts or Spades
J. Ten of Hearts or Spades
K. Jack of Hearts or Spades
L. Queen of Hearts or Spades
M. King of Hearts or Spades

N. Ace of Diamonds or Clubs
O. Two of Diamonds or Clubs
P. Three of Diamonds or Clubs
Q. Four of Diamonds or Clubs
R. Five of Diamonds or Clubs
S. Six of Diamonds of Clubs
T. Seven of Diamonds or Clubs
U. Eight of Diamonds or Clubs
V. Nine of Diamonds or Clubs
W. Ten of Diamonds or Clubs
X. Jack of Diamonds or Clubs
Y. Queen of Diamonds or Clubs
Z. King of Diamonds or Clubs

How to Proceed

Shuffle the cards thoroughly, and lay them out on the table in front of you, backed up in a fan shape.

Now let your hand be directed by your "instinct." Choose one of the cards, and take it out of the deck. Lay it face up, to your left. This is the initial of your future husband's or wife's first name. Next draw another card, and place it face up beside the first one, to its right. This is the initial of the middle name. Now let your hand be guided again in selecting the third and last card, and place it face up to the right of the second card. Now look in the list to see what letters the cards signify, and discover the three initials of your future husband or wife. If you have followed your "instinct or unconscious" in choosing these cards, they will be reasonably accurate. If two of the cards are black and one red, the person will be a brunette. If two are red and one black, the person will be a blond. If all black, it will be a dark brunette.

You should never ask the cards to choose the initials of your future husband or wife more than once, unless they tell you that you are to be married more than once. However, this system may be used over and over again to tell you the initials of your next new friend, new neighbors, next business partner, or next employer. Remember: The cards deal with future associates, not past or present ones.

Securing Quick Answers to Questions

Shuffle all the cards thoroughly while you are silently asking the question. Cut the cards once, and note if a red or black card turns up. Repeat the shuffling and cutting three times. If two out of the three cuts are red, the answer is "yes." However, if two of the three cuts are black cards, the answer is "no." If all three cuts are red, the answer is "absolutely yes." If the three cuts are all black, the answer is "positively no."

Future Trips

Shuffle the cards, spread them before you in a fan shape, and carefully select ten cards. Look up the letters that these ten cards represent in the preceding table. By rearranging these letters and changing them around, you will find that they almost spell a certain state or city. The city or state that they come the nearest to spelling is the one you will likely visit on your trip.

How to Tell How Many Children You Will Have

Remove all of the face cards from the deck. Shuffle the cards thoroughly, and cut them three times, shuffling them for each cut.

Write down the number of the card you cut each time. Thus: If the Six of Diamonds was the first cut, write down 6. If the Act of Clubs was the second cut, write down 1. If the 4 of Diamonds was the third cut, write down 4. Now total these numbers, which in this case is 12, and divide by 3, which gives the number 4. You will likely have 4 children. If your sum is indivisible by 3, use the nearest number, and discard the remainder. This way, if the total of your three cuts should be 11, we find that 3 will go into 11 only 3 times, with a remainder of 2. We discard the 2 and say you will have 3 children.

How to Tell a Person's Age with the Cards

For this aspect of fortune-telling, prepare in advance an ordinary deck of playing cards that may then be used over and over.

Pick out the deck the Ace, Two, Three, Four, Five, Six, and Seven of Diamonds, Clubs, and Hearts. Across the tops of the cards write the following numbers:

Ace of Hearts:	8	29	50
2 of Hearts:	9	30	51
3 of Hearts:	10	31	52
4 of Hearts:	11	32	53
5 of Hearts:	12	33	54
6 of Hearts:	13	34	55
7 of Hearts:	14	35	56
Ace of Clubs:	15	36	57
2 of Clubs:	16	37	58
3 of Clubs:	17	38	69
4 of Clubs:	18	39	60
5 of Clubs:	19	40	61
6 of Clubs:	20	41	62
7 of Clubs:	21	42	63
Ace of Diamonds:	22	43	64
2 of Diamonds:	23	44	65
3 of Diamonds:	24	45	66
4 of Diamonds:	25	46	67
5 of Diamonds:	26	47	68
6 of Diamonds:	27	48	69
7 of Diamonds:	28	49	70

★

Shuffle these twenty-one cards and lay them face up on the table in three rows of seven each. Let them overlap each other in each row, but leave enough of the top of each card showing so the numbers are visible. Ask a person to tell you which row the card is in that has his or her age written on it. When he tells you which row it is in, pick up the three rows one at a time, but put the row just indicated in the middle. Proceed to lay them out in the same manner, without shuffling them. Ask him to point out the row that the card is in this time. When he has done so, put that row in the center, and deal them out once more. Now take up the deck and deal off ten cards from either the top or the bottom, then look at the eleventh card. The eleventh card will be the one containing his age. You will be able to tell by looking at the person which one of the three numbers is his age, since there is enough difference in the numbers to tell if a person is 8, 29, or 59 years of age.

You will note, of course, that the range of ages is from eight to seventy. It is quite unlikely that you will have anyone younger than eight or older than seventy to work with.

If you have made no mistake in laying out these cards and placing the proper row in the center each time, it will automatically work out that the eleventh card is always the one containing the person's age. You can make yourself very popular among your friends by telling their ages in this manner, if you do not reveal the secret of the center row and the eleventh card to them. Practice this with yourself until you become thoroughly familiar with the principle before attempting to do it for someone else.

★
The Modern System

The modern method is one in which fifty-two cards of the deck are used, and in which the older interpretations of the cards have been amplified by more modern, twentieth-century definitions.

HEARTS

Ace. An important card whose meaning is affected by its environment. Among Hearts, it implies love, friendship, and affection; with Diamonds, money and news of distant friends; with Clubs, festivities and social or domestic rejoicing; with Spades, disagreements, misunderstandings, contention, or misfortune; individually, it stands for the house.

King. A good-hearted man, with strong affections, emotional, and given to rash judgments, possessing more zeal than discretion.

Queen. A fair woman, loving and lovable, domesticated, prudent, and faithful.

Knave. Not endowed with any sex. Sometimes taken as Cupid; also as the best friend of the inquirer or as a fair person's thoughts. The cards on either side of the knave are indicative of the good or bad nature of its intentions.

Ten. A sign of good fortune. It implies a good heart, happiness, and the prospect of a large family. It counteracts bad cards and confirms good ones in its vicinity.

Nine. The wish card. It is the sign of riches and of high social position, accompanied by influence and esteem. It may be affected by the proximity of bad cards.

Eight. The pleasures of the table, convivial society. Another meaning implies love and marriage.

Seven. A faithless, inconstant friend who may prove an enemy.

Six. A confiding nature, liberal, openhanded, and an easy prey for swindlers; courtship and a possible proposal.

Five. Jealousy without cause in a person of weak, unsettled character.

Four. One who has remained single until middle life from being too hard to please.

Three. A warning card as to the possible results of the inquirer's own want of prudence and tact.

Deuce Prosperity and success in a measure dependent on the surrounding cards; endearments and wedding bells.

DIAMONDS

Ace. A ring or paper money.

King. A fair man, with a violent temper and a vindictive, obstinate turn of mind.

Queen. A fair woman given to flirtation, fond of society and admiration.

Knave. A near relative who puts his own interests first, is opinionated, easily offended, and not always quite straight. It may mean a fair person's thoughts.

Ten. Plenty of money, a husband or wife from the country, and several children.

Nine. This card is influenced by the one accompanying it; if the latter is a court card, the person referred to will have his capacities negated by a restless, wandering disposition. It may imply a surprise connected with money; if in conjunction with the Eight of Spades, it signifies crossed swords.

Eight. A marriage late in life, which will probably be somewhat checkered.

Seven. This card has various meanings. It cautions of the need for careful action. It may imply a decrease of prosperity. Another reading connects it with uncharitable tongues.

Six. An early marriage and speedy widowhood. A warning with regard to a second marriage is also indicated.

Five. To young married people this portends good children. In a general way it means unexpected news or success in business enterprises.

Four. Breach of confidence. Troubles caused by inconstant friends, vexations, and disagreeableness.

Three. Legal and domestic quarrels and probable unhappiness caused by wife's or husband's temper.

Deuce. An unsatisfactory love affair; sudden opposition from relatives or friends.

CLUBS

Ace. Wealth, a peaceful home, industry, and general prosperity.

King. A dark-complexioned man of upright, high-minded nature, calculated to make an excellent husband, faithful and true in his affections.

Queen. A dark woman, with a trustful, affectionate disposition, with great charm for the opposite sex, and susceptible to male attractions.

Knave. A generous, trusty friend, who will take trouble on behalf of the inquirer. It may also mean that the inquirer is in a dark man's thoughts.

Ten. Riches suddenly acquired, probably through the death of a relation or friend.

Nine. Friction through opposition to the wishes of friends.

Eight. Love of money and a passion for speculating.

Seven. Great happiness and good fortune. If troubles come they will be caused by one of the opposite sex to the inquirer.

Six. Success in business both for self and children.

Five. An advantageous marriage.

Four. A warning against falsehood and double-dealing.

Three. Two or possibly three marriages, with money.

Deuce. Care is needed to avert disappointment and avoid opposition.

SPADES

Ace. It may concern love affairs or convey a warning that troubles await the inquirer through bad speculations or ill-chosen friends.

King. A dark man, ambitious and successful in the higher walks of life.

Queen. A widow of malicious and unscrupulous nature, fond of scandal and open to bribes.

Knave. A well-meaning, lazy person, slow in action though kindly in thought.

Ten. An evil omen; grief or imprisonment. Has power to detract from the good signified by cards near it.

Nine. An ill-fated card meaning sickness, losses, troubles, and family dissensions.

Eight. A warning with regard to any enterprise in hand. This card close to the inquirer means evil; also opposition from friends.

Seven. Sorrow caused by the loss of a dear friend.

Six. Hard work brings wealth and rest after toil.

Five. Bad temper and a tendency to interfere the inquirer, but happiness to be found in the chosen wife or husband.

Four. Illness and the need for great attention to business.

Three. A marriage that will be marred by the inconstancy of the inquirer's wife or husband, or a journey.

Deuce. A removal or possibly death.

In connection with the foregoing detailed explanation of the meaning of each card in an ordinary pack, we append a short table that may be studied either separately or with the preceding definitions. It gives at a glance certain broad outlines that may be of use to one who wishes to acquire the art of reading a card as soon as it is laid face up.

GENERAL INTERPRETATIONS

Prudence

Ace of Clubs
Six of Spades

Wealth

Nine of Hearts
Two of Hearts
Seven of Clubs
Ten of Diamonds
Ten of Clubs

Rejoicing

Eight of Hearts

Presages Misfortune

Ten of Spades
Nine of Spades
Eight of Spades
Seven of Spades
Three of Spades
Two of Spades
Three of Diamonds
Nine of Clubs

Credibility

Six of Hearts

★

Early Marriage

Two of Clubs
Six of Diamonds
Three of Clubs
Five of Clubs

Late Marriage

Eight of Diamonds
Three of Clubs

Prosperity

Ten of Hearts
Two of Hearts
Seven of Clubs
Six of Clubs

Discretion Needed

Three of Hearts
Seven of Diamonds
Two of Diamonds
Two of Clubs
Four of Spades

Jealousy

Five of Hearts

Unfaithfulness

King of Diamonds
Four of Diamonds
Four of Clubs
Seven of Hearts

The Method

The fifty-two cards are shuffled and cut into three piles face up, with the left hand toward the inquirer. Before starting the deal, select the card that represents the person whose fortune is being told. (See signification of the cards.) This card, representing the inquirer, is not withdrawn but is shuffled with the pack.

Lay all the cards out, nine in a row, from right to left in six rows. Only seven cards will be in the sixth row. (To save space, overlap the cards in each row, leaving about one-third of each card uncovered.)

After all fifty-two cards have been dealt out in six rows, find the first Key Card by counting nine cards from right to left from the inquirer's card.

If the inquirer's card happens to be in the sixth row, you must count straight upward from the inquirer's card to the top row, and then from right to left.)

When you come to the last card in a row, continue the count in the next row below, moving from left to right. Repeat this process until there are not enough cards left to count nine before coming back to the inquirer's card. This locates the remaining Key Cards, which reveal the inquirer's fortune.

Three readings are required to complete telling a fortune. The first reading usually represents the past, the second the present, while the third reveals the future.

The following example, using the Queen of Hearts as the inquirer's card, illustrates a typical reading. Lay out the cards as follows:

First Reading (The Past)

First Line. Seven of Clubs, Seven of Spades, King of Spades, Ace of Diamonds, Ace of Hearts, Jack of Clubs, Four of Hearts, Eight of Hearts, Jack of Spades

Second Line. Two of Diamonds, Three of Diamonds, Two of Hearts, Six of Hearts, King of Diamonds, Five of Clubs, Two of Clubs, Five of Spades, Three of Hearts

Third Line. Five of Hearts, Six of Diamonds, Four of Clubs, Queen of Clubs, Five of Diamonds, Three of Spades, King of Hearts, Four of Diamonds, Ten of Spades

Fourth Line. Nine of Spades, Queen of Spades, Eight of Diamonds, Ace of Spades, Six of Clubs, Queen of Diamonds, King of Clubs, Jack of Hearts, Six of Spades

Fifth Line. Ten of Diamonds, Eight of Clubs, Seven of Diamonds, Ace of Clubs, Nine of Diamonds, Nine of Clubs, Jack of Diamonds, Ten of Hearts, Ten of Clubs

Sixth Line. Eight of Spades, Queen of Hearts, Seven of Hearts, Four of Spades, Three of Clubs, Two of Spades, Nine of Hearts

After you have laid out the cards according to instructions note where the inquirer's card is located. (Should it be in the very last row, remember to count upward and over to the left from the top row.) Count nine cards from the inquirer's card, and mark the card on a piece of paper, or take the card out of the layout so that you can look up its meaning. Continue until there are no longer nine cards between the final count and the inquirer's card. Should the inquirer's card be the ninth card, eliminate the count. Remember there must be nine cards from or between each Key Card.

★

According to this example, the Key Cards would be the Jack of Clubs, Six of Hearts, Three of Spades, Ace of Spades, and Nine of Clubs. Referring to the information given above, you can interpret the significance of the cards.

Jack of Clubs. A generous, trustworthy friend who will go out of his way to help the inquirer.
Six of Hearts. An early marriage and a speedy separation. A warning with regard to a second.
Three of Spades. A marriage that may be marred by infidelity or incompatibility, or a journey.
Ace of Spades. Concerns ill-fated love affairs, also trouble through speculation and ill-chosen companions.
Nine of Clubs. Friction and opposition to the wishes and advice of friends.

The interpretation of the above fortune could be: Should the Queen of Hearts represent an unmarried woman, it would indicate a warning against an unhappy marriage that would bring displeasure to her friends and family. She will disregard the advice of a sincere friend or suitor and marry in haste, which may result in a speedy separation. Foolish speculations will also add to her sorrows. She can avoid this only by heeding the advice of a trusty friend.

Should the Queen of Hearts represent a married woman, the fortune would indicate that if the events have not already occurred, she must be careful not to give too much credence to the reports of doubtful friends and must guard her own conduct carefully.

Note that the cards must be reshuffled between each reading, but for the purpose of this lesson we will pick up the cards in suits and lay them out as follows.

The Second Reading (The Present)

First Line. Eight of Clubs, Queen of Hearts, Six of Spades, Eight of Spades, Eight of Hearts, Six of Diamonds, Ten of Hearts, Nine of Clubs, Six of Hearts

Second Line. Three of Spades, Ace of Spades, Three of Diamonds, King of Spades, Ace of Diamonds, Ace of Hearts, King of Diamonds, King of Clubs, Ace of Clubs

Third Line. Ten of Spades, Five of Clubs, Two of Hearts, Five of Hearts, Ten of Diamonds, Four of Hearts, Two of Clubs, Jack of Spades, Three of Hearts

Fourth Line. Five of Spades, Four of Clubs, Six of Clubs, Queen of Diamonds, Four of Diamonds, King of Hearts, Nine of Spades, Five of Diamonds, Seven of Clubs

Fifth Line. Jack of Clubs, Ten of Clubs, Three of Clubs, Nine of Diamonds, Queen of Spades, Seven of Spades, Jack of Hearts, Eight of Diamonds, Seven of Diamonds

Sixth Line. Seven of Hearts, Four of Spades, Queen of Clubs, Two of Spades, Jack of Diamonds, Two of Diamonds, Nine of Hearts

When you have completed the layout, following previous instructions, the Key Cards will be the King of Clubs, Five of Clubs, Five of Diamonds, Ten of Clubs, Two of Diamonds, and Three of Spades.

As to the signification of the cards, we find:

King of Clubs. A dark upright man. An excellent husband, faithful and true.

Five of Clubs. An advantageous marriage.

Five of Diamonds. To young people this portends good children. In a general way it means unexpected good news or success in business.

Ten of Clubs. Riches suddenly acquired, possibly through the death of a relation or friend.

Two of Diamonds. An unsatisfactory love affair with opposition from relatives or friends.

Three of Spades. A marriage that will be marred by infidelity or incompatibility.

The definition of the above fortune could be: Should the Queen of Hearts be unmarried and young, she would marry an upright dark man who will make an excellent husband. They will have good children and may receive a gift or legacy of a considerable sum of money. Should she be a married woman, it would indicate an unsatisfactory love affair, marred by infidelity and incompatibility, notwithstanding the receipt of a legacy. It could also mean that a second marriage would prove to be happy and successful, with financial security.

After picking up the suits, lay the cards out again for the third reading.

The Third Reading (The Future)

First Line. Ace of Clubs, Eight of Clubs, Queen of Hearts, Ten of Spades, King of Clubs, Five of Diamonds, Ten of Clubs, Nine of Spades, Jack of Spades

Second Line. Three of Spades, Two of Spades, Six of Hearts, Eight of Spades, Five of Spades, Jack of Clubs, Seven of Hearts, Four of Spades, Queen of Clubs

Third Line. Five of Hearts, Two of Diamonds, Three of Diamonds, Queen of Diamonds, Eight of Hearts, Three of Clubs, Ace of Diamonds, Six of Diamonds

Fourth Line. Four of Diamonds, Six of Clubs, Seven of Diamonds, Seven of Clubs, Six of Spades, Nine of Diamonds, Jack of Diamonds, Nine of Hearts, Eight of Diamonds

Fifth Line. Ten of Hearts, King of Spades, Two of Hearts, Ten of Diamonds, Ace of Hearts, Four of Hearts, King of Hearts, King of Diamonds, Queen of Spades

Sixth Line. Two of Clubs, Seven of Spades, Jack of Hearts, Nine of Clubs, Three of Hearts, Four of Clubs, Ace of Spades

When you complete this layout, you will have the following Key Cards: Seven of Hearts, Three of Diamonds, Jack of Diamonds, Two of Hearts, Three of Hearts, and Ace of Clubs. Referring to the signification of the cards, we find:

Seven of Hearts. A faithless, inconstant friend who may prove an enemy.

Three of Diamonds. Legal and domestic quarrels and unhappiness caused by bad tempers.

Jack of Diamonds. A male relative who puts his own interests first.

Two of Hearts. Endearments and wedding bells.

Three of Hearts. A warning card to the inquirer who lacks prudence and tact.

Ace of Clubs. Wealth, a peaceful home, industry, and general prosperity.

This fortune again warns the inquirer about the possibilities of disaster in marital and business affairs unless good judgment and careful consideration are given to dealing with friends and associates.

It points out the pitfalls and dangers, as well as the rewards and good fortune, if the inquirer will heed the warnings and advice given.

Study these examples carefully. Make up your own interpretation, using these same cards. After a little practice you will become a proficient fortune-teller.

★
A Simple Method

For this very simple method of studying the past, the present, and the future in the light of cartomancy, a selected pack of thirty-two cards from the Sevens to the Aces is required. The pack must be shuffled and cut in the ordinary way. After the cut, the top card of the lower pile and the bottom card of the upper one are set aside to form the surprise. The remaining thirty cards are then to be dealt into three equal packs that, beginning at the left, represent respectively the past, the present, and the future.

We will suppose that the Knave of Hearts, a pleasure-seeking young bachelor, is the inquirer.

Signification of the Cards

The individual meaning attached to the thirty-two cards employed is as follows.

Clubs

Ace of Clubs. Signifies money, joy, or good news; if reversed (upside-down), the joy will be of brief duration.

King of Clubs. A frank, liberal man, fond of serving his friends; if reversed, he will meet with a disappointment.

Queen of Clubs. A clever and enterprising young man; reversed, a heartless flirt and flatterer.

Knave of Clubs. A fair young man, possessed of no delicacy of feeling, who seeks to injure.

Ten of Clubs. Fortune, success or grandeur; reversed, want of success in some small matter.

Nine of Clubs. Unexpected gain or a legacy; reversed, some trifling present.

Eight of Clubs. A dark person's affections, which, if returned, will be the cause of great prosperity; reversed, those of a fool, with attendant unhappiness if reciprocated.

Seven of Clubs. A small sum of money or unexptectedly recovered debt; reversed, a yet smaller amount.

Hearts

Ace of Hearts. A love letter or some pleasant news; reversed, a friend's visit.

King of Hearts. A fair, liberal man; reversed, will meet with disappointment.

Queen of Hearts. A mild, amiable woman; reversed, has been crossed in love.

Knave of Hearts. A carefree young bachelor who dreams only of pleasure; reversed, a discontented military man.

Ten of Hearts. Happiness, triumph; if reversed, some slight anxiety.

Nine of Hearts. Joy, satisfaction, success; reversed, a passing chagrin.

Eight of Hearts. A fair person's affections; reversed, indifference on his or her part.

Seven of Hearts. Pleasant thoughts, tranquillity; reversed, ennui, weariness.

Diamonds

Ace of Diamonds. A letter, soon to be received; reversed, containing bad news.

King of Diamonds. A fair man, generally in the army, but both cunning and dangerous; if reversed, a threatened danger caused by machinations on his part.

Queen of Diamonds. An ill-bred, scandal-loving woman; if reversed, she is to be greatly feared.

Knave of Diamonds. A tale-bearing servant or unfaithful friend; if reversed, will be the cause of mischief.

Ten of Diamonds. Journey or change of residence; if reversed, it will not prove fortunate.

Nine of Diamonds. Annoyance, delay; if reversed, either a family or a love quarrel.

Eight of Diamonds. Wooing; if reversed, unsuccessful.

Seven of Diamonds. Satire, mockery; reversed, a foolish scandal.

In order to know whether the Ace, Ten, Nine, Eight, and Seven of Diamonds are reversed, make a small pencil mark on each to show which is the top of the card.

Spades

Ace of Spades. Pleasure; reversed, grief, bad news.

King of Spades. The envious man, an enemy, or a dishonest lawyer who is to be feared; reversed, impotent malice.

Queen of Spades. A widow; reversed, a dangerous and malicious woman.

Knave of Spades. A dark, ill-bred young man; reversed, he is plotting some mischief.

Ten of Spades. Tears, a prison; reversed, brief affliction.

Nine of Spades. Tidings of a death; if reversed, it will be some near relative.

Eight of Spades. Approaching illness; reversed, a marriage broken off or offer refused.

Seven of Spades. Slight annoyance; reversed, a foolish intrigue.

The court cards of Hearts and Diamonds usually represent persons of fair complexion, Clubs and Spades the opposite.

Signification of Different Cards of the Same Denomination

Four Aces. Coming together, or following each other, announce danger, failure in business, and sometimes imprisonment. If one or more of them are reversed, the danger will merely be lessened.

Three Aces. Coming in the same manner, good tidings; if reversed, folly.

Two Aces. A plot; if reversed, will not succeed.

Four Kings. Rewards, dignities, honor; reversed, they will be less, but sooner received.

Three Kings. A consultation on important business, the result of which will be highly satisfactory; it reversed, success will be doubtful.

Two Kings. A partnership in business; if reversed, a dissolution of the same. Sometimes this only denotes friendly projects.

Four Queens. Company, society; one or more, reversed, denotes that the entertainment will not go off well.

Three Queens. Friendly calls; reversed, chattering and scandal, or deceit.

Two Queens. A meeting between friends; reversed, poverty, troubles, in which one will involve the other.

Four Knaves. A noisy party mostly of young people; reversed, a drinking bout.

Three Knaves. False friends; reversed, a quarrel with some low person.

Two Knaves. Evil intentions; reversed, danger.

Four Tens. Great success in projected enterprise; reversed, the success will not be so brillant but it will be sure.

Three Tens. Improper conduct; reversed, failure.

Two Tens. Change of trade or profession; reversed, denotes that the prospect is only a distant one.

Four Nines. A great surprise; reversed, a public dinner.

Three Nines. Joy, fortune, health; reversed, wealth lost by imprudence.

Two Nines. A little gain; reversed, trifling losses at cards.

Four Eights. A short journey; reversed, the return of a friend or relative.

Three Eights. Thoughts of marriage, reversed, folly, flirtation.

Two Eights. A brief love affair; reversed, small pleasures and trifling pains.

Four Sevens. Intrigues among servants or low people, threats, snares, and disputes; reversed, their malice will be impotent to harm, and the punishment will fall on themselves.

Three Sevens. Sickness, premature old age; reversed, slight and brief indisposition.

Two Sevens. Levity; reversed, regret.

Any picture card between two others of equal value—as two Tens or two Aces—denotes that the person represented by that card runs the risk of prison.

It requires no great effort to commit these significations to memory, but it must be remembered that they are but what the alphabet is to the printed book; a little attention and practice, however, will soon enable the learner to from these mystic letters into words and words

into phrases, to assemble these cards together, and to read the events
past and to come that their faces reveal.

There are several ways of doing this, and we will give them all, so
as to afford our readers a choice of methods of delving into the future.

The Past

We will suppose that the Knave of Hearts, a pleasure-seeking
bachelor, is the inquirer and create below a sample ordering of the
cards. We deal first with the past, for which the cards are as follows.

Queen of Clubs, reversed
King of Diamonds, reversed
Ten of Clubs, reversed
Nine of Diamonds
Eight of Clubs
Ace of Diamonds, reversed
Ace of Hearts, reversed
Queen of Spades, reversed
Eight of Diamonds

There are three pairs among the ten. Two Queens, both reversed,
remind the inquirer that he has had to suffer from the consequences of
his own actions. The two Aces, also both reversed, refer to partnership
into which he entered with good intentions but which was doomed to
failure. The two Eights speak of his frivolous pleasures and countless
evanescent love affairs.

After analyzing the groupings, we see what the cards have to say
individually, taken in order. We begin with the Queen of Clubs,
reversed, a dark woman tormented by jealously, in which she was
encouraged by the King of Diamonds, reversed, who is a treacherous
schemer, wishing no good to the inquirer. The Ten of Clubs tells of a
sea voyage and is followed by the Nine of Diamonds, showing that
there were vexations and annoyances on that voyage. The Eight of
Clubs speaks of the inquirer's having engaged the affections of a dark
woman, who would have contributed to his prosperity and happiness.
The Ace of Diamonds, reversed, represents evil tidings that reached
him in connection with the Ace of Hearts, reversed, which stands for a
change of abode, and from the Knave of Spades, reversed, a legal
agent who was not to be trusted. There was also the Queen of Spades,

a designing widow with whom he had a romantic involvement indicated by the Eight of Diamonds.

The Present

The ten cards in center pack are as follows.

Ace of Spades, reversed
Seven of Diamonds
Eight of Hearts
Queen of Hearts
Seven of Hearts
Queen of Diamonds, reversed
Nine of Spades
King of Hearts, reversed
Knave of Hearts, reversed
Ten of Diamonds

In this pack we have only two pairs: two Sevens, speaking of mutual love; and two Queens, one suggesting rivalry.

Taken in order, the pack reads as follows. The Ace of Spades, reversed, speaks of sorrow in which the inquirer will be treated with a certain amount of heartless chaff and want of sympathy, as it is followed by the Seven of Diamonds. The Eight of Hearts tells us that he is entertaining thoughts of marriage with the Queen of Hearts, a fair, lovable girl; but the Seven of Hearts shows that he is very contented with his present condition and in no hurry to change it. He is amusing himself with the Queen of Diamonds, reversed, who is a born flirt but more spiteful than he suspects, and who is next placed to the worst card in the pack, the Nine of Spades, indicative of the harm she does to him and the failure of his matrimonial plans. He is cut out by the King of Hearts, who thus causes him a serious disappointment, and we see him, himself, reversed as the lover with a grievance; the last card is the Ten of Diamonds: he has decided to ease his heartache by traveling.

The Future

This pack contains the following cards.

Knave of Diamonds, reversed
Seven of Clubs

Eight of Spades, reversed
Seven of Spades, reversed
Ten of Spades
Nine of Hearts
King of Clubs
Ten of Hearts
King of Spades
Ace of Clubs, reversed

The presence of four Spades foretells that trouble awaits our bachelor. We again have a pair of Sevens, but one is reversed, so he may expect deceit to be at work. The two Tens promise him an unlooked-for stroke of luck to be met with a new walk of life, while the two Kings speak of cooperation in business and of the success that will crown his upright and practical conduct. The wish card, the Nine of Hearts, and the Ten of Hearts in a great measure counteract the mischief represented by the Spades.

The inquirer must beware of the Knave of Diamonds, reversed, who is a mischief maker, who will make use of the Seven of Clubs, trifling financial matters, either to break off an engagement or to cause an offer of marriage to be refused, as shown by the Eight of Spades, reversed. The chagrined lover will have recourse to silly stratagems in his courting, the Seven of Spades, reversed, and this error will cause him grief, even to the shedding of tears, the Ten of Spades. The wish card, the Nine of Hearts, however, brings him better luck in his love affairs through his trusty, generous friend, the King of Clubs. His ill fortune is further counteracted by the next card, the Ten of Hearts, which promises him prosperity and success. He will find an enemy in the King of Spades, a dark widower who is a lawyer by profession and none too scrupulous in his ways. He may expect a good deal of troublesome correspondence with this man, as shown by the last card, the Ace of Clubs, reversed.

The subject of this correspondence is possibly to be found in the surprise, which consists of the Nine of Clubs, reversed, meaning an unexpected acquisition of money under a will. He will do well to take heed when in the company of the Knave of Clubs, reversed, the second card of the surprise, for he is a flatterer and a somewhat irresponsible character.

★

Dealing the Cards by Threes

Take the pack of thirty-two selected cards—that is the Ace, King, Queen, Knave, Ten, Nine, Eight, and Seven of each suit—having decided upon the one intended to represent the inquirer. In doing this, it is necessary to remember that the card chosen should be according to the complexion of the chooser: King or Queen of Diamonds for a very fair person, ditto of Hearts for one somewhat darker, Clubs for one darker still, and Spades only for one who is very dark. The card chosen also loses its signification and simiply becomes the representative of a dark or fair man or woman, as the case may be.

This point having been settled, shuffle the cards and either cut them or have them cut, taking care to use the left hand. That done, turn them up by threes, and every time there appears in these triplets two of the same suit, such as two Hearts or two Clubs, withdraw the highest card and place it on the tble. If the triplet should be all of the same suit, the highest card is the only one withdrawn; but should it consist of three of the same value but of different suits, such as three Kings, they are all to be appropriated. We will suppose that after having turned up the cards three by three, six had been withdrawn, leaving twenty-six to be shuffled and cut and again turned up by threes as before, until either thirteen, fifteen, or seventeen cards have been obtained. Remember that the number must always be uneven and that the card representing the inquirer must be one of them. If the requisite thirteen, fifteen, or seventeen have been obtained and the inquirer's card has not made its appearance, the operation must be done over.

Now let us suppose that the inquirer is a lady, represented by the Queen of Hearts, and that fifteen cards have been obtained and laid out—in the form of a half-circle—in the folowing order: the Seven of Clubs, the Ten of Diamonds, the Seven of Hearts, the Knave of Clubs, the King of Diamonds, the Queen of Hearts, the Nine of Clubs, the Seven of Spades, the Ace of Clubs, the Eight of Spades.

The cards include two Queens, two Knaves, two Tens, three Sevens, two Eights, and two Nines and would prompt the observations below.

The two Queens signify the reunion of friends, the two Knaves that there is mischief being made between them. The two Tens denote a change of profession, which, from one of them being between two Sevens, will not be made without some difficulty, the cause of which, according to the three Sevens, will be illness. However, the two Nines promise some small gain, resulting—so say the two Eights—from a love affair.

Now, to analyze the cards individually, begin to count seven cards from right to left, beginning with the Queen of Hearts, who represents the inquirer. The seventh being the King of Diamonds means the inquirer often thinks of a fair man in uniform.

The next seventh card (counting the King of Diamonds as one) proves to be the Ace of Clubs, signifying receipt from him of some very joyful tidings; also he intends to give the inquirer a present.

Count the Ace of Clubs as one and proceed to the next seventh card, the Queen of Spades, which indicates that a widow is endeavoring to injure the inquirer; and (the seventh card, counting the Queen as one, being the Ten of Diamonds) this annoyance will oblige the inquirer either to take a journey or change residence; but (the Ten of Diamonds being imprisoned between two Sevens) the journey or move will meet with some obstacle.

Counting as before, calling the Ten of Diamonds one, the seventh card will prove to be the Queen of Hearts, the inquirer's card, and it may be safely concluded that the inquirer will overcome these obstacles without needing anyone's aid or assistance.

Now look at the two cards at either end of the half-circle, which are, respectively, the Eight of Spades and the Seven of Clubs. Together they may be read as a sickness that will lead to the receipt of a small sum of money.

Repeat the same maneuver, which brings together the Ace of Clubs and the Ten of Diamonds: good news that will make the inquirer decide to take a journey, destined to prove a very happy one, and that will occasion the receipt of a sum of money.

The next pair, the Seven of Spades and the Seven of Hearts, brings tranquillity and peace of mind, followed by slight anxiety but quickly succeeded by love and happiness.

Then come the Nine of Clubs and the Knave of Clubs, foretelling a certain receipt of money, through the exertions of a clever, dark young man, Queen of Hearts and King of Diamonds, which comes from the fair man in uniform; this announces great happiness in store and complete fulfillment of wishes, Knave of Diamonds and Nine of Diamonds, although this happy result will be delayed for a time through a fair young man not famed for his delicacy. Eight of Hearts and Ten of Hearts, love, joy, and triumph. The Queen of Spades, who remains alone, is the widow who is endeavoring to injure the inquirer and who finds herself abandoned by her friends.

Now gather up the cards, shuffle, and cut them with the left hand, and proceed to make them into three packs by dealing one to the left, one in the middle, and one to the right; a fourth is laid aside to form a surprise. Continue to deal the cards to each of the three packs in turn until their number is exhausted. It will be found that the left and middle pack each contain five cards, while the one on the right hand has only four.

Now ask the inquirer to select one pack at a time. The first is "for the inquirer," and we will suppose this to be the middle one, and that the cards comprising it are the Knave of Diamonds, the King of Diamonds, the Seven of Spades, the Queen of Spades, and the Seven of Clubs. These, by recalling our previous signification of the cards, are easily interpreted as follows.

The Knave of Clubs, a fair young man of no delicacy of feeling who seeks to injure, the King of Diamonds, a fair man in uniform, Seven of Spades, and will succeed in causing him some annoyance, the Queen of Spades, at the instigation of a spiteful woman, Seven of Clubs, but, by means of a small sum of money, matters will finally be easily arranged.

Next take up the left-hand pack, which is "for the house." Supposing it to consist of the Queen of Hearts, the Knave of Clubs, the Eight of Hearts, the Nine of Diamonds, and the Ace of Clubs, they would read as follows.

Queen of Hearts, the inquirer, is or soon will be in a house, Knave of Clubs, where she will meet a dark young man who, Eight of Hearts, will entreat her assistance to forward his interest with a fair girl, Nine of Diamonds, he having met with delays and disappointments, Ace of Clubs, but a letter will arrive announcing the possession of money that will remove all difficulties.

The third pack is "for those who did not expect it" (a surprise) and is composed of four cards, let us say the Ten of Hearts, Nine of Clubs, Eight of Spades, and Ten of Diamonds, signifying as follows.

The Ten of Hearts, unexpected good fortune and great happiness, Nine of Clubs, caused by an unlooked-for legacy, Eight of Spades, which may perhaps be followed by a slight sickness, Ten of Diamonds, the result of a fatiguing journey.

There now remains on the table only the card intended for the surprise. This, however, must be left untouched, the other cards gathered up, shuffled, cut, and again laid out in three packs, not forgetting at the first deal to add a card to the surprise. After the different packs have been examined and explained, they must again be gathered up and shuffled, repeating the whole operation, after which the three cards forming the surprise are examined. Supposing them to be the Seven of Hearts, the Knave of Clubs, and the Queen of Spades, they are to be interpreted as follows.

Seven of Hearts, pleasant thoughts and friendly intentions, Knave of Clubs, of a dark young man, Queen of Spades, related to a malicious dark woman or widow who will cause him much unhappiness.

Dealing the Cards by Sevens

After having shuffled the pack of thirty-two selected cards, either cut them or let the inquirer cut them, taking care to use the left hand. Then count seven cards, beginning with the one lying on the top of the pack. Since the first six are useless, put them aside and retain only the seventh, which is placed face upward on the table. Repeat this three times more, then shuffle and cut the cards that were thrown to one side together with those remaining in your hand, and deal them out in sevens, as before, until twelve cards are obtained. It is, however, indispensable that the one representing the inquirer should be among the number; therefore, the whole operation must be done again if it doesn't make its appearance. Once the twelve cards have been spread out in the order in which they have been dealt, the explanation may begin as described in the manner of dealing the cards in threes— always bearing in mind both their individual and relative signification. Count the cards first by sevens, beginning with the one representing the inquirer, going from right to left. Then take the two cards at either end of the line or half-circle and unite them. Afterward form the three packs and the surprise precisely as before. The only difference between the two methods is the manner in which the cards are obtained.

★

Dealing the Cards by Fifteens

After the cards have been well shuffled and cut, deal them out in two packs containing sixteen cards each. Ask the inquirer to choose one of them, lay aside the first card to form the surprise, turn up the other fifteen, and arrange them in a half-circle from left to right, placing them in the order in which they come to hand, and taking care to notice whether the one representing the inquirer is among them. If not, the cards must be gathered up, shuffled, cut, and dealt as before. This must be repeated until the missing card shows up in the pack chosen by the inquirer.

Now proceed to explain them—first by interpreting the meaning of any pairs, triplets, or quartets among them, then by counting them in sevens (going from right to left and beginning with the card representing the inquirer) and finally by taking the cards at either end of the line and pairing them. Then gather up the fifteen cards, shuffle them, cut, and deal so as to form three packs of five cards each. From each of these three packs remove the topmost card, and place them on the one laid aside for the surprise, thus forming four packs of four cards each.

As before, ask the inquirer to choose one of these packs for herself or himself, as the case may be. Turn it up and spread out the four cards from left to right, explaining their individual and relative significance. Next proceed with the pack on the left, which will be "for the house"; then the third one, "for those who do not expect it"; and lastly, "the surprise."

For example, let us suppose that the pack for the inquirer is composed of the Knave of Hearts, the Ace of Diamonds, the Queen of Clubs, and the Eight of Spades, reversed. With the aid of the list of meanings we have given, it will be easy to interpret them as follows.

The Knave of Hearts is a carefree young bachelor, the Ace of Diamonds, who has written or will very soon write a letter, the Queen of Clubs, to a dark woman, Eight of Spades, reversed, to make a proposal to her that will not be accepted.

We will suppose that the pile "for the house" consists of the Queen of Hearts, the Knave of Spades, reversed, the Ace of Clubs, and the Nine of Diamonds, which reads thus.

The Queen of Hearts is a fair woman, mild and amiable in disposition, who, Knave of Spades, reversed, will be deceived by a dark, ill-bred young man, the Ace of Clubs, but she will receive some good news that will console her, Nine of Diamonds, although it is probable that the news may be delayed.

The pack "for those who do not expect it," consisting of the Queen of Diamonds, the King of Spades, the Ace of Hearts, reversed, and the Seven of Spades, would signify that the Queen of Diamonds is a mischief-making woman, and the King of Spades is in league with a dishonest lawyer, Ace of Hearts reversed, they will hold a consultation together, Seven of Spades, but the harm they do will be repaired.

Last comes the surprise, formed by, we will suppose, the Knave of Clubs, the Ten of Diamonds, the Queen of Spades, and the Nine of Spades, of which the interpretation is that the Knave of Clubs is a clever, enterprising young man, Ten of Diamonds, about to undertake a journey, Queen of Spades, for the purpose of visiting a widow, Nine of Spades, but one or both of their lives will be endangered.

Dealing Twenty-one Cards

After having shuffled the thirty-two cards and cut or had them cut with the left hand, deal from the pack the first eleven and lay them on one side. The remainder—twenty-one in all—are to be again shuffled and cut. That done, lay the topmost card on one side to form the surprise, and range the remaining twenty before you, in the order in which they come to hand. Then see whether the card representing the inquirer is among them; if not, one must be withdrawn from the eleven useless ones and placed at the right end of the row to represent the missing card, no matter what it may really be. We will, however, suppose that the inquirer is an officer in the army and is represented by the King of Diamonds, and that the twenty cards ranged before you are the Queen of Diamonds, the King of Clubs, the Ten of Hearts, the Ace of Spades, the Queen of Hearts, reversed, the Seven of Spades, the Knave of Diamonds, the Ten of Clubs, the King of Spades, the Eight of Diamonds, the King of Hearts, the Nine of Clubs, the Knave of Spades, reversed, the Seven of Hearts, the Ten of Spades, the King of Diamonds, the Ace of Diamonds, the Seven of Clubs, the Nine of Hearts, and the Ace of Clubs.

Proceed to examine the cards as they lie and seeing that all the four Kings are there, it can be predicted that great rewards await the inquirer, and that he will gain great dignity and honor. The two Queens, one of them reversed, announce the reunion of two sorrowful friends; the three Aces foretell good news; the two Knaves, one of them reversed, danger; the three Tens, unchanged conduct.

Now you can begin to explain the cards commencing with the first on the left hand, the Queen of Diamonds. The Queen of Diamonds is a mischief-making, underbred woman, the King of Clubs, endeavoring to win the affections of a worthy and estimable man, Ten of Hearts, over whose scruples she will triumph, Ace of Spades, the affair will make some noise, Queen of Hearts, reversed, and greatly distress a charming, fair woman who loves him, Seven of Spades, but her grief will not be of long duration, Knave of Diamonds, an unfaithful servant, Ten of Clubs, will make off with a considerable sum of money, King of Spades, and will be brought to trial, Eight of Diamonds, but saved from punishment through a woman's agency. King of Hearts, a fair man of liberal disposition, Nine of Clubs, will receive a large sum of money, Knave of Spades, reversed, which will expose him to the malice of a dark youth of course manners. Seven of Hearts, pleasant thoughts followed by, Ten of Spades, great chagrin, King of Diamonds, await a man in uniform, who is the inquirer, Ace of Diamonds, but a letter he will speedily receive, Seven of Clubs, containing a small amount of money, Nine of Hearts, will restore his good spirits, Ace of Clubs, which will be further augmented by some good news. Now turn up the surprise. We will suppose it to prove the Ace of Hearts, a card that predicts great happiness caused by a love letter, but which by making up the four Aces shows that this sudden job will be followed by great misfortune.

Now gather up the cards, shuffle, cut, and form them into three packs, laying one aside at the first deal to form the surprise. By the time they are all dealt out it will be found that the two first packets are each composed of seven cards, while the third contains only six. Ask the inquirer to select one of these, take it up, and spread out the cards from left to right, explaining them as earlier described.

Gather up the cards again, shuffle, cut, form into three packs (dealing one card to the surprise), and proceed as before. Repeat the whole operation once more; then take up the three cards forming the surprise and give their interpretation.

No matter how the cards are dealt, whether by threes, sevens, fifteens, or twenty-one, when those lower than the Knave predominate, it foretells success; if Clubs are the most numerous, they predict gain and considerable fortune; if Diamonds dignity and honor; if Hearts, gladness and good news; if Spades, death or sickness.

These significations are necessarily very vague and must of course be governed by the relative positions of the cards.

★
A Reduced Pack

Like the Simple Method, this method requires a pack of thirty-two cards, although only twenty-one of them are actually used in the process. The whole pack must be well shuffled and cut with the left hand. The dealer then removes the first eleven cards and puts them aside. From the twenty-one in his hand, he takes the uppermost card and places it apart for the surprise before dealing out the other twenty and placing them in order on the table before him. If the card representing the inquirer is not among them, the whole process must be repeated from the beginning.

The signification of the cards must then be read, taking care to notice any set of two, three, or four of a kind, as their collective meaning should be added to the individual explanation. After this has been done, the twenty cards should be taken in order, starting from the left, and their meanings linked together as a continuous message.

The cards must now be taken up again, shuffled, and cut as before. The dealer then makes them into three packs. Two of the packs will consist of seven cards, the third of only six, as one card has been held for the surprise.

The inquirer is then asked to choose one of the packs, which must be exposed face upward, moving from left to right, and these six or seven cards, as the case may be, should be read according to their significations. This operation is repeated three times, so that at the finish the surprise consists of three cards that are exposed and read last of all.

An Example

The accompanying example will make the foregoing explanation more lucid and interesting.

We will take the Knave of Clubs, a dark, clever, well-intentioned young man, as the representative of the inquirer. Then suppose that the twenty-one cards come out in the following order, beginning from the left.

King of Spades
Queen of Hearts, reversed

Ace of Hearts
King of Clubs
Ace of Spades, reversed
Ace of Clubs
Knave of Hearts
King of Hearts
Queen of Spades, reversed
Nine of Hearts
Knave of Diamonds
Ten of Spades
Ace of Diamonds, reversed
King of Diamonds
Seven of Diamonds
Eight of Diamonds
Eight of Spades
Seven of Clubs, reversed
Nine of Clubs, reversed
Nine of Diamonds
The surprise, placed apart

Before interpreting the individual significance of each card, we will look at some of the combinations. There are four Aces, telling of bad news relating to trouble through the affections, but two, being reversed, mitigate the evil and give a ray of hope to the inquirer. The three Kings tell of an important undertaking that will be discussed and carried through successfully by the young man, who has excellent abilities. The two Queens, both reversed, warn the inquirer that he will suffer from the result of his own actions, more especially as the Queen of Spades in an inverted position represents a malicious and designing widow. She is very much to the fore with regard to the inquirer's affairs. The three Knaves confirm the foregoing reading, for they foretell annoyances and worries from acquaintances, ending even in slander. The three Nines, one of them reversed, speak of happiness and entire success in an undertaking, though the inversion shows that there will be a slight passing difficulty to overcome. The two Eights refer to flirtations on the part of the inquirer, and the reversed one warns him that he will have to pay for some of his fun. The two Sevens tell of mutual love between the young man and the lady of his choice, but as the one is reversed there will be deceit at work to try to separate them.

Now let us see what the twenty cards have to say taken consecutively. We start off with the King of Spades, a clever, ambitious but unscrupulous man who has been instrumental in thwarting the love affairs of the fair, lovable, and tenderhearted woman, the Queen of Hearts, upon whom the inquirer has set his affections. The Ace of Hearts following her is the love letter she will receive from the inquirer, the Knave of Clubs; but he is next to the Ace of Spades, reversed, foretelling grief to him that may affect his health, and the Ace of Clubs coming immediately after points to the cause being connected with money. The next three cards are court cards and that means gaiety in which the inquirer will be mixed up with a lively young bachelor, the Knave of Hearts, a fair, generous but hot-tempered man, the King of Diamonds, and the malicious, spiteful widow represented by the Queen of Spades, reversed. The inquirer will meet with pleasure caused by success, the Nine of Hearts; but this is closely followed by the Knave of Diamonds, an unfaithful friend who will try to bring disgrace, represented by the Ten of Spades, upon his betters and will write a letter containing unpleasant news, the Ace of Diamonds, reversed, which will concern or be prompted by the King of Diamonds, a military man who has a grievance with regard to his love affairs and who is not above having recourse to scandal, signified by the Seven of Diamonds, to avenge his wounded vanity. The next card is the Eight of Diamonds, the sign of some courting, but our young people are not at the end of their troubles yet, for the Eight of Spades, reversed, tells us that his offer of marriage will be rejected. The Seven of Clubs is a card of caution and implies danger from the opposite sex, so we gather that the spiteful widow has been at work and is possibly to blame for his rejection; this idea is further strengthened by the Nine of Clubs, also reversed, coming immediately, which suggests letters that may have done the mischief. The Nine of Diamonds tells of the annoyance caused by these events and their effect upon the affections of a dark person, the inquirer.

In the first deal the inquirer chooses the middle pack, which contains the following cards: the Knave of Diamonds, the Seven of Diamonds, the Ace of Clubs, the Queen of Spades, reversed, the Ace of Spades, the Ace of Diamonds, the Eight of Diamonds.

We notice that three Aces come out in this pack and show passing troubles in love affairs. The Knave of Diamonds, an unfaithful friend, is mixed up in scandal, the Seven of Diamonds, conveyed in a letter,

THE THREE PACKS

	One Chosen by Inquirer	

What the first selected pack contains–

Knave of Diamonds	Seven of Diamonds	Ace of Clubs	★ Queen of Spades ★

Ace of Spades	Ace of Diamonds	Eight of Diamonds

The three cards forming the surprise–

King of Spades	Queen of Hearts	★ Nine of Hearts ★

★ Means "reversed"

the Ace of Clubs, written or instigated by the spiteful widow, the Queen of Spades. The Ace of Spades betokens sickness, but it is followed by the Ace of Diamonds, the wedding ring, and the pack closes with the Eight of Diamonds, telling of a happy marriage for the inquirer after all his worries.

In the second deal he again selects the middle pack, and we see the following: the Queen of Spades, reversed as usual, the Nine of Clubs, reversed, the Seven of Clubs, reversed, the Nine of Hearts, the Seven of Diamonds, the Eight of Clubs, small worries, and the Seven of Clubs and the Seven of Diamonds, one reversed. The pack reads thus: The Queen of Spades, the spiteful widow, who seems to be ubiquitous, is followed by the Nine of Clubs, representing the letter referred to above. The Seven of Clubs standing next to it sounds a word of caution to the inquirer as to his lady.

There are two Nines, one reversed, speaking of a friend, so-called; he will probably succeed in outwitting the widow, for the next card is the Nine of Hearts, implying joy and success in spite of scandal, the Seven of Diamonds, with reference to his affections, represented by the Eight of Clubs.

In the third deal, the inquirer is still faithful to the middle pack, and we find the following cards: the Ace of Diamonds, Ten of Spades, reversed, Queen of Spades, reversed, Nine of Diamonds, reversed, Seven of Clubs, reversed, Ace of Clubs, reversed.

The two Aces, one of them reversed, tell of a union between two parties, but as there is one red and one black and one is reversed, the result is ambiguous. Here we get the wedding ring, the Ace of Diamonds, followed by the Ten of Spades, reversed, which speaks of brief sorrow, occasioned doubtless by the spiteful widow, who again appears reversed and intent upon mischief; next to her comes the Nine of Diamonds, reversed, signifying a love quarrel; the Seven of Clubs, reversed, gives a word of caution to the inquirer with regard to the opposite sex; the last card is the Ace of Clubs, reversed, which means joy soon followed by sorrow.

This sample fortune is remarkable in that the Queen of Spades comes out in each of the packs and is reversed every time.

The Surprise

The surprise is now turned up and contains the King of Spades, a dark, ambitious, unscrupulous man who has interfered with the love affairs of the fair woman, the Queen of Hearts, to whom the inquirer has made an offer, so far without success; the Nine of Hearts, reversed, tells that what separates the lovers is but a passing cloud.

The Seven Packs Method

This method uses a reduced pack with an uneven number of cards, sometimes as little as fifteen or seventeen, though this example uses twenty-three. The cards are shuffled and dealt into seven piles, representing, respectively, yourself, your house, what you expect, what you don't expect, a great surprise, what is sure to come true, and the wish.

The cards are shuffled and cut once, then dealt out in the manner described. Let us assume the following combinations:

First Pack. Queen of Spades, Queen of Hearts, Ten of Clubs, Seven of Hearts.

Second. Ace of Spades, Knave of Clubs, Ace of Diamonds, and Ten of Spades.

Third. Knave of Spades, King of Diamonds, Knave of Hearts.

Fourth. Queen of Clubs, Seven of Spades, King of Spades.

Fifth. Ten of Diamonds, Eight of Clubs, and Queen of Diamonds.

Sixth. King of Hearts, Ten of Hearts, King of Clubs.

Seventh. Ace of Hearts, Knave of Diamonds, Ace of Clubs.

For this example we will assume that the inquirer is a woman, represented by the Queen of Hearts.

The first pack represents the meeting of the inquirer with a dark or elderly woman, for whom she has a strong affection. Water is crossed before that meeting takes place.

The second pack suggests that a dark man will offer a ring or a present of jewelry, and also that he is considering a journey by land. He is probably a professional man or in government service.

The third pack, with its combination of Knaves and King, has reference to business transactions that will most probably be favorable to the interests of the Queen of Clubs.

The fourth pack presages some slight disappointment, illness, or unhappiness in connection with some friends.

The fifth pack tells us that some brilliant fortune is awaiting a fair friend, which will lead to a higher social position.

The Sixth pack tells us that perhaps our seemingly indifferent Queen of Hearts has a slight tenderness for someone. He is older than she is and is only waiting for an opportunity to declare his affection. If the wish is related to such a man as I have described, she may be certain of its fulfillment, even should there be a slight delay.

The seventh or wish pack is extremely good and tells us that many affairs will be transacted by writing.

The future of the Queen of Hearts is fair and bright, her disposition is lovable, and she will bring happiness to other people.

This example is not made up of selected cards. They were shuffled, cut, and drawn in the ordinary way. I say this because so few cards of bad import have appeared, and it might be thought that these were chosen in order to avoid prophesying disappointments.

When a smaller quantity of cards is used, there is an optional way of concluding operations. After having read the pairs, the cards are gathered up, shuffled, and cut into three packs instead of seven. These three are placed in a row, and a fourth card is put aside for the surprise. The inquirer is requested to choose one of the three packs, which represent respectively the house, those who did not expect it, and the inquirer—the last being decided by the choice of the person in question.

When these three packs have been read, all the cards are again taken up except the surprise (which is left face downward on the table) and dealt out again; the same process is repeated three times, until there are three cards set aside for the surprise. These are read last of all and form the concluding message to the inquirer.

★

The Gypsy Method

This method also uses thirty-two cards, the cards from Two to Six, inclusive, being discarded.

The Meaning of the Cards

Court Cards

In this system the court cards represent people, and the King, Queen, and Knave in each suit suggest relationships. The Kings also indicate profession or vocation, as follows.

Spades— a literary man or one whose ambition would lead him to the pulpit or the platform.

Hearts—the symbol of a wealthy man, who deals with large sums of money, for instance, a banker, capitalist, or stockholder.

Clubs—indicates the mental side of business, and here we look for the lawyer or attorney.

Diamonds—a businessman, one who depends on both his brain and hands for work. Diamonds are eminently the practical suit and must always be consulted with reference to the subject's condition in life. Since they signify the material side of life, this suit indicates success; or the absence of it, failure.

Numbers

HEARTS

Ace. Quietness and domestic happiness
Seven. Love
Eight. A surprise
Nine. A wish
Ten. A wedding

★

SPADES

Ace. Government service
Reverse Ace. A death
Seven. Unpleasant news
Eight. Sorrow or vexation
Nine. Quarrels
Ten. A disappointment

DIAMONDS

Ace. A letter or ring
Seven. A journey
Eight. Society
Nine. Illness or news of a birth
Ten. Money, joy, success

CLUBS

Ace. A present
Seven. Gain, good business
Eight. Pleasure
Nine. A proposal
Ten. A journey by water

How to Consult the Cards

The inquirer is to shuffle the pack of cards and cut it into three. Take up the cards and let your subject draw any chance card that he pleases. Place this card on the table. The suit from which it is drawn will determine the representative card, as it is an indication of the character of your subject.

A lady is represented by a Queen, a man by a King, and the Knave stands for the male relations or thoughts.

After the card is drawn, place the remainder on the table in four rows, beginning each row from left to right.

The cards that immediately surround the King or Queen aid us in our judgment of the inquirer—remember that the right-hand card is the more important one.

An Illustration

For this illustration we will suppose the inquirer to be a woman.

The cards being shuffled and cut into three, the card was drawn, and as this proved to be a seven of clubs, so the Queen represented the subject in this instance. When the cards were placed in order, this is how they appeared.

First line. Seven of Clubs, Eight of Clubs, King of Clubs, Seven of Hearts, King of Diamonds, Nine of Diamonds, Ten of Diamonds, King of Hearts.

Second line. Seven of Spades, Nine of Spades, Knave of Hearts, King of Spades, Eight of Spades, Queen of Spades, Ten of Spades, Ace of Diamonds.

Third line. Ace of Spades, Knave of Clubs, Queen of Clubs, Ten of Hearts, Ace of Hearts, Queen of Diamonds, Ace of Clubs, Nine of Hearts.

Fourth line. Knave of Spades, Seven of Diamonds, Eight of Hearts, Nine of Clubs, Eight of Diamonds, Knave of Diamonds, Queen of Hearts, Ten of Clubs.

Now we can proceed with the reading. As the suit of Clubs is a pleasant one, we may conclude that the lady is of a cheerful temperament. The Seven signifies gain and prosperity, and the Eight pleasure, which come to the inquirer through the King of Clubs, typical of a lawyer. The Seven of Hearts indicates that a fair man is in love with the inquirer. The Nine of Diamonds, with the joyful Ten beside it, seems to foretell a birth, and the King of Hearts stands for a good friend. But the Seven and Nine of Spades, in conjunction, inform us that some annoyance is coming that is possibly connected with the King of Hearts.

The King of Spades, accompanied by the Eight of that suit, tells that this man is suffering considerable grief and vexation on account of the Queen of Clubs, suffering that will cause another woman to be jealous.

The Queen and Ten of Spades, with the Ace of Spades, imply disagreeable tidings; but as the Knave of Clubs appears side by side with the Queen of that suit (the inquirer) and they are followed by the Ten of Hearts, it will in no way disturb the affection of either. The Knave here may be taken to indicate the thoughts or intentions of the King. The Ace of Hearts seems to promise great tranquillity and happiness in the domestic life. A near relation, one deeply interested in the Queen of Clubs, is represented by the Queen of Diamonds. The Ace of Clubs shows that a letter is on its way.

The Nine of Hearts, the wish or betrothal card, follows, and from this I should infer that a proposal of marriage will come by letter, one that will most probably be accepted. The Knave of Spades is followed by the Seven of Diamonds and the Eight of Hearts, which shows that the Queen of Clubs has been much loved by someone and that an offer of marriage will have to be considered either directly before or immediately after a journey. The inquirer will have a great deal of pleasure on a journey. The Queen of Hearts and Knave of Diamonds indicate good friends who show her much kindness, and there will be welcome tidings for her across the water.

Now count the rows. Should the betrothal card (the Nine of Hearts) appear in the third or fourth row, that number of years must elapse before she becomes engaged.

Count the rows again until the one in which the Ten of Hearts (the marriage card) appears. In this example the betrothal and marriage card both appear in the third row, which indicates that the inquirer will be engaged in about three years and that marriage will take place soon after.

The French Method

Take the pack of thirty-two cards, shuffle them thoroughly, cut them in the usual way, and deal them out in two packs of sixteen cards each. The inquirer must choose one of the packs. The first card in the pack is placed apart, face down, to supply the surprise. The remaining fifteen cards must then be turned face upward and placed in order from left to right before the dealer. It is essential that the card representing the inquirer should be in the pack selected by him or her; otherwise it is useless to proceed.

The Reading

The reading is conducted as follows. First take any two, three, or four of a kind—Kings, Knaves, Eights, or whatever may appear—and give their explanation as pairs, triplets, or quartets; then start from the representative card and count in sevens from right to left; finally, pair the end cards together and consider their meaning. The next move is to shuffle the fifteen cards again, cut, and deal them out into three packs, each of which will have five cards. The first card of the three packs is removed and placed with the card that has been set apart for the surprise. In this way there will be four packs containing an equal number of cards (four in each pack).

The inquirer must then be asked to choose one of these packs for himself or herself, after which the four cards are exposed on the table from left to right, and their individual and collective meanings are read. The left-hand pack will be for the house, the third pack is for those who do not expect it, and the fourth for the surprise.

An Example

We will suppose that the inquirer is represented by the Queen of Clubs. Her choice falls on the middle pack, which contains the following cards: the Knave of Clubs, the Eight of Diamonds, reversed, the

Eight of Hearts and the Queen of Spades as shown below.

Starting from the left, the reading suggests that thoughts of the inquirer are running upon an unsuccessful love affair, and though moving in a good society, she is exposed to the interference of a dark, malicious widow.

Knave of Clubs	★ Eight of Diamonds ★	Eight of Hearts	Queen of Spades

The next pack, standing for the house, is made up of the Knave of Spades, the Ace of Spades, the King of Spades, and the Knave of Hearts. Taking the meaning of the group, three Spades mean disappointment. The presence of two Knaves together speaks of evil intentions. The legal agent, Knave of Spades, is employed in some underhand business by his master, the King of Spades, the dishonest lawyer, whoh is an enemy to the inquirer as he is to her friend, the festive, thoughtless young bachelor, the Knave of Hearts, who follows him.

Knave of Spades	Ace of Spades	King of Spades	Knave of Hearts

The third pack is composed of the Nine of Clubs, reversed, the Ace of Clubs, the Ten of Spades, and the Queen of Hearts. We find short-lived joy and good news, followed by tears for the fair, soft-hearted lady, who is susceptible to the attractions of the other sex.

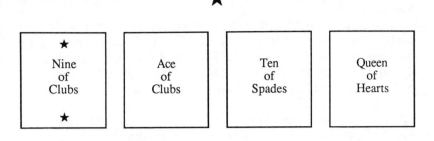

The surprise is very closely connected with the inquirer herself, for we find her included in the four cards. These are the Ace of Hearts, the Queen of Clubs, the Nine of Diamonds, and the Seven of Diamonds. From this we gather that there is a love letter for the inquirer, which, however, may be delayed by some accident, and that she will be exposed to the foolish ridicule of tactless, unkind persons. But she will get the letter all the same.

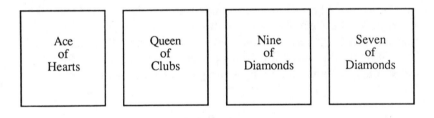

The Grand Star

In any system using the star configuration, the number of cards must be uneven—an even number of cards placed around one in the center. Some systems use as few as thirteen cards, but the traditional grand-star method uses twenty-one.

The Method

Supposing the inquirer be a fair man, the King of Hearts would be the card selected to form the center of the star. This representative card is placed face upward on the table. The remaining thirty-one cards of the pack (the Twos, Threes, Fours, Fives, and Sixes having been removed) must then be shuffled and cut with the left hand.

The cards are numbered in the order in which they are placed upon the table, taking the representative as 1. The mode of withdrawing the cards from the pack is as follows. The first ten cards are thrown aside after the first cut, and the eleventh card is placed below 1; then cut a second time and place the top card of the pack on the table above 1; cut a third time, take the bottom card of the pack and place it to the left of 1. The cards must be cut every time a card is to be withdrawn, and they are taken alternately from the top and bottom of the pack. Great care should be observed in the placing of the cards in proper order, as any deviation will affect the reading at a subsequent stage of the process. The last card, 22, is placed across the foot of the representative.

When the grand star has been formed, the cards must be read first for the significance of the various combinations and duplications, and then in pairs, taking the outside circle in this order: 14 and 16, 21 and 19, 15 and 17, 20 and 18. Then take the inner circle, moving from left to right, thus: 6 and 10, 9 and 12, 8 and 13, 7 and 11; the four center points are paired thus: 4 and 2, 5 and 3; and the last card, 22, is taken separately. The significations are, of course, taken with regard to the relative positions of the cards, and their special reference to the central figure of the inquirer. This is a picturesque and simple way of consulting the cards and will probably be a favorite with most people.

An Example

Assume that the twenty-one cards come out in the following order:

1. King of Hearts
2. Ten of Spades
3. Ten of Hearts
4. Ace of Hearts
5. Nine of Spades
6. Ace of Spades
7. Nine of Diamonds, reversed
8. Queen of hearts
9. Knave of Diamonds
10. Queen of Spades
11. Knave of Clubs
12. King of Clubs
13. Eight of Clubs

14. Queen of Diamonds
15. Nine of Clubs, reversed
16. King of Spades
17. Queen of Clubs
18. Eight of Diamonds, reversed
19. Ace of Diamonds
20. Knave of Spades
21. Knave of Hearts
22. Ace of Clubs

Before taking these in pairs as directed, it will be well to glance at the groups contained in the star as it lies before us. We find the following.

Four Aces. Love troubles and hasty news for the inquirer
Three Kings. Success in an important undertaking
Four Queens. A good deal of social intercourse
Four Knaves. Somewhat noisy conviviality
Two Tens. Unexpected good luck
Three Nines. Health, wealth, and happiness, discounted by imprudence since one is reversed
Two Eights. Passing love fancies, one being reversed

The King of Hearts, a fair, openhanded, good-natured man, is the starting point in reading the pairs that surround him. He is connected with (14) the Queen of Diamonds, a fair woman with a tendency to flirtation. She is amusing herself with (16) a very dark man, probably a lawyer, of an ambitious and not too scrupulous character, who does not wish well to the inquirer. The next pair (21) shows the Knave of Hearts, representing Cupid or the thoughts of the one concerned, linked with (19) the Ace of Diamonds, a wedding ring. While this important item is occupying his thoughts he gives a small present (15), the Nine of Clubs, reversed, to (17) the Queen of Clubs, a charming dark lady who is the real object of his affections. (20) The Knave of Spades, representing a legal agent or the wily lawyer's thoughts, makes mischief, and (18) the Eight of Diamonds, reversed, causes the inquirer's courting to be unsuccessful. (6) The Ace of Spades warns the inquirer against false friends who will frustrate his matrimonial projects, and in (10) we find one of them, the Queen of Spades, a widow with possible designs upon him herself; (9) the Knave of

Diamonds, reversed, shows the mischief maker trying to breed strife with the inquirer's trusty friend (12), the King of Clubs, and (8) the Queen of Hearts, a fair, lovable woman possessing (13) Eight of Clubs, a dark person's affections; (7) the Nine of Diamonds, reversed, tells of a love quarrel, owing to (11) the Knave of Clubs, reversed, a harmless flirt. The inquirer will get (4) the Ace of Hearts, a love letter, but his happiness will be succeeded by (2) the Ten of Spades, a card of bad import; (5) the Nine of Spades tells of grief or sickness, possible news of a death; but (3) the Ten of Hearts counteracts the evil and promises happiness to the inquirer, who will triumph over the obstacles in his path and find (22) joy in love and life.

Important Questions and Games of Chance and Romance

When an answer to an important question is required and the inquirer wishes to consult the cards on the subject, the following simple method may be adopted.

Let the question be asked by the inquirer, then let the dealer take the pack of thirty-two cards, which must be shuffled and cut in the usual manner. The dealer throws out the first eleven cards, which are not used, and proceeds to turn up the others upon the table. The answer is determined by the absence or presence of the special cards applying to each question among the exposed twenty-one.

Specimen Questions

Let us suppose the question to be "How far off is the wedding?" The necessary cards in this case are the Queen of Spades, who should come out with or near the Queen of Hearts, and the Ace of Spades, which should accompany the Eight of Diamonds. These must be taken in conjunction with the other Eights—each of which signifies a year; the four Nines—each of which stands for a month; and the four Sevens—each of which represents a week. Supposing the above-named cards—the two Queens, the Ace of Spades, and the Eight of Diamonds—should not come out in this order or be absent altogether, it may be feared that the date is postponed to the vanishing point.

"Have I real cause for jealousy?" If the Seven of Diamonds comes out in the first fifteen cards, the answer is "Yes." If the Five of Hearts and the Seven of Clubs appear instead among the first fifteen, it is "No."

"Shall we be parted?" or "Shall I sustain the loss of my goods?" If the four Nines are included in the twenty-one cards, the answer is "Yes." Should the four Kings and the four Queens come out, the meaning is "No, never!"

331

"Shall I succeed in my present or projected undertaking?" To insure a favorable answer, the four Aces and the Nine of Hearts must come out. Should the Nine of Spades appear just before the card representing the inquirer, it foretells failure.

"Will the change of residence or condition that I am considering be satisfactory?" Should the question be asked by the master or mistress of a house or an employer of labor, a favorable answer is obtained by the presence of the four Knaves, the Eight and Ten of Diamonds, and the Ten of Clubs. In the event of the inquirer being an employee or a paid worker of any grade, the twenty-one cards must include the Ten and Seven of Diamonds the Eight of Spades, and the four Queens to insure a satisfactory reply. In both cases the Nine of Diamonds means hindrances and delay in attaining success.

"What fortune does the future hold for this child?" The four Aces foretell good luck and a suitable marriage. If the child in question is a girl, the four Eights and the King of Hearts should come out to secure peace and concord for her in the home of her husband.

Cupid and Venus at Work

Among the many ways in which cards can be used to provide entertainment, seasoned with a spice of the unexplainable, the following round game may be given a prominent place.

The pack of fifty-two cards is used.

The Ace of Diamonds is the most valuable asset in winning tricks, as it takes all the other cards.

The Queen of Hearts represents Venus.

The Knave of Hearts stands for Cupid.

The Knave of Clubs represents a sweetheart.

The Knave of Diamonds represents a sweetheart.

The Knave of Spades represents a sweetheart.

The Ace of Hearts, a new house.

The Ace of Clubs, conquest.

The Two of Diamonds, the ring and marriage.

The Twos of Clubs, Spades, and Hearts, good luck.

The Threes show surprise.

The Fours indicate that present conditions will remain unchanged.

The Fives stand for lovers' meetings.
The Sixes, pleasure.
The Eights, mirth.
The Nines, change.
The Tens, marriage settlements.
The Queens represent women.
The Kings represent men.

Any number may take part in the game. The dealer is chosen by lot, and when this has been settled, he or she proceeds to deal out the cards, leaving ten face downward on the table. The stakes are agreed upon, and each player puts into the pool, the dealer being expected to pay double for the honor done to him by the fates.

The cards are then taken up, and each player looks at his own hand. The dealer calls for the Queen of Hearts, Venus, who ranks next to the Ace of Diamonds in value. Should anyone have the Ace of Diamonds in his hand, he plays it straight out. Should the Ace not be among those that have been dealt, the Queen of Hearts is supreme, and the happy holder of Venus may look confidently forward to standing before the altar of Hymen during the current year. If the Ace of Diamonds player holds both Cupid and Venus in his hand, he wins the pool and so ends the game right off. In the event that the holder of these cards is married, their presence promises him some special stroke of good fortune.

When the matrimonial cards are out or proved absent, the game is played on similar lines to whist, the same order of precedence being observed in taking tricks, and the larger the number taken, the better the luck of the winner during the current year.

The Nine of Spades is the worst in the pack, and the unfortunate holder has to pay for its presence in his hand by a triple stake to the pool. Should any player fail to win any tricks, he must pay in advance the stakes agreed upon for the next game.

Marriage by Lot System

For this appeal to the fates we require a full pack of cards, a bag, and stakes either in money or counters. When the players have fixed upon their stakes and placed them in the pool, one of those playing

★

must thoroughly shuffle the pack of cards and place them in the bag. The players then stand in a circle and draw three cards in turn from the bag as it is handed to each of them. Pairs of any kind win back the stakes paid by the holder and promise good luck in the immediate future. The Knave of Hearts is proclaimed to represent Hymen. He wins double stakes and is a happy augury that the holder will soon be united to the partner of his or her choice. Should Venus, the Queen of Hearts, be found in the same hand, the owner takes the pool and wins the game. Fours and Eights are losses and crosses, compelling a prearranged payment to the pool in addition to the usual stakes. A lady who draws three Nines may resign herself to a single life, and the one who has three Fives must prepare to cope with a bad husband

Twenty-Cards Method

This method is traditionally used to answer romantic questions for women, and only three or four are required to pursue this search for hidden knowledge. All the Kings, Queens, Knaves, Aces and Threes must be taken from the pack and dealt round to the players. Each one examines her hand for an answer to her inward questionings. The one who holds the most Kings possesses the largest number of friends. The one with the most Queens has a proportionate number of enemies. Where Kings and Queens are united, there is a promise of speedy and happy marriage. Should a Queen come out with Knaves, we may be sure that intrigues are being woven round some unlucky person. Knaves by themselves represent lovers. Threes are evil omens betokening great sorrow. A Knave with four Threes means that the fair holder will not enter the holy estate. A King with four Threes encourages her to hope, for she has a good chance of matrimony. A Queen with four Threes is the worst combination a woman can draw, for it speaks of sorrow deepened by disgrace. Mixed hands have no special significance, nor is there any great meaning attached to the four Aces. Where only two or three of one kind of card fall together, the meaning ascribed to the four collectively is lessened in proportion to the number held.

Hearts Are Trumps

This method of fortune-telling might be considered an apology for whist. Four players, or three and a dummy, are necessary, and the whole pack is dealt out in the usual way. Hearts are trumps in every deal and carry everything before them. The highest card is the Queen, who is the goddess of love and takes precedence to the Ace, which counts only as one. The person on the left hand of the dealer leads trumps, and the stronger the hand, the better the chances for love and marriage. The one who wins the largest number of tricks has, or will have, the most lovers. The presence of the King and Queen of trumps in one hand is the sign of a speedy union of hearts and of the approaching sound of wedding bells. A sorry fate awaits the luckless maid or youth who is without a Heart—in the hand—for Cupid and Hymen have turned their faces away, and no luck will come of a love affair in that quarter. Where only one or two small trumps can be produced, the holder will have to wait long for wedded bliss. Each person plays quite independently of the others, and the one who acts as dummy must not connect its cards in any way with those he holds himself.

Another Lottery Method

This method is also used to determine romantic questions. Put a well-shuffled pack of cards into a bag deep enough to prevent the contents from being seen. An uneven number of women must then form a ring around the one holding the bag, and each must draw a card. The cards drawn must then all be exposed as they have to be compared. The lucky lady who draws the highest card will be the first to be led to the altar. She who draws the lowest will have to resign herself to the fact that "he cometh not" for many weary days to follow. Anyone drawing the Ace of Spades may cheerfully prepare for the pleasures of the single life. The Nine of Hearts is an omen of serious trouble coming to the holder through loving "not wisely but too well."

★

Italian Method

Only thirty-two cards are used for the Italian method of fortune-telling, all the numbers under Seven, except the Ace, being taken out of each suit. This reduced pack—containing the Ace, King, Queen, Knave, Ten, Nine, Eight, and Seven of the four suits—must be carefully shuffled and cut, with the left hand, of course, by the inquirer. The one who is going to act as interpreter then takes the pack and turns them up three at a time. Should three cards of one suit be turned up at once, they are all laid upon the table face upward; if only two of a suit come out together, the higher card is selected; if all three belong to different suits, they are all rejected.

When the pack has been dealt out in this manner, the cards that have not been chosen are taken up, shuffled, and cut a second time. The deal by threes is then repeated until there are fifteen cards upon the table. They must be placed in line from left to right as they appear.

It is absolutely necessary that the card representing the inquirer should be among those on the table. Some authorities maintain that in the event of its not showing up during the deals, the whole process must be repeated until it makes its appearance. Others simply take the card out of the deck and place it on the table when fourteen others have been selected.

The next step is to count five cards from the representative one and to continue counting in fifths from each fifth card until all have been included or the counting has come back to the representative. The signification of every card is read as it is reached, notice being taken as to whether it is reversed or not. The surrounding circumstances must also be balanced by the interpreter.

When this reading is complete, the fifteen cards must be paired, one from each end of the line being taken, and read together, while the remaining odd one must be dealt with separately.

The third process is to shuffle and cut the fifteen cards and deal them out into five small packs: one for the inquirer; one for the house; one for those who do not expect it; one for the surprise; and one, which is not to be covered, for consolation. When the fifteen cards have been dealt out, it will be seen that four of the packs contain three cards and the fifth only two. These must all be turned face upward and read in separate packs, but their meanings will interconnect.

An Example

Let us imagine that a very fair lady, represented by the Queen of Diamonds, is seeking to read her fortune.

The fifteen cards come out in the following order: the Queen of Diamonds; Nine of Diamonds, reversed; Queen of Hearts; King of Spades; Ten of Diamonds; Seven of Diamonds, reversed; Knave of Hearts, reversed; Ten of Hearts; Knave of Diamonds; Ace of Diamonds, reversed; Knave of Spades; Nine of Spades; King of Clubs; Ten of Spades, reversed; Ace of Hearts.

We begin to count from the Queen of Diamonds, the representative card, and find the Nine of Diamonds to be the fifth from it. By this first count we see from the Nine being reversed that there is a love quarrel troubling the inquirer. Starting again from the Nine, we come to the Queen of Hearts, a mild, good-natured, but not very wise woman who is probably the tool of the next fifth card, the King of Spades, a crafty, ambitious man and an enemy to the Queen of Diamonds.

Our next count is to the Ten of Diamonds, which speaks of a journey for the inquirer. Passing on the Seven of Diamonds, reversed, we find a foolish scandal connected with, if not entirely caused by, the next card in the count, which is the Knave of Hearts, reversed, standing for a military man who is very discontented with the treatment he has received at the hands of the fair inquirer. She will, however, triumph over this foolish annoyance, for the Ten of Hearts comes next in order and counteracts the harm indicated by the other cards.

Our gentle lady has, unfortunately, an unfaithful friend in the Knave of Diamonds, reversed, which portends a letter on the way, containing bad news. The writer of this is a dark young man of no social position, and he probably is the servant of one who is dear to the Queen of Diamonds. The bad news is found in the next count, the Nine of Spades, which tells of sickness affecting the King of Clubs, the warm-hearted, chivalrous man who occupies first place in the inquirer's affections. The last count but one brings us to the Ten of Spades, reversed, by which we know that the lady's sorrow will be but brief. It is followed by the Ace of Hearts, a love letter containing the good news of her lover's recovery.

As earlier, before proceeding to pair the cards, we should interpret the groups as they have come out in the fifteen. The six Diamonds point to there being plenty of money; the two Tens tell of a change of residence either brought about by marriage or by the journey read in the Ten of Diamonds; the presence of three Knaves betokens false friends, though as one is reversed their power of doing harm is lessened; two Queens indicate gossip and the revealing of secrets; the two Aces imply an attempted plot, frustrated by the one being reversed; the two Nines also point to riches.

Now consider the pairs, which are taken from each end, beginning with the Queen of Diamonds and the Nine of Spades.

The Queen of Diamonds and the Nine of Spades imply that sickness and trouble will affect the inquirer; the Ten of Diamonds pairs with the Ten of Hearts to signify a wedding; the Knaves of Diamonds and Spades coming together show evil intentions toward the inquirer; the King of Clubs and the Ace of Hearts tell of the lover and the love letter; the inverted Nine of Diamonds pairing with the Knave of Spades tells of a love quarrel in which a dark young man, wanting in refinement, is concerned; the reversed Seven of Diamonds pairs with the Knave of Hearts, also inverted, and tells of a foolish scandal instigated by the ungallant soldier who is suffering from wounded vanity; the inverted Ace of Diamonds comes out with the Queen of Hearts, telling of a letter containing unpleasant news from a fair, good-natured woman; while the remaining card, the Ten of Spades, being inverted, speaks of brief sorrow for the inquirer.

Our next step is to deal out the five packs as already directed. The first one—for the lady herself—contains three cards, two of which are bad, but their harm is largely discounted by the Ten of Hearts. In the Nine of Spades we read of the trouble caused by her lover's illness; the Ten of Spades betokens the tears she will shed while the beloved's life is in danger; the Ten of Hearts speaks of happiness triumphing over sorrow.

The second pack—for the house—contains a flush of Diamonds, the Ten, the Ace, and the Knave. There is plenty of money in the house; the Ten speaks of a journey, possibly resulting in a change of residence; the Ace, being reversed, tells of a letter on the way containing unpleasant news, probably connected with the removal of the Knave, who is a faithless friend and is to blame for the annoyance.

The third pack—for those who do not expect it—consists of three court cards that taken together foretell gaiety of some sort. We find the inquirer, personified by the Queen of Diamonds, in the society of the Knaves of Spades and Hearts, the latter reversed, and consequently we know that she will be troubled by some unfriendly schemes, in which the dark, undesirable young man and the disappointed officer will be concerned. The inversion of the one Knave counteracts the intended harm.

The fourth pack—for those who do expect it—contains the Queen of Hearts, the King of Spades, and the Seven of Diamonds, reversed. These indicate that the fair woman of gentle and affectionate nature will be exposed to scandal, Seven of Diamonds, reversed, through the agency of the King of Spades, an ambitious, untrustworthy lawyer, who is her enemy.

The fifth pack, consisting of only two cards (the Ace of Hearts and the Nine of Diamonds), is for the surprise, and we learn that a love letter, the Ace, will be delayed, the Nine; but the consolation card is the King of Clubs, the dark, warm-hearted man, who will come in person to his lady love.

The above example has been given in the plainest, most straightforward manner, with the most apparent reading of the cards given as an illustration of the method. Those who spend time and thought on the subject will soon get to see more of the true nature of the cards with respect to their relative positions and their influence one upon another. Various experiments with this method of fortune-telling will give rise to curious combinations and perhaps startling developments, as the one interpreting for the inquirer gains in knowledge and confidence.

★
The Professional Method

This is a detailed and exhaustive method for reading the cards. The beginner may feel somewhat alarmed at the mass of explanatory matter there is for him to study, but when the information has been acquired, the would-be cartomancer will find he possesses a sense of power and comprehension that will give both confidence and dexterity to his attempts to unravel the thread of destiny.

The Pack

The selected pack of thirty-two cards, which have been mentioned in connection with several of the preceding methods, is in this case augmented by the addition of the four Twos, one of which is sometimes taken as the representative of the inquirer. There is no hard and fast rule about this, however, and another card may be taken if preferred. Not only does each card have its own signification but every position upon the table within the cube in which the cards are arranged has its own meaning. These must be carefully studied, first separately and then together. It would be a help to the beginner to make a separate chart for his own use, and to have it at hand when laying the cards according to this system.

The thirty-six cards must be shuffled and cut in the usual way and then be placed upon the table in six rows of six cards each, starting from the left-hand corner, where square 1 is marked on the chart. The position of the inquirer must be carefully noted, and then all the cards in his immediate neighborhood must be read in all their individual bearing, with regard to their position and their influence upon the representative card.

We will examine the meanings of the thirty-six squares in connection with the several cards that may appear in them.

1. The Project in Hand

When covered by a Heart, the inquirer may hope that the project will be successfully carried out.

When covered by a Club, kind and trustworthy friends will help foward the project.

When covered by a Diamond, there are serious business complications in the way of the project's accomplishment.

When covered by a Spade, the inquirer will have his trust abused, and those in whom he has confided will play him false, to the detriment of the project in hand.

2. Satisfaction

When covered by a Heart, the inquirer may look for the realization of his brightest hopes and his dearest wishes.

When covered by a Club, satisfaction will be derived by the help of true friends who will do all in their power to promote the inquirer's happiness.

When covered by a Diamond, there will be jealousy at work to mar the inquirer's satisfaction.

When covered by a Spade, the hope of success will nearly be shattered by deceit and double-dealing.

3. Success

When covered by a Heart, the inquirer may hope for complete success.

When covered by a Club, any success will be due to the help of friends.

When covered by a Diamond, there is only a slim chance for success.

When covered by a Spade, all chance of success will be eventually destroyed by underhand means.

4. Hope

Covered by a Heart, the inquirer may look for the fulfillment of his dearest hopes.

Covered by a Club, hopes will be realized through the agency of helpful friends or be due to the obstinate determination of the inquirer.

Covered by a Diamond, it shows that the hopes are groundless and impossible of realization.

Covered by a Spade, wild hopes are indicated, tending to mania and provocative of grave trouble or even tragedy.

5. Chance, Luck

Covered by a Heart, good luck will attend the hopes and plans of the inquirer.

Covered by a Club, moderately good luck, especially due to the kindly offices of friends.

Covered by a Diamond, not much luck for the inquirer; rather an evil than a good influence.

Covered by Spade, bad luck, robbery, financial ruin, disaster, and possibly death.

6. Wishes, Desires

Covered by a Heart and surrounded by good cards, it promises the immediate fulfillment of the inquirer's highest desires.

Covered by a Club, a partial gratification of the inquirer's wishes may be expected.

Covered by a Diamond, the earnest efforts of both the inquirer and his friends will be crowned only with imperfect success.

Covered by a Spade, disappointment and nonfulfillment of desires.

7. Injustice

Covered by a Heart, any injustice done to the inquirer will be rectified and removed, so that the passing cloud will turn to his ultimate advantage.

Covered by a Club, the wrong already done will require long and courageous efforts to wipe out its effects, and the inquirer will need the support of his best friends.

Covered by a Diamond, the harm done will not be entirely remedied, but the inquirer's good name will be reestablished.

Covered by a Spade, injustice will bring about sore trouble and serious misfortunes.

8. Ingratitude

The four suits have exactly the same iinfluence upon the situation in this number as in the preceding one.

TABLE OF THE POSITIONS
AND THEIR MEANINGS

No. 1 Project in Hand	No. 2 Satisfaction	No. 3 Success	No. 4 Hope
No. 5 Chance Luck	No. 6 Wishes Desire	No. 7 Injustice	No. 8 Ingratitude
No. 9 Association	No.10 Loss	No. 11 Trouble	No. 12 State or Condition
No. 13 Joy	No. 14 Love	No. 15 Prosperity	No. 16 Marriage
No. 17 Sorrow Affliction	No. 18 Pleasure Enjoyment	No. 19 Inheritance Property	No. 20 Fraud Deceit
No. 21 Rivals	No. 22 A Present Gift	No. 23 Lover	No. 24 Advancement A Rise In The World
No. 25 Kindness A Good Turn	No. 26 Undertaking Enterprise	No. 27 Changes	No. 28 The End (of Life)
No. 29 Rewards	No. 30 Misfortune Disgrace	No. 31 Happiness	No. 32 Money Fortune
No. 33 Indifference	No. 34 Favor	No. 35 Ambition	No. 36 Ill-health Sickness

9. Association

Covered by a Heart, the partnership will be successful and have the best results.

Covered by a Club, good results of cooperation or partnership will be effected through the agency of true friends.

Covered by a Diamond, the inquirer will need to use all possible caution and diplomacy, and even then the results will be unsatisfying.

Covered by a Spade, the connection will not benefit the inquirer; in fact he may suffer terribly from it, but his friends will profit thereby.

10. Loss

Covered by a Heart, shows loss of a benefactor, which will be a great grief to the inquirer.

Covered by a Club, the loss of dear friends and the failure of cherished hopes.

Covered by a Diamond, loss of money, goods, property, and personal effects.

Covered by a Spade, the best interests of the inquirer will be seriously compromised, and he will have to renounce them.

11. Trouble

Covered by a Heart, very great trouble caused by near relations or born of love for another.

Covered by a Club, trouble with friends.

Covered by a Diamond, money troubles.

Covered by a Spade, trouble arising from jealousy.

12. State or Condition

Covered by a Heart, the conditions of life are steadily improving.

Covered by a Club, the improvement will be slower and more uncertain; hard work and good friends are essential to ensure advancement.

Covered by a Diamond, the inquirer will only attain a satisfactory position in life after he has overcome numerous and powerful enemies. He will never get very far, however.

Covered by a Spade, the inquirer's circumstances are bound to go from bad to worse in spite of all he may do.

13. Joy, Delight

Covered by a Heart, deep, unruffled delight, joy of a pure and disinterested nature.

Covered by a Club, joy from material causes, better luck, or greater prosperity.

Covered by a Diamond, joy springing from success in profession or business, gained in spite of jealous opposition.

Covered by a Spade, joy from having been able to render a service to a superior, who will not forget it.

14. Love

Covered by a Heart, the inquirer will be blessed and happy in his love.

Covered by a Club, he may rely absolutely upon the fidelity of his beloved.

Covered by a Diamond, love will be troubled by jealousy.

Covered by a Spade, love will be slighted and betrayed.

15. Prosperity

Covered by a Heart, the inquirer will enjoy complete and well-merited prosperity.

Covered by a Club, foretells moderate prosperity, due to hard work and the kindly offices of friends.

Covered by a Diamond, prosperity will be damaged by the jealousy of others.

Covered by a Spade, serious misfortunes will arise in business, brought about by the malice and fraud of other people.

16. Marriage

Covered by a Heart, the inquirer may look forward to a happy marriage.

Covered by a Club, foretells a marriage prompted by practical or financial considerations alone.

Covered by a Diamond, the married life will be troubled by the jealousy of one or both partners.

Covered by a Spade, inquirer will lose the chance of a wealthy marriage through the deceit and jealousy of his enemies.

17. Sorrow, Affliction

Covered by a Heart, the inquirer will pass through a love trouble, but it will be of only short duration.

Covered by a Club, trouble will arise from a quarrel with a dear friend, but it will end in complete reconciliation.

Covered by a Diamond, there will be sorrow caused by jealousy.

Covered by a Spade, bad faith and underhand dealings will bring affliction upon the inquirer.

18. Pleasure, Enjoyment

Covered by a Heart, the inquirer will enjoy the bliss of mutual love, undimmed by even passing clouds.

Covered by a Club, there will be love of a more imperfect and superficial character.

Covered by a Diamond, love will be tormented and distracted by jealousy.

Covered by a Spade, love will be unreal and fleeting, unable to bear the test of time or survive the first disagreement.

19. Inherited Money or Property

Covered by a Heart, the inquirer will come into a large inheritance to which he has a legitimate and undisputed right.

Covered by a Club, a friend will bequeath a portion of his property or money to the inquirer.

Covered by a Diamond, the inquirer will lose part of his rights owing to the jealousy of another person.

Covered by a Spade, an entire estate will be stolen from the inquirer by intriguing rivals.

20. Fraud, Deceit

Covered by a Heart, the deceiver will be caught in the trap he has laid for the inquirer.

Covered by a Club, by the aid of true friends the inquirer will escape from the effects of an act of treachery.

Covered by a Diamond, the inquirer will have to suffer great pain as the consequence of deceit, but it will only be a passing trouble.

Covered by a Spade, deceit and underhand dealings will culminate in slander that will cost the inquirer many friends and have serious consequences for him.

21. Rivals

Covered by a Heart, the inquirer will obtain his desire in spite of powerful or puny rivals.

Covered by a Club, rivals will be overcome with difficulty, the help of generous friends.

Covered by a Diamond, a rival will so far outwit the inquirer as to obtain some of the advantage, wealth, or favor for which he is striving.

Covered by a Spade, the rival will triumph over the inquirer, robbing him and plunging him into disgrace both with his benefactors and with members of his own immediate circle.

22. A Present or Gift

Covered by a Heart, the inquirer will have a very handsome and unexpected present.

Covered by a Club, the inquirer will receive a gift that is bestowed upon him from motives of self-interest or in a spirit of vulgar display.

Covered by a Diamond, points to a gift intended to act as a bribe.

Covered by a Spade, indicates a present that is given to further deceitful ends of the donor.

23. Lover

Covered by a Heart, the gentleman or the lady, as the case may be, will be both fond and faithful in life and death.

Covered by a Club, the beloved will be faithful but somewhat faulty in other respects.

Covered by a Diamond, the inquirer may be prepared to find the beloved both jealous and disposed to sulk.

Covered by a Spade, the beloved will prove faithless, selfish, and vindicative.

24. Advancement

Covered by a Heart, the inquirer will soon see a rapid improvement in his worldly position that will exceed his wildest hopes.

Covered by a Club, there will be a moderate and satisfying advance in the inquirer's circumstances, which will be the result of his own hard work, aided by the sympathy and help of his friends. He will be contented and happy.

Covered by a Diamond, advancement will be obtained only after a hard struggle against difficulties, caused by the jealous ill will of others.

Covered by a Spade, the underhand dealings of his enemies will destroy all hopes of a rise in the world.

25. Kindness, Good Turn

Covered by a Heart, the inquirer will receive a kindness that far exceeds both his expectations and his deserts.

Covered by a Club, this good turn will be well deserved but only obtained by the help of disinterested friends.

Covered by a Diamond, the inquirer will obtain only a modicum of kindness, and that after he has surmounted serious obstacles built up by the jealousy and self-seeking of some people concerned in it.

Covered by a Spade, the inquirer must prepare for failure in his enterprise as a result of the malicious intrigues of his rivals.

26. Undertaking, Enterprise

Covered by a Heart, whatever undertaking the inquirer has in hand will meet with success.

Covered by a Club, the enterprise will be a financial success owing to the help of friends.

Covered by a Diamond, the success of the undertaking will be hindered and decreased by the jealousy and self-seeking of some people concerned in it.

Covered by a Space, the inquirer must prepare for failure in his enterprise, owing to the malicious intrigues of his rivals.

27. Changes

Covered by a Heart, the change contemplated by the inquirer is a good one.

Covered by a Club, a change for the better will take place in the inquirer's circumstances as a result of the good offices of friends.

Covered by a Diamond, the inquirer will make an earnest attempt to change his position in life, but his efforts will be fruitless.

Covered by a Spade, a change, very much for the worse, is to be apprehended. It will be brought about by the malice and double-dealing of those who seek to harm him.

28. The End (of Life)

Covered by a Heart, by the death of a relation or friend, the inquirer will come into a considerable fortune.

Covered by a Club, a handsome legacy from a friend may be expected by the inquirer.

Covered by a Diamond, one who wishes ill to the inquirer will depart this life.

Covered by a Spade, this portends the untimely death of the inquirer's greatest enemy.

29. Reward

Covered by a Heart, the inquirer will be rewarded out of all proportion to his efforts.

Covered by a Club, a due and fitting reward will be meted out in response to industry and perseverance.

Covered by a Diamond, a well-merited reward will be hindered and reduced by the unscrupulous action of others.

Covered by a Spade, the inquirer will be done out of his just reward by the double-dealing and dishonesty of certain people.

30. Disgrace, Misfortune

Covered by a Heart, misfortune will come to the inquirer, but it will not do him any permanent harm.

Covered by a Club, the inquirer will suffer through the disgrace of a friend.

Covered by a Diamond, misfortune will be brought about by jealousy and will indirectly affect the inquirer.

Covered by a Spade, dishonesty and double-dealing will cause disgrace from which the inquirer will suffer long and acutely.

31. Happiness

Covered by a Heart, the inquirer will experience unexpected happiness that will be both deep and lasting.

Covered by a Club, a stroke of luck will come to the inquirer through the good offices of friends.

Covered by a Diamond, the jealousy and ambition of false friends will result in good fortune to the inquirer.

Covered by a Spade, the life of the inquirer will be in danger from the malice of his enemies. Their murderous schemes will be happily defeated by the vigilance of his friends.

32. Money, Fortune

Covered by a Heart, the inquirer will rapidly acquire a large fortune by achieving success in his profession or by a lucky speculation.

Covered by a Club, through hard work and sustained effort, the inquirer will secure an income and will receive both help and encouragement from his friends.

Covered by a Diamond, through misplaced confidence in unworthy friends, the inquirer will see his fortune pass into dishonest hands.

Covered by a Spade, not only will the inquirer be tricked out of his money by dishonest acquaintances, but he will have to suffer for their misdeeds in his business or profession.

33. Indifference

Covered by a Heart, thanks to his indifference and lack of heart, the inquirer will lead an unruffled if somewhat joyless life.

Covered by a Club, lack of interest and energy will allow the inquirer to let slip things that would give him pleasure.

Covered by a Diamond, the inquirer will forfeit the love and regard of valuable friends owing to indifference and utter unresponsiveness.

Covered by a Space, as a result of culpable indifference the inquirer will be robbed and impoverished.

34. Favor

Covered by a Heart, the inquirer will enjoy all that love can bestow upon the beloved.

Covered by a Club, the inquirer will honestly seek and acquire the favor of influential persons.

Covered by a Diamond, the favor of the great will be long and earnestly sought by the inquirer, who will not succeed single-handed.

Covered by a Spade, no effort of any kind will admit the inquirer to the favor to which he aspires.

35. Ambition

Covered by a Heart, the inquirer will shortly arrive at the highest point of his ambition.

Covered by a Club, the moderate ambition of the inquirer will be realized.

Covered by a Diamond, the lawful ambitions of the inquirer will be partially frustrated by the ill will and jealousy of certain acquaintances.

Covered by a Spade, the principal ambition of the inquirer will be defeated by underhand transactions, and he will even suffer from the consequences of justifiable steps that he may take to accomplish his desire.

36. Sickness, Ill Health

Covered by a Heart, the inquirer will suffer from passing ailments that will leave no bad results.

Covered by a Club, a rather serious illness may be expected.

Covered by a Diamond, an acute attack of a definite disease.

Covered by a Spade, a very severe illness that may materially interfere with the inquirer's career or happiness.

Tendencies of the Suits

It will be seen in the foregoing definitions that Hearts are almost invariably the sign of good luck, love, and happiness. Even where the position is indicative of misfortune, the presence of a Heart has a mitigating effect upon the evil. Clubs rank next in order of good fortune and seem specially connected with the precious gift of true friendship. Diamonds seem accompanied by the disquieting elements of jealousy and rivalry, which strew obstacles in the path of success and happiness, while for sheer bad luck and dire disaster the ill-omened suit of Spades stands unrivaled.

Hearts

The King of Hearts. In this method he represents a married man or a widower. Should the inquirer be a woman and this card fall upon squares 14, 22, 23, or 32, he then denotes a lover. Should the inquirer be a man, the King falling in the above-named squares signifies a rival.

When this card falls on any of the following numbers, 2, 3, 4, 13, 14, 15, 16, 18, 19, 23, 24, 29, 31, 32, 34, the situation is favorable, and the inquirer will have his wishes granted with respect to the special meaning of the square.

When the King falls on square 1, 5, 6, 9, 12, 22, 26, 27, or 28, there will be a satisfactory solution of any matter connected with the subject represented by the squares.

Should he fall upon an unlucky square, namely, 7, 8, 10, 11, 17, 20, 21, 30, 33, 35, or 36, the King mitigates the evil fortune of the positions.

The Queen of Hearts. She signifies a married woman or a widow who desires the happiness of the inquirer and does her best to promote it.

If the inquirer is a man, this card falling on squares 14, 22, 23, 24, or 32 represents his ladylove. In the event of his being already engaged, his fiancée will possess all the most lovable and desirable qualities.

When the inquirer is a woman and the Queen of Hearts falls on any of the above-named squares, it shows that she has a rival to reckon with. Should she be engaged, it indicates that her future husband is both young and well equipped for social and professional success.

When a very elderly person consults the cards, the above combination foretells a peaceful, contented old age.

To anyone interested in agriculture, the same combination promises abundant crops.

The Knave of Hearts. This card represents a good-natured, amiable, but rather insipid young man, devoid alike of violent passions and exalted aspirations.

When a young girl consults the cards, this Knave falling on the squares 14, 22, 23, 24, or 32 may be taken to personify her fiancé.

When the inquirer is a young, unmarried man, the same combination indicates that he will marry the object of his choice after he has surmounted considerable obstacles by his tact and quiet determination.

The Ten of Hearts. The signification of this card does not differ from that given in the general definitions save in the following cases. When it falls on square 10, it signifies success. When it falls on square 14, it signifies success in love. When it falls on square 16, it signifies a happy marriage.

If in the last-named case, a Knave or a Seven falls on 7, 15, 17, or 25, there will be several children born of the union.

If the Ten of Hearts falls on squares 18, 19, 31, or 32, there will be wealth, intense enjoyment, and real happiness.

The Nine of Hearts. The only addition to the general signification is that when this card falls near the Seven of Clubs, it denotes that a promise already made to the inquirer will shortly be fulfilled.

The Eight of Hearts. This card is the special messenger of good things when it falls on one of the following squares: 5, 9, 15, 18, 19, 22, or 31.

The Seven of Hearts. If this card falls on 14, 22, 23, 24, or 32, when the inquirer is a bachelor, it signifies that he will very soon take a wife.

The Two of Hearts. This is frequently taken as the representative card, and in that case it is entirely influenced by its position on the chart in relation to the cards that touch or surround it.

The Ace of Hearts. This card represents the house of the inquirer as it does in other methods. It is very important to note its position on the chart and its surroundings.

Clubs

The King of Clubs. Taken generally, this card represents a married man or a widower whose worth as a friend is not to be excelled.

When the inquirer is a young girl and this King falls on 14, 22, 23, 24, or 32, she may rejoice for she will shortly be united in marriage to the man she loves.

Should a young man be consulting the cards, this King falling on any of the above-named squares denotes a generous, high-minded rival who will meet him in fair fight, and who is far above anything like taking a mean advantage.

When this card falls on 18, 19, 20, 27 or 28, it represents the guardian of a minor, whose line of conduct will be determined by the cards that surround or touch it.

The Queen of Clubs. When a bachelor consults the cards, and this Queen falls on 14, 22, 23, 24 or 32, it promises him a ladylove whose beauty will be her strongest attraction.

Should a woman be seeking to know her fate, this Queen falling on either of the above-named squares warns her that she has a rival. In the case of the inquirer being a married man or woman, this card represents a woman of high position and great influence who is attractive to the inquirer and who will be the means of bringing him or her valuable and pleasing intelligence.

In the case of a businessman, the above combination denotes that he will be entirely successful in the enterprise that is engrossing all his thoughts at the moment.

The Knave of Clubs. This card may be taken to represent a sincere and lasting friendship founded upon a basis that will endure.

When the inquirer is a young girl and this card falls upon either of the matrimonial squares, namely, 14, 22, 23, 24, or 32, it signifies some man who wants to marry her.

In the case of a bachelor, this card on the same squares tells him that he has a rival, either in love or in his business career.

The Ten of Clubs. This card is the harbinger of good luck if it falls on 3, 5, 15, 18, 19, 22, 25, 28, 31, or 32.

Should this card fall on squares 10, 17, or 36, it implies that the inquirer will be asked for a loan of money that he will be unable to lend.

The Nine of Clubs. This card means a present. If it follows a Club, the gift will be in money; if it follows a Heart, the inquirer may look for a present of jewelry; if it follows a Diamond, the gift will be trifling in value; and if it follows a Spade, the recipient of the present will derive no pleasure from it.

The Eight of Clubs. Has no special significance outside the general definition.

The Seven of Clubs. This represents a young girl capable of the highest self-devotion, even to risking her life in the interests of the inquirer.

The exact nature of her relations and services to the object of her affection will be decided by the surrounding cards.

In the case of a bachelor, this card falling on any of the squares 14, 22, 23, 24, or 32 represents the lady of his choice.

In the case of an unmarried girl or a widow, the same combination points to a generous rival.

Whenever this Seven comes out near the Nine of Hearts, the wish card, it is a token of some signal success for the inquirer.

The Two of Clubs. This represents the trusted friend of the inquirer, and the square on which it falls will give the requisite information, if its meaning is taken in conjunction with those of the surrounding cards.

The Ace of Clubs. This card is the sign of a well-ordered life and legitimate hopes, and foretells success in an ordinary career, or the attainment of celebrity in special cases.

Should the inquirer be a soldier, it signifies a fortunate turn of events that will secure him a rapid rise in the army.

To one interested in agriculture, it promises plentiful crops.

To a traveler, it foretells a most satisfactory result from his journey.

To an actress, it promises phenomenal success in a leading role. Should the inquirer or one of his parents be a dramatic or musical author, this card is the omen of theatrical success.

Diamonds

The King of Diamonds. Should the inquirer be a young girl, she will do well to note whether this card falls on any of the matrimonial squares, 14, 22, 23, 24 or 32, for in that case her present admirer is not to be trusted unless he has cards of good import touching him or is preceded by either a Heart or a Club.

The Queen of Diamonds. If this card falls on any of the matrimonial squares, 14, 22, 23, 24, or 32, it signifies to a bachelor that he will be engaged to one whose character is to be read in the surrounding cards. If this Queen is preceded by a Heart or a Club, it promises good luck on the whole; but if by a Diamond or a Spade, the augury is bad.

Should the inquirer be a young unmarried woman or a widow, this card indicates that she has a rival whose character is revealed by the cards touching it.

The Knave of Diamonds. For an unmarried woman or a widow, this card represents a lover from a foreign country. If it is accompanied by a Heart, he has many good points to recommend him; if by a Club, he is kind and generous; if by a Diamond, he is bad-tempered, exacting, undesirable, and she had better have nothing to do with him.

The Ten of Diamonds. The general meaning of this card is a journey.

If it falls between two Hearts the journey will be short. If it falls between two Clubs, the journey will be successful. If it falls between two Diamonds, the journey will have bad results.

The Nine of Diamonds. This card signifies news. If preceded by a Heart or a Club, the news will be good. If preceded by a Diamond or a Spade, the news will be bad.

The Eight of Diamonds. The card signifies a short journey. If it falls between two hearts, the expedition will be an enjoyable pleasure trip.

If between two Clubs, it denotes a satisfactory business journey.

If between two Diamonds, it signifies a trip begun for pleasure and ending in misadventure.

If between two Spades, it signifies an unsuccessful business journey.

The Seven of Diamonds. This card stands for a young girl of foreign birth and breeding. Taken by itself it means love sorrows and heart searchings.

Should the inquirer be a bachelor and this card fall on one of the matrimonial squares, 14, 22, 23, 24, or 32, it signifies a ladylove as described above.

This Seven is an excellent augury when it falls on 2, 3, 15, 16, 18, or 27.

The Two of Diamonds. Has practically the same significance as the Deuce of Clubs, unless it is selected as the representative card.

The Ace of Diamonds. The significance of this card is a letter. If preceded by a Heart, it is a letter from a lover or friend. If preceded by a Club, it is a letter on business or one containing money. If preceded by a Diamond, the letter is dictated by jealousy. If preceded by a Spade, the letter contains bad news.

Spades

The King of Spades. When the inquirer is an unmarried woman or a widow, this card falling on the squares, 14, 22, 23, or 32 is indicative of a false lover whose character is mean and base.

When the inquirer is an unmarried man, the above combination signifies that he has a rival.

This card falling on the squares numbered 10, 18, 19, 20, 27, 28, or 29 represents a guardian or the executor of a will.

To a married man, this King is a warning that there are domestic ructions in store for him.

To a married woman, the card cautions her to be very much on her guard when in the society of an attractive but unprincipled man whom she has to meet frequently, and who will bring scandal upon her if she is not most careful.

The Queen of Spades. When the inquirer is a bachelor, this card falling on 14, 22, 23, 24, or 32 represents the lady to whom he will be engaged.

In the case of an unmarried woman or a widow, the combination signifies a rival in love.

The Knave of Spades, Ten of Spades, Nine of Spades, and Eight of Spades have no special signification other than that given in the general definitions.

The Seven of Spades. This card signifies all troubles and worries connected with the tender passion.

Should the inquirer be a man, this Seven falling on squares 14, 22, 23, 24, or 32 foretells faithlessness on the part of his fiancée, a betrayal of trust by some other woman, or a robbery.

When the inquirer is a woman, this card on any of the same squares points to a rival who will be preferred before her.

The Two of Spades. May be taken as a representative card but otherwise has no special signification.

The Ace of Spades. Is a card of good omen, meaning perseverance followed by possession, a happy marriage, success, and rapid advancement in business or profession.

An Example

We have taken the Deuce of Hearts as the representative card of the inquirer, who is a fair young girl seeking to know her fate. We will give the order in which the thirty-six cards come out, but intend to leave the bulk of them for the reader to solve according to the instructions given.

We have taken the inquirer and her immediate surroundings as an example of the working of the method and feel sure that any intelligent reader will be able to complete the reading for himself.

1. Ace of Clubs
2. Eight of Spades
3. Two of Clubs
4. Knave of Hearts
5. King of Diamonds
6. King of Hearts

7. Eight of Diamonds	22. King of Clubs
8. Ten of Clubs	23. Nine of Clubs
9. Ten of Hearts	24. Eight of Hearts
10. Seven of Spades	25. Queen of Clubs
11. Nine of Spades	26. Knave of Diamonds
12. Two of Spades	27. Queen of Spades
13. Nine of Hearts	28. Seven of Diamonds
14. Eight of Spades	29. Seven of Hearts
15. Queen of Diamonds	30. Ten of Diamonds
16. Two of Hearts	31. Knave of Clubs
17. King of Spades	32. Ace of Diamonds
18. Queen of Hearts	33. Ace of Hearts
19. Ace of Spades	34. Seven of Clubs
20. Ten of Spades	35. Two of Diamonds
21. Knave of Spades	36. Nine of Diamonds

We find the inquirer in 16, which square, when covered by a Heart, indicates a happy and well-suited marriage. On her left in 15 (prosperity) she has the Queen of Diamonds, a very fair woman who is fond of gossip and somewhat wanting in refinement of feeling. She will interfere with the inquirer's prosperity through jealousy, but on the whole she will bring good luck because she is preceded by a Club. To the right in 17 (sorrow) we have the King of Spades, a dark, ambitious, but unscrupulous man who is the inquirer's legal adviser and will bring grave sorrow upon her by his underhand dealings. Immediately above her we have in 10 (loss) the Seven of Spades, a card representing troubles connected with a love affair. This square being covered by a Spade indicates that she will be unjustly compelled to relinquish her rights and that her chance of marriage may be lessened or postponed by the loss of her fortune.

On the left above her we get in 9 (association) the Ten of Hearts, a most cheering and excellent card promising her success and happiness in a partnership that she is contemplating. On the right, above, in 11 (trouble) we have the Nine of Spades, a bad omen signifying the failure of her hopes through the jealousy of some other person.

Immediately below her we find in 22 (a gift) the King of Clubs, who is her true and valued friend, either a married man or a widower. He will make her a present and will be actuated by certain motives of self-

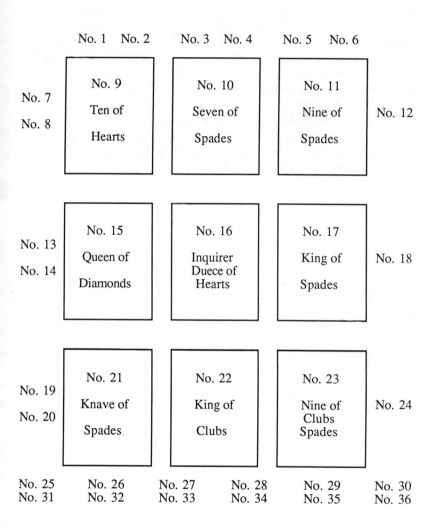

No. 1   No. 2   No. 3   No. 4   No. 5   No. 6

No. 7

No. 9

Ten of

Hearts

No. 10

Seven of

Spades

No. 11

Nine of

Spades

No. 8

No. 12

No. 13

No. 15

Queen of

Diamonds

No. 16

Inquirer

Duece of

Hearts

No. 17

King of

Spades

No. 14

No. 18

No. 19

No. 21

Knave of

Spades

No. 22

King of

Clubs

No. 23

Nine of

Clubs

Spades

No. 20

No. 24

No. 25   No. 26   No. 27   No. 28   No. 29   No. 30
No. 31   No. 32   No. 33   No. 34   No. 35   No. 36

interest in so doing; but she may keep a good heart, for his presence in that position on the chart indicates that she will soon be united to the man of her choice. On the left, below, in 21 (rival) we find the Knave of Spades, a legal agent whose influence will be instrumental in enabling a rival to triumph over and bring discredit upon the inquirer. On the right, below, we have in 23 (a lover) the Nine of Clubs, which in this case means a gift in money. We may take it that her faithful lover, uninfluenced by her pecuniary losses, has decided to make her a present, probably in the form of a marriage settlement.

The remainder of the chart will provide the student with many more interesting particulars regarding the fate of this fair inquirer and at the same time prove an excellent exercise in the art of cartomancy.

★

Wishing with the Cards

The Fifty-two-card System

The fifty-two cards must be shuffled and cut into three packs by the person who wishes to have his or her fortune told, and the fortune-teller must be careful to note what cards appear as the various packs are turned face upward.

The card representing the inquirer must first be selected. Then lay the cards nine in a row, beginning from right to left with each row; only seven will be in the last row.

The cards being in order on the table, begin by counting nine from your representative card and nine again from the ninth, until you come to a card that has already been counted.

The court cards represent the various people with whom the inquirer is brought into contact, and their relation and attitude are easily determined by the meaning of the cards between. Three deals are necessary for a good reading.

An Example

I give an example of fortune-telling by the combination of nines because an illustration is of practical help.

The First Reading. The pack having been dealt in the manner described, we find the cards have resolved themselves thus, reading from left to right in each row.

First line. Seven of Clubs, Seven of Spades, King of Spades, Ace of Diamonds, Ace of Hearts, Knave of Clubs, Four of Hearts, Eight of Hearts, Knave of Spades.

Second line. Two of Diamonds, Three of Diamonds, Two of Hearts, Six of Hearts, King of Diamonds, Five of Clubs, Two of Clubs, Five of Spades, Three of Hearts.

Third line. Five of Hearts, Six of Diamonds, Four of Clubs, Queen of Clubs, Five of Diamonds, Three of Spades, King of Hearts, Four of Diamonds, Ten of Spades.

Fourth line. Nine of Spades, Queen of Spades, Eight of Diamonds, Six of Clubs, Ace of Spaces, Queen of King of Clubs, Knave of Hearts, Six of Spades, Nine of Hearts.

Fifth line. Ten of Diamonds, Eight of Clubs, Seven of Diamonds, Ace of Clubs, Nine of Clubs, Nine of Diamonds, Knave of Diamonds, Ten of Hearts, Ten of Clubs.

Sixth line. Eight of Spades, Queen of Hearts, Seven of Hearts, Four of Spades, Three of Clubs, Two of Spades.

We will take the Queen of Hearts to Represent the inquirer and, as she is in the lowest line of all, will count upward. The ninth card is the Knave of Clubs, and the next ninth the Six of Hearts, then the Three of Spades, the Ace of Spades, and Nine of Clubs, which brings us back to our Queen.

According to the signification given by this method, the reading would be as follows.

Knave of Clubs. A generous friend
Six of Hearts. Implies credulity
Three of Spades. Difficulties. Be careful in making friends.
Nine of Clubs. Displeasure of friends

My general reading of this would be that if the Queen of Hearts were an unmarried woman she would be in danger of making an unhappy marriage bringing the displeasure of her friends upon her. If she will avoid forming hasty friendships and take the advice of a man who is older and darker than herself, she will avoid much misfortune.

If married, the Queen is the victim of an ill-matched union, but she must be careful not to give too much credence to the reports of friends and must guard her own conduct carefully.

We will now proceed with the next deal to see if we can find a more favorable augury.

The Second Reading. *First line.* Eight of Clubs, Queen of Hearts, Six of Spades, Eight of Spades, Eight of Hearts, Six of Diamonds, Ten of Hearts, Nine of Clubs, Six of Hearts.

Second line. Three of Spades, Ace of Spades, Three of Diamonds, King of Spades, Ace of Diamonds, Ace of Hearts, King of Diamonds, King of Clubs, Ace of Clubs.

Third line. Ten of Spades, Five of Clubs, Two of Hearts, Five of

Hearts, Ten of Diamonds, Four of Hearts, Two of Clubs, Knave of Spades, Three of Hearts.

Fourth line. Five of Spades, Four of Clubs, Six of Clubs, Queen of Diamonds, Four of Diamonds, King of Hearts, Nine of Spades, Five of Diamonds, Seven of Clubs.

Fifth line. Knave of Clubs, Ten of Clubs, Three of Clubs, Nine of Diamonds, Queen of Spades, Seven of Spades, Knave of Hearts, Eight of Diamonds, Seven of Diamonds.

Sixth line. Seven of Hearts, Four of Spades, Queen of Clubs, Two of Spades, Knave of Diamonds, Two of Diamonds, Nine of Hearts.

Here our inquirer does not prove to be a very wise person. In spite of the warning and displeasure of friends, regardless of the affection of a good man, and elated through unexpected riches, she listens with credulous mind to one who will cause her much unhappiness. Let us hope she will stop short of one fatal step and take the good honorable love that is awaiting her.

The ninth card is the King of Clubs, and the Five of the same suit following in our arranged plan, then the Five of Diamonds, the Ten of Clubs, the Two of Diamonds, the Six of Hearts, and the Three of Spades complete this reading. A reference to the signification will show the importance of these cards.

Perhaps in the third reading we may have more success.

The Third Reading. *First line.* Ace of Clubs, Eight of Clubs, Queen of Hearts, Ten of Spades, King of Clubs, Five of Diamonds, Ten of Clubs, Nine of Spades, Knave of Spades.

Second line. Three of Spades, Two of Spades, Six of Hearts, Eight of Spades, Five of Spades, Knave of Clubs, Seven of Hearts, Four of Spades, Queen of Clubs.

Third line. Five of Hearts, Two of Diamonds, Three of Diamonds, Queen of Diamonds, Eight of Hearts, Three of Clubs, Five of Clubs, Ace of Diamonds, Six of Diamonds.

Fourth line. Four of Diamonds, Six of Clubs, Seven of Clubs, Seven of Diamonds, Six of Spades, Nine of Diamonds, Knave of Diamonds, Nine of Hearts, Eight of Diamonds.

Fifth line. Ten of Hearts, King of Spades, Two of Hearts, Ten of Diamonds, Ace of Hearts, Four of Hearts, King of Hearts, King of Diamonds, Queen of Spades.

Sixth line. Two of Clubs, Seven of Spades, Knave of Hearts, Nine of Clubs, Three of Hearts, Four of Clubs, Ace of Spades.

The cards here are more promising, though still full of warning. The ninth card is the Seven of Hearts, which means unfaithfulness, followed by another card indicating domestic dissension. The next is the Knave of Diamonds and treachery is to be feared. But there is considerable success if care is exercised, and later on there appears to be a happy marriage with comfort and even luxury.

Throughout her life the inquirer will have to be on her guard against forming hasty friendships and refrain from listening to scandal about those near and dear to her. In this care I should think there will be two marriages, the first not happy (probably dissolved by law), then a happier time later in life with one who had been content to wait.

"Your Heart's Desire" System

This method uses fifteen cards. Having shuffled the cards well, select the card that will represent the inquirer—a King for a man, a Queen for a woman—and place this card on the table; then request your subject to wish for some one thing while he or she is shuffling the pack (which must include only the selected thirty-two cards). The pack must be cut once.

Take the cards, and holding them easily in your own hands, let the inquirer draw fifteen cards, placing them face downward on the table, one on top of the other in the order drawn. The fifteen cards having been drawn, discard the others and place the selected ones in position according to the following plan. The representative card is to be in the center, and the other cards are to be placed to the left—to the right—above—below—and on the center, one by one. Thus on the left you will have the first, sixth, and eleventh; on the right, the second, seventh, and twelfth; above, the third, eighth, and thirteenth; below, the fourth, ninth, and fourteenth; and on the representative card you will have placed the fifth, tenth, and fifteenth. (See diagram.)

Then take the left packet and turn and read according to the meaning in the combination of sevens. The next packet to be taken is the one on the right, then the one above, and following that the packet below. The left and top packets represent events that may influence your wish in the future; the packets on the right and below show those events that have influenced it in the past while those cards covering the representative card indicate affairs that may be expected immediately and are to be read in strict reference to the wish.

YOUR WISH IN FIFTEEN CARDS

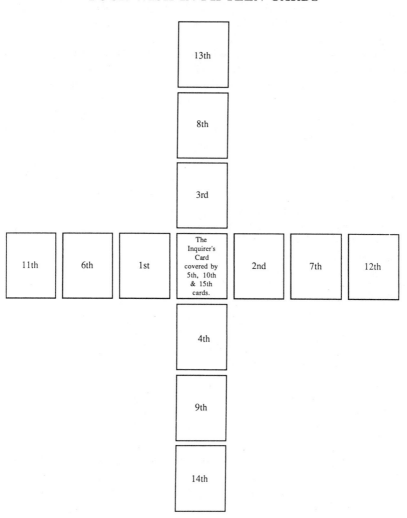

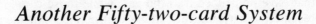

Another Fifty-two-card System

Let the inquirer shuffle the cards well, and cut them into three packs, having first selected your representative card as in the former method and placed it in the center of a circle.

Take up the packs and lay the cards in a circle using forty-two, and with the remaining nine form a triangle inside the circle. The cards must be laid face down.

Now let the inquirer choose any fifteen cards, which must be faced upward as he makes his selection. When fifteen cards are chosen, read the signification according to the meaning given in the combination of nines.

Generally speaking, if Diamonds predominate, the fortune will be fair; if Hearts appear in the ascendant, love affairs are prosperous; Clubs will show how material interests are progressing; and Spades will prepare us for sorrow.

The Wish with Thirty-two Cards

Take out all the Twos, Threes, Fours, Fives, and Sixes from an ordinary pack. The inquirer must then shuffle the remaining thirty-two, cut with the left hand, and wish from the depths of his heart. The dealer places eight cards face downward upon the table in a row before him. He next turns them up one by one, beginning from the left, and as soon as a pair of any kind, it does not matter what, be exposed, they must both be covered by cards taken from the pack in his hand. If they all pair off exactly, it may be taken as a sign that the inquirer's wish will be gratified, but if at any moment there are no pairs exposed, the fates are unpropitious, and the search for a favorable answer must be abandoned. Should most of the cards pair off, leaving only one, two, or three unmated, it portends delay and disappointment before the realization of the desire.

Take the thirty-two cards up again, shuffle them, and mentally register your wish. The first thirteen cards must be turned up and a careful search made for any Aces that may be there. If found, place them on one side. The rest of the cards must be shuffled again and thirteen more dealt out, with a second search for Aces. This is done a third time if all four have not appeared; and if they still refuse to come, there is no hope of the wish being granted. It is the best possible omen if the four Aces come out in the first deal, and very good luck if they arrive with only two attempts; but the third is the last chance, so the turning up of those thirteen cards is fraught with much excitement.

The Wish in Seven Packs

This is a very simple method, but it is by no means always propitious to the inquirer; if, however, he does get the desired answer, we take it that the capricious goddess is in a very smiling mood.

Thirty-two cards are required, and they must be arranged in suits in the following order: Ace, King, Queen, Knave, Ten, Nine, Eight, Seven. The cards must not be shuffled, but the arranged pack is cut with the left hand into seven smaller packs and all are placed face downward upon the table.

The dealer must then proceed to turn up the top cards of each pack, and as a pair of Queens, Nines, Knaves, or whatever they may happen to be becomes visible, he must remove them from the packs. Should all the cards pair off in this manner, the wish may be taken as one that will speedily be granted. Should the cards come out awkwardly, literarlly in Sixes and Sevens instead of pairs, the inquirer must adapt his desires to the inevitable with the best grace he can.

The Wish-Card System

Yet a sixth way that will give some idea whether the heart's desire will be gratified is as follows.

Shuffle the whole pack of cards and give them to the inquirer, who must then divide the pack into three, wishing intently all the time. Take up the packs separately and glance through them; the Nine of Hearts is the most important card as that is the symbol of the wish. Should this be in juxtaposition to the card—the King or Queen—representing the inquirer and with favorable surroundings, then you may conclude that the things hoped for will come to pass. Also, if the wish card is in combination with cards that are an indication of the inquirer's desires, it is a favorable augury.

For instance, if the wish referred to business and the suit of Clubs surrounded the Nine of Hearts, then it might be concluded that the matter would terminate in a prosperous manner. Diamonds, as they foretell wealth, would also promise prosperity; Hearts imply good wishes and good will, while Spades carry a sinister meaning.

A Rhyming Divination

There are those to whom the more elaborate forms of fortune-telling by cards may seem a trifle wearisome or possibly too intricate to be followed without an exhausting effort of attention. The method we give in this chapter has the advantage of being at once simple, diverting, and varied.

As the rhyming significations concern both sexes, a great deal of fun can be provided where there is a party of young people, and who can tell whether the long arm of coincidence may not use this old practice to bring some loving pair together?

Take a new pack of cards, or at any rate one in which there are no telltale marks on the reverse sides, and spread them face downward upon the table. Before anyone draws a card, he or she is requested to close the eyes, place the right hand on the heart, and say, "Honi soit qui mal y pense" ("Shamed be he who thinks evil of it," the motto of the Order of the Garter). The card must then be drawn with the left hand, and its meaning will be read by the one who holds the key contained in the verses below.

Diamonds

Ace

Since that this Ace is now your lot,
You will wed one that's fierce and hot;
But if a woman does draw it,
She will wed one with wealth and wit.

Two

Hast thou not drawn the number Two?
Thy spouse shall be both just and true.
But if a woman this now have,
Beware a sly and crafty Knave!

Three

You that have drawn the number Three,
Great honor will your fortune be;
But if a female draw the same,
She must beware of fickle shame.

Four

The man that draws the number Four
Shall quite forsake his native shore;
But if the same a woman finds,
Both hand and heart in love she joins.

Five

He that draweth the number Five,
Where he was born he best will thrive;
But if it's drawn by womankind,
Good luck abroad they sure will find.

Six

He that can catch the number Six
Will have cunning and crafty tricks;
But if a woman draw the same,
'Twill show that she is free from blame.

Seven

Since that the Seven does appear,
Crosses thou hast great cause to fear;

Women, whene'er the same they draw,
Shall not fear crosses more than straw.

Eight

Hast thou then drawn the number Eight?
Thou sure wilt be a rascal great;
Females that chance the same to take,
They never will the truth forsake.

Nine

Hast thou turn'd up the merry Nine?
Then guineas will thy pocket line;
She that doth draw it to her hand
Will die for love or leave the land.

Ten

O brave! the Ten, 'tis very well!
There's none in love shall thee excel.
Only the maid who draws the Ten
May wed, but nobody knows when.

King

This noble King of Diamonds shows
Thou long shalt live where pleasure
    flows;
But when a woman draws the King,
Sad, melancholy songs she'll sing.

Queen

Now is the Queen of Diamonds fair,
She shows thou shalt some office share;
Oh, woman! if it fall to you
Friends you will have not a few.

Knave

Is now the Knave of Diamonds come?
Be sure beware the martial drum;
Yet if a woman draw the Knave,
She shall much better fortune have.

Hearts

Ace

He that draws the Ace of Hearts
Shall surely be a man of parts;
And she that draws it, I profess,
Will have the gift of idleness.

Two

He who can draw the Deuce shall be
Endowed with generosity;
But when a woman draws the card,
It doth betide her cruel hard.

Three

The man who gets hold of this Trey
Always bound, always obey;
A woman that shall draw this sort
Will surely drink brandy by the quart.

Four

He that draws this Four shall make
A faithful love for conscience's sake;
But if it's drawn by fair womankind,
They will prove false, and that you'll find.

Five

Note that this Five of Hearts declares
Thou shalt well manage great affairs;
But if it's drawn by fair women,
They sure will love all sorts of men.

Six

The Six of Hearts surely foretells
Thou shalt be where great honor dwells;
If it falls on the other side
It then betokens scorn and pride.

Seven

Now this old Seven, I'll maintain,
Shows that thou hast not loved in vain;
Thou shalt obtain the golden prize,
But, with the maids, 'tis otherwise.

Eight

Having drawn the number Eight,
Shows thou'rt servile, born to wait;
But if a woman draw the same,
She'll mount upon the wings of fame.

Nine

By this long Nine be well assured
The lovesick pains must be endured;
But the maid tha draws this Nine
Soon in wedlock hands shall join.

Ten

This Ten it is a lucky cast,
For it doth show the worst is past;
But if the maids the same shall have,
Love will their tender hearts enslave.

King

By this card surely 'twill appear
Thou shalt live long in happy cheer;
And if a woman draw this card,
She shall likewise be high preferred.

Queen

Now by this card it is well known
Thou shalt enjoy still all thine own;
But women, if they draw the same,
Shall sure enjoy a happy name.

Knave

He that doth draw the Knave of Hearts
Betokens he hath knavish parts;
But if a woman draw the Knave
Of no man shall she be the slave.

Spades

Ace

Thou that dost draw the Ace of Spades
Shall be sore flouted by the maids;
And when it is a damsel's lot,
Both love and honor go to pot.

Two

Always this Deuce betokens strife,
And with a scolding, wicked wife;
But if a woman's lot it be,
Honor, great love, and dignity.

Three

Thou that are happy in this Trey
Shalt surely wed a lady gay;
Whilst maids who now the same shall take,
Join marriage with a poor town rake.

Four

Now this same Four betokens you
Shall lead a dissipated crew;
Maids that do draw the same shall meet
With certain joys always complete.

Five

The Five of Spades gives you to know
That you must through some troubles go;
But, if a woman, it foretells
Her virtue others' far excels.

Six

The Six foretells whene'er you wed
You'll find your expectations fled
But if a maid the number own
She'll wed a man of high renown.

Seven

Now the Seven comes to hand,
It does entitle you to land;
But maids with this shall wed with those
That have no money, friends, or clothes.

Eight

This Eight of Spades foretells you shall
Wed a young maid fair, straight, and tall;
if to a maid the same shall come,
She weds the brother of Tom Thumb.

Nine

Now by this Nine thou are foretold,
Thou shalt wed one deaf, lame, and old.
Females, when they draw this odd
   chance,
Shall of themselves to wealth advance.

Ten

'Tis seen by this long Ten of Spades
That thou shalt follow many trades
And thrive by none. But women, they
By this chance shall not work but play.

King

By this brave King observe and note,
On golden streams you e'er shall float;
But women, by the self-same lot,
Shall long enjoy what they have got.

Queen

Here is the Queen of Spades likewise
Thou soon shalt unto riches rise;
A woman by the same shall have
What her own heart doth sorely crave.

Knave

This is a Knave, pray have a care
That you fall not into despair.
Women, who the same shall choose,
Shall prove great flats, but that's no
   news!

Clubs

Ace

He that doth draw the Ace of Clubs,
From his wife gets a thousand snubs;
But if maids do it obtain,
It means that they shall rule and reign.

Two

Note that this Deuce doth signify
That thou a loyalist shalt die;
The damsels that the same shall take
Never will their good friends forsake.

Three

You that by chance this Trey have drawn
Shall on a worthless woman fawn.
A maiden that shall draw this Trey
Shall be the lass that ne'er says nay.

Four

Now by this four we plainly see
Four children shall be born to thee;
And she that draws the same shall wed
Two wealthy husbands, both well bred.

Five

Now by this Five 'tis clear to see
Thy wife will but a slattern be.
This same Five drawn by virgins, they
Shall all wed husbands kind and gay.

Six

By this Six thou'rt wed, we know,
To one that over thee will crow;
Maids that can draw the same shall be
Blest with good husbands, kind and free.

Seven

Thou that hast now the Seven drawn
Shall put thy Sunday clothes in pawn;
Maids that draw the same shall wear
Jewels rich without compare.

Eight

By this Club Eight, tho' Whig or Tory,
Thy life will prove a tragic story;
Ye maids that draw the same are born
To hold both fools and fops in scorn.

Nine

By this brave Nine, upon my life,
You soon shall wed a wealthy wife;
She that shall draw the same shall have
One that is both fool and knave.

Ten

Now for this number, half a score,
Shows that thou wilt be wretched poor;
Maids that can draw this number still
Shall have great joy and wealth at will.

King

Here comes the King of Clubs and
    shows
Thou hast some friends as well as foes;

Maids that do draw this court card shall
Have very few or none at all.

Queen

If the Queen of Clubs thou hast,
Thou shalt be with great honor graced.
And women, if the same they find,
Will have things after their own mind.

Knave

See how the surly Knave appears!
Pray take care of both your ears!
Women, whene'er the same they see,
Will be what oft they used to be.

The Significance of Combinations

Combinations of Court Cards

Four Aces. When these fall together they imply danger, financial loss, separation from friends, love troubles, and, under some conditions, imprisonment. The evil is mitigated in proportion to the number that are reversed.

Three Aces. Passing troubles, relieved by good news, faithlessness of a lover, and consequent sorrow. If reversed, foolish excess.

Two Aces. These portend union; if Hearts and Clubs, it will be for good; if Diamonds and Spades, for evil, probably the outcome of jealousy. If one or both are reversed, the object of the union will fail.

Four Kings. Honors, preferment, good appointments. Reversed, the good things will be of less value but will arrive earlier.

Three Kings. Serious matters will be taken in hand with the best result unless any of the three cards be reversed, in which case the outcome will be doubtful.

Two Kings. Cooperation in business, upright conduct, and prudent enterprises to be crowned with success. Each one reversed represents an obstacle.

Four Queens. A social gathering that may be spoilt by one or more being reversed.

Three Queens. Friendly visits. Reversed, scandal, gossip, and possibly bodily danger to the inquirer.

Two Queens. Petty confidences interchanged, secrets betrayed, a meeting between friends. When both are reversed, there will be suffering for the inquirer resulting from his own acts. Only one reversed means rivalry.

Four Knaves. Roistering and noisy conviviality. Any of them reversed lessens the evils.

Three Knaves. Worries and vexations from acquaintances, slander calling the inquirer's honor in question. A reversed card foretells a passage at arms with a social inferior.

380

Two Knaves. Loss of goods, malicious schemes. If both are reversed, the trouble is imminent; if one only, it is near.

Combinations of Plain Cards

Four Tens. Good fortune, wealth, success in whatever enterprise is in hand. The more there are reversed, the greater the number of obstacles that are in the way.

Three Tens. Ruin brought about by litigation. When reversed, the evil is decreased.

Two Tens. Unexpected luck that may be connected with a change of occupation. If one is reversed, it will come soon, within a few weeks possibly; if both are reversed, it is a long way off.

Four Nines. Accomplishment of unexpected events. The number that are reversed stand for the time to elapse before the fulfillment of the surprise.

Three Nines. Health, wealth, and happiness. Reversed, discussions and temporary financial difficulties caused by imprudence.

Two Nines. Prosperity and contentment, possibly accompanied by business matters, testamentary documents, and possibly a change of residence. Reversed, small worries.

Four Eights. Mingled success and failure attending a journey or the taking up of a new position. Reversed, undisturbed stability.

Three Eights. Thoughts of love and marriage, new family ties, honorable intentions. Reversed, flirtation, dissipation, and foolishness.

Two Eights. Frivolous pleasures, passing love fancies, an unlooked for development. Reversed, paying the price of folly.

Four Sevens. Schemes and snares, intrigue prompted by evil passions, contention, and opposition. Reversed, small scores of impotent enemies.

Three Sevens. Sadness from loss of friends, ill health, remorse. Reversed, slight ailments or unpleasant reaction after great pleasure.

Two Sevens. Mutual love, an unexpected event. Reversed, faithlessness, deceit, or regret.

★

Various Cards Read Together

The Ten of Diamonds next to the Seven of Spades means certain delay.

The Ten of Diamonds with the Eight of Clubs tells of a journey undertaken in the cause of love.

The Nine of Diamonds with the Eight of Hearts foretells a journey with certainty.

The Eight of Diamonds with the Eight of Hearts means considerable undertakings; with the Eight of Spades there will be sickness; and with the Eight of Clubs there is deep and lasting love.

The Seven of Diamonds with the Queen of Diamonds tells of a very serious quarrel; with the Queen of Clubs we may look for uncertainty; with the Queen of Hearts there will be good news.

The Ten of Clubs followed by an Ace means a large sum of money; should these two cards be followed by an Eight and a King, an offer of marriage is to be expected.

When the Nine, Ace, and Ten of Diamonds fall together, we may look for important news from a distance; and if a court card comes out after them, a journey will become necessary.

The Eight and Seven of Diamonds in conjunction imply the existence of gossip and chatter to be traced to the inquirer.

When the King, Queen, Knave, and Ace of one color appear in sequence, it is a sign of marriage; should the Queen of Spades and the Knave of Hearts be near, it shows there are obstacles in the way; the proximity of the Eight of Spades bodes ill to the couple in question, but their happiness will be assured by the presence of the Eight of Hearts and the Eight of Clubs.

The Ace of Diamonds and the Ten of Hearts also foretell wedding bells.

The Seven of Spades, with either a court card or the Two of its own suit, betrays the existence of a false friend.

The Eight and Five of Spades coming together tell of jealousy that will find vent in malicious conduct.

A number of small spades in sequences are significant of financial loss, possibly amounting to ruin.

The King of Hearts and the Nine of Hearts form a lucky combination for lovers.

The Nine of Clubs joined to the Nine of Hearts is indicative of affairs connected with a will likely to benefit the inquirer.

The Queen of Spades is the sign of widowhood, but if accompanied by the Knave of her own suit, she is symbolic of a woman who is hostile and dangerous to the inquirer.

General Meaning of the Several Suits

Hearts, as might well be supposed, are specially connected with the work of Cupid and Hymen. The suit also has close reference to affairs of the home and to both the domestic and social sides of life.

Diamonds are mainly representative of financial matters small and great, with a generally favorable signification.

Clubs are the happiest omens of all. They stand for worldly prosperity and a happy home life with intelligent pleasures and successful undertakings.

Spades, on the other hand, forebode evil. They speak of sickness, death, monetary losses and anxieties, separation from friends and dear ones, to say nothing of the minor worries of life. They are also representatives of love unaccompanied by reverence or respect and appealing exclusively to the senses.

When a number of court cards fall together, it is a sign of hospitality, festive social intercourse, and gaiety of all kinds.

Married people who seek to read the cards must represent their own life partner by the King or Queen of the suit they have chosen for themselves, regardless of anything else. For example, a very dark man, the King of Spades, must consider his wife represented by the Queen of Spades, even though she may be as fair as a lily and not yet a widow.

Bachelors and spinsters may choose cards to personify their lovers and friends according to their coloring.

Two red Tens coming together foretell a wedding, and two red Eights promise new garments to the inquirer.

A court card placed between two cards of the same grade—for instance, two Nines, two Sevens—shows that the one represented by that card is threatened by the clutches of the law.

It is considered a good augury of success when, in dealing the cards out, those of lesser value than the Knave are in the majority, especially if they are Clubs.

Should a military man consult the cards he must always be represented by the King of Diamonds.

It is always essential to cut cards with the left hand, there being a long-established idea that it is more intimately connected with the heart than the right. A round table is generally preferred by those who are in the habit of practicing cartomancy. It is a matter of opinion as to whether the cards speak with the same clearness and accuracy when consulted by the inquirer without an intermediary. The services of an adept are generally supposed to be of great advantage, even when people have mastered the rudiments of cartomancy themselves.

Patience, the power of putting tow and two together, a quick intuitive perception, and a touch of mysticism in the character are all useful factors in the pursuit of this pastime.

The Combination of Sevens

This method is very simple and, as it takes but a short time, is more suitable when there are many fortunes to read. A little practice will soon enable a would-be cartomancer to construe the various combinations, as there are so few cards to remember.

It may be objected that meanings are now given that are different from those taught in earlier methods. This is certainly a fact, but it also is an advantage; one method may suit one person's abilities and intuitiveness better than another and so enable a more comprehensive reading to be given from the diminished pack than from the full pack.

The Method

Thirty-two cards only are selected from an ordinary pack of playing cards. In each suit the Ace, King, Queen, Knave, Ten, Nine, Eight, and Seven are retained; all the others, those from Two to Six inclusively, are discarded.

The cards must be shuffled and cut into three sections by the inquirer, each cut being turned face upward. The manipulator must carefully note the result of these cuts, as they give an indication of what is coming. The center pack is to be taken first, the last next, and the first last of all.

Holding this newly arranged pack in the left hand, draw off three cards, and facing them upward, select the highest card of any suit that may appear. Retain this one and put the others aside for the next deal. Proceed in this way until you have finished the pack, then shuffle all the discard together, and repeat until you have any number over twenty-one on the table. If three cards of any suit should appear, or three cards of the same value, they are all to be taken.

It must not be forgotten that the cards are also selected from the "cuts," and should the lifting of one card reveal another of greater value of the same suit exposed, then that also is retained.

The first question to decide is which card will represent the inquirer. This is generally settled according to the complexion: Diamonds for the very fair; Hearts for those of medium coloring; Clubs for brunettes with brown hair; and Spades for those of dark complexion. This suit also represents elderly people. A King represents a man and a Queen a woman. This representative card is not to be drawn out; it is shuffled with the others and taken when it is the highest of its suit. The only exception to this rule is when there have already been twenty-one or more cards selected; then it must be taken from the remainder and placed last of all.

Reading of the Cards

The reading in this method is from left to right, and the cards are to be placed in a semicircle or horseshoe, in the order they are drawn.

Court cards represent people, and the numbers relate to events. Generally Diamonds relate to money and interest; Hearts, to the affections; Clubs, to business; Spades, to the more serious affairs of life.

The signification of each card is given separately, as well as some of the combinations, and an example of a fortune is worked out, the study of which will more easily enable a student to understand this method.

HEARTS

King.   A man with brown hair and blue eyes
Queen. A woman of similar complexion
Knave. A friend with good intentions
Ten.   Marriage
Nine.   Wish
Eight. Affection
Seven. Friendship
Ace.   Home

DIAMONDS

King.   A fair man
Queen.   A fair woman
Knave.   A friend
Ten.   Wealthy marriage
Nine.   Rise in social position
Eight.   Success with speculation
Seven.   A good income
Ace.   A wedding or present of jewelry

CLUBS

King.   A man who is neither fair nor dark
Queen.   A woman in middle life
Knave.   A business friend
Ten.   Journey by water
Nine.   Successful business
Eight.   Pleasure in society
Seven.   A business affair
Ace.   A letter, check, or legal document

SPADES

King.   A dark man
Queen.   A dark woman (or widow)
Knave.   Personal thoughts
Ten.   A journey by land
Nine.   Illness or sorrow
Eight.   A loss
Seven.   A disagreement
Ace.   Responsible position in the service of the government

A Typical Example

Now we will proceed to read a fortune. For the subject we will take the Queen of Hearts. The first shuffle and division of the pack into three reveals three Hearts—King, Knave, and Seven—which indicates that the lady whom the Queen represents has a firm male friend, who is neither fair nor dark. These three cards are taken and laid in order, beginning on the left hand.

Then the packs having been taken in order as described and held in the left hand, the fortune-teller proceeds to draw off three cards and make his selection according to the rule. The pack being finished, the process is repeated twice more.

In three deals the fortune of the Queen of Hearts revealed the following cards, and if a student will take a pack of cards and select the same, he can judge how the various combinations may be read.

King, Knave, Seven of Hearts, Ace of Clubs, King of Spades, Queen of Clubs, Queen of Diamonds, Queen of Spades, King of Clubs, Knave of Diamonds, Ace of Hearts, Knave of Spades, King of Diamonds, Knave of Clubs, Queen of Hearts, Ace of Diamonds, Ten of Hearts, Eight of Clubs, Seven of Spades, Ace of Spades, Ten of Clubs, Ten of Spades, Ten of Diamonds.

Now, from the Queen of Hearts we will proceed to count seven, in the direction in which the lady's face is turned. Since it is to the left, the seventh card from her is the Queen of Spades, the seventh from which is the King of Hearts, and the seventh again is the Ten of Hearts. I read this to mean that the lady has some good friends but that the woman whom the Queen of Spades represents will resent her marriage, without effect. The next card is the Knave of Diamonds followed by the Seven of Hearts and the Seven of Spades—a combination that represents some speedy news, not exactly to the advantage of the inquirer. The Knave of Spades followed by the King and the Ten of Clubs denotes that a dark man, who is separated from the Queen of Hearts, is constantly thinking of her and hoping for a speedy reunion.

The Knave of Clubs and the Queen of Diamonds come next. Knaves and women form a conjunction that never brings good luck; but in this case they are followed by the Ten of Diamonds, one of the most fortunate cards in the pack. The Ace of Diamonds and the King of Clubs follow, which means an offer of marriage shortly. The Queen of Hearts is indeed a sad coquette, for there is no indication that she accepts this, as the Knave of Hearts with the Eight of Clubs and the Ace of Hearts are quickly on the scene. It appears that there is another wooer who comes to her home and is received with pleasure.

More serious affairs appear now; the Ace of Clubs with the Ace of Spades and the King of Diamonds signifies that the lady is likely to have some business with which a woman darker than herself is connected. This will lead to a considerable journey that she will immediately take, as the card denoting this counts seven directly to her.

Now we will look at the cards as they lie on the table. In a reading taken at random, they foretell a very good future. All the court cards and the Aces and Tens are out, with the Seven of Hearts and the Eight of Clubs, and all are cards of favorable import.

Three Queens together generally betoken some mischief or scandal, but as they are guarded by Kings it will probably not amount to much. The Ace of Diamonds and the Ten of Hearts placed so near the representative card would surely tell us of a forthcoming marriage except that the Queen has her face turned away from it. The three Tens placed as they are tell of prosperity after journeys by land and water.

Now we will pair the cards and see if any more meaning can be extracted from them. On land and on the water this lady will meet a rich man who will entertain a strong affection for her. I must not omit to mention that the cards are paired from the extreme ends of the horseshoe. Thus are paired the King of Hearts and the Ten of Diamonds, the Knave of Hearts and Ten of Spades, and so forth. The business appears again, and a dark man seems to be in some perplexity. The three Queens are not yet separated and are in closer connection with the inquirer than ever. There will be chatting over the teacups about a marriage. The fair damsel herself appears to be a little more inclined to matrimony, but the three Knaves imply that she will have some difficulty in settling her affairs.

The two Kings imply that she has some staunch friends and that the result will be quite satisfactory. A general reading gives the impression that the Queen of Hearts is of a lovable disposition and fond of society, as so many court cards came out and if the three Queens meant a little gossip it was in a kindly spirit.

There is another little ceremony to be gone through that will tell us if she is likely to have her "heart's desire" realized. Since the Nine of Hearts, which is the symbol of a wish, did not appear, she is apparently very cool and neutral. However, the other cards may tell us something.

The used cards are to be shuffled and cut once by the inquirer; she may wish for anything she likes during the process. Then the cards are laid out one at a time in seven packs—six packs in a semicircle and one in the center—the cards of the last are to be turned face upward, but none of the other cards are to be exposed until the end.

★

The Seven Packs

The seven packs represent, respectively, yourself, your house, what you expect, what you don't expect, a great surprise, what is sure to come true, and the wish.

The cards, having been shuffled and cut once, are dealt out in the manner described, and these are the resulting combinations.

First Pack. Queen of Spades, Queen of Hearts, Ten of Clubs, Seven of Hearts.

Second. Ace of Spades, Knave of Clubs, Ace of Diamonds, Ten of Spades.

Third. Knave of Spades, King of Diamonds, Knave of Hearts.

Fourth. Queen of Clubs, Seven of Spades, King of Spades.

Fifth. Ten of Diamonds, Eight of Clubs, Queen of Diamonds.

Sixth. King of Hearts, Ten of Hearts, King of Clubs.

Wish. Ace of Hearts, Knave of Diamonds, Ace of Clubs.

In a reading of these cards, the first pack is likely to represent the meeting of the inquirer with a dark or elderly woman for whom she has a strong affection. Water is crossed before that meeting takes place.

The second pack reads as if a dark man would offer a ring or a present of jewelry, and also that he is contemplating a journey by land. He is probably a professional man or in government service.

The third pack, with its combination of Knaves and King, has reference to business transactions that will most probably be favorable to the interests of the Queen.

The fourth pack presages some slight disappointment, illness, or unhappiness in connection with some friends.

The fifth pack tells us that some brilliant fortune that will lead to a higher social position is awaiting a fair friend.

The sixth pack tells us that perhaps our seemingly indifferent Queen of Hearts has a slight tenderness for someone. He is older than she is and is only waiting for an opportunity to declare his affection. If the wish is related to such a man, she may be certain of its fulfillment even should there be a slight delay.

The seventh or wish pack is extremely good and tells us that many affairs will be transacted in writing.

The future of the Queen of Hearts is fair and bright, her disposition is lovable, and she will bring happiness to other people.

This example is not made up of selected cards. They were shuffled, cut, and drawn in the ordinary way. I say this because so few cards of bad import have appeared, and it might be thought these were chosen in order to avoid prophesying disappointments.

In the foregoing example twenty-three cards were dealt out, but the number may vary. It must, however, be an uneven number. Sometimes only fifteen or seventeen cards are taken, and with the smaller quantity of selected cards there is an optional way of concluding operations. After having read the pairs, the cards are gathered up, shuffled, and cut into three packs instead of seven. These three are placed in a row, and a fourth card is put apart for the surprise. The inquirer is requested to choose one of the three packs, which represent, respectively, the house, those who did not expect it, and the inquirer—the last being decided by the choice of the person in question.

When these three packs have been duly read, all the cards are again taken up except the surprise (which is left face downward on the table) and dealt out again, the same process being repeated three times until there are three cards set aside for the surprise. These are read last of all and form the concluding message to the inquirer. Let's hope it may be a cheerful one!